Thinking About Movies

THINKING ABOUT
MOVIES

WATCHING, QUESTIONING, ENJOYING

SECOND EDITION

PETER LEHMAN
AND
WILLIAM LUHR

Blackwell
Publishing

350 Main Street, Malden, MA 02148-5018, USA
108 Cowley Road, Oxford OX4 1JF, UK
550 Swanston Street, Carlton South, Melbourne, Victoria 3053, Australia
Kurfürstendamm 57, 10707 Berlin, Germany

First edition published 1999 by Harcourt Brace & Company
Second edition published 2003 by Blackwell Publishing Ltd

Library of Congress Cataloging-in-Publication Data

Lehman, Peter.
    Thinking about movies : watching, questioning, enjoying / Peter Lehman
and William Luhr. – 2nd ed.
        p.   cm.
Includes index.
    ISBN 0-631-23357-1 (hardcover : alk. paper) – ISBN 0-631-23358-X
(pbk. : alk. paper)
1. Motion pictures.   I. Luhr, William.   II. Title.
    PN1994 .L373 2003
    791.43 – dc21

                                                                2002008044

A catalogue record for this title is available from the British Library.

Set in 10½ on 13pt Galliard
by SNP Best-set Typesetter Ltd, Hong Kong
Printed and bound in the United Kingdom
by T. J. International, Padstow, Cornwall

For further information on
Blackwell Publishing, visit our website:
http://www.blackwellpublishing.com

For my son, David, with admiration and love
William Luhr

For Susan Hunt, a true teacher, educator, and friend
Peter Lehman

CONTENTS

PREFACE

Film studies continues to grow both in popularity and enrollment, with course offerings found in a wide variety of departments: film, art, theater, English, and communications. The second edition of *Thinking About Movies: Watching, Questioning, Enjoying* has been written specifically for the student with no previous film background, who has never taken a film course, and who, in many cases, may never take another. This textbook provides a valuable introduction to the plurality of critical approaches that characterizes current studies of film.

This book's goal is to make students more perceptive and critical viewers of the kinds of film that they already watch, as well as to expand their tastes to include a broader variety of material. The book is structured so that teachers can organize classes to include a weekly film screening chosen from the films we analyze in detail or, if they desire, from other films raising related issues. These film examples have been selected with careful consideration of their availability on DVD and video, since the reality of the current academic situation is that those are the formats used in most film courses. Most of the titles are available on DVD in their proper aspect ratio. Our analyses, however, are written and illustrated in a manner that should be useful to students regardless of which films are screened in class to accompany our text.

The first half of each chapter introduces critical issues in a broad manner and illustrates them with brief references to a variety of films. The second half analyzes one or two films in detail in relation to the issues raised in the preceding portion of the chapter. Numerous stills from the films will facilitate discussion and criticism. Throughout the book, films have been chosen that represent a balance between those that are likely to be familiar to most students, such as recent Hollywood films, and those that are likely to represent styles of filmmaking that most students have not previously encountered, such as films from various national cinemas and historical time periods. Following each chapter is a brief, annotated bibliography, the primary purpose of which is to provide students with further reading related to the broad theoretical and critical ideas presented in the text. We also annotate and acknowledge articles and books upon which we have drawn in our discussions.

This book devotes attention to aesthetic as well as social and cultural issues. We believe that all are equally important and, in fact, inseparable. It is hard to speak insightfully about how women or people of color are represented in films without knowledge of how films function as a representational system. It is equally limiting to talk about visual composition as if it had no social significance. Learning to see in a more sophisticated fashion what is transpiring on the screen should be linked to thinking more critically about what is represented, how it is represented, and how it affects its audience. *Thinking About Movies: Watching, Questioning, Enjoying* is based upon that conviction.

The second edition of *Thinking About Movies* expands upon the first in many ways. We have added a glossary of specialized film terms that are highlighted in the text and updated our film examples throughout, drawing upon films that have been released since the first edition. We have also expanded chapters by adding new sections such as, for example, an overview of Bruce Willis's acting career in chapter 7, and a discussion of the Broadway musical version of *Victor/Victoria* as well as stage adaptations of *The Strange Case of Dr Jekyll and Mr Hyde* that enable expanded consideration of theater in relation to literature and film in chapter 9. In several instances we have replaced one of the major film examples with a different film, as in chapter 3 where *The Sixth Sense* replaces *Mr Hulot's Holiday* and chapter 13 where *LA Confidential* and *Out of the Past* replace *Greystoke*. Most importantly, we have added a new final chapter on the increasingly important impact of digital technology on cinema. We have made these and other changes in the belief that the new material makes this edition stronger, clearer, and more relevant to today's introductory film student.

We have both written, together and separately, on a variety of areas in film studies and have drawn upon our research in the writing of this book. Although we feel an obligation as scholars to cite published sources of our own from which we have drawn, we do not consider it appropriate, with one exception, to do so in the chapter bibliographies for fear of appearing to give undue attention to our own work. Consequently, we will place those citations here:

Chapter 1 (Introduction): Peter Lehman analyzes the X motif and relations between men and women in the 1932 *Scarface* in *Running Scared: Masculinity and the Representation of the Male Body* (Philadelphia: Temple University Press, 1993).

Chapter 2 (Narrative Structure): William Luhr and Peter Lehman give a formal account of narrative, including a discussion of free and bound motifs and the distinction between story and plot, in *Authorship and Narrative in the Cinema: Issues in Contemporary Aesthetics and Criticism* (New York: G. P. Putnam's, 1977).

Chapter 4 (Authorship): Peter Lehman analyzes *The Searchers* utilizing a detailed discussion of visual motifs, narrative structure, and issues of race and gender in "Texas 1868/America 1956: *The Searchers*" in *Close Viewings: An Anthology of New Film Criticism*, edited by Peter Lehman (Tallahassee: Florida State University Press, 1990).

Chapter 5 (Genres): William Luhr analyzes *Murder, My Sweet*, including the roles of the disoriented, blinded detective and the sexually alluring black widow, in *Raymond Chandler and Film*, 2nd edn (Tallahassee: Florida State University Press, 1991). Luhr discusses changing film and television representations of Wyatt Earp in "Reception, Representation, and the OK Corral: Shifting Images of Wyatt Earp" in *Authority and Transgression in Literature and Film*, edited by Bonnie Braendlin and Hans Braendlin (Tallahassee: University Press of Florida, 1996), pp. 23–44.

Chapter 8 (Audiences and Reception): William Luhr discusses the position of *A Woman of Paris* in Chaplin's work in "*A Woman of Paris* and Charles Chaplin's Career," *Griffithiana*, 40/42 (October 1991), pp. 104–17. Peter Lehman analyzes the representation of the male genitals in *The Crying Game* in "When a Man Loves a Man: Crying over the Melodramatic Penis," *Society for the Philosophical Study of the Contemporary Visual Arts Newsletter* (February 1994), p. 9.

Chapter 9 (Film and the Other Arts): Peter Lehman analyzes the differences between how language functions in plays and movies in "Texas 1868/America 1956: *The Searchers*," in *Close Viewings: An Anthology of New Film Criticism*, edited by Peter Lehman (Tallahassee: Florida State University Press, 1990). William Luhr and Peter Lehman discuss the distinctions between literature and film, using *Dr Jekyll and Mr Hyde* as an example, in *Authorship and Narrative in the Cinema* (New York: G. P. Putnam's, 1977). William Luhr analyzes the relationship of Robert Louis Stevenson's novel to both stage and film versions of *Dr Jekyll and Mr Hyde*, as well as narrative structure, visual motifs, and issues of sexuality in *Dracula* and *Nosferatu*, in *Victorian Novels on Film* (Ann Arbor: University Microfilms International, 1979).

Chapter 12 (Gender and Sexuality): Peter Lehman analyzes male power and sexuality in *Cyrano de Bergerac, Rio Bravo, Rio Lobo*, and *American Gigolo* in *Running Scared: Masculinity and the Representation of the Male Body* (Philadelphia: Temple University Press, 1993) and *Silence of the Lambs* in "In the Dark Basement: *Silence of the Lambs* and Female Vision in the Hollywood Cinema," lecture delivered at the Contemporary Arts Center, New Orleans, 1992.

Chapter 13 (Race): William Luhr examines racial and national representation as well as the influence of *film noir* in *Out of the Past* and *LA Confidential* with relation to the cultural shifts in the fifty-year period between the films in "Border Crossings in *Out of the Past* and *LA Confidential*," *The Bilingual Review/La Revista Bilingue*, 23 (3) (1998), pp. 230–6.

ACKNOWLEDGMENTS

Our special thanks go to Jayne Fargnoli at Blackwell whose strong belief that a second edition of *Thinking About Movies* should see the light of day has been nothing less than inspirational to us. She is that rare editor who has complete knowledge of a manuscript and stays on top of all the publication details and deadlines. We are also grateful to Sue Ashton for helpfully and conscientiously copy-editing the manuscript. Thanks also go to the reviewers of the second edition of this textbook, all of whom offered sound advice based upon their experiences of using the earlier edition in their classrooms: Robert Eberwein, Oakland University; Krin Gabbard, SUNY-Stony Brook; Pamela Grace, New York University; Martha Nochimson, Mercy College; Kevin S. Sandler, University of Arizona; and Don Staples, University of North Texas. Thanks go to Keith Meunzes for his help and expertise in preparing the many illustrations that are so central to this volume. We also want to thank once again the reviewers who read the early drafts of the manuscript for the first edition and made countless valuable revision suggestions: Rick Altman, University of Iowa; Charles Harpole, University of Central Florida; Brian Henderson, SUNY-Buffalo; Gary London, Everett Community College; Paul Pilger, Florida State University; David Popowski, Mankato State University; Gerry Veeder, University of North Texas; and Mark Zalk, Nassau Community College.

Peter Lehman would also like to thank Gary Keller, the Director of the Hispanic Research Center at Arizona State University, for his strong commitment to film studies curriculum development and research. Aaron Baker, the coordinator of the Film Concentration in the Interdisciplinary Humanities Program, has been an invaluable colleague and friend throughout and he generously gave chapter 16 a "test run" in a Fall 2001 class. Joaquin Alvarado of the Hispanic Research Center also provided generous advice and expertise.

Justine Kleiback did a superb job reading page proofs. Once again, Melanie Magisos helped in more ways than can ever be acknowledged. A week never goes by in which I don't discuss movies with my brother, Steve; and no list of thanks can ever be complete without mentioning my daughter, Eleanor, who always keeps me up on which movies I should run, not walk, to see. She shares my enthusiasm at the same time as she chuckles at it.

William Luhr would like to thank the New York University Faculty Resource Network, along with Bill Simon, Robert Sklar, and Chris Straayer of the Department of Cinema Studies, who have been invaluable in providing research help and facilities, as have Charles Silver, Steve Higgins, and the staff of the Film Study Center of the Museum of Modern Art. Generous assistance has also come from the members of the Columbia University Seminar on Cinema and Interdisciplinary Interpretation, particularly my co-chair, David Sterritt, as well as Krin Gabbard and Christopher Sharrett, and Robert L. Belknap, Director of the University Seminars. At Saint Peter's College, gratitude goes to Academic Dean Eugene Cornacchia, Bill Knapp and the staff of the Instructional Resources Center, the members of the Committee for the Professional Development of the Faculty, Dr John M. Walsh, Mrs Diane Nelson, Mrs Barbara Pedone, Dr Thomas Kenny, Dr Alessandro Calianese, David X. Stump, SJ, Oscar Magnan, SJ, and Dr Leonor I. Lega for generous support, technical assistance, and research help. As always, I am deeply indebted to my father, Helen, and Grace; Walter and Richie; Bob, Carole, Jim, Randy, Roger, Judy, and David. My brother Richard and my oldest friend, Robert Banka, passed away during the writing of this book and I want most particularly to remember them here.

The authors and publishers gratefully acknowledge the following for permission to reproduce copyright material.

Figures

Chapter 1   Figure 1.1: *Dragon: The Bruce Lee Story*, copyright © 1992, Universal; Figure 1.2: *Breakfast at Tiffany's*, copyright © 1961, Paramount; Figure 1.3: *Psycho*, copyright © 1960, Universal; Figure 1.4: *Jaws*, copyright © 1975, Universal; Figure 1.5: *Schindler's List*, copyright © 1993, Universal; Figure 1.6: *Breakfast at Tiffany's*, copyright © 1961, Paramount; Figures 1.7–1.16: *Fatal Attraction*, copyright © 1987, Paramount; Figures 1.17–1.28: *Scarface*, copyright © 1932, Caddo Co., Inc.

Chapter 2   Figure 2.1: *Jurassic Park*, copyright © 1993, Universal; Figures 2.2–2.4: *She Wore a Yellow Ribbon*, copyright © 1949, RKO; Figure 2.5: *Alien*, copyright © 1979, Fox; Figures 2.6–2.8: *A Perfect World*, copyright © 1993, Warners; Figures 2.9–2.12: *The Man who Shot Liberty Valance*, copyright © 1962, Paramount; Figures 2.13–2.14: *Fatal Attraction*, copyright © 1987,

Paramount; Figure 2.15: *Scarface*, copyright 1932, Caddo/Universal; Figures 2.16–2.17: *The Man who Shot Liberty Valance*, copyright © 1962, Paramount; Figure 2.18: *A Perfect World*, copyright © 1993, Warners; Figure 2.19: *Psycho*, copyright © 1960, Universal; Figure 2.20: *In the Realm of the Senses*, copyright © 1976, Argos Films; Figures 2.21–2.24: *Jurassic Park*, copyright © 1993, Universal; Figures 2.25–2.27: *Rashomon*, copyright © 1950, RKO.

Chapter 3   Figures 3.1–3.2: *2001: A Space Odyssey*, copyright © 1968, MGM; Figure 3.3: *Dr Strangelove: Or How I Learned to Stop Worrying and Love the Bomb*, copyright © 1963, Hawk Films; Figure 3.4: *Psycho*, copyright © 1960, Universal; Figure 3.5: *Alien*, copyright © 1979, Fox; Figure 3.6: *Jurassic Park*, copyright © 1993, Universal; Figure 3.7: *Schindler's List*, copyright © 1993, Universal; Figures 3.8–3.9: *Carrie*, copyright © 1976, United Artists; Figures 3.10–3.11: *Stagecoach*, copyright © 1939, W. Wanger; Figures 3.12–3.13: *The Pink Panther Strikes Again*, copyright © 1976, United Artists; Figures 3.14–3.18: *The Man who Shot Liberty Valance*, copyright © 1962, Paramount; Figures 3.19–3.33: *Rules of the Game*, copyright © 1939, Les Grandes Films.

Chapter 4   Figure 4.1: *Big*, copyright © 1988, Fox; Figure 4.2: *A League of their Own*, copyright © 1992, Columbia; Figure 4.3: *Renaissance Man*, dir. Penny Marshall, copyright © 1994, Cinergi; Figures 4.4–4.5: *Scarface*, copyright © 1983, Universal; Figure 4.6: *The Birds*, copyright © 1963, A. J. Hitchcock; Figure 4.7: *Notorious*, copyright 1946, RKO; Figure 4.8: *North by Northwest*, copyright 1959, Loews, Inc.; Figure 4.9: *Unforgiven*, copyright © 1992, Warners; Figure 4.10: *A Perfect World*, copyright © 1993, Warners; Figure 4.11: *The Man who Shot Liberty Valance*, copyright © 1962, Paramount; Figure 4.12: *She Wore a Yellow Ribbon*, copyright © 1949, RKO; Figure 4.13: *The Man who Shot Liberty Valance*, copyright © 1962, Paramount.

Chapter 5   Figure 5.1: *The Texas Chainsaw Massacre*, copyright © 1974, Vortex, Inc.; Figure 5.2: *The Stepfather*, copyright © 1986, ITC Prod., Inc.; Figure 5.3: *Dances with Wolves*, copyright © 1990, TIG Prod., Inc.; Figure 5.4: *Posse*, copyright © 1993, Polygram; Figure 5.5: *Geronimo*, copyright © 1993, Columbia; Figure 5.6: *Tombstone*, dir. George P. Cosmatos, copyright © 1994, Cinergi; Figure 5.7: *Bad Girls*, dir. Jonathan Kaplan, copyright © 1994, Fox; Figure 5.8: *Wolf*, dir. Mike Nicholls, copyright © 1994, Columbia; Figure 5.9: *Letter from an Unknown Woman*, copyright © 1948, Rampart; Figure 5.10: *A Fistful of Dollars*, copyright © 1964, Jolly Film; Figures 5.11–5.14: *Murder, My Sweet*, copyright © 1944, RKO; Figures 5.15–5.20: *Gunfight at the OK Corral*, copyright © 1956, Paramount.

Chapter 6   Figure 6.1: *The Pink Panther*, copyright © 1963, Mirisch-G-E; Figure 6.2: *Lethal Weapon*, copyright © 1987, Warners; Figure 6.3: *Lethal*

Weapon 2, copyright © 1989, Warners; Figure 6.4: *Lethal Weapon 3*, copyright © 1992, Warners; Figure 6.5: *Terminator 2: Judgment Day*, copyright © 1991, Carolco; Figure 6.6: *The Pink Panther Strikes Again*, copyright © 1976, United Artists; Figure 6.7: *Terminator 2: Judgment Day*, copyright © 1991, Carolco; Figure 6.8: *True Lies*, dir. James Cameron, copyright © 1994, Lightstorm; Figure 6.9: *Goldfinger*, copyright © 1964, Danjaq; Figure 6.10: *The Fugitive*, copyright © 1993, Warners; Figure 6.11: *Rio Bravo*, copyright © 1958, Armada Prod.; Figure 6.12: *Rio Lobo*, copyright © 1970, Malabar Prod.; Figure 6.13: *El Mariachi*, copyright © 1992, Los Houligans; Figures 6.14–6.22: *Psycho*, dir. Alfred Hitchcock, copyright © 1960, Shamley Productions and Universal Pictures.

Chapter 7   Figure 7.1: *The Terminator*, copyright © 1984, Cinema 84; Figure 7.2: *The Last Action Hero*, copyright © 1993, Columbia; Figures 7.3–7.4: *The Searchers*, copyright © 1956, Warners; Figure 7.5: *It Happened One Night*, copyright © 1934, Columbia; Figure 7.6: *Gone with the Wind*, copyright © 1939, Selznick International; Figures 7.7–7.8: *The Public Enemy*, copyright © 1931, Warners; Figure 7.9: *White Heat*, copyright © 1949, Warners; Figures 7.10–7.16: *Morocco*, copyright © 1930, Paramount; Figure 7.17: *Shanghai Express*, copyright © 1932, Paramount; Figure 7.18: *The Blue Angel*, copyright © 1930, UFA; Figures 7.19–7.21: *Morocco*, copyright © 1930, Paramount; Figures 7.22–7.29: *Dirty Harry*, copyright © 1971, Malpaso/Warners; Figure 7.30: *The Good, the Bad, and the Ugly*, copyright © 1966, PEA; Figure 7.31: *Coogan's Bluff*, copyright © 1968, Universal; Figure 7.32: *Sudden Impact*, copyright © 1983, Warners; Figure 7.33: *The Outlaw Josey Wales*, copyright © 1976, Warners.

Chapter 8   Figure 8.1: *Basic Instinct*, copyright © 1992, Carolco; Figure 8.2: *Forrest Gump*, dir. Robert Zemeckis, copyright © 1994, Paramount; Figure 8.3: *Fantasia*, copyright © 1940, Disney; Figure 8.4: *The Crow*, dir. Alex Proyas, copyright © 1994, Miramax; Figure 8.5: *The Wizard of Oz*, copyright © 1939, MGM; Figure 8.6: *It's a Wonderful Life*, copyright © 1946, Republic; Figure 8.7: *The Birth of a Nation*, copyright © 1915, David W. Griffith Corp.; Figure 8.8: *The Rink*, copyright © 1916, Mutual; Figure 8.9: *Easy Street*, copyright © 1917, Mutual; Figure 8.10: *The Immigrant*, copyright © 1917, Mutual; Figure 8.11: *A King in New York*, copyright © 1957, Archway; Figures 8.12–8.19: *A Woman of Paris*, copyright © 1923, United Artists; Figures 8.20–8.29: *The Crying Game*, copyright © 1992, Miramax.

Chapter 9   Figure 9.1: *M. Hulot's Holiday*, copyright © 1953, Cady/Discina; Figure 9.2: *The Untouchables*, copyright © 1987, Paramount; Figures 9.3–9.4: *Gone with the Wind*, copyright © 1939, Selznick International; Figures 9.5–9.18: *Dr Jekyll and Mr Hyde*, copyright © 1932, Paramount; Figures 9.19–9.29: *Nosferatu*, copyright © 1922, Prana Films, G.M.B.H.

Chapter 10   Figure 10.1: *Village of the Damned*, dir. John Carpenter, copyright © 1995, Universal; Figure 10.2: *Driving Miss Daisy*, copyright © 1989, Warners; Figure 10.3: *Village of the Damned*, dir. John Carpenter, copyright © 1995, Universal; Figure 10.4: *Jurassic Park*, copyright © 1993, Universal; Figure 10.5: *Gone with the Wind*, copyright © 1939, Selznick International; Figure 10.6: *North by Northwest*, copyright © 1959, Loews; Figure 10.7: *Miami Vice*, copyright © 1984, Universal; Figure 10.8: *Blue Velvet*, copyright © 1986, Warners; Figure 10.9: *Twin Peaks*, copyright © 1987, Lynch/Frost Prod.; Figure 10.10: *Murder, My Sweet*, copyright © 1944, RKO; Figures 10.11–10.21: *Peter Gunn:* "Skin Deep" copyright © 1958, International Creative.

Chapter 11   Figure 11.1: *Basic Instinct*, copyright © 1992, Carolco; Figure 11.2: *The Birds*, copyright © 1963, A. J. Hitchcock Prod.; Figure 11.3: *Wolf*, dir. Mike Nichols, copyright © 1994, Columbia; Figure 11.4: *Bonfire of the Vanities*, copyright © 1990, Warners; Figures 11.5–11.6: *The Untouchables*, copyright © 1987, Paramount; Figure 11.7: *The Battleship Potemkin*, copyright © 1925, Goskino; Figure 11.8: *Carrie*, copyright © 1976, United Artists; Figure 11.9: *Last Tango in Paris*, copyright © 1972, United Artists; Figures 11.10–11.22: *The Battleship Potemkin*, copyright © 1925, Goskino; Figures 11.23–11.30: *Umberto D*, copyright © 1952, Rizzoli Films.

Chapter 12   Figure 12.1: *Geronimo*, copyright © 1993, Columbia; Figure 12.2: *Aliens*, copyright © 1986, Carolco; Figure 12.3: *Terminator 2: Judgment Day*, copyright © 1991, Carolco; Figure 12.4: *The Man who Shot Liberty Valance*, copyright © 1962, Paramount; Figure 12.5: *Scarface*, copyright © 1983, Universal; Figure 12.6: *The Terminator*, copyright © 1984, Cinema 84; Figure 12.7: *Every Which Way but Loose*, copyright © 1978, Warners; Figure 12.8: *Point of No Return*, copyright © 1993, Warners; Figure 12.9: *Way Down East*, copyright © 1920, D. W. Griffith Corp.; Figure 12.10: *Stagecoach*, copyright © 1939, W. Wanger Prod.; Figure 12.11: *Single White Female*, copyright © 1992, Columbia; Figure 12.12: *She Wore a Yellow Ribbon*, copyright © 1949, RKO; Figure 12.13: *Marnie*, copyright © 1964, Universal Pictures; Figure 12.14: *Rio Bravo*, copyright © 1958, Armada Prod.; Figure 12.15: *Single White Female*, copyright © 1992, Columbia; Figure 12.16: *Alien*, copyright © 1979, Fox; Figure 12.17: *True Lies*, dir. James Cameron, copyright © 1994, Lightstorm; Figure 12.18: *Rio Bravo*, copyright © 1958, Armada Prod.; Figure 12.19: *The Good, the Bad, and the Ugly*, copyright © 1966, PEA; Figure 12.20: *Cyrano de Bergerac*, copyright © 1950, Stanley Kramer.

Chapter 13   Figure 13.1: *Do the Right Thing*, copyright © 1989, 40 Acres & Mule; Figure 13.2: *Dances with Wolves*, copyright © 1990, Tig Productions, Inc.; Figures 13.3–13.4: *Lethal Weapon*, copyright © 1987, Warners; Figure 13.5: *Bonfire of the Vanities*, copyright © 1990, Warners; Figures 13.6–13.7: *Stagecoach*, copyright © 1939, W. Wanger Prod.; Figures 13.8–13.9: *Dirty*

Harry, copyright © 1971, Malpaso/Warners; Figure 13.10: *Higher Learning*, dir. John Singleton, copyright © 1994, Columbia; Figure 13.11: *Gone with the Wind*, copyright © 1939, Selznick International; Figure 13.12: *The People Under the Stairs*, copyright © 1991, Universal; Figure 13.13: *Dances with Wolves*, copyright © 1990, Tig Productions, Inc.; Figure 13.14: *Jungle Fever*, copyright © 1991, Universal; Figure 13.15: *Boyz N the Hood*, copyright © 1991, Columbia; Figures 13.16–13.21: *LA Confidential*, dir. Curtis Hanson, copyright © 1997, Warner Brothers.

Chapter 14 Figures 14.1–14.2: *The Wizard of Oz*, copyright © 1939, MGM; Figure 14.3: *The Pink Panther*, copyright © 1964, Mirisch-G-E; Figures 14.4–14.5: *Gone with the Wind*, copyright © 1939, MGM; Figure 14.6: *The Birth of a Nation*, copyright © 1915, David W. Griffith Corp./Epoch Producing Corp.; Figure 14.7: *It's a Wonderful Life*, copyright © 1946, Republic; Figure 14.8: *The Adventures of Robin Hood*, copyright © 1938, Warners; Figure 14.9: *Young Mr Lincoln*, copyright © 1939, Fox; Figure 14.10: *The Godfather, Part II*, copyright © 1974, Paramount; Figure 14.11: *The Invasion of the Body Snatchers*, copyright © 1956, Allied Artists; Figure 14.12: *The Texas Chainsaw Massacre*, copyright © 1974, Vortex; Figure 14.13: *Double Indemnity*, copyright © 1944, Paramount; Figure 14.14: *Little Caesar*, copyright © 1930, Warners; Figure 14.15: *The Man who Shot Liberty Valance*, copyright © 1962, Paramount; Figure 14.16: *Dr Jekyll and Mr Hyde*, copyright © 1932, Paramount; Figures 14.17–14.27: *Pretty Woman*, copyright © 1990, Touchstone, Figures 14.28–14.38: *The People Under the Stairs*, copyright © 1991, Universal.

Chapter 15 Figures 15.1–15.3: *Citizen Kane*, copyright © 1941, RKO; Figure 15.4: *Stagecoach*, copyright © 1939, W. Wanger Prod.; Figure 15.5: *Touch of Evil*, copyright 1958, Universal; Figures 15.6–15.9: *Citizen Kane*, copyright © 1941, RKO; Figure 15.10: *His Girl Friday*, copyright © 1939, Columbia; Figures 15.11–15.18: *Citizen Kane*, copyright © 1941, RKO; Figure 15.19: *The Third Man*, copyright © 1949, London Films; Figures 15.20–15.39: *Citizen Kane*, copyright © 1941, RKO.

Plates

Plates 1–3: *Schindler's List*, copyright © 1993, Universal; Plates 4–6: *Dead Ringers*, copyright © 1988, Morgan Creek Productions; Plates 7–20: *The Sixth Sense*, dir. M. Knight Shyamalan, copyright © 1999, Hollywood Pictures and Spyglass Entertainment; Plates 21–33: *The Searchers*, copyright © 1956, Warners; Plates 34–40: *Jungle Fever*, copyright © 1991, Universal; Plates 41–48: *Goldfinger*, copyright © 1964, Danjaq; Plates 49–53: *Psycho*, dir. Gus Van Sant, copyright © 1998, Universal Pictures and Imagine Entertainment; Plates 54–56: *Victor/Victoria*, copyright © 1982, Ladbroke for M-G-M; Plate

57: *A Shot in the Dark*, copyright © 1964, Mirisch-G-E; Plates 58–59: *The Pink Panther*, copyright © 1964, Mirisch-G-E; Plates 60–66: *Victor/Victoria*, copyright © 1982, Ladbroke for M-G-M; Plates 67–74: *The Silence of the Lambs*, copyright © 1990, Orion; Plates 75–80: *American Gigolo*, copyright © 1980, Paramount; Plates 81–89: *Boyz N the Hood*, copyright © 1991, Columbia; Plate 90: *Gladiator*, dir. Ridley Scott, copyright © 2000, Dreamworks SKG and Universal Pictures; Plate 91: *Forrest Gump*, dir. Robert Zemeckis, copyright © 1994, Paramount; Plate 92: *Jurassic Park*, copyright © 1993, Universal; Plates 93–94: *Conceiving Ada*, dir. Lynn Hershman Leeson, copyright © 1997, Hotwire Productions; Plates 95–97: *Armageddon*, dir. Michael Bay, copyright © 1998, Touchstone; Plate 98: *Marnie*, copyright © 1964, Universal Pictures; Plate 99: *Natural Born Killers*, dir. Oliver Stone, copyright © 1994, Warner Brothers; Plates 100–120: *The Matrix*, dir. The Wachowski Brothers, copyright © 1999, Warner Brothers; Plates 121–127: *Timecode*, dir. Mike Figgis, copyright © 2000, Red Mullet Productions and Screen Gems Inc.

Every effort has been made to trace all the copyright holders, but if any has been inadvertently overlooked, the publishers will be pleased to make the necessary arrangement at the first opportunity.

1

INTRODUCTION

Fatal Attraction and *Scarface*

How We Think about Movies

People respond to movies in different ways, and there are many reasons for this. We have all stood in the lobby of a theater and heard conflicting opinions from people who have just seen the same film. Some loved it, some were annoyed by it, some found it just OK. Perhaps we've thought, "Well, what do they know? Maybe they just didn't get it." So we go to the reviewers whose business it is to "get it." But often they do not agree. One reviewer will love it, the next will tell us to save our money. What thrills one person may bore or even offend another. Disagreements and controversies, however, can reveal a great deal about the assumptions underlying these varying responses. If we explore these assumptions, we can ask questions about how sound they are. Questioning our assumptions and those of others is a good way to start thinking about movies. We will soon see that there are many productive ways of thinking about movies and many approaches that we can use to analyze them.

In *Dragon: The Bruce Lee Story* (1992), the actor playing Bruce Lee sits in an American movie theater (figure 1.1) and watches a scene from *Breakfast at Tiffany's* (1961) in which Audrey Hepburn's glamorous character awakens her upstairs neighbor, Mr Yunioshi. Half awake, he jumps up, bangs his head on a low-hanging, "Oriental"-style lamp, and stumbles around his apartment crashing into things. The audience in the theater laughs uproariously at this slapstick comedy but Lee does not. To the contrary, he becomes more and more enraged until finally he and his girlfriend leave the theater.

Lee is Chinese, his girlfriend is white, and *Dragon: The Bruce Lee Story* has shown him to be the victim of anti-Asian prejudice in the

Fig. 1.1

Fig. 1.2

United States. In this scene, the butt of the humor, Mr Yunioshi, is an Asian man played by a white man (Mickey Rooney); the character's appearance (exaggerated make-up that makes him appear to be bug-eyed with buck teeth), dialect (he speaks with an exaggerated accent), and actions (comic ineptness), all reinforce stereotypical and degrading views of Asian behavior (figure 1.2). Lee feels that this representation, combined with the audience's laughter, reflects and contributes to his own assimilation problems. Others in the audience, however, do not see the movie in this way at all. They respond, or think they respond, only to the slapstick: the same scene, but very different responses. Furthermore, Lee's girlfriend initially joins in the laughter but becomes uncomfortable when she senses his pain.

Movies and Entertainment

Why do we go to the movies? Most of us go for entertainment. Indeed, Bruce Lee and his girlfriend are on a date when they see *Breakfast at Tiffany's*, a common context in which young people see movies. Going out on a date, having fun, and eating popcorn may all make it seem as if movies are fairly simple things that do not require much thought. But, as *Dragon* illustrates, having fun is not isolated from serious issues. Lee does not go to the movies in order to contemplate his social oppression but, in the midst of a light-romantic comedy, that is precisely what happens. He comes to an awareness that motivates his entire career: he dedicates his life to offering alternative representations of Asian men in the cinema.

Far from being frivolous, entertainment may actually provide a pleasurable smokescreen beneath which disturbing issues can be either reinforced or, more helpfully, contemplated. Different genres lend themselves to the examination of particular social and cultural issues. The modern horror film, beginning with *Psycho* (1960, figure 1.3, see chapter 6) and including such films as *The Texas Chainsaw Massacre* (1974) and *The Hills Have Eyes* (1977), locates the most hideous horror at the center of the home and family. People go to those films, of course, to get scared to death, shriek, and jump out of their seats, not to

Fig. 1.3

contemplate whether the once joyous nuclear family with a working father and housewife mother is an outmoded institution that has become the breeding ground for psychotic murderers. Yet, as we will see in chapter 5, it may be precisely because we enjoy being scared to death that these films can take such an unflinching look at the family. Similarly, most people go to Westerns because they enjoy the action and the scenery, not because they want to contemplate the tensions within American society between the wilderness and the frontier and between white civilization and Native Americans. Yet, a film like *Dances with Wolves* (1990) makes very clear that that, in part, is what the genre is about.

At times, different films or genres reflect virtually opposed responses to common cultural concerns. As the modern horror film has focused upon the collapse of traditional images of the supportive nuclear family, a number of recent historical epics have championed a return to conservative family values and linked the maintenance of those values with grand issues of national identity and continuity. Films like *Braveheart* (1995), *Saving Private Ryan* (1997), *Gladiator* (2000), *The Patriot* (2000), and *Pearl Harbor* (2001) begin with devastations to or dysfunctions within traditional families and show their damaged heroes going on to help save their nation during a time of national crisis; these films conclude with a sense of a triumphant society realigned to "proper" values. *Saving Private Ryan, The Patriot*, and *Pearl Harbor* all close with images of strong nuclear families that signify national continuity. *Gladiator* closes with the dying hero envisioning an Elysian reunion with his lost family, and the implication that his sacrifice has made the Roman Empire safe for such families in the future. Such endings could hardly be more different from the endings of recent horror films, but modern horror films and historical epics both respond to a common cultural impulse – anxiety about the decline of the traditional family at the end of the twentieth century.

Part of understanding movies is understanding the complex ways in which they relate to the society that produced them. People frequently assume this with movies like the Nazi propaganda film, *Triumph of the Will* (1935), but we will see that it is just as useful in exploring issues of race, class, and gender in a wide variety of genres including horror films, historical epics, action films, comedies, and Westerns. A Western like *Posse* (1993), for example, with its large cast of central black characters, seems odd when compared with most Westerns, such as *High Noon* (1952) and *Shane* (1953), which have no central black characters and frequently do not even contain marginalized images of blacks. The "civilized" West, these films assume, was a West peopled with whites. *Posse*, however, explicitly refers to the fact that the historical "West" contained many blacks; this implicitly leads the viewer to question their absence in traditional Westerns. When we look at the vast majority of Westerns from 1900 to 1970 and see virtually no blacks anywhere, we begin to learn about the racial priorities of American society and of the film industry during that period. We can often learn a great deal not only from what we see in a film but also from what we do not see.

Certain films "push all the buttons" to stimulate widespread enthusiasm or anger at the time of their release. Such a widespread reaction can reveal a great deal about the ways in which we look at films and think about them. In 1915, *The Birth of a Nation* became a lightning rod for both adoration and anger for its representation of blacks and the Ku Klux Klan. In 1993, both *Jurassic Park* and *Schindler's List* pushed all the buttons, but they were different buttons.

Jurassic Park is, worldwide, one of the largest grossing box-office movies ever made. Half a year after *Jurassic Park* appeared, its director, Steven Spielberg, released *Schindler's List*, one of the most critically acclaimed films

Fig. 1.4

Fig. 1.5

of that year. They are very different kinds of film. *Schindler's List* received twelve Academy Award nominations, whereas *Jurassic Park* received only three, but earned much more money. *Jurassic Park* was, in many ways, exactly what Spielberg's fans expected – a fantasy filled with childlike wonder and moments of great terror, like Spielberg's *Jaws* (1975, figure 1.4). *Schindler's List* (figure 1.5) seemed to come from a "different" Spielberg, since it is a three and a half hour, intensely serious, black-and-white film about the Nazi Holocaust. Most of the critical respect went to *Schindler's List*; most of the money went to *Jurassic Park*.

Yet we must question rather than simply accept the seeming dichotomy between these two films. The Academy Awards typically honor serious films that represent Hollywood in a respectable light. That may help explain why many of the most successful genre directors such as Alfred Hitchcock, Howard Hawks, and Blake Edwards never won best director awards during the years in which their best mysteries, Westerns, and comedies were made. It may also help explain why comedies seldom win best film of the year and why, when they do, they are likely to be comedies with overtly serious subject matter. From this perspective, *Jurassic Park* is too much of an action-adventure, science-fiction film to be taken seriously. But this may tell us more about the Academy of Motion Picture Arts and Sciences than it tells us about anything intrinsic to *Jurassic Park*.

If we switch perspectives to that of authorship, as we will in chapter 4, we may begin to notice unexpected similarities between Spielberg's genre entertainments and *Schindler's List*. Although the latter film is about the Jews during the Nazi Holocaust, its central character is an Aryan played by Liam Neeson, a handsome young actor. He thus parallels the character of Indiana Jones played by Harrison Ford in the series of popular films featuring that character. Furthermore, the Jews are reduced to an historical backdrop of undifferentiated people who show no active agency on their part; they must be saved by Schindler, who thus becomes a hero figure like Indiana Jones. Is this a whole new Steven Spielberg?

Critical Approaches to Movies

Throughout this book, we will be encouraging a critical process that is, by definition, never finished. As soon as we stop questioning, we are in danger of accepting easy and obvious "truths" that can, in fact, blind us to important issues. Let us return for a moment to *Dragon: The Bruce Lee Story* to illustrate how this works. As we have suggested, the film provocatively dramatizes the evils of racial stereotyping in Hollywood films. As such, many might think that it should simply be embraced as a progressive step forward. Notice, however, that in the movie theater scene that we have discussed, Lee, the central character, is with his girlfriend. He is the one who has insight and, when she sees his rage, she adopts his position. If we just look at this scene, there is no problem. He, after all, is Asian and she is white, so it makes perfect sense that he would recognize the ugly racism of the film they are watching and she would adopt his insights. This, however, is not an isolated incident. *Dragon* constantly reinforces traditional gender roles by marginalizing her role and limiting her to comparatively brief scenes in which she is seen primarily as a girlfriend or wife/mother. She is narratively subordinate to the central male character in a manner that, like most contemporary Hollywood films, *Dragon* never questions or challenges. At every level, *Dragon* asks us to unquestioningly accept current stereotypes of women in film that are equivalent to the racial stereotypes in *Breakfast at Tiffany's* that so anger Lee. Yet, how many people watching *Dragon* are equally angered by its treatment of women as passive, marginalized characters who are beautiful to look at and whose primary function is to support important men?

People respond differently to films depending upon their gender, race, class, sexual orientation, and personal background. In *Dragon*, Lee's race and American experience make him respond to *Breakfast at Tiffany's* differently from the rest of the audience. In actuality, *Breakfast at Tiffany's* received many different responses at the time of its release. A brief survey of them complements the fictionalized Lee's response in *Dragon* and points to many central issues we will be exploring in the following chapters. In 1961, *Breakfast at Tiffany's* was dominantly perceived as a sophisticated romantic comedy. It was also seen as a star vehicle for Audrey Hepburn. Holly Golightly, the character that she plays, was, by early 1960s' standards, a free-wheeling, daringly sexual woman (figure 1.6). This image departed significantly from Hepburn's previous roles. During production of the film she was concerned that her character should not be too shocking for her fans. She wanted, in other words, to change her image but not to change it too drastically. But Audrey Hepburn was not the only famous name associated with this film. It was based on Truman Capote's well-known novella of the same name. As always happens in such cases, many people focus attention on similarities and differences between the novel and the film: how "faithful" is the movie to the novel; what changes have been made?

Within the industry, and increasingly for the public, another famous name associated with the film was that of its director, Blake Edwards. He had his first major box-office success with the immensely popular service comedy, *Operation Petticoat* (1959), which starred Cary Grant and Tony Curtis, two hugely successful stars of the time. But Edwards had never directed a sophisticated comedy. For some, this film was seen as marking a shift within the career of a director

Fig. 1.6

not unlike the manner in which *Schindler's List* is currently seen within Spielberg's career. Yet, another film director, Radley Metzger, primarily saw the film at the time of its release as opening the door to treating disturbing sexual topics and themes in a manner that would not offend audiences. Based upon his perception of *Tiffany's* as a sexually daring and groundbreaking film, Metzger made a series of successful and critically acclaimed films such as *Carmen, Baby* (1967) with much more overt and graphic sexuality than that in *Tiffany's*. Perhaps related to this, *Tiffany's* has remained an immensely popular film within the gay male community, where it still receives theatrical screenings.

Some of these responses to *Tiffany's* may seem bewildering. How is it possible that the same film can be seen by mainstream audiences as a nice romantic comedy, by another film director as the inspiration for making heterosexual soft-core pornography, and by gay men as a cult classic? Is one of these perceptions more correct than the other? Is someone "misreading" the film? For those who respond to the film primarily as a literary adaptation, we should ask, "What is the relationship between a novel and a film based on it?" Can a film be "faithful" to its literary source, or is the concept of "faithfulness" a murky one that may obscure rather than illuminate its subject? In what sense can the film be seen as a Blake Edwards film, particularly one such as this for which he receives no screenwriting credit? What are the assumptions behind attributing a film's authorship to its director? What can we learn from studying *Tiffany's* in relation to Edwards's following films, *The Days of Wine and Roses* (1962) and *The Pink Panther* (1964)? For those who see the film as a star vehicle, in what sense does an actor like Audrey Hepburn shape and control her performance in a film? Is it her performance, or is her performance part of something larger that someone else controls? How does the character of Holly Golightly differ from those of previous Hepburn parts such as Sabrina in the film of the same name? Questions like these lie at the center of each of the following chapters. They are complex and require careful consideration. In many cases, assumptions that many of us share about the nature of movies will have to be revised or discarded.

Outline of the Book

The following chapters employ the structure of this one, with the first half introducing the chapter's basic critical focus and the second half illustrating it with close readings of individual films. The second half of this chapter uses *Fatal Attraction* (1987) and *Scarface* (1932) to introduce approaches that later chapters will develop more fully. The book's underlying premise remains constant: that there are many productive ways to think about movies; that we must never think we know everything about a movie; and that the more we learn about movies, the more that knowledge will help us to understand not only those films but also important aspects of our culture. Far from destroying our pleasure from movies, this process enhances our appreciation of the complexities of this popular, influential art form.

We have arranged the chapters in such a way as to systematically expand our understanding of film while avoiding potential pitfalls and confusions. Chapter 2 discusses **narrative** structure or the manner in which a film's story is told and organized. Most people, when asked what a movie is "about," think first in terms of its storyline, so a look at the ways in which movies tell stories is a useful place to begin a study of their meaning. We will examine the standard narrative techniques as well as alternatives to them, and then illustrate those techniques with a detailed look at two films from different narrative traditions. *Jurassic Park* (1993) is a popular film which uses classical Hollywood narration; *Rashomon* (1950) is a widely respected one which works in an entirely different tradition, that of the international art cinema. Studied together, these films reveal a good deal about how movies tell stories.

Movies do much more than tell stories, however, and they also tell stories differently from other narrative forms. The novel *Jurassic Park*, for example, is not the same thing as the movie. We cannot begin to think with any sophistication about movies until we understand their formal workings, the things that make them different from other art forms such as plays or novels. Chapter 3, on **formal structure**, discusses the properties of film, such as cinematography, sound, and editing and shows how these formal properties function in two films from different periods and different national cinemas, *Rules of the Game* (1939) and *The Sixth Sense* (1999).

These early chapters deal with approaches that help us to understand the workings of individual films. The remainder of the book explores larger contexts that enable us to understand the relation of individual films to other films or to cultural issues. It is essential, however, for the student to begin with the specifics of the individual film because, unless we have a detailed sense of the construction of a film, we cannot intelligently and accurately relate it to larger issues.

The first of these issues, discussed in chapter 4, is **authorship**. One traditional way of relating artworks to larger issues is by raising the issue of authorship. This is a complicated issue since film is a collaborative form, but we show why the director is commonly considered the author of a film and then examine two films by quite different American directors from different decades, *The Searchers* (1956) by John Ford and *Jungle Fever* (1991) by Spike Lee. We show how placing these films within the perspectives of their directors' other works can give us valuable insights.

An entirely different context into which film can fruitfully be placed is **genre**, the subject of chapter 5. Genre study relates films not to other works by the same author but to other works of the same type, such as Westerns, musicals, or horror films. It shows us how different eras have treated similar material in different ways and helps us to understand the role of both formula and creativity in genre films. We discuss *Murder, My Sweet* (1944) in relation to both the detective genre and *film noir*, and *Gunfight at the OK Corral* (1956) in relation to the Western.

Chapter 6 looks at a major phenomenon of the past twenty years: **series**, **sequels**, and **remakes**. This approach explores individual films within the context of films that are either sources for them or other films to which they are related by sharing common characters or continuing stories. We examine as examples the classic 1960 horror film, *Psycho*, and the 1998 remake of it, as well as *Goldfinger* (1964) from the popular James Bond series, which has continued over decades.

Stars constitute a major part of the appeal of some films as well as a substantial part of their budgets. Some people, in fact, think of films mainly in terms of the actors in them. Chapter 7 looks at the difference between **stars** and actors and at how an actor's "image" can contribute substantially to a film's meaning. We show how such an image changes over time and examine the careers of a major female and male star from the perspective of their work in two films made decades apart, Marlene Dietrich in *Morocco* (1930) and Clint Eastwood in *Dirty Harry* (1971).

Up to this point, this book explores ways in which film can be understood by either examining internal aspects of the films themselves or by relating them to patterns within the world of cinema, but that world does not account for much of the significance that film has or what we can learn from it. To understand this, we have to consider wider areas. The first context, explored in chapter 8, is audiences and **reception**. The same film can mean different things at different times and even different things at the same time to different spectators and audiences. Much of this depends on the reception context in which the film is viewed. Reception contexts include how a movie is advertised and publicized as well as such things as public outcries and protests. This chapter will look at the initial reception of Charles Chaplin's *A Woman of Paris* (1923) within the context of the popular comedian's career at that time and how its meanings shifted at different points in his career, and at *The Crying Game* (1992), a controversial film whose initial reception context included a highly successful advertising campaign with which popular reviewers initially played along, creating a reception context that was soon to be altered.

Another way in which we can learn about film by stepping outside its world is to look at its relation to other art forms, the subject of chapter 9. We will look at areas of similarity and difference with art forms to which film is often compared: theater (a performance art) and fiction (a narrative form). We will illustrate these relations by means of two movies based upon novels, *Dr Jekyll and Mr Hyde* (1932), one of the many movies based upon Robert Louis Stevenson's novel *The Strange Case of Dr Jekyll and Mr Hyde* (and influenced by plays based upon the same novel), and *Nosferatu* (1922), a German film from the silent era based upon Bram Stoker's novel *Dracula*.

As well as being an art form, film is part of the mass media, and chapter 10 examines film's relation to the other mass media of radio and television. While all three use narrative, the formal properties and industrial practices of each make of them very different things with different capabilities and traditions. Blake Edwards has had a long, successful career that includes work in radio and television narrative series and many Hollywood feature films. We will illustrate the differences and similarities among these media using one of his works from each medium: the radio show *Richard Diamond, Private Detective*, the television show *Peter Gunn*, and the movie *Victor/Victoria* (1982).

At this point, with a number of critical perspectives behind us, it is important to look at some of the major theories of film. Most people assume that film is in some ways "realistic," though they mean many things by this. We examine the theoretical assumptions underlying *The Battleship Potemkin* (1925), a Russian formalist film from the silent era, and *Umberto D* (1952), an Italian film made within a realist tradition. Film theorists help us explore and understand such notions as **realism**, and it is important that we do so before moving on to discuss social and cultural issues, since naïve notions about realism block exploration of such issues.

The next three chapters take up the vital issues of gender, race, and class in film. All of us are in part defined through the nexus of these three categories, whether we are a white, middle-class man living in the suburbs or an African American woman living in the inner city. Films draw upon, promulgate, and challenge common ideas about race, class, and gender in our culture. They frequently do so implicitly rather than explicitly and by invoking invisible norms by which we judge characters and actions: masculinity is the norm against which femininity is judged; the middle class is the norm against which the lower and upper classes are judged; heterosexuality is the norm against which homosexuality is judged; and white is the norm against which people of color are judged.

Chapter 12 examines how movies construct gender (e.g., masculinity and femininity) and sexuality (e.g., heterosexuality and homosexuality). These assumptions affect not only characterization but also narrative structure and visual style. We have chosen *American Gigolo* (1980) as a film that represents masculinity in an unusual way and *The Silence of the Lambs* (1990) as a film that represents femininity in a challenging departure from Hollywood norms. Yet, both films contain contradictions that caution us from simply thinking of these representations as all good or all bad.

Chapter 13 similarly examines representations of race and ethnicity in film. To do so, we raise questions about what stereotypes are, how they function, and whether they affect all people in the same manner. We also consider the related issue of role models and show how seemingly progressive films with positive role models may nevertheless be racially troubling. Close readings of *LA Confidential* (1997) and *Boyz N the Hood* (1991), films which both engage and challenge traditional racial representations from profoundly different perspectives, conclude the chapter.

Chapter 14 explores class in a comparable way. Characters are stereotyped by **economic class** much as they are by race and gender. Frequently these issues intertwine, as in the common representation of certain minorities as belonging almost exclusively to a servant class. Our culture also promulgates class myths such as the ones that rich people are miserable and that we are all better off being middle class or that class injustices exist only in other societies, not in the contemporary United States. We then analyze two Hollywood films, one of which, *Pretty Woman* (1990), simply affirms common notions of class; the other, *The People Under the Stairs* (1991), challenges those notions.

Chapter 15 breaks the pattern of the book and concentrates entirely upon one film, *Citizen Kane* (1941). Undoubtedly the most heralded and praised American film of all time, it enables us to illustrate how the major approaches of the book can be applied to a single film and gives students a model that integrates many useful methods for thinking about any film, including those that they will see in the years to come.

The ways in which movies are made, distributed, and understood are currently changing radically and will continue to do so in the coming decades. Chapter 16 surveys digital technology and its impact on 35 mm filmmaking as well as the emergence of digital video features that use no film at all in the shooting, editing, and projection process. We will also relate new digital technologies to "realism" and the **pro-filmic event** (see chapter 11). The emergence of home theaters with large, high-definition digital projection systems with Dolby surround sound and of DVDs (digital video disks) is also an important part of the digital revolution. Our primary film examples are *The Matrix* (1999) and *Timecode* (2000).

Our approach to understanding movies will take us on a quite different path from the one we are used to from reading movie reviews in newspapers and magazines or watching reviews on television. The purpose of reviews is to tell the reader whether or not the reviewer likes the movie and thinks people should see it. Accordingly, most people read reviews to help decide which films they should see; they commonly have a favorite reviewer with whom they frequently agree. The purpose of this book is quite different. Our primary purpose is not to tell students which films to see or which films are good or bad but, rather, to help students understand all the films they see and to learn ways of thoughtfully evaluating and talking about them. This process may lead some students to change their previous opinions about some movies and to become more responsive to others than they have been in the past.

We offer a close analysis of two films at the end of most chapters not because we think our interpretation is correct or the best one but, rather, because we want to demonstrate how a particular critical method or approach can be applied to specific films. As such we encourage students to think critically about our interpretations, questioning our readings and formulating their own. A textbook such as this is not just a presentation of factual information to be memorized. We offer our readings of films not to tell students what those films mean for all viewers at all times but, rather, to show what they mean to us within a particular critical framework. As such, we have chosen the films for their illustrative value, not because we think they are all good or favorites of ours. We have drawn heavily on popular Hollywood films and recent films since many students will have seen them. But one of the purposes of a text-book such as this is to broaden students' viewing habits and introduce them to films with which they are not familiar. Thus, we have selected films from different national cinemas and older, classical Hollywood films to augment those with which most students will already be familiar. There is nothing priv-ileged about the list of films except that they work for us and supply a balance between the familiar and the unfamiliar.

We turn now to two analyses that will briefly introduce the wide variety of topics with which the following chapters deal in detail. We have chosen *Fatal Attraction* (1987) and *Scarface* (1932), commercially successful films from dif-ferent genres and different eras in film history that attracted a great deal of attention at the time of their release, generating controversy and conflicting interpretations. They provide us with useful springboards from which to introduce many of the topics with which the remainder of this book will be concerned.

Fatal Attraction (1987)

When Vice-President Gore appeared on the *Late Show with David Letterman* in 1993, during an attempt to lighten and popularize his image, he joked that his security code name was "Buttafuoco." He was referring to the widely pub-licized case in which Joey Buttafuoco's teenaged lover attempted to murder his wife. It was often called the "Fatal Attraction" case and was not alone. At around the same time, national attention focused upon the case of a Long Island schoolteacher, Carolyn Warmus, who actually murdered her lover's wife. This was also called the "Fatal Attraction" case.

"Fatal Attraction" has become a popular expression to describe almost any romantic triangle that ends badly. It comes from the 1987 movie that became the second highest grossing film of that year, behind *Beverly Hills Cop II*. But, unlike *Beverly Hills Cop II*, *Fatal Attraction* generated widespread and pas-sionate debate. That controversy is helpful to us because it reveals common assumptions about movies.

Reception

One of the most helpful assessments of the film came from one of its pro-ducers, Sherry Lansing, who called it a Rorshach test for everyone who sees it. Different people see it in different ways. This happens with all films but the differences are more immediately obvious with controversial ones like *Fatal Attraction*.

Perhaps the best place to begin is with the film's unexpected and widespread popularity, not only in the United States but also in Europe. This came despite the fact that many critics did not consider the film particularly good, tending

Fig. 1.7

Fig. 1.8

to describe it as overly manipulative. Its popularity can be seen not only in the film's box-office success but also in the number of newspaper and magazine articles written about it, widespread reports of intense and vocal responses in theaters, talk-show discussions in which the term "Fatal Attraction Syndrome" was used as a pop psychological term to describe ruinous erotic attractions, a *Saturday Night Live* parody, and the widespread use of the title to characterize and popularize situations like the Joey Buttafuoco and Carolyn Warmus cases. Much of the talk-show interest focused in particular on women who were characterized as resembling the Glenn Close character, successful single women frustrated by the lack of a traditional husband and family.

The movie is about a brief affair (figure 1.7) between a married man (Dan, played by Michael Douglas) and a single woman (Alex, played by Glenn Close). When the man tries to end it, she refuses and, after first attempting suicide to gain his sympathy, she begins to menace him and his family. She finally invades his house brandishing a knife and is shot dead by his wife (Beth, played by Anne Archer).

While Alex, who has a traditionally masculine name, is established as an independent career woman, her independence is shown to be a veneer hiding her desperate envy of Dan's close relationship with his wife and daughter. In a key scene, she stands outside his house and secretly watches as he gives his daughter a pet rabbit while the whole family sits cozily beside a fireplace (figure 1.8). The domestic serenity of the scene is so disturbing to Alex that she staggers away to vomit uncontrollably (figure 1.9). Her frustration, which she first turned suicidally against herself, she then turns against the family. She kills the child's rabbit and later tries to kill the wife.

Different reviews described the film as "about" many things: a warning about the dangers of casual sexual relationships, even a masked warning about the dangers of sex in the age of AIDS; a melodrama about the importance of and dangers to family life; a condemnation of independent career women who express sexual desire; a half-horror film that turns such a woman into a monster; or even a feminist slant on a triangular relationship, since it is the woman who initiates the affair, the man who is weak, and the wife who kills the threatening Alex.

Its story was considered particularly appropriate for its times, the late 1980s, in which the conservative Reagan administration sought to reverse what it considered the excesses of 1960s' liberalism and, most appropriately in this case, those of the "sexual revolution" and the rise of feminism, by emphasizing "family values." From this perspective, the film can be seen as a corrective to many movies of the 1960s and 1970s in which people experiment with different sexual partners without harmful consequences. Here, there are brutal consequences that imperil the husband's cherished family life and lead to Alex's death.

Fig. 1.9

In the 1970s and early 1980s, many films such as *The Turning Point* (1977), *An Unmarried Woman* (1978), *Norma Rae* (1979), and *Private Benjamin* (1980) showed single women living productive lives without the necessity of marriage to be happy. This film depicts such a lifestyle as a cover-up for desperate unhappiness and a yearning to belong to a family unit. Many feminists argued that the film was part of a brutal backlash against feminism that removed the option of a happy, single life for women and, in fact, represented single women with sexual desires as monstrous threats to society. Others countered that, although the film undoubtedly strove to that end, it nevertheless created a strong point of identification and sympathy with the "monstrous" woman and made the "normal" family appear smug and repulsive. Rather than accept the film's family values and condemnation of the independent career woman at face value, such a response rejects those very values and opinions. We will see in chapter 12 that such gender issues comprise an important aspect of film criticism.

Fig. 1.10

The Film as a Construct rather than Reality

Part of the response brought attention to the fact that a film is not a "natural" but a constructed object. Many reviewers called the film overly manipulative and attributed this quality to the director (Adrian Lyne), who had a background as a maker of television commercials. They considered him clever with "surface" effects but as having little depth. Such a response reveals many assumptions. In calling the film manipulative and excessive, the reviewers presumed that certain moments in the movie were "more" than the material "required." They particularly cited the scene in which the child's rabbit is found killed and the ending, which depicts Alex as a knife-wielding monster resembling the supernatural killers in the *Halloween* movies.

Fig. 1.11

Alex appears to be killed twice, by two people. When she attacks Beth, Dan comes to Beth's rescue and pushes Alex into the bathtub, attempting to drown her (figure 1.10). A number of close-ups show her apparently dead – under water, eyes open, the water no longer rippling from the struggle; everything is still and quiet (figure 1.11). Suddenly, she rises from the water, brandishing the knife, as if returning from the dead to kill Dan (figure 1.12). Beth enters the room and shoots her through the heart (figure 1.13). Such an ending strongly mimics endings in horror films like *Nightmare on Elm Street* (1984) in which the monster is apparently killed only to rise again and, in some cases, to be killed yet again. Since *Fatal Attraction*, such endings have appeared in a number of mainstream films such as *The Jackal* (1997) in which Bruce Willis's character, a brutal international assassin, is apparently killed by his nemesis,

Fig. 1.12

Fig. 1.13

played by Richard Gere, only to rise again and then be shot dead by another character. In fact, what was once an exciting plot surprise in thrillers can become, over time, an expected one. After John Travolta's villain appears to be blown up before the audience's eyes in *Swordfish* (2001), and even after his scorched body is graphically displayed on an autopsy table, some opening-day audience members said aloud, "He's coming back," and he does.

Norms for Judging the Film

Reviewers' objections to the excesses of *Fatal Attraction*'s ending point to their assumption of a proper dramatic norm. Deviation from this norm becomes excess, or manipulation. Such an assumption, however, obscures the fact that the norm is equally manipulative, although it is likely to go unnoticed since it conforms to expectations. Furthermore, norms for different types of movies are different. The ending would not be excessive in a horror film; on the contrary, if many recent horror films did not have such endings, they would be considered deficient. Most of *Fatal Attraction* conforms to norms for romantic thrillers; its use of devices more appropriate to horror films at the end violated many reviewers' notions of what is "realistic" for romantic thrillers. It is important to note, then, that many notions of realism conform less to any correspondence with "real life" than with the standards accepted for films of a certain type.

The DVD of *Fatal Attraction* includes two endings shot for the film, the one in the **release print** and the original one. The release ending probably accounted for most of the excitement in theaters during the movie's release. It did so by turning Alex into a homicidal monster, and then by letting the audience revel in her brutal destruction. It is not only the fact of her demonization and obliteration that contributed to the film's success with audiences, but also the formal, technical skill with which Adrian Lyne shot and edited it. A look at some of the shots in the sequence preceding the attack will illustrate this and point not only to the role of a director in making a film but also to the value of close formal analysis of the films we see.

The Style of the Ending

The sequence opens with a shot of water swirling into a bathtub drain. The bright light makes the porcelain ominously white, recalling a similar shot of water in a drain during the famous shower murder scene in Hitchcock's *Psycho* (see chapter 6). Here, Beth, dressed in white, is filling the bathtub. During the following scene, the bathroom is brightly white, with the light becoming more and more diffused by steam (figure 1.14).

Fig. 1.14

The bathroom shots are **intercut** with shots of Dan downstairs as he goes about the house checking the locks, so the sense of danger from Alex outside builds. He puts a kettle of water on the stove. The lighting downstairs is a warm amber, which contrasts sharply between cuts with the bright white of the bathroom. In the bathroom, Beth looks vulnerable with her black eyes from an auto accident (figure 1.15). When she wipes steam from a mirror, she, and we, are shocked to see Alex in the room. We then get a full shot of Alex holding a large knife (figure 1.16).

Fig. 1.15

The scene is intensified by a number of carefully organized elements. Alex, also dressed in white, does not lunge right at Beth but, with a puzzled look on her face, asks Beth what she is doing there – as if Alex belonged in the house and Beth were the intruder. This adds an aspect of insanity to her menace, which is further intensified with shots of her absentmindedly cutting her thigh with the knife and not reacting to the pain. A number of shots of overflowing liquids builds the explosive tension in the scene. The bathtub overflows, blood drips on Alex's foot, and finally the kettle downstairs boils and whistles. Then Alex attacks. The audience-pleasing excitement of the ending comes from much more than the simple story element of an attack; it comes in part from the way in which the director organizes and edits the specific images and sounds of that attack.

Fig. 1.16

The original ending

The debate over manipulation would not have been so intense had the original ending been used. When the film was test-marketed with the original ending, audiences objected because they did not feel that Alex suffered enough. Where the ending in the release version borrows its violent impact from horror movies, the original one has more muted associations of artistic drama.

In the original ending, Dan and Beth are quietly raking leaves when the police arrest Dan for murder. Alex has been found with her throat cut and his fingerprints on the knife. When Beth searches for their lawyer's telephone number, she comes across a menacing audiotape that Alex had sent Dan in which she threatens suicide. Alex has killed herself in a way that implicates Dan who has been arrested, and it seems as if the tape will exonerate Dan. In the final shot we see a flashback of Alex in her bathroom. As *Madam Butterfly* plays loudly, she slowly begins to cut her throat.

This ending is much quieter than that of the release version. It makes Alex less of a monster and gives Dan no chance to partially redeem himself by coming to his wife's rescue. The test audiences specifically objected to the fact that Alex's fate was not punishment enough for her behavior.

Unity

By the standards of **classical Hollywood** filmmaking this ending is, however, more complex and unified than that of the release version. A standard rule of Hollywood filmmaking is that there should be no irrelevant plot elements: things introduced should be woven tightly into the fabric of the film. The original ending provides an ideal example. First, it reintroduces the threatening audiotape that Alex had sent Dan and that we have heard earlier. Secondly, the last shot shows Alex in her bathroom where she had originally attempted suicide by slashing her wrists when Dan prepared to leave for the first time. It is also where Dan had cared for and comforted her. Thirdly, the knife is the knife with which each had menaced the other during the brutal fight that occurred when Dan broke into her apartment after Alex had briefly kidnapped his daughter. Finally, *Madam Butterfly* works on a double level. It is not only an opera about a woman who commits suicide after a man abandons her but it is also a favorite of both Alex's and Dan's. Their love of the opera helped bring them together; it also signifies their estrangement when she bought two tickets to a performance and he refused to go. On the night of the performance we see her alone in her apartment dementedly switching her light off and on as *Madam Butterfly* plays on the soundtrack. Now it plays as she kills herself.

The two endings point to an important aspect of movies: they are shaped by a multitude of forces, from screenwriters to directors to producers to actors to audiences. Even when "finished," a film isn't necessarily finished. Movies are often changed extensively as a result of audience testing.

Even when "finished" again, films are not necessarily finished. They are often cut or cropped or even colorized for television viewing; footage is often added for European or video or DVD release; and, years after a movie's release, a "director's cut" is sometimes assembled from material never shown in theaters (as is the case with the DVD version of *Fatal Attraction*). It is useful, then, to question what a film is or if a film is ever a single thing. Not only is it possible to interpret a film from a number of perspectives, but it is also possible to develop a number of perspectives about what the film itself actually is.

The Development of the Movie

Fatal Attraction is based upon a story that became the basis for a 45-minute short film, *Diversion*, by screenwriter James Dearden. Producer Sherry Lansing originally supported the development of the film as a big studio feature because she felt it was important to develop sympathy for the single woman and show the guilt and responsibility of the man. By the time the script had gone through several stages of development, the final film did exactly the opposite. It soft-pedaled the man's guilt and made a monster out of the woman. The original developers of the script – Dearden, Lansing, and her partner Stanley Jaffe – were involved with the project until the end. They got screen credit and did not claim that the project was taken away from them. They participated in the complex process of developing an idea into a commercial film, even though basic aspects of its meaning changed along the way.

Directors often have a great role in this, since they not only shape the form of a film in areas such as composition, lighting, and editing, but they also, generally without screen credit, shape and reform the story. Adrian Lyne admits to this quite readily in the interview on the DVD of the film. He speaks of his dissatisfaction with the ending in the script and the reasons for reforming it into his original ending for the movie. In that version, Beth does not find the tape and Alex has succeeded in framing Dan for killing her. Lyne also speaks of the preview reactions to his ending that led him to change the film into its release form. Comparably, Blake Edwards, responding to preview reactions, added a number of slapstick scenes to the end *of Blind Date* (1987), drastically altering the final third of the movie. Like Adrian Lyne, he gets no screenplay credit.

Glenn Close's Star Image

Fatal Attraction involved another transformation of an entirely different kind – that of a **star's image**. Glenn Close changed her image entirely with *Fatal Attraction*. Previously, after success as a stage actress, she was largely known for playing "good," largely asexual, women in movies like *The World According to Garp* (1982) and *The Big Chill* (1983). No one considered her for this role and, unusual for an important actress, she campaigned and tested for it. Her success with it turned her into a major star and has affected the kind of roles in which she has subsequently been cast, such as the ruthless and sexual manipulator in *Dangerous Liaisons* (1989) and, in a role directly reminiscent of *Fatal Attraction*, the ruthless, independent, sexually active career woman in *The Paper* (1994), as well as the crazed, jaded movie star in Andrew Lloyd Webber's stage musical, *Sunset Boulevard*, the greedy heiress in *Cookie's Fortune* (1999), and the sinister Cruella de Vil in Disney's *101 Dalmatians* (1996) and *102 Dalmatians* (2000). As we will see in chapter 7, a star's image is a carefully constructed entity, often an enormous financial asset, and something that helps create a film's meaning in basic ways.

Scarface (1932)

When Paul Muni appeared in the title role in *Scarface*, he had no star image. A successful stage actor, associated with the Jewish art theater in the 1920s, he had appeared in a few undistinguished and virtually unknown films. The success of *Scarface* led to his becoming one of the most prestigious star actors of the 1930s, but one with a profile very different from that of Glenn Close. As we discuss in chapter 7, there is a major difference in films between stars and star actors. Stars like Clint Eastwood, Marilyn Monroe, and John Wayne establish charismatic star images that follow them throughout their careers. Audiences tend to perceive all of their roles as variations upon their dominant image, such as sexpot or rugged cowboy. Many such stars often play a greater variety of roles than they are given credit for, but their fans' perception of them returns to the dominant star image. Star actors, to the contrary, often have no dominant image and often pride themselves on the diversity of roles they play: examples are Marlon Brando, Meryl Streep, Tom Hanks, and Laurence Olivier.

In the 1930s, Paul Muni was a pre-eminent star actor, so much so that some critics commented that he never looked the same from film to film. He became associated with roles in "prestige" historical dramas and commonly played highly ethnic or foreign characters, often using elaborate make-up. His ethnically Italian gangster in *Scarface* was only one example; others included the title French physician in *The Story of Louis Pasteur* (1936, for which he won a Best Actor Academy Award), a Chinese peasant in *The Good Earth* (1937), another nineteenth-century Frenchman in *The Life of Emile Zola* (1937), and the eponymous Mexican revolutionist in *Juarez* (1939).

Interestingly, *Scarface* also produced an actor with an indelible star image, George Raft. From the time of *Scarface*'s release, Raft became associated with gangster characters and, although he tried repeatedly, he could never divest himself of the typecasting. His attempts to break from his gangster image and develop a more "wholesome" one made him legendary for poor script decisions. He purportedly rejected the lead in *High Sierra* (1939) because he did not want to play another gangster, and the lead in *The Maltese Falcon* (1941) because he did not want to play a private detective with questionable morals. Both roles went to Humphrey Bogart and helped establish his career as a major star. Raft's attempts to avoid his gangster image, combined with Bogart's successes, became something of an industry joke. Hearing that a film about Mark Twain was to be made, Bogart quipped that he hoped the studio would offer it to Raft because he (Bogart) would love to play it. Raft never divested himself of the image. A quarter of a century after *Scarface*, in *Some Like it Hot* (1959), and nearly a decade after that, in *Casino Royale* (1966), he was still playing parodies of his coin-tossing, gangster role.

The Gangster Genre

Along with *Little Caesar* (1930) and *The Public Enemy* (1931), *Scarface* helped establish the urban gangster **genre**, one which began in the early sound era and generally involved the meteoric rise and violent end of a young male criminal. His rise frequently involves the murder of the previous mob boss and his frenzied acquisition of extravagant consumer goods (clothes, automobiles, apartments) as well as women. The genre has often been seen as a critique of consumer capitalism of the 1920s, with the gangster as stand-in for the successful businessman.

Each of the three films mentioned launched the career of a major actor (Edward G. Robinson in *Little Caesar*, James Cagney in *The Public Enemy*, and Muni) and the genre became a male action genre. The films generated much controversy since they were accused of glorifying crime and reveling in violence. The stars created by the genre soon distanced themselves from it for more law-abiding roles and the genre itself, for a number of reasons, soon became marginalized as a "B" genre, seen as unsavory, overly formulaic and repetitive, receiving little critical attention and seldom drawing established stars or major studio financing. As we see in chapter 5, however, the components and industry profile of genres change over time, and by the 1970s the genre would achieve a new respectability with films like *Bonnie and Clyde* (1967), *The Godfather* (1972), and the 1983 remake of *Scarface* starring Al Pacino.

Set during the Prohibition era, *Scarface* tells the tragic story of the rise and fall of Tony Camonte (Paul Muni), a small-time Italian mobster who takes over a crime organization before being killed by the police in a shoot-out. Although the Depression backdrop of bootleg liquor and Camonte's rise and fall typify conventions of 1930s' gangster films, *Scarface* is in other ways highly unusual for the genre.

Scarface is not only a cornerstone of the gangster genre but it was also significant for the careers of important Hollywood figures. Independently produced by the legendary Howard Hughes and directed by Howard Hawks, it began the star careers of Paul Muni and George Raft. Its cinematographer, Lee Garmes, and one of its writers, Ben Hecht, are among the most respected in film history.

We will discuss *Scarface* in ways that continue where we left off with *Fatal Attraction*, introducing various approaches that this book will take. We have already looked at star image and genre. We will now consider the film's reception and social context (see chapter 8), then develop its formal construction (see chapter 3), discuss a remake (see chapter 6), and touch upon issues such as race, ethnicity, and class (see chapters 13 and 14).

In pairing *Scarface* with *Fatal Attraction* at the beginning of this book, we hope to make another point. It is not unusual for older people to declare that "Movies today just aren't what they used to be" and complain that things such as sexual content, graphic violence, and profanity render contemporary films inferior to those of Hollywood's "Golden Age." Comparably, students sometimes adopt a condescending attitude toward older films in black and white, or silent films. Even when praising such films, some students use patronizing terms like "It was good for films back then." We hope to break down both prejudices and show that, regardless of their era, films can manifest a great deal of complexity and are worthy of serious and rewarding study.

Social Context

Scarface was as controversial a film in its day as *Fatal Attraction* was in 1987. In 1932 there was widespread concern that gangster films glorified violence and might corrupt the young. This tapped into the extensive publicity of the era given to actual gangsters like "Scarface" Al Capone and anxiety that a wave of violence was overtaking the country. Many films in the genre were marketed as coming "from the headlines," or directly representing contemporary urban reality. Studio attempts to avoid censorship led to a number of significant changes in *Scarface* before its release and, even when it was released, it appeared in different versions in different states (many of which had different censorship boards). What we now accept as the standard release version of *Scarface* opens with a written prologue directly asking the viewer what should be done about violence in society. The prologue, along with a scene of a newspaper editor meeting concerned citizens, was added after censors objected to the film's violence. The studio responded by claiming that the film was centrally concerned with violence as a real social problem. Yet nothing in the film hints either at the causes of its characters' violence or at what might be done to eliminate such behavior. In fact, *Scarface* is notable for its lack of any real social context. The film represents gangsterism as a form of male bonding and contrasts it with the family sphere and the home, which is the traditional place for women. This narrative structure gives central importance to Tony's obsessive concern with keeping his sister at home with their mother and thus far removed from his world of male violence. He fails in this mission: Cesca (Ann Dvorak), his sister, ends up dying in a hail of police fire.

Such thematic observations contribute to the important awareness that film is never an unmediated reality but always a construction. *Scarface* might have had its inspiration from "the headlines" but is not equivalent to them, just as the headlines themselves are mediations of the events they report. *Scarface* has a rigorous formal structure.

Fig. 1.17

Fig. 1.18

Fig. 1.19

The X Motif and Male Violence

Howard Hawks, the director, structures the film around a visual **motif** of Xs (see chapter 3 on formal analysis). Initially, the X motif is associated exclusively with male violence but it later becomes complexly interwoven with the world of women and romance. Indeed, this is already hinted at in an early use of the X motif. An X-shaped scar on a close-up of Tony's face in a barbershop identifies him as the title character (figure 1.17). Shortly after, a woman

Fig. 1.20

Fig. 1.21

asks him how he got the scar and he replies, "In the war." Another gangster cynically interjects, "Yeah, some war with a blonde in a Brooklyn speakeasy." Scars resulting from wars are traditional signs of masculinity that show that a man has been tested in violence and survived. The scars imply that he is tough, not weak. Tony's scar, however, implies an inability to control women.

Fig. 1.22

Scarface begins with Tony killing a gangster. At the moment that he fires the shot, we see his shadow fall directly upon the shadow of a large cross or upright X (figure 1.18). From this moment on, all the killings will be marked by the presence of the X motif. During a montage of violence, for example, we see a body lying directly over a shadow of an X on the ground and, in a high angle, we see the X shape of street signs above the body (figure 1.19). We see a wounded gangster lying in a hospital bed with an X behind the bed (figure 1.20); moments later, he is shot dead. Another gangster, hiding in a dark room, sits beneath and then stands in front of a large white X on the wall (figure 1.21). He leaves to go bowling and, in a comic variation of the motif, we see him bowl a strike and die while the X is marked on the scoring sheet (figure 1.22). A mass murder of gangsters in a garage takes place beneath a rafter lined with Xs (figure 1.23) and, after the shooting, we see a bright X shape on their bodies (figure 1.24).

Fig. 1.23

The X Motif and Male–Female Relationships

In all of these instances, the X motif characterizes the world of male violence. As in the old cliché, X does, indeed, mark the spot. It even functions as a form of foreshadowing, marking some who will soon be dead. Somewhat ominously, then, the X appears in the first scene between Cesca and Guino Rinaldo (George Raft), one of Tony's comrades. Cesca looks down at Guino, who stands on the street below her balcony. The shape of an X appears in the grill-work of the balcony railing (figure 1.25) and is visible in shots

Fig. 1.24

Fig. 1.25

Fig. 1.26

representing both his and her points of view. From the start, their relationship is doomed and they are marked for death. Later, we see Cesca at a party and Tony flies into a rage at her sexual behavior. After Tony confronts her, she turns around and the straps of her sleeveless dress form a large X across her bare back (figure 1.26). She leaves the party and we see a midshot of the X on her back as she stands looking out of her bedroom window, from which she first saw Guino. Although Tony has been obsessed with keeping Cesca out of his world, the X motif of male violence has now literally migrated on to her body.

The uses of the X motif both as a sign of male violence and as signifying a breakdown of Tony's effort to keep Cesca from that world come together in two remarkable scenes. Cesca and Guino, unbeknown to Tony, have got married. Tony, enraged at Cesca's presumed immoral behavior, approaches their apartment. As he rings at the door, we see the Roman numeral X, indicating apartment number ten (figure 1.27). When Guino opens the door, he stands directly in front of a huge, white X on the wall behind him (figure 1.28). Seconds later, Tony shoots him.

Fig. 1.27

Whereas the Roman numeral for ten has a "realistic" explanation for its presence, there is no such explanation for the X on the wall. Like the white X on the bodies of the massacred men in the garage, it appears painted on. The use of the motif, then, cannot always be explained by reference to the fictional world of the film, as can the doorway motif in *The Searchers* (discussed in chapter 4). Unusual for a Hollywood film, the development of the motif takes precedence over both concerns with realism and the invisible style. The large X on the wall behind Guino is there only because the filmmakers put it there, not because it appears, for example, to be a shadow cast from light coming through a window.

Incest Theme

Fig. 1.28

The film ends ironically with Cesca being killed not only with Tony, but in the very sanctuary that he built to protect himself. He virtually imprisons himself in a fortress and yet Cesca enters it. Just as he fails to keep her home with his mother and fails to keep her from entering into a relationship with Guino, he fails to keep her out of his inner sanctuary and then fails to protect her after she enters it. Once again, both death and the failure to separate the two worlds are marked by the X. We see an X on the wall of Tony's room as he carries his mortally wounded sister to a sofa. That and other Xs are now at the very center of his private sanctuary.

The scene of Cesca's death points to the unusual relationship Tony has with her. From the very beginning of the film, Cesca talks of something strange about her brother's relationship with her, and this initiates a sexual **subtext** in the film. Such a subtext deals implicitly rather than overtly with a sexual theme. The iconography of the climax makes Tony and Cesca appear more like lovers than brother and sister. Her death in Tony's arms recalls countless scenes of a lover dying in a lover's embrace. Within the film's subtext, Tony's obsession with keeping his sister safely at home with his mother has strong incestuous implications; the intensity of his response at the dance, for example, stems from jealousy rather than protective brotherly love. He must keep Cesca out of his world and, paradoxically, keep her for himself because of his illicit desires for her.

Neither the X motif nor the incest theme is necessary to an understanding of the film's plot; indeed, many people have enjoyed the film with no awareness of their presence. They do work, however, to develop the complexity and artistic individuality of the film and an awareness of such things can increase our enjoyment of it. Interestingly, the 1983 remake of the film does not develop an X motif and the incest theme is represented quite differently.

The 1983 Remake of *Scarface*

In chapter 6 on series, sequels, and remakes we discuss ways in which films use works of the past. The **remake** of *Scarface* appeared not only during a time in which the gangster genre enjoyed a renewed respectability but also during one in which films of the classical Hollywood era were widely quoted. Brian De Palma, the film's director, has developed a reputation for citing the works of older Hollywood directors like Howard Hawks and Alfred Hitchcock in his own films. He did not do this in isolation but as part of the first generation of Hollywood directors who received their training not as apprentices within the film industry but in academic film schools. These directors appeared after the **studio system** had collapsed but often referred extensively and nostalgically to its products in their own work. It is indicative of this climate that just a year before De Palma's *Scarface* remake appeared, John Carpenter, another film-school graduate, remade Howard Hawks's production of *The Thing* (1951).

De Palma's remake of *Scarface* seems to tell a story similar to the original. Once again, an ambitious gangster who is overly protective of his sister rises to prominence in the mob and dies. The obvious differences are that De Palma's film is set in Florida during the 1980s and deals with the drug trade and with emigrés from Castro's Cuba, while Hawks's film deals with bootleg liquor and Italian Americans during the 1930s. A closer examination of the relationship between the two films reveals some of the ways in which remakes both differ from and refer back to the original film.

De Palma's film makes no attempt to slavishly reproduce dominant structures in Hawks's film but rather deals with Hawks's material in an innovative fashion. A simple illustration lies in its non-use of the X motif so central to Hawks's film. Aside from the scar on the title character's face, there is no X motif in De Palma's film; it might as easily have a different title. Why, then, is it called *Scarface*?

Part of the reason points to the film's profoundly different narrative implications from those of Hawks's film. The title of Hawks's film referred to a contemporary reality. Viewers would have associated the name "Scarface" with that of "Scarface" Al Capone, a Chicago gangster active in 1932; this would have underscored the "from the headlines" appeal of the film. For 1983 viewers, however, Al Capone was a long-dead historical figure and the term "Scarface" was likely to invoke not a contemporary gangster but rather a famous old film. This invocation of history is also evident in the narrative context.

The movie opens with newsreel footage of Fidel Castro. We soon see an internment camp in the United States for Cuban refugees in which we witness Tony Montana (Al Pacino), the title character, being interrogated about his criminal past. The historical context of the Cuban migration and later scenes of Montana working in a low-class Cuban restaurant create a social context for Montana's character and his actions. He is a man motivated by his experiences as a poor immigrant and turns to violence as a way of elevating his class status.

No such scenes nor similar motivations exist for Camonte in Hawks's film, and the difference is crucial. Hawks's film focuses so entirely on the role of male violence and the separate sphere of the family that the "real" social world is virtually non-existent. The Depression and Prohibition are reduced to backdrops for the personal relationships. De Palma's film, to the contrary, literally throws its characters into an international context with several scenes taking place in South America. Here, the "real" world of social, economic, and class experience is anything but a backdrop; it is a central presence. And just as the film develops much of its meaning from its relationship to then contemporary "headline" issues, it also in its status as a remake courts its relationship to Hollywood history. This makes it an engagement of Hawks's film, but one with fundamentally different imperatives.

Ethnicity and Class

Issues of class and ethnicity figure prominently in each film. Neither of the central characters conforms to the cultural ideal of white, middle-class male but, rather, they come from marginalized immigrant classes in the United States and seek elevation through violent crime. Marked by their accented English, clothes, and social deportment, their behavior engages contemporary **stereotypes** about "those" types of people being "inherently" criminal. The immigrant class for each film is different – Italian Americans in the 1930s as opposed to Cuban Americans in the 1980s – as is the outlawed business they enter – liquor during Prohibition as opposed to illegal drugs in the 1980s – but both films engage contemporary prejudices against immigrant classes. A very real question for us is whether or not the films promote or deflate ethnic stereotypes. And if they promote stereotypes, what significance does that have? We will return to racial and ethnic stereotyping in chapter 13. A related issue emerges in the fact that the working-class gangsters of both films desire to leapfrog the middle class and rise directly into the wealthy, upper class. As we will see in chapter 14 on class, this simply places them in comparably untenable positions.

The study of film tells us not only about artistic objects but also about the cultures from which they come. If we are used to simply going to movies to have a good time, it may seem that thinking about such things as visual style and the manner in which women are represented will take the fun away. We hope in the following chapters, however, to show that the opposite is the case: the more ways one learns about watching and thinking about movies, the more one will get out of them and the more one will enjoy them.

SELECTED READINGS

Susan Faludi describes the shift from sympathy for the single woman to the construction of her as evil in the various story and script versions of *Fatal Attraction* in *Backlash* (New York: Doubleday, 1991). Deborah Jermyn rejects Faludi's notion that the film is a simple backlash against feminism in "Rereading the Bitches from Hell: A Feminist Appropriation of the Female Psychopath," *Screen*, 37: 3 (Autumn 1966), pp. 251–67. Chris Holmlund analyzes the reception context for the movie, as well as different approaches to character construction in it, in "Reading Character with a Vengeance: The *Fatal Attraction* Phenomenon," *The Velvet Light Trap*, 27 (Spring 1991), pp. 25–36.

Todd McCarthy outlines the censorship problems that the 1932 *Scarface* encountered, as well as the different versions of the release print of the film produced to deal with them, in *Howard Hawks: The Grey Fox of Hollywood* (New York: Grove Press, 1997). Robin Wood analyzes the themes, visual motifs, and sexual subtext of the 1932 *Scarface* in *Howard Hawks* (London: British Film Institute, 1981).

Noël Carroll discusses the extent and manner in which 1970s' and 1980s' films directed by film-school graduates refer to and remake older films in "The Future of Allusion: Hollywood in the 70s (and Beyond)," *October*, 20 (Spring 1982), pp. 51–81.

2

NARRATIVE STRUCTURE

Jurassic Park and *Rashomon*

What is a Film About?

If, after seeing a movie, we run into friends who ask us, "What was it about?" we are likely to answer by telling them the story or at least the premise of the story. If the film is *Jurassic Park* (1993), we might say something like: "After scientists bring dinosaurs back to life from fossilized DNA fragments, a dinosaur expert is coerced into inspecting a dinosaur park in the hopes that his approval will calm the fears of investors in the park. The dinosaurs break loose, terrifying everyone and killing several people. The survivors escape and the park is closed down." We might mention the exciting chases and describe some of the main characters and their relationships. Two of the scientists, for example, are potential lovers who are united at the end.

Our friends would probably be happy with this answer. If, however, we answered by saying, "It's all about this great tracking shot . . ." and then describe a moving camera shot in detail, they would probably look at us strangely. Even with a film like *Jurassic Park*, which is known for its amazing special effects, audiences are not likely to say that the film is about those effects but that, rather, it is about its story and characters. This leads us to the issue of narrative, which is a term for the way in which the story events of a movie are organized; in exploring narrative we explore the structure of those events or the way the story is told.

Feature films are generally perceived first in narrative terms; everything else is secondary. If Steven Spielberg, the film's director, had employed the same special effects in a documentary about dinosaurs, it is unlikely that he would have ended up with one of the biggest, worldwide box-office hits of all time. In fact, when he made its popular sequel, *The Lost World: Jurassic Park* (1997), he not only used comparable effects but also placed them in a comparable narrative structure. Even though *Jurassic Park* has a strong emphasis on spectacle, that spectacle is part of a narrative. The dinosaurs at the center of the spectacle are even presented like human characters with, for example, the dreaded, deadly Velociraptors becoming "the bad guys."

Narrative Primacy

In chapter 3, we will see that this dominance of narrative in feature filmmaking is not as simple as it seems and that films are as much about their style of storytelling as about the stories they tell; the two may not even be separable. But, for now, let's assume that the story is what interests us in a film. Even that is more complicated than it seems at first. As daily experience tells us, there are many ways to tell a story. We have all been bored by someone telling us a story by relating every detail in exactly the order in which the events happened. We would like to reveal our impatience by saying, "Get on with it" or "Cut to the chase." The latter expression is revealing for our purposes since it refers to several aspects of filmmaking – cutting and excitement. The term "cut" quite rightly implies that we don't need to hear or see everything to appreciate a story; parts can, and probably should, be left out. The word "chase" implies that some parts of a story, such as the climax of an action film where the hero finally catches up with the villain, are more exciting than other parts, and we want to get to that excitement. Storytelling involves decisions about what gets told and what does not as well as how the events that are told should be arranged. This chapter deals with ways of understanding such narrative decisions.

Let's return to *Jurassic Park*. It begins with a mysterious, darkly lit, night scene in which a group of men transport a cage (figure 2.1). Although we do not see what is in the cage, we hear scary animal sounds, witness violent shaking, and see looks of great anxiety on the faces of the workers, all of which suggest a ferocious beast inside. Moments later, something goes wrong and one of the workers is gruesomely killed. The film then cuts to an entirely different time, place, and setting. This is one instance of the result of a narrative decision. The film could just as easily have started at the chronological "beginning" of its events, with a group of scientists theorizing about how fossilized

Fig. 2.1

traces of DNA could be used to return an extinct species to life. We could then have seen their experiments, their efforts to determine where such fossil remains could be found, their journey to the site, and the laborious excavation of the fossils. Had the filmmakers chosen such a route, *Jurassic Park*, instead of being one of the biggest grossing box-office films of all time, might have quickly wound up in second-run theaters and video store shelves. *The Lost World: Jurassic Park* and its sequel *Jurassic Park III* (2001) would probably never have been made.

At the simplest level of storytelling, the opening of the film involves us with the events by raising many questions: who are these men and what are they doing? Are they engaged in some forbidden activity that they attempt to hide in the darkness of night? What is in the cage? In addition to all of these story questions, the first scene of the film introduces an important theme: no matter how extreme the precautions and no matter how careful the workers, some unforeseen disaster can take place. This becomes one of the film's main themes as the story develops to show the dinosaurs that are supposedly safely contained within the theme park break loose and go on a rampage. As with many science-fiction films, *Jurassic Park* develops a theme that apparent scientific progress can be dangerous and threaten the human race.

The decision to begin *Jurassic Park* in mid-action has important implications. In the above-described alternative of following the scientists, audiences would be likely to say, "Cut to the chase." And that is precisely what Spielberg has done. Or, more accurately, he has cut to a chase but not *the* chase, for part of the art of storytelling is to build anticipation by delaying the outcome. Thus, Spielberg also knows when to cut to the next portion of the story. After the exciting but mystifying opening scene, we do not learn anything about who the victim was or how anyone in charge of the operation responded to the accident. Many things that could have been told have been left out. The filmmakers proceed from what they consider one important event to another, implicitly telling us that some things are not worth taking the time to relate, or that we will have to wait for the outcomes of some events. These filmmakers do not make such decisions in a vacuum: they have mastered a long-established and highly profitable tradition of narrative filmmaking – the classical Hollywood style.

Private and Public Goals

The **classical Hollywood narrative style** was established around 1915. One of its major requirements is that a film's plot have a clear forward direction. One event should logically lead to the next and all should fit together. Such plots generally focus on a small group of people whose goals are very clear; everything in the movie must contribute toward the resolution of those goals. The goals tend to be twofold: a private and a public one. The private one is frequently a heterosexual romance and the public one involves the accomplishment of an important deed or the attainment of something valuable.

Hollywood movies do not need to have happy endings, although many do. What they need are endings that clearly resolve their goals, one way or the other. In one of the most beloved of Hollywood films, *The Maltese Falcon* (1941), the hero (Humphrey Bogart) fails in both goals. He does not have a successful romance with the leading lady and he never finds the Maltese Falcon, but the audience clearly understands why these things do not happen and, therefore, the movie is very much a classical Hollywood narrative. In one sense of the term, all such endings are happy endings since they satisfy audience expectations by tying up all loose ends.

Fig. 2.2

Fig. 2.3

Fig. 2.4

Fig. 2.5

Plots and Subplots

There are many ways that we can understand narrative patterns such as those in *Jurassic Park*. Hollywood films frequently have a main dramatic **plot** with subplots. In *She Wore a Yellow Ribbon* (1949), for example, the main dramatic plot involves the final mission of a retiring cavalry captain (figure 2.2). A comic **subplot** revolves around the impending retirement of his sergeant who drinks heavily and thereby risks his pension (figure 2.3). A romantic subplot centers on two young lieutenants who want to marry the same woman (figure 2.4). Near the end of the film, all three plots are resolved when we learn that a new position has been created for the retiring captain, that he has found a way to guarantee that his sergeant's drunkenness will be contained until retirement, and that the young woman has chosen the suitor she will marry.

Not all films conform to this pattern. *Alien* (1979) is notable for its lack of either a romantic or a comic subplot. The entire film is structured around the dramatic mission of a space crew that encounters alien life forms. Only one crew member is left alive at the end of the film (figure 2.5). *Alien* may be one of the earliest examples of some recent films that resist conventional romantic subplots. We will see in chapter 12 that there are important gender implications in these plot decisions. Unlike *Alien*, which has no romantic subplot, *The Silence of the Lambs* (1990, which we shall discuss in detail in chapter 12) seems to set up a conventional romantic pairing between a young, beautiful female FBI agent and her attractive, older male supervisor. There is, however, never a moment of romance between them. In the classical Hollywood cinema, they would be united when the crime is solved at the end of the film. This more conventional plot structure can be seen in *In the Line of Fire* (1993), in which an older Secret Service agent falls in love with a younger woman who is assigned to a case with him. By the film's conclusion, they are romantically coupled.

The Silence of the Lambs even points to its unconventional plot structure by including moments in which two powerful male characters in the film, a doctor and a scientist, attempt to initiate a romantic relationship with the female agent, only to be quickly rebuffed. *A Few Good Men* (1992) is another film that promises the likelihood of a romantic subplot and then thwarts it. The film stars Tom Cruise and Demi Moore, and the star system, which we discuss in chapter 7, implies that these two young, attractive leads are likely to be involved with each other. The plot has the conventional structure of having the young man and woman work together on the same case. There is even a scene where they go out to dinner together, a moment that generally signals the beginning of a romance, but they talk only about work. There is never a moment in which they kiss or even look at each other in a romantic manner.

Story and Plot

Our awareness of the significance of such plot decisions will be helped by understanding the distinction between a story and a plot. The term "story" refers to the events that must be narrated and the term "plot" refers to the arrangement of those events as they are told. Story events occur in chronological order; plot events occur in the order the filmmakers choose to present them, and such choices often reveal a good deal about the meaning of the film. The above-cited example of the exciting scene at the beginning of *Jurassic Park* is an example of a filmmaker presenting an event out of story order for plot purposes.

The story of *A Perfect World* (1993) involves two escaped convicts who kidnap a boy and the law-enforcement team that pursues them. Anyone telling that story must include the information about how one of the convicts is killed by the other and how the boy eventually shoots and mortally wounds the remaining convict, who dies as he is about to be captured. The film begins with a brief scene of haunting images with Kevin Costner, the film's star, lying in a field (figure 2.6). He appears to be sunning himself on a beautiful day. Dollar bills drift through the air, stirred up by the blades of a helicopter (figure 2.7). Were it not for the somewhat ominous presence of the helicopter (figure 2.8), we would accept these images as the ideal world to which the title refers. After this brief prologue, the film cuts to the convicts making their escape. We only learn near the end of the film that, far from sunning himself in a utopia bountiful with money, Costner's character lies dead or dying as the police helicopter circles in for a landing.

Fig. 2.6

Fig. 2.7

Fig. 2.8

This kind of rearrangement of narrated events constitutes one significant way in which stories become structured as plots. Other filmmakers could have chosen to begin the story chronologically with the prison escape. Or, if they had chosen to begin with a brief glimpse of the end, they probably would have made that end clear rather than ambiguous. Indeed, the poetic ambiguity arising from the opening of *A Perfect World* supplies a highly unusual plot structure, since the audience is left wondering about what they have just seen and what its importance is for what follows. In this regard, the prologue to *Jurassic Park* is more conventional, since it clearly establishes the idea of a threat that humans cannot adequately contain and control.

Flashbacks and Plot Structure

Intersection (1994) uses a related device for structuring story events into a plot. It begins with its central character driving in his car. To avoid an accident, he slams on his brakes and goes into a skid. The film cuts to shots of a clock's mechanism and then to a **flashback**. Near the end of the film, we recognize the same shots the film opened with and the skid leads to a crash. The film then continues in present time. This flashback structure, which is emphasized by repeated shots of the clock's mechanism, creates a plot with added suspense. Instead of just watching the story events unfold, we keep wondering when the skidding car will reappear and what will happen to its driver.

Since the 1940s, flashbacks have been a common device filmmakers use to structure their plots. *Citizen Kane* (1941), perhaps the most critically praised American film ever made (which we analyze in detail in chapter 15), begins with the mysterious death of its central character. He drops an object and utters a meaningless word as he dies. The entire film is structured around a reporter's quest to learn what the final word spoken by this powerful man meant. As the reporter interviews acquaintances, we get flashback segments about Kane's life. The story of his life would have begun with his birth and proceeded to the writing of the story of his death; the plot, however, begins near the end of that story, and then jumps back and forth among its events.

The Man who Shot Liberty Valance (1962) also makes important use of a flashback structure, but in a different manner. It begins and ends with a frame story. A US senator and his wife come to a Western town for the funeral of an old, forgotten man (figure 2.9). Rather than supplying a brief prologue, the frame story introduces many of the main characters and delineates relationships among them. The senator then tells his story about meeting the man whose funeral he is attending (figure 2.10). At this point, a flashback begins and the main portion of the film takes place within the time of the flashback when the senator and his wife were young (figure 2.11). *The Man who Shot Liberty Valance* contains the unusual plot structure of a flashback within a flashback. Within the tale the senator narrates, another character tells him that he is mistaken about what happened during a shoot-out (figure 2.12). We then see the shoot-

Fig. 2.9

Fig. 2.10

Fig. 2.11

out again, this time from that other character's perspective. When he finishes, the film returns to the senator's flashback and, shortly after that, it returns to the frame story. Now we know the truth about who shot Liberty Valance.

Fig. 2.12

Citizen Kane and *The Man who Shot Liberty Valance* are particularly instructive for illustrating the crucial difference between a story and a plot because they both structure their plots around people telling stories. *Citizen Kane* could have told the same story by beginning with the events in the life of the little boy and progressing through his education, career as a politician and newspaper editor, marriage, divorce and remarriage, and ending with his reclusive old age and death. Similarly, *The Man who Shot Liberty Valance* could have begun with the senator arriving in the town as a young man and progressed through his election as senator and ended with his return to the town for the funeral of his old friend. By presenting these story events out of temporal order and from the perspective of various characters, these films show how not only what we learn, but also when we learn it and from whom, can be important parts of narration. The same story can yield an infinite number of plots, some of which will be more interesting and exciting than others.

Free and Bound Motifs

Learning the significance of these kinds of reorderings of story events is one of the most important reasons for making the distinction between a story and a plot, but other narrative distinctions are helpful also. An equally important one involves the difference between a **free motif** and a **bound motif**. Motifs result from the repetition of visual images or sounds in a manner that forms a perceptible pattern. These patterns may or may not have thematic meaning (in Hollywood cinema they usually do), but they structure the film by ordering sights and sounds.

Fig. 2.13

A bound motif is one that is necessary for telling a story. In *Fatal Attraction* (see chapter 1), the child's pet rabbit is a bound motif since it is a necessary part of the story that we see it boiled in a pot by Alex (figure 2.13), demonstrating just how far she will go to terrorize Dan. The images of slaughtered animals that we constantly see outside Alex's apartment, however, are a free motif (figure 2.14). By situating her apartment in a meat-packing area, the film implies that the kind of one-night-stand, no-commitment sex in which the lovers engage dehumanizes human beings and reduces them to little more than meat. In *Intersection*, cars are a bound motif in that any filmmaker must include the car crash in narrating that story. The story cannot be told without cars but repeated shots of the clock mechanism, on the other hand, are a free motif that stresses the idea that time is running out for the central male character, who is having a midlife crisis. In *Stagecoach*

Fig. 2.14

Fig. 2.15

(1939), the stagecoach referred to in the title and in which the passengers travel is a bound motif. Any film that narrates the story of those passengers taking that trip through the Western wilderness must include the coach. In this film, however, two of the characters on the coach, the Ringo Kid and Hatfield, both wear similar large white hats. In many ways, they are opposite characters. The Ringo Kid is the Western hero and Hatfield is a displaced Southern gentleman who has become a gambler. The similarity in their hats, however, suggests a similarity between them and, in fact, they each live their lives and even risk death to follow a strict code of behavior. This hat motif, which also includes other characters in the film, is a free motif since the story of the journey can be told (and, in fact, has been told in remakes) without a hat motif.

Scarface (1932), which we analyzed in chapter 1, includes the careful use of an X motif, which initially refers to an X-shaped scar on a gangster's face (figure 2.15). Since the film's title refers to its central character's face and since the dialogue in one scene refers to it, the scar is a bound motif. Throughout the film, however, Xs are carefully placed in scenes in which gangsters are killed. Sometimes they are presented as a natural part of the setting, such as a street sign, a Roman numeral on apartment ten, or an "X" mark on a score sheet in a bowling alley (see figures 1.19, 1.22 and 1.27 in chapter 1). On other occasions, however, they simply appear in the frame with no plausible explanation of where they are coming from. Before the gangster in apartment ten is killed, for example, we see the Roman numeral on the door (figure 1.27). When he opens the door, we see a large white X on the wall behind him (figure 1.28). No object or light source accounts for its presence; it simply appears painted on the wall. The X motif, which characterizes male violence in the film and which indicates that someone will be killed, is also then a free motif. The story can be told (and has been in a remake) without the motif.

Similarly, the film has a major sound motif linked to its central character. During the film's opening scene, the gangster with the scarred face whistles as he prepares to shoot his first victim. Later, when we see him walking down the hall to apartment ten, we hear him whistle the same tune. In this case the sound motif signals the same thing that the visual motif of the X does: the gangster in apartment ten is doomed. This sound motif is also a free one. The gangster's story can be told without hearing him whistle before he shoots someone.

Free Motifs, Aesthetic Complexity, and Thematic Meaning

Free motifs frequently give aesthetic complexity and thematic meaning to films. In *The Man who Shot Liberty Valance*, we have seen how the rearrangement of the story events into a complex flashback structure creates an interesting plot. That plot is further structured around several free visual motifs including door-

Fig. 2.16

Fig. 2.17

ways and letters of the alphabet. The doorway motif relates primarily to Tom Doniphon, a central character. He is frequently framed through and by doorways which suggest that he is separated from the spaces and characters within – that he somehow does not fit in the social order (figure 2.16). The narrative action in the film confirms this when Doniphon loses both his "girlfriend" and his political power in the town of Shinbone, dying a forgotten old man. He is associated with the old West at a time of transition and he does not fit into the new order. The new order is associated with literacy, as opposed to the law of the gun, and its chief proponent is Ransom Stoddard, a lawyer and schoolteacher. He is associated with the letters of the alphabet that he teaches to the townspeople and with which he introduces new ideas about law and order. At a key point in the film, he stands in the street outside the newspaper office at night and the shadow of a letter on the window falls on his body (figure 2.17). As he prepares for a gunfight, he does so in the name of literacy.

We have also seen how the opening of *A Perfect World* rearranges narrative events to create its plot. Like *The Man who Shot Liberty Valance*, *A Perfect World* uses free visual motifs to give complexity to its plot. After one of the kidnappers has been killed, the other takes the boy to a clothing store, since he is only wearing underwear. Due to a strict religious upbringing, the boy has never worn a Halloween costume, and he takes a ghost costume with a mask from the store. Excited by the opportunity to wear the mask, which had been forbidden, the boy wears it for most of the rest of the film. When he's not wearing the mask on his face, it is pushed up on his head. Several shots emphasize this strange costume by placing the mask prominently in the composition (figure 2.18). This motif strongly affects the tone of many scenes by juxtaposing this image of child's play with the deadly serious circumstances of crime, violence, and death in which this child finds himself. The child's invocation of fear and death by playfully pretending to be a ghost reflects the truly adult world of fear and death that we witness.

In *Psycho* (1960) birds and mirrors are important free motifs. Norman Bates, the psychotic murderer of the

Fig. 2.18

Fig. 2.19

film's title, pursues taxidermy as a hobby. His room is full of stuffed birds, which associate him with attack birds (see figure 6.22 in chapter 6) and a woman he is about to kill with innocent songbirds. He talks about his life as if he were a bird trapped in a cage. At one point, he even stands in front of a tree branch, seemingly perched upon it as he nibbles at food reminiscent of bird seed. The action takes place near Phoenix, a city named after a bird.

At the end of the film, we discover that birds are not all Norman has been stuffing. He has stuffed his mother and, at times, taken her place by dressing and talking like her; he is really two people – himself and his mother. This duality is not, however, limited to Norman. Nearly all the characters in the film lead some sort of double life. Marion, who becomes Norman's victim, is a decent, hard-working woman who takes care of her younger sister, but she also hides an affair from her and steals money. At several points in the film we see her image reflected in a mirror – in an hotel after an illicit lunchtime affair (figure 2.19), in her apartment after she has stolen the money, and in the Bates Motel when she checks in under an assumed name. These mirror images are free visual motifs that develop her character as one with a hidden, double side. Norman is literally two people and Marion is figuratively two people.

Color can be used as a free visual motif. *Dead Ringers* (1988) tells the story of twin gynecologists who operate a fertility clinic for women. The opening credit sequence is set against a bright red background. There is much talk in the film about menstruation and, during the film's climax, we see blood as one of the twins kills the other. Furthermore, red has strong cultural connotations that associate it with blood. During several scenes in the film, we see surgical procedures in which the brothers as well as the entire surgical team are dressed in bright red robes and hoods that cover their entire bodies, again, strongly connoting blood.

The Revelation of Narrative Truth

Another way of understanding narratives focuses on how they reveal their "truth" to us. By the time most films are over, we feel that we know what has happened. In fact, the common feeling that the film is about to end usually means we know that the main plot elements have been resolved. In *Jurassic Park* the entrepreneur declares the park unsafe and several of the main characters, including the romantic couple, escape unharmed; in *Scarface* the gangster is killed; in *Stagecoach* most of the passengers survive the dangerous journey and the hero is romantically united with the woman he loves; in *Independence Day* (1996) the alien invasion is defeated and the two Americans who destroyed the alien mothership return safely to earth; and in *A Perfect World* the kidnapper dies and the boy is safely returned to his mother. But how do narratives maintain our interest until they are resolved, and what is the significance of the fact that we walk out of the theater feeling that we "know" what has happened? Indeed, this feeling is so standard with Hollywood films that it comes as a surprise to many viewers to discover that in some styles of filmmaking the audience does not always know either what has happened or why it has happened.

We mentioned at the beginning of this chapter that filmmakers frequently begin their films by cutting to the chase; that is, by placing a significant or exciting piece of action at the beginning of the film: the death of the old man in *Citizen Kane* or the death of the worker transporting the beast in the cage in *Jurassic Park*. Yet, these are obviously not the chase that implies the end of the action and the end of the story. These instances raise many questions that remain unanswered. What is the importance of the object that the old man holds in his hands and what does his dying word mean? What additional threats do the beasts in the cage pose to the humans who attempt to control them?

Narrative Questions: Delays, Snares, and Answers

Hollywood films typically pose a variety of **narrative questions** and then answer them using delays and snares. The viewer of *The Man who Shot Liberty Valance*, for example, is snared into believing that Ransom Stoddard, the Eastern lawyer, shot Liberty Valance, the outlaw of the title, in a fair gunfight. Even Stoddard believes that. However, later in the film, we learn that Tom Doniphon secretly shot Valance from an alley. Both Stoddard and we, the spectators of the film, were fooled into believing Stoddard had done it.

Delays sustain spectator interest. In *Fatal Attraction*, if, after the first time that Dan rebuffs Alex's attempts to continue their affair, Alex entered his home, threatened his wife with a knife, and was shot dead, the film would be over too quickly – there would not be "enough" story. This simple example shows us that we have come to expect movies to resolve their main narrative questions at a certain rate because, when those questions are resolved, we presume the story will soon be over – which indeed is the case when we see Alex killed or learn that Tom Doniphon, not Ransom Stoddard, killed Liberty Valance. *Citizen Kane* supplies a simple variation: the reporters trying to find out what the dying man's word meant fail at their mission, but we the spectators are privy to a shot that at least partially answers the question for us – Kane died referring to a childhood sled on which we saw him playing in the snow during one of the flashbacks. The snow also explains the glass ball with snow that he holds in his hands and drops at the moment of his death.

Our interest in Hollywood films is not sustained, however, solely by awaiting the answer to a big question that is usually delayed for ninety minutes or more. Some questions are posed and then answered quickly but nevertheless intensify our interest for short periods of time. In *Fatal Attraction*, as soon as we learn that the mother is surprised to find a pot boiling on the stove, we see the little girl running to her rabbit's cage. We wonder and probably fear what the connection between these two seemingly disparate actions is but, after a few moments of cross-cutting, we learn the answer when we simultaneously see the mother discover the rabbit in the pot and the girl discover it missing from the cage.

Other narrative questions are posed and answered at different rates from that of the extremely long delay of the major question or the extremely brief delay of a question such as what's in the pot and what does it have to do with the girl running to her pet's cage? After Dan sleeps with Alex and she pursues the relationship, we wonder: will he leave his wife for Alex? Will his wife find out and, if so, how will she respond? Will this affair wreck their marriage? The answers to these questions are somewhat delayed but, after the rabbit is killed, Dan decides to tell his wife that he knows who did it. She asks if he is having an affair and he replies truthfully that he is. We now know the answer to the question "Will she find out?" Although she tells him to get out of the house and he packs and leaves, we still wonder whether or not they will reconcile. The answer comes when she has a car accident and Dan rushes to her side in the hospital. She decides to forgive him. Dan notifies the police of Alex's crimes and harassment but, when they go to question her, they cannot find her. Thus, a new question is opened immediately: what will this deranged woman do next? We learn the answer in the next scene when she invades the home with a knife. The climax includes a snare, since the audience breathes a sigh of relief when they think Alex has been drowned, but she suddenly rises from the tub, knife in hand, and is then shot by the wife. Now we know what the word "fatal" refers to in the film's title, and the main question as to how these relationships will be resolved is answered.

We will see in chapter 12 that this ending and indeed Alex's behavior throughout the film reveal strong assumptions about gender and sexuality. But for now the important thing to notice is how the structure of posing and then delaying the answers to various questions moves the viewer through the film by promising that everything will be explained and that, when all the important questions have been answered, he or she will know the truth about this story. A film like *Stage Fright* (1950) wreaks temporary havoc with these assumptions when the audience learns that what they have accepted as the truth in a flashback is in actuality a lie. In most films, such as *The Man who Shot Liberty Valance*, flashbacks normally reveal what "really" happened. *Stage Fright* tricks us by giving us a duplicitous flashback. In this case, however, both the character and the film lie to us. But since the lie is revealed, everything is set right in the end and we do know the truth about what has happened.

Classical narrative films operate upon the assumption that there is a truth to every story and that revealing that truth is the goal of storytelling. Other traditions of narrative filmmaking do not operate on such presumptions. We will see shortly with *Rashomon* that it is possible to deny the single truth of a story. It is also possible not to explain what has happened or why it has happened. The "what" and the "why" are central to Hollywood narration and, therefore, in *Fatal Attraction* we learn that part of Alex's psychological problems derive from her relationship with her father. We similarly learn that Dan is ripe for an affair since his domestic life is full of interruptions ranging from the dog to his daughter and visiting friends that constantly frustrate his sexual desires for his wife. Thus we understand why Dan and Alex do what they do.

Fig. 2.20

Art Cinema and Narrative Ambiguity

By way of contrast, in Nagisa Oshima's *In the Realm of the Senses* (1976), a Japanese film about an obsessive affair, we learn nothing about why the husband leaves his wife and enters into the affair with the woman (figure 2.20) and, although we learn that the woman is "hypersensitive," we learn nothing about what caused this hypersensitivity or anything else about the woman's background. The lovers simply devote themselves totally to their passion. Similarly, in Oshima's *Death by Hanging* (1968) and *The Man who Left his Will on Film* (1970), we never even learn what has taken place. In the former film, we repeatedly see the same man executed but, if he has already been killed, how can he be killed again? In the latter film, we see two people try to understand the death of a third but we never really learn what happened to the title character, who died with his camera recording his death.

Films within the post-World War II European and international **art cinema** tradition frequently present characters whose actions are psychologically unexplained. Why they do what they do remains unknowable. Their behavior cannot be explained with reference to their childhood or to a past traumatic event. The title character of the French film *Pickpocket* (1959) devotes his life to pickpocketing. Yet, we never learn why he has become this kind of criminal or why, at the end of the film, he suddenly accepts the love of a woman. In *Last Year at Marienbad* (1961), another French art film, we see an encounter between three people in a luxury hotel but are totally confused as to what is real and what is not; the film's conclusion does nothing to resolve that confusion.

The "Real" World and Narrative Truth

Narratives employ various kinds of references to the "real" world as a way of explaining the actions of their characters. Hollywood films draw a close connection between these references to the "truth" of life and the truth we learn at the end of the story when the main question posed by the narrative is answered. In *Looking for Mr Goodbar* (1977), a woman finds herself in danger from a man she picks up in a New York singles bar. The audience is likely to understand the man's bizarre behavior by saying to themselves, "That's the kind of person who's likely to hang out at that kind of bar." Although most people have never been to New York singles bars in the 1970s or met a man like the pervert in the film, they feel that they "know" what such bars and such perverts are like. This supposed "knowledge," however, is based upon cultural assumptions about the way things are. If some people do not share those assumptions, they may be puzzled or outraged by what they see. At times cultural assumptions can shift. A simple example is assumptions about space aliens. In the 1950s, in films like *The Thing* (1951) or *Invaders from Mars* (1953), they were usually evil and murderous. In the 1970s and 1980s, however, with films like *Close Encounters of the Third Kind* (1977) and *ET: The Extra-Terrestrial* (1982), they often appeared benign. More recently, films like *Predator* (1987) and *Independence Day* (1996) have returned to the evil representational pattern.

Imagine someone with no knowledge of our culture watching a film in which a woman in a dangerous situation suddenly starts screaming and behaving irrationally until a man slaps her and brings her to her senses. The action would be inexplicable. If, however, spectators share (this does not necessarily mean accept) the knowledge of the common cultural assumption that women get hysterical in the face of danger and that men retain their composure, then the action is comprehensible. We will see in the following chapters that these apparent "truths" have strong political implications and that narratives often confirm for us what we think we already know. But, for now, it is sufficient to note that the manner in which narratives refer to commonly accepted truths about the real world and the manner in which they relate the "truth" of the story they are telling combine to give spectators a strong sense of possessing truth about life.

We now turn to a detailed analysis of *Jurassic Park* and *Rashomon* to illustrate many of the general observations we have just made about narrative. We have chosen *Jurassic Park* since it is likely that most students will already have seen it and since its box-office success is directly related to the manner in which it successfully characterizes the current Hollywood style of narration. We have chosen *Rashomon*, a Japanese film, as a contrasting example of a distinctly alternative style of film narration with which most students will not be familiar.

Jurassic Park (1993)

Jurassic Park is the most popular movie ever made, and the reasons, at first, seem obvious – dinosaurs and the "realistic" **special effects**. As we pointed out earlier, however, those effects would not have had nearly the popularity of *Jurassic Park* if the movie had been a documentary study of dinosaurs. But if those "realistic" and terrifying dinosaurs alone did not bring people to the theaters in droves, what did? Part of the answer lies in the film's use of narrative.

Public and Private Narrative Goals

The public goal of *Jurassic Park* is established very early in the film. Multi-millionaire John Hammond has nearly completed an amusement park with real dinosaurs but, because a dinosaur kills a worker, his investors want a dinosaur expert, Alan Grant, to assure them that the park will be safe and that they will not lose their investment. Throughout the movie, we see what Grant sees, or soon learns, about the park. At the end, he declares the park unsafe, and John Hammond agrees with him.

The movie does not show us any of the investors. We see few of the scientists who achieved the startling accomplishment of creating the dinosaurs, and few of the people who designed the park. They might be important to the park but not to the way this classical narrative deals with the park. This story focuses on the small group who takes the first tour of the park and the exciting dangers they encounter. Unlike what we will soon learn about *Rashomon*, the truth of what we see is never called into question. It is all so clearly and unambiguously "true" that even Hammond eventually agrees with Grant that the park should not open.

Virtually every event in the plot moves toward this conclusion. Once the major question is established, everything in the movie contributes directly to its resolution. If an event does not do this, it has no place in this type of movie. When Hammond's grandchildren arrive, we learn nothing of their parents, their past history with Hammond, or their homelife. A different kind of film might have developed some of those aspects; here, the children matter only in so far as they further the plot. They are in this movie as evidence that Hammond will risk his family to ensure the park's safety and to provide innocent and vulnerable potential victims to enhance the dinosaurs' threats.

The children also relate to the private goal of the film. Hollywood narration is flexible and has modified over the years to accommodate a wide variety of structures. Indeed, *Jurassic Park*, like many other contemporary films, has much more emphasis on spectacle and less time devoted to its character development than did most classical Hollywood films of the 1930s and 1940s. Nor does every movie need an explicit romantic plot, and Spielberg's films tend to have minimal interest in romance, focusing more on displaced children and family concerns. Here, while a romantic subplot exists, little time is spent developing it. Alan Grant is living with Ellie Sattler and, although there is a potential rival for her affections, none of this is developed in any detail. Rather, Alan's dislike of children is established near the beginning of the film. He even takes pleasure in terrifying one smug youngster with a tale of a Velociraptor attack. As the film develops, however, he saves the lives of Hammond's grandchildren and, through them, becomes more tolerant of children, thus apparently deepening his relationship with Ellie. The movie ends with a strong sense of them as an intact "couple."

Fig. 2.21

Fig. 2.22

Narrative Unity

At the beginning of the movie, when all arrive on the island in a helicopter, we see Hammond walking toward the camera in smiling anticipation of the wonders his park has to display (figure 2.21). At the end of the film, as all are escaping, Hammond is on the same helicopter pad and again walks toward the camera in much the same way as he had in the beginning of the film, only now the look on his face is sad: his dream has been destroyed (figure 2.22). These two rhyming shots provide a unifying frame for the whole film. Their similarity reminds the viewer at the end of the beginning and how the whole film, in a way, falls between the two states of Hammond's mind. His goal was clear at the beginning; its failure is now clear at the end.

Everything in the movie contributes to our awareness of the failure of Hammond's dream, even the major subplot, which concerns the efforts of a traitorous employee, Dennis, to steal some of Hammond's discoveries for a rival corporation. He places important embryos in a specially rigged aerosol shaving-cream can and shuts down some of the park's systems so that he can escape with the can. His efforts fail, however, when he gets his jeep stuck in the jungle and is killed by a Dilophosaurus. The shaving-cream can rolls off and disappears in the mud.

This at first seems to be a trivial deviation from the main plot but, upon closer inspection, we can see its relationship to the rest of the movie. First, it does influence the main plot since Dennis's shutting down of the computer systems in the park causes the breakdown of the safety systems that allows the

Fig. 2.23

dinosaurs to escape. Secondly, the very non-success of his plan gives a prophetic parallel for the failure of the park as a whole. The safety systems are a **bound motif** since his shutting them down is directly related to the progress of the plot. The aerosol can is a **free motif**. The plot would have progressed in exactly the same way whether or not it was lost, but it provides symbolic reinforcement for the notion that the park is dangerous because too many things can go wrong. The free motif of the aerosol can, which includes the image of it now worth millions of dollars but lost in the jungle (figure 2.23), is a reinforcement of the major theme that humanity at its most powerful and ambitious is no match for the forces of nature.

Fig. 2.24

All the film's subplots provide complications to and commentary on the main plot. Late in the film, Hammond's two grandchildren are in the visitor center recuperating from a dinosaur attack. On the wall behind them is a backlit mural of dinosaurs in a prehistoric setting. Suddenly the silhouette of a real dinosaur appears behind the painting and covers the figure of a painted dinosaur; the children are now in real danger (figure 2.24).

This tells us a good deal about the movie's narrative priorities. The children are in the foreground; the ancient world of the dinosaurs is depicted in the background. The movie is not a documentary about the world of dinosaurs. It gives only as much information about them as we need to make the story of the characters' plight understandable. As soon as we get the background sketched out, we go on to the real threat to the children.

Plot Confusion and Clarification

In a similar way, the movie does not immediately give us its main narrative goal but first, although very briefly, establishes a context to make that goal compelling and meaningful. Its first three **scenes** mystify and tease us as much as they inform us. In the first, shot at night and near Costa Rica, we see a man killed by something ferocious in a closed container. We are not shown what it is but we do know that the stern, well-armed men surrounding it are afraid of it. All we see of it are brief glimpses, including a shot of a sinister eye looking out.

In the second scene, set in the Dominican Republic, we see a lawyer, looking out of place in his suit, come awkwardly ashore on a raft. He speaks with a scientist about the investors who are anxious about the "accident" and want verification of their investment by Alan Grant. The scientist is skeptical about Grant's willingness to become involved but, during the scene, becomes excited by the discovery of a mosquito mummified in amber. Now the viewer is even more puzzled. Is the "accident" the death we saw in the first scene? If so, why was that scene set near a country in Central America and this one set in an island in the Caribbean? Who are the investors and why are they insecure? Who is Alan Grant? What is the significance of the mosquito?

In the third scene we see paleontologists on a dig in Montana delicately uncovering the bones of a dinosaur. We now see Alan Grant, the respected leader of the group. When he talks of a Velociraptor, a boy makes fun of it, saying it sounds like a six-foot turkey. Grant, using a real Velociraptor claw, describes the dinosaur's hunting methods in ways so detailed and dramatic that he makes the dinosaur "come alive" for the now-awestruck boy.

This scene resembles the one with the children in front of the mural since the plot first gives the viewer enough information to understand what is going on, then makes it "come alive" or enter the action, whether by terrifying the boy with the claw or having the Velociraptors attack the children. The two scenes are further related in that Alan's knowledge is of a danger millions of years removed from his reality. By the time he meets the children in Jurassic Park, the dinosaurs he animates through words are very real and life-threatening.

Later in the scene the dig is disturbed by John Hammond's aggressive helicopter landing, his intrusion into Grant's trailer and coercion of Grant and his companion to accompany him to Jurassic Park to restore investor confidence. We still know nothing about what is going on at the park, and we have a number of unexplained or barely explained pieces of evidence to try to piece together.

This is a traditional way of beginning a Hollywood movie by structuring the story into a plot that puzzles the viewer but then quickly draws all the threads together to inform the viewer of the major issues at stake. In *Jurassic Park* we see Hammond, Grant, and others arrive at the park, the nature of which is still unexplained until, driving through a meadow, Grant suddenly becomes awestruck by the sight of a number of real Brachiosaurus dinosaurs. Soon after, he gets a tour in which the rationale for the park is explained. We see an educational film and tour showing how dinosaur DNA was extracted from mosquitoes who had drunk dinosaur blood and become trapped and mummified in amber. The tour also shows how the dinosaurs are bred, hatched, and contained in the park.

Where the beginning of the film seemed concerned with mystifying, the film suddenly goes out of its way to clarify. It almost parodies Hollywood narrative techniques by literally incorporating an educational film into itself, in case anyone does not realize that major questions are now being answered. We now know why the scientist was so excited to find the mosquito in amber, why the "accident" threatened investor confidence in the park, which was to open soon if it could be proved safe, and why Alan Grant, a noted dinosaur expert, is needed to declare the park safe.

By this point in the movie, Spielberg and his screenwriters have given us enough information to make the plot credible, and given it in ways tantalizing enough to whet our interest. The major question of the plot has been clearly defined, "Will Alan Grant declare the park safe?"

Now the delaying begins. Alan and a number of characters take a tour of the park. First, they go to the Dilophosaur area. A recorded message tells them what to look for, but no Dilophosaurs show up. Then they go to the area of the Tyrannosaurus Rex but, again, it doesn't show up. One of the characters even sarcastically asks Hammond if there are going to be any dinosaurs on his dinosaur tour. They then come upon a sick and disabled Triceratops.

The movie's first scene presented a scary and murderous dinosaur. Even though we never see it fully, its threat is real. But once we reach Jurassic Park, the threat is muted. The first dinosaurs we see are the graceful and unthreatening Brachiosauruses, not at night but in sunny daylight. Then we don't see either the expected Dilophosaurus or the Tyrannosaurus Rex; then we see a virtually comatose Triceratops. But then the action begins. A storm comes and the traitorous Dennis shuts down the park's safety mechanisms. The Tyrannosaurus Rex attacks the tour cars and kills the lawyer, and a Dilophosaurus kills Dennis.

The beginning of the movie does what the rest of the movie never does – it confuses us. We do not know what is going on. This does not happen in the body of the film, which certainly scares us, but we know very clearly what is going on, how it has been developing, and what is at stake. We follow the fate of a few people, and the action moves forward unrelentingly. We may be scared but we are never confused, especially at the end. Such things make *Jurassic Park* very much a classical Hollywood narrative, but very few of them are at work in *Rashomon*.

Rashomon (1950)

Fig. 2.25

Rashomon, which is probably the most praised Japanese movie ever made, begins like many Hollywood movies: we are presented with a mystery, an unanswered question. A woodcutter mutters over and over again to a priest, "I don't understand it. I don't understand it at all" (figure 2.25). A commoner arrives and asks what it is that he does not understand. The priest amplifies the confusion by saying that even Abbot Konin of Kiyomian Temple would not understand it. The woodcutter starts to tell the story, and we see a flashback from three days earlier that begins to define the question for us. The woodcutter, walking through a forest, comes upon a hat, a rope, and an amulet case strewn along the way. He is then shocked to find a dead body.

Narrative Confusion without Clarification

At this point, nothing could be more like a classical Hollywood narrative. *Citizen Kane* (1941) opens with a dying man saying "Rosebud" and nobody knows what the word means, so the movie becomes a quest to learn its meaning. *Murder, My Sweet* (1944) opens with the main character blindfolded in a sinister interrogation room asking a police officer, "Boys tell me I did a couple of murders. Anything in it?" The rest of the movie answers the question. And *Jurassic Park* opens with an attack by something monstrous and a number of other confusing events.

In *Citizen Kane* we learn what "Rosebud" means – it was the name of a sled that the man cherished as a boy; in *Murder, My Sweet*, we learn who committed the murders and why the main character is blindfolded; in *Jurassic Park*, the confusing events are quickly cleared up. *Rashomon* does not work that way. We see testimony at a trial from the priest who saw the man and his wife before the man was killed and then testimony from a man who captured the bandit who confesses to the killing. The man claims that the bandit had fallen from his horse. The bandit interrupts this testimony, saying he didn't fall off the horse at all but was sick from drinking from a poisoned stream and was resting. He then admits killing the man with a sword and raping his wife.

Unresolved Contradictions

The question of whether the bandit fell from his horse or climbed off to rest seems like a minor one but it points to major aspects of the movie. It is the first outright contradiction in the film, and it is never resolved. Later, the wife tells the story of the rape and killing, but her story contradicts that of the bandit. In her version she, and not the bandit, may have killed her husband with a dagger. One would think that, since the killing is only days old and the body was found, it would be a simple matter to check to see if the body had a sword or dagger wound in it, but we never learn why this apparently wasn't done. Nor do we even learn the outcome of the trial or see the judges.

Furthermore, the priest says that not only was the woman's story completely different from the bandit's but that he also disagrees entirely with the bandit's characterization of the woman. The bandit found her strong, the priest found her pitiable. Now we not only have contradictions about the events but also contradictions about perceptions of the people involved. Since much of the material is given to us in flashbacks, we also see the contradictory material played out. The commoner, the only character with no direct experience of the events, says that, the more he hears, the more confused he becomes. Viewers share his confusion.

In a classical Hollywood movie like *Jurassic Park*, this would be the time for Steven Spielberg to come galloping to the rescue with an educational-type film clarifying things and focusing on the main question posed by the film. Instead of clarifying the situation, however, Kurosawa now gives us another version that contradicts the first two. To compound the confusion, this version is told by the dead man through a medium. Granted, the movie is set in the twelfth century, but it is for twentieth-century audiences who are likely to seriously question the reliability of a dead man's testimony told through a dancing conjurer. However, the flashbacks of the medium's tale are shown in the same manner and with equal reliability as the first two, and the very presence of the conjurer at the trial implies that the testimony is given equal weight by the judges. In this tale the husband is not murdered at all but commits suicide with the dagger.

Citizen Kane might be seen as comparable to this movie since we get incidents from Kane's life told by people with different perceptions of him. They agree, however, about factual information and disagree only in their perceptions of the man. And the "Rosebud" question is cleared up at the end. *Rashomon* does nothing of the sort. Virtually nothing is cleared up, and we do not even learn the outcome of the trial.

Narrative Unity and Closure

As with *Jurassic Park*, we get a frame for the plot. *Rashomon* opens and closes with shots of the dilapidated Rashomon gate where the story is recounted

Fig. 2.26   Fig. 2.27

(figures 2.26 and 2.27). The movie begins in the pouring rain, and the priest and the woodcutter are in the building, apparently for shelter. The commoner arrives seeking shelter and the others tell their tale to him. When the rain ends, the commoner leaves and the film closes with shots of the gate. Like the two shots of Hammond on the helipad in *Jurassic Park*, the shots of the gate frame the film – it opens and closes there – but, unlike the shots of Hammond, nothing is resolved between them.

It is not the resolution of the narrative question that ends the film but simply the fact that the rain ends. In a sense, the film simply stops rather than ends. The storytellers disperse without resolving the questions raised by the different versions of the story. To underline the arbitrary quality of the ending, an entirely new story element is introduced when an abandoned baby is discovered by Rashomon gate. The commoner steals its clothing, the priest cuddles it, and the woodcutter takes it home to be raised with his other children as the film ends.

Integrated versus Separated Plot Events

Like much in the movie, the baby is presented without being integrated into the plot. In a classical Hollywood movie, exactly what happened with the rape and killing would be clarified by this point. It is quite traditional in classical movies for the official truth-seekers to fail and for only the viewer or a privileged few characters to learn the truth. In *Citizen Kane*, for example, only the viewer learns what "Rosebud" is. In *The Man who Shot Liberty Valance*, only the participant and a few reporters learn who shot Liberty Valance, and they decide to conceal the truth. But in both movies the viewer knows. In *Rashomon*, however, no one knows.

This does not indicate in any way that *Rashomon* is a failure as a narrative film but simply that it operates under different conventions from those of classical Hollywood narration. It more readily fits into the international art cinema, which at times explicitly critiques presumptions of classical narration, such as those of rigorous clarity and knowability of basic plot elements. There are many narrative traditions.

Classical narration integrates the elements of the plot in such a manner that everything fits together in a related way and nothing is random. In *Jurassic Park*, Alan Grant terrifies a boy with a tale of the Velociraptor's hunting techniques; later, we see a real Velociraptor kill an experienced hunter using those techniques. In *Rashomon*, the woodcutter finds an amulet case at the murder scene. At the end, an amulet is found on the foundling child. A Hollywood screenwriter would be tempted to make the baby the child of the devastated couple and thereby link up those parts of the story in an integrated manner by means of the amulet. This movie makes no such attempt; they are separate, unrelated events.

This lack of clear and integrated story development makes it difficult to separate free from bound motifs. In classical films it is easy. Bound motifs are what directly contribute to the resolution of the basic narrative question. But here, that question is only multiplied, never really clarified and never resolved. What relevance does the poisoned stream have, the bandit's prized Korean sword, the amulet case? On a larger scale, why doesn't the wife's tale agree with the bandit's, or the husband's with the wife's? A traditional explanation for lying at a murder trial might be that they were trying to escape guilt, but this hardly makes sense since all three claim they killed the husband, and the bandit freely admits to the rape. Furthermore, traditional logic gives all three strong motivation to be truthful since all exist under the shadow of death. The bandit presumes that he will be executed, the wife has tried to drown herself, and the husband is already dead. Why lie? Of course, reasons could be created, but this movie is not concerned with looking for them.

The woodcutter's story is slightly different, since he may have stolen the dagger and would, therefore, have reason to testify falsely, but this does nothing to clarify the rest.

Rashomon clearly violates basic rules of classical narration. Like other films within the international art cinema tradition, the story it tells is not clear but confusing and it does not build logically to a clear resolution of its plot threads but rather leaves them unresolved. Part of the "point" of the movie is that the events in the wooded grove will never be known and that the testimony of the participants is not reliable for reasons no one can ever know. Yet, even as the movie undercuts nearly everything about the story of the killing in the grove, it undercuts virtually nothing about the frame story.

The Frame Story and Narrative Reliability

The frame story is much more conservative in its narrative techniques; it bears many resemblances to classical narration. Most obviously, it is reliable. Nothing contradicts its presentation of a story being told under Rashomon gate. Nothing makes us question the fact that it is raining or that each of the characters is a certain type of personality. In the story of the grove, on the contrary, we question everything. We see characters presented in entirely different ways; we do not even know basic facts about the incident, like how the man died or whether it was murder, suicide, or an accident. The constant cuts back to the people giving testimony at the trial do not help. In a classical film we would scrutinize their demeanor while they testify, looking for clues as to whether or not they are telling the truth. But here we get no such clues; we just get more contradictions. We do not know what to believe about the story of the grove. We do, however, know what to believe about the Rashomon gate. We know that three men gathered there seeking shelter from a downpour and that they exchanged details of a puzzling story. They found a baby, the rain ended, and they dispersed. Nothing contradicts these things; they are quite clear.

The commoner intrudes upon the quieter world of the woodcutter and priest in ways similar to the intrusion of the bandit into the journey of the man and woman. Like the bandit, the commoner is loud, aggressive, and abrasive in his manner, given to outbursts of derisive laughter and indifferent to traditional morality. The woodcutter and priest tell him the story of the grove and he frequently admits to being confused, but this confusion does not particularly bother him. The priest tries to give the story apocalyptic significance, but the commoner cannot be bothered with the priest's pious and overblown interpretations, saying he would rather listen to the rain than to the priest's sermonizing. He also says that stories of murders are plentiful and that this is only one of many. He is not disturbed by plot contradictions, saying simply that he enjoys a good story. At the end he sees the contradictions clearly enough to pressure the woodcutter into admitting that he saw more than he testified to and then into giving his eyewitness account. He also implies that the woodcutter stole the dagger and, therefore, that his story was compromised.

But none of this interests him beyond the level of a good yarn. When the baby is discovered, he steals most of its clothes and leaves. He has listened as long as he was interested and, now that he has a good reason, he leaves. But his reason has nothing to do with the plot resolution. The only storyline in the movie that fully makes sense is his. He arrives at the beginning, listens for a while to an interesting story, and leaves. He leaves, however, not because the story is resolved but because he wants to escape with the clothing he has grabbed, because the rain is stopping, and because he has had enough. The film ends with the priest uselessly announcing that he once again has faith in humankind and with the woodcutter taking the foundling off. But the priest's interpretations of things are not particularly reliable, and the woodcutter acts from unknown and unknowable motives.

Rashomon has been widely praised for nearly half a century as powerful and provocative in its probing of the nature of truth, but it is clearly not a classical Hollywood narrative and never attempted to be. Movies tell their stories in many ways.

SELECTED READINGS

David Bordwell applies neoformalist theory to film, including the international art cinema and the classical Hollywood cinema, in *Narration in the Fiction Film* (Madison: University of Wisconsin, 1985), and he, Janet Staiger, and Kristin Thompson define and trace the evolution of classical film narration in *The Classical Hollywood Cinema: Film Style and Mode of Production to 1960* (New York: Columbia University Press, 1985). Roland Barthes offers a poststructuralist account of narration, including an analysis of how narrative questions are posed and answered and how classical texts seem to reveal the "truth" by answering all pertinent questions and referring to the "real" world for validation, in *S/Z* (New York: Hill and Wang, 1974 [1970]). Patricia Erens gives a good introduction to the major issues in *Rashomon* with a particular concentration upon its representation of women in *Japanese Women in Film* (New York: Japan Society, 1992). Donald S. Richie has placed *Rashomon* within the context of Kurosawa's career in *The Films of Akira Kurosawa* (Berkeley, CA: University of California Press, 1970); he has also edited a collection of essays, *Rashomon* (New Brunswick, NJ: Rutgers University Press, 1987), which also contains a helpful narrative continuity.

3

FORMAL ANALYSIS

Rules of the Game and *The Sixth Sense*

Most of us will have had the experience of flipping through the television channels with the remote control and coming upon a movie we have previously seen. Typically, we think to ourselves, "I've already seen that," and continue searching the channels for something new. This response implies that, once we have seen a movie, we have used it up: we know what happens so we are bored by the prospect of watching it again. Why watch a movie if we know how the story ends? In this chapter we will explore many reasons why one might want to watch movies again and, indeed, why one might even enjoy them more on repeated viewings than one did the first time.

Let us return to our example of flipping channels for something to watch. No doubt on many such occasions we said that, although we had already seen the film, it was so long ago that we would like to watch it again. This response implies that one reason for watching a film again is that we have forgotten part of it. In such a case, it is still the story that is primary; if we can't remember how it ends, our interest will be maintained. At times we rewatch a film because it stars a favorite actor and we want to enjoy the performance again. We might even delight in remembering and anticipating a particular moment, such as when Clint Eastwood, aiming his gun at a criminal in *Sudden Impact* (1983), sadistically taunts him to go for his own gun by saying, "Go ahead. Make my day."

While the above reasons for rewatching movies are certainly valid, in this chapter we discuss other reasons related to the formal properties of films. By **formal properties**, we are referring to the elements of the medium which shape what we see and hear when we watch a film. We do not simply or directly see a story when we go to a movie; we see images and hear sounds from which we construct or make a fictional world. Formal properties of images include techniques of composition such as what is in the foreground and what is in the background of the image or what is at the left, center, and right side of the image. Similarly, we might hear the dialogue in the scene accompanied by street noises such as police sirens or by music coming either from a radio in the scene or from soundtrack music. These sounds comprise the aural aspect of film. The manner in which the visual and aural elements of a film are shaped and formed are our concern in this chapter.

Generally, we do not go to the theater two Saturdays in a row to watch the same movie, but most of us can probably think of exceptions. *Titanic* became a phenomenon, not to mention a financial blockbuster, upon its release in 1997, due to the number of people seeing the 3-hour-and-14-minute movie repeatedly. When *Star Wars* (1977) first appeared, many people also saw it repeatedly. Indeed, the movie and its two sequels even had an unprecedentedly successful theatrical re-release in 1997. Furthermore, the re-release whetted audience appetites for three announced **prequels**, beginning with *Star Wars Episode I: The Phantom Menace* in 1999. The reason may seem obvious: like *Jurassic Park* (1993) and *Titanic*, much of *Star Wars* is full of spectacle and special effects. It is fun to re-experience those effects while they are fresh in our minds or even after the passage of many years. We may eagerly anticipate a favorite moment, relishing the sensation we felt the first time and hoping that we will feel it again. Or, in the case of the *Star Wars* trilogy theatrical re-release, young people who had only previously seen it on video may look forward to the theatrical experience involving a large, high-definition, widescreen image accompanied by stereo Dolby sound. Since most movies don't emphasize spectacle and special effects, we might think that *Star Wars*, *Jurassic Park*, and *Titanic* are exceptions that tell us little or nothing about how we respond to movies like *Driving Miss Daisy* (1989). We should not be too quick, however, to jump to this conclusion.

Visual Images

Fig. 3.1

Fig. 3.2

While it is true that most of the time, after we have seen a movie, we remember the story, once in a while a visual image or a **scene** is so vivid that we remember it equally well, and maybe even better. As time passes, we may even forget the story but remember the image. Who can forget the moment in *2001: A Space Odyssey* (1968) when the camera follows a club thrown by a primitive man as it sails high in the air and the image suddenly cuts to that of a futuristic space ship similarly flying through the skies (figures 3.1 and 3.2)? Or, to pick another example from another film directed by Stanley Kubrick, the moment in *Dr Strangelove: Or How I Learned to Stop Worrying and Love the Bomb* (1963) when a bomber pilot rides a nuclear bomb like a bucking bronco as it plunges downward to destroy the planet (figure 3.3)? Long after we have forgotten the plot details of *The*

Quiet Man (1952), we are likely to remember the vivid image of the lovers, played by John Wayne and Maureen O'Hara, as they romantically embrace during a windswept rainstorm. Similarly, viewers of *Titanic* might be fuzzy in their remembrance of the various character interactions but are unlikely to forget the spectacular overhead shot in which the stern of the ship rises almost vertically out of the water, with people and objects suddenly plummeting down as if falling from a tall building.

Fig. 3.3

Nearly everyone who has seen *Psycho* (1960, see chapter 6) remembers the famous shower murder scene where a woman is brutally stabbed to death (figure 3.4). Those who saw *The Gold Rush* in 1925 invariably remember the scene in which a starving Charlie Chaplin cooks and eats his shoe. Similarly, nearly everyone who has seen *Alien* (1979) remembers the moment when the creature bursts forth from the abdomen of a crew member (figure 3.5). Yet, within a short time of seeing *Alien*, it is quite likely that we will forget the name of the crew member, what he looked like, and what kind of character he was. The visual impact of that shockingly unexpected moment, in other words, will dominate the narrative. It is also quite likely that anyone who has seen *Jurassic Park* will vividly recall some of the images of horror as the vicious Velociraptors stalk two children who hide in a kitchen (figure 3.6). At the same time, however, we will probably quickly forget the names and appearances of the

Fig. 3.4

children as well as what narrative circumstances account for their being alone in the kitchen. We might remember them crouching down against the stainless steel of the kitchen, but we can't remember what they are doing there.

Moments like the primitive club turning into the futuristic spaceship, the "cowboy" riding the bomb, the lovers embracing in the storm, the sinking of the *Titanic*, the shower murder, the shoe-eating scene, the birth of the alien monster bloodily boring its way out of its host's body, and the children hiding from the deadly Velociraptors illustrate that, regardless of the primacy of narrative in most films, visual images do at times come to the fore. We may remember a precise moment such as the blade of the knife being thrust at the woman's body in the shower or the blank stare in the close-up of her eye after she has fallen dead. If the scene had been filmed differently, perhaps it would

Fig. 3.5

Fig. 3.6

not be so memorable. In actuality, however, such moments tell us something fundamental about all narrative filmmaking: that how the story is told is inseparable from and as important as the story itself.

Departures from the Stylistic Norm

Creative filmmakers sometimes employ surprising stylistic features that are unusual for the time of their release precisely because such departures from the **stylistic norm** may have a strong impact on the audience. Such moments offer particularly good examples of style since we are likely to be struck by something novel. *Schindler's List* (1993), for example, is a black-and-white movie over three hours long. It came at a time when nearly all films were made in color, so the mere fact of it being in black and white made it stand out (figure 3.7). Spielberg did, however, use brief moments of color in the film. We repeatedly see a little girl wearing a red coat (plate 1) and, in one scene, we see the flames of candles lit during a religious ceremony burning in color (plate 2). Finally, the epilogue is a full-color scene in the cemetery where the historical character upon whom the film is based is buried (plate 3). This color scheme will surely be remembered by spectators who have never seen anything like it. Other films do similar things, including *Raging Bull* (1980), which is photographed entirely in black and white with the exception of a sequence using color home movies, and *Shock Corridor* (1963), which similarly contains brief color footage.

Audiences who saw *Bonnie and Clyde* (1967) and *The Wild Bunch* (1969) at the time of their release were mesmerized by the unexpected use of violence seen in slow motion, a technique that created an almost ballet-like effect as bodies slowly moved through the air and fell to the ground. Critics and the public alike spoke incessantly about the slow-motion finale in *Bonnie and Clyde* when the gangster lovers of the title die in a hail of bullets. In *The Wild Bunch*, scenes of violence that had long been characteristic of Westerns are presented in graphic slow motion throughout the film. We see bodies slowly writhing and twisting as bullets hit them and blood spurts out. Although audiences of the time expected such shoot-outs in Westerns, they had never seen them in such extended slow motion. Once again, there had been previous instances of slow-motion violence in Westerns, such as a brief moment in *Forty Guns* (1957), but such extended use of slow-motion violence did not constitute an expected technique of the time. Since then, it has been used so often that, to many viewers now, these scenes may appear like the norm.

The D-Day invasion sequence in *Saving Private Ryan* (1997) became instantly famous for its horrifying and oppressive sense of mass slaughter of the Allied troops landing on the beach. Mass slaughter is nothing new to films, and there have been other D-Day films, but the combination of the images of soldiers being mowed

Fig. 3.7

down, even before they could leave their boats, with a soundtrack that emphasized the various and unrelenting sounds of bullets – hitting men, the metal walls of the boats, the water, ricocheting around – in a way that created a virtual wall of sounds of unavoidable death gave viewers a sense of a new way of presenting violence. In the remainder of the film, however, the violence is presented in much more conventional ways.

A final such example comes from two Brian De Palma films. In *Sisters* (1973) and *Carrie* (1976, figures 3.8 and 3.9), De Palma used a **split screen**, but only in certain scenes. Throughout most of the films, De Palma composes the shots in accordance with the then current conventions of filmmaking, which presented one unified image filling the entire scene. During certain highly dramatic scenes, however, he suddenly shows two images juxtaposed directly next to each other with only a dividing frame line separating the images. Furthermore, both images show the same action, but photographed from a drastically different camera position. Unlike films like *Dr Jekyll and Mr Hyde* (1932), which occasionally used split screens to show different characters in different settings (see chapter 9), De Palma used the device to simultaneously show two different views of the same characters in the same setting (we examine a related technique in *Timecode* (2000) in chapter 16). Again, audiences unused to this style are likely to be jolted into an awareness of stylistic technique that they might not normally notice.

Fig. 3.8

Fig. 3.9

Visual Style and Narrative Effect

The above examples show moments when elements of film style are foregrounded and noticed as much as, if not more than, the narrative elements they represent. In chapter 2 we explored how the story and the manner in which it is told are inseparable. We might think that the mere fact of a woman being killed in the shower in *Psycho* supplies the horror, but it is really how Alfred Hitchcock, the film's director, shoots and edits the scene that makes it so horrifying. The scene is composed of many brief shots and, although it seems graphically violent, we mostly see stabbing motions when the knife does not pierce the skin of the victim. Had another director simply used a few shots of the killer plunging the knife into the woman's body, the scene would have had an entirely different effect. We have all had the experience of watching remakes of films we love, such as *Dracula* (1931), *Dr Jekyll and Mr Hyde*, *The Big Sleep* (1946), or even *Psycho* (see chapter 6), and being disappointed. The story might be very similar, the film technology might be more current, but the specific formal techniques that made the first film compelling are absent. We are not, by the way, suggesting that the original is always superior. The extremely popular *The Maltese Falcon* (1941) was the third, not the first, film based upon Dashiell Hammett's novel, but easily the one that has affected audiences most intensely. Our point is that much of a film's effect comes from the formal skill with which it is made and in this chapter we will help students to recognize this.

In *Return of the Pink Panther* (1975), a comic moment occurs when Inspector Clouseau appears at the scene of the crime. The fabled Pink Panther jewel has been stolen from a museum, and the camera is placed in the room where the theft has occurred. The camera remains stationary as we see a local police officer and Clouseau arrive to investigate. The officer enters the room, but Clouseau idiotically marches right past the door without even slowing down. The camera remains stationary as we and the officer await Clouseau's reappearance. When he finally returns, he has a serious look on his face as if he were in control of everything and had done nothing stupid. What makes the moment so funny is the use of **offscreen space**. The wall blocks our view of Clouseau after he walks past the doorway. We do not see him discover his error, react to his blunder, and reassert his composure; we simply see his ludicrous reappearance after he has recovered his composure. Had the camera been placed so that we had followed Clouseau and seen everything, the scene would have had an entirely different effect.

Few of us go to an art museum because we have a particular interest in looking at fruit but we might spend hours looking at still-life paintings composed of nothing but bowls of fruit. Similarly, few of us sit at home and stare at fruit for long periods of time. Implicitly, what fascinates and pleases us in the museum is how the apples, pears, and bananas are painted. We can easily purchase a bowl of fruit for a few dollars; a painting of one might sell for millions. The subject matter is secondary; how it is represented is primary. We pay careful attention to the shapes, arrangements, colors, and brush strokes – in other words, the formal properties of painting. *Jurassic Park* may seem to present a totally different situation from the still-life paintings: the exciting story and the opportunity to see dinosaurs as opposed to something as ordinary as a bowl of fruit make it appear as if those are the only things we care about, not how they are represented. The truth, however, is that these two divergent experiences are on a continuum rather than being totally different. The ways in which painters and movie directors compose their compositions, use color, shape, and light are an important part of our experience of their works.

Much as art-appreciation classes can make us more sensitive to the nuances of style in a still-life, film criticism can increase our awareness of the stylistic features of movies. Once we have this increased awareness, we will notice, appreciate, and respond to different elements of a film. Most listeners to classical music enjoy a symphony more after they have heard it several times. They hear new things on repeated listenings but also enjoy hearing the various elements with which they are already familiar take shape and form. As with painting, experiencing the shape and form of the music is pleasurable. From this perspective, movies, including Hollywood genre entertainments, are more like painting and music than we may realize. As we become aware of their techniques, we can repeatedly enjoy watching them, even while the story is fresh in our minds. Indeed, as we become familiar with them, we may even enjoy them more than we did on first viewing.

Common Stylistic Techniques

Many films are not particularly noteworthy in terms of their styles. They follow predictable patterns of, for example, camera positioning and cutting from one camera position to the next. Style is only minimally noticeable and perhaps even invisible. Such films are like some best-selling novels that tell their story with little creative use of language or chapter organization. Readers may devour such "page turners" to find out what happens but are unlikely to come away remembering sentences that they will quote or complexities in the point of view from which the story is narrated.

Cutting on dialogue

The same is true for some films. Some techniques are used so widely that they become unquestioned norms, and many filmmakers use them unthinkingly, almost as a "knee-jerk response." A major example in Hollywood filmmaking involves **shot/reverse-shot editing** and **cutting** on action, reaction, and dialogue. Shot/reverse-shot editing refers to a pattern whereby first a **shot** shows one character and then there is a **cut** to a reverse shot that shows us a nearly opposite view, typically another character who is talking to or interacting with the first. The shots sometimes include a small portion of the back of the head, neck, and shoulders of the character in the prior shot. For example, if two characters are in a room talking to each other, a common pattern shows one of the characters talking and then cuts to the other character when he or she either starts talking or reacts to something that the first character has said. If a character says, "I'll tell you who shot the butler!" we are likely to see that character make the important pronouncement followed by the stunned reaction of a listener. The cut to the listener is the **reaction shot**, since it shows how the listener reacts to the revelation. The purpose of the cut is to allow us to witness the impact of the dialogue just spoken. Then the film may cut back to the first character, who continues by naming the suspect, and then another cut may return to the listener, who exclaims in disbelief. In this example, both shots are motivated by showing the character who is speaking or, in other words, the shot/reverse-shot cutting is determined by dialogue. Many scenes simply go back and forth between such shots until all the significant dialogue has been spoken.

Cutting on action

Another variation on this common pattern involves action rather than dialogue. In a Western fight scene, for example, we might see a character pull his arm back, make a fist, and prepare to throw a punch in one shot. We might then see a cut to the character who receives the punch and staggers backward. The structure here is exactly the same as in the dialogue scenes, but the action (drawing the arm back) replaces the important line of dialogue; the reaction (being hit and staggering backward) replaces the responsive line of dialogue or the reactive facial expression. This is an example of cutting on action and reaction. As with shot/reverse-shot editing, many films use such formulaic cutting patterns throughout. The reliance upon such well-established editing patterns results from the ease with which experienced filmmakers can set up shots. Rather than spending long periods of time grappling with original camera positions and cutting patterns, filmmakers can quickly and efficiently complete a scene using these traditional techniques. Such techniques are also clear to spectators already familiar with them and there is, therefore, no risk of unwanted confusion.

Establishing shots

Another such pattern in Hollywood films involves the use of **establishing** or **master shots**. An establishing shot is an extreme **long shot** that shows (or establishes) the entire space in which the ensuing scene will take place. Many scenes begin with such shots to show the spectator where the characters are in relation to each other and to important elements of the set, such as a loaded gun. Sometimes there are two establishing shots, one exterior and one interior. We might, for example, see an exterior long shot of a building and then cut to an interior shot showing a room with two angry men standing by a desk with a gun lying on top of it. The establishing shots serve to anchor the space: we know the building and we know the room and who is in it and where they are. If one of the men stands closer to the desk and the two lunge for the gun, we understand the spatial dynamics of who gets there first and why.

Many Hollywood scenes not only begin with establishing shots but end with similar shots. Thus, we start with a full view of the room, move into closer shots that include the shot/reverse-shot cutting patterns discussed above, and then end by pulling back to the full view where we started. This pattern of beginning with a long shot that establishes the space, moving into that space and becoming part of the dialogue and action through shot/reverse-shot editing, and then being extricated from the conversation and/or action and returned to our original vantage point is so common that it is likely to go unnoticed by contemporary viewers. When it goes unnoticed we have what is frequently referred to as the **invisible style** of filmmaking, a style that encourages us to follow the action and dialogue without noticing the cuts or where the camera is placed. This style is intended to make us feel as if we were watching the events themselves, rather than the events as staged for and recorded by the camera.

If, in the middle of a cutting on action and reaction interior fight scene, for example, a director cuts to an exterior shot of a tree and then cuts back to the fight, nearly every spectator would take note of the unexpected exterior view of the tree. It wouldn't "fit" into the illusion of the "real" fight unfolding before them. In fact, something similar to this occurs in the climactic shoot-out near the end of *Face/Off* (1997). A number of characters are gathered in a church, pointing guns at one another. We see some of the characters' reactions and gazes as they size up the situation, but when the shooting starts, the film cuts away to shots of flowers, a dove flying, and a religious icon. Instead of seeing who shoots whom when, in a manner that represents the illusion of an actual fight taking place before us, we are surprised to see imagery from another part of the church. When we return to the fight, many of the characters are lying dead. Far from being invisible, spectators of the film will notice and probably even remember the unexpected cut to the shot of the dove flying, since the cutting in the film is likely to startle the spectator.

The 180-degree rule

Many rules of classical cinema, such as that which forbids the crossing of the **180-degree line**, help maintain the **invisible style**. Typically, after a scene is established, an imaginary line is drawn between the camera and the participants; all subsequent action in the scene is shot from only one side of that line. It is not important which side it is, right or left, just that the camera positions consistently keep to that side to prevent viewer disorientation. Let us take the example of a dialogue scene with two characters facing each other. As long as the camera remains on one side of the 180-degree line, the positioning and movements of both characters will retain the same screen direction in each shot – that is, one will look left to right and the other right to left. If the camera crossed the line and shot the characters from the other side, their screen direction would reverse. Even though the characters had not moved, they would appear to be looking in the opposite direction. Obviously this calls attention to itself and makes the cut anything but invisible. It might also confuse viewers used to the stylistic norm, since they expect a character to be facing in a different direction only if that character has moved.

The same is true with action. As long as the camera stays on one side of the imaginary line, the action will appear to move in one direction; if the line is crossed, the direction reverses. *Stagecoach* (1939) contains an exception that proves the rule. During a climactic fight scene, Indians chase the coach. After many shots showing the coach moving in one screen direction (figure 3.10), there is a cut to the coach moving in the opposite direction (figure 3.11). Technical

Fig. 3.10

Fig. 3.11

lighting considerations forced the filmmakers to move the camera to the opposite side of the 180-degree line, thus making it seem as if the coach suddenly reversed direction. Director John Ford, however, was not concerned about this, since he felt that spectators would be so caught up in the excitement of the chase and the fight that they would not even notice it. Although in this instance he was right, the rule in Hollywood is to avoid any such extreme situations where the cutting patterns could become noticeable.

More Departures from Stylistic Norms

If the invisible style of filmmaking often involves little more than the unnoticeable use of normative patterns, many films develop a formal style that departs from expectations, frequently foregrounding techniques in a noticeable and even startling manner. Blake Edwards frequently employs such departures from norms for comic effect. In his musical comedy *Darling Lili* (1970), for example, a scene starts with an extreme **close-up** of a rose. The camera slowly pulls back and reveals another, and then another and, as it moves and shifts focus, we begin to see an extraordinary number of rose bouquets, which eventually reach ludicrous proportions as the camera finally shows us the long shot of the space in which the flowers are placed. Now we recognize the room as that belonging to Lili Smith (one of the central characters) and realize that the roses have been sent by Major Larabee (another central character) as a romantic gesture after a first date. The entire effect of the scene (the revelation of Larabee's grandiose romantic gesture) is contingent on denying us the usual full view of the scene at its beginning. If we knew where we were and saw the room full of flowers, the entire effect would be lost; Larabee's excessive romantic nature would simply be a piece of narrative information we had about the character (he sends flowers after dates) rather than being a formally shaped experience that reveals in a startling manner the character's romantic proclivities. The scene, in other words, is shaped by the denial of the expected establishing shot.

Fig. 3.12

Fig. 3.13

Another comic use of space occurs in *The Pink Panther Strikes Again* (1976) when Inspector Clouseau mounts a set of parallel bars. As he dismounts by swinging off the bars (figure 3.12), we see him disappear from sight as we hear his offscreen scream. Suddenly, we cut to a shot of a room full of seated people as we see Clouseau tumbling down the stairs in the rear of the shot (figure 3.13). The humor is premised upon two spatial confusions resulting from a lack of establishing shots. First, Edwards has not shown us enough of the room with the parallel bars for us to see that they are located next to a descending staircase. Had we seen that we would not have been surprised that the accident-prone inspector would have such a mishap. The cut to the room of seated people seems initially like a cut away to an entirely unrelated space. We have neither seen the room before nor the characters in it. Suddenly, when Clouseau tumbles into view, we realize that the room is directly under the one with the parallel bars. Had this been established previously, we would, once again, have expected his typically ungracious entrance. As it is, we are surprised and then amused at the manner in which he tries to recover his composure and conduct an interrogation of those who have just witnessed his bumbling incompetence.

An example from another of the Inspector Clouseau films reveals how variations of shot/reaction-shot patterns can also be used in refreshingly creative ways. Near the end of *A Shot in the Dark* (1964), Clouseau assembles a room full of criminal suspects and announces that he is going to reveal which one of them is a murderer. We cut to a series of seven reaction shots of startled faces, all of which contain guilty looks and shifting eyes, as each of those present nervously surveys the others. Then we see a close-up of Clouseau's eyes similarly darting back and forth. The humor comes from disrupting several aspects of the expected shot/reaction-shot pattern. First, the sheer number of reaction shots is bewildering. We expect perhaps one such shot but not a series of everyone in the room that stops the action dead in its tracks. In fact, the film literally stops for the purpose of showing reaction shots rather than maintaining the predictable rhythm of integrating one such shot into the flow of a cut back to the original speaker. Secondly, when we next see Clouseau, he engages in the same suspicious darting of the eyes as the others. Normally, we expect that the look of the person who initiates a reaction shot will be different from that of the person in the reaction shot when we return to him or her. But in this unusual scene, the two kinds of shot are virtually identical; Clouseau suspiciously looks at the suspects in the same way as they suspiciously look at each other. In this scene, Edwards has created a refreshing variation on a clichéd formula.

Structuring Screen Space

Film form has many elements that can be structured in complex ways. Filmmakers can use these elements in ways that do not simply embellish the action and dialogue but rather significantly structure it. *The Man who Shot Liberty Valance* (1962) is another interesting example since many people consider Westerns, like comedies, simple genre entertainments. This film organizes screen space in a meaningful, complex manner.

The Man who Shot Liberty Valance draws creatively upon the fact that, when we watch a film, in addition to the space we see on the screen at any moment, there are six potential areas of **offscreen space** surrounding the image. Four of the six areas of offscreen space are fairly easy to pick out and identify: the

Fig. 3.14

Fig. 3.15

Fig. 3.16

Fig. 3.17

spaces at the left, right, top, and bottom of the image. The remaining two are a little more complicated: the space behind the camera and the space beyond the horizon. Imagine, for example, an exterior, stationary shot in a forest. We see trees all around but no characters. If a woman walks into the shot from the left, she has entered from offscreen space that we do not see but which we presume extends beyond the **frame** line at the left side of the image. The same thing would happen if she entered from the right. If she dropped into the frame from the top, we would presume she had been perched on a tree branch that lies above our view; if she suddenly leapt up from the bottom, we would similarly presume she had been crouched beneath our view. If she appeared with her back toward us walking into the forest, we would surmise that she entered from behind the camera and was walking away from it; if she suddenly appeared as a small figure in the distance, facing us and coming closer, we would conclude that she came from beyond the horizon of our vision and was approaching the camera. These spatial aspects of film form are simple enough but can be used in sophisticated and complex ways.

In *The Man who Shot Liberty Valance* every major entrance of the character of the villain, Liberty Valance, takes place in relation to offscreen space. In the first shot of a flashback, a stagecoach comes toward the camera when suddenly the figure of an armed bandit rises into the frame (figure 3.14): it is our introduction to Valance, who, in this case, bursts into the frame from below the frame line. The next time we see him it is in the town of Shinbone. We see the interior of a peaceful restaurant when suddenly the doors at the left of the frame are thrown open and the menacing outlaw appears and disrupts the atmosphere (figure 3.15). Later, an important town meeting takes place with the sheriff posted outside. Suddenly we hear the sound of galloping horses and see the frightened look on the face of the sheriff, who withdraws in the frame as Valance forcefully enters from offscreen behind and at an angle to the right of the camera (figure 3.16). He interrupts the town meeting and threatens the participants. In the final example, we see the interior of a newspaper office as the editor enters and lights a lamp. When the dark room (figure 3.17) lights up, we suddenly see Valance standing against the back wall in a threatening posture (figure 3.18). He savagely beats the editor for being a political foe. In this case, the sudden shift in lighting extends our view of the horizon within the frame, turning what had been dark, offscreen space into well-lit screen space. Notice that in each of these examples Valance is a disruptive force and that the manner in which he enters from offscreen intensifies his disruptive nature. Offscreen space, in other words, complexly structures this character's impact on us.

Color and Sound

Fig. 3.18

Many other elements of film such as sound and color can be structured in a similar manner to create formal complexity. The color red is used in such a way in *Dead Ringers* (1988). The opening credits appear over a deep red backdrop (plate 4). The plot, dealing with twin brothers who operate a gynecological clinic, raises issues of menstruation. In several scenes we see surgical teams dressed in bright red gowns and masks (plate 5), which recall the red of the credit sequence. Finally, we see a bloody body when, at the film's conclusion, one of the now-demented brothers fatally operates on the other (plate 6). Red becomes a free **motif** with connotations of blood. In the opening shot of *Scarface* (1932), we hear a man whistling as he approaches another man with a gun and then shoots him. Later, we see the same man walk down the hallway of an apartment house, once again with a gun and whistling the same tune. As soon as we hear the whistling, we know that he will soon kill another man and, moments later, he does.

The spaces, colors, and sounds that we see and hear when we watch a movie can all lend formal complexity to the stories the movies tell. Sometimes these formal elements may create an effect in just one scene, or they may be repeated and structured to create **free motifs** that become part of character and thematic development. In either case, thinking about movies means learning to perceive the presence of many visual and aural components and the complex patterns they form within the plot. Narrative is one of the elements that shapes film form, but it is by no means the only or always the primary one. To become attentive film viewers, we have to sharpen both our looking and listening skills.

To illustrate this, we turn now to two films made in different national cinemas, styles, and time periods. *Rules of the Game* (1939) holds a position in French cinema not unlike *Citizen Kane* (1941) in American cinema: it has been widely praised since it appeared and is notable for its creative use of **long takes**, moving camera, and **deep focus cinematography** in its exploration of serious cultural issues in France on the brink of World War II. *The Sixth Sense*, a Hollywood film that was a surprise hit in 1999, at first appears to tell a deceptively simple story about the relationships of a lonely, disturbed boy who tells his psychologist that he sees dead people. As it unfolds, however, we learn a "secret" that gives the film an unexpected and entirely different meaning. The "secret" is developed and made credible by formally complex strategies that use our expectations about Hollywood filmmaking to manipulate our responses to what has been before our eyes all along.

Rules of the Game (1939)

Rules of the Game (directed by Jean Renoir) tells the story of a group of upper-middle-class French people and their servants, who spend a week at a country chateau. The events seem simple enough: the guests gather to enjoy such things as a hunt and a costume party, but the large number of characters and the intrigues between them create a complex plot. Indeed, there are so many characters that no one emerges as the film's central character. To add to the complexity, nearly all of the main characters are involved in affairs. The Marquis Robert de la Chesnaye (Marcel Dalio) and his wife, Christine (Nora Gregor), host the party. He has a mistress, Genevieve de Marras (Mila Parely), and she has an affair with Andre Jurieux (Roland Toutain), a famed aviator. Similar marital intrigue exists among the servants. Schumacher (Gaston Modot), the groundskeeper, is in a constant jealous rage at Marceau (Julien Carette), a newly hired domestic who flirts with Lisette (Paulette Dubost), his wife. And so it goes.

The Chateau as Microcosm

The film begins at an airport as radio reporters eagerly await the landing of a record-setting, transatlantic flight by Andre Jurieux, who immediately becomes a national hero. Renoir establishes several important motifs in this scene; one is that radio and airplanes represent technological "progress" in a rapidly changing world. A guest at the chateau will remark in surprise that Robert has bought a radio, and one of the film's main themes is that the upper class is a dying breed. The scene also introduces the theme of marital infidelity, since Andre is heartbroken to find that Christine, the married woman for whom he undertook the flight, is not waiting for him at the airport. His friend Octave (Jean Renoir) succeeds in getting him an invitation to the chateau so that he may see Christine.

Once all the guests have arrived, Renoir builds a complex set of motifs that intertwine to create a sense of impending doom for the upper class way of life, yet the members of that class themselves seem blithely unaware of this. Since the film was made in 1939, when Hitler's threat was apparent, the film also symbolically addresses the imminent danger of the Nazis to France. As such, the chateau becomes a microcosm of French society, which enables Renoir to explore class issues, ethics, and politics. What emerges is the image of a society engaged in playing childish and dangerous games, all the while blind to inevitable tragedy.

Robert collects mechanical musical toys, and his child-like passion for the instruments lends a sense of immature innocence to the character. Everything he does seems like childish play, and therein lies one of the meanings of the film's title: for Robert it is all a game. If his collection of musical instruments forms a motif of childish innocence, the motifs during the hunt suggest a brutal dimension to the game. Renoir shows many images of innocent and frightened rabbits and birds as they are systematically forced into the paths of hunters. Suddenly the games of the idle rich resemble a disgusting slaughter. The party following the hunt literally introduces the motif of disguises and game-playing that characterize the actual lives of these characters. They have all been playing roles as faithful husbands and wives, for example, while in reality they have been engaged in a dance of romantic intrigue and marital infidelity that now literally takes the form of dancing. Violence literally erupts into that dance, first comically, then dramatically, and finally tragically.

During the party we see the comic spectacle of Schumacher dragging Lisette around with one hand while waving his pistol in the other as he pursues Marceau, occasionally shooting wildly. One of the guests mistakenly mis-interprets it all as another act and, when Robert finally orders one of the ser-vants to "stop this farce," he responds "Which one?" By this point in the film, the entire party has degenerated into a farce of such proportions that the ludi-crous spectacle of the enraged, jealous Schumacher fits in perfectly well with the other goings-on. Soon Robert himself is engaged in a fistfight with Andre, who wants to leave with Christine. Before the evening is over, events escalate to truly tragic proportions when Schumacher mistakes Andre for Octave, whom he has mistaken for Lisette's lover, and kills him.

The film ends as the guests gather outside the chateau and hear Robert cover up the tragic events by telling them that Schumacher accidentally shot Andre, mistaking him for a poacher. When one of the guests says that that gives a new meaning to the word "accident," the General (Pierre Magnier) replies that, on the contrary, Robert is the last of a dying race, and the final shot of the film shows the eerie shadows of the guests being cast in giant shadow on a wall of the chateau as they enter. The actual death of Andre, the General's ref-erence to Robert as part of a dying breed, and the shadows on the wall all combine to give a profoundly symbolic sense of death to the scene. Andre's tragic death is much more than a literal loss of one life; it is the harbinger of the tragic end of a whole way of life that has merrily proceeded as if it were all a game. Near the beginning of the movie, Octave tells Andre that there are rules to the game and, near the end, Andre tells Christine the same thing as they prepare to run away together. What they and no one else realize is that, in addition to rules, there are consequences and that the consequences are so shattering that they destroy the illusion that it is all a game.

Deep Focus Cinematography

In addition to the formal development of the visual motifs discussed above, *Rules of the Game* has a sophisticated visual style based upon **deep focus cinematography** with long takes and moving camera. It also makes complex use of sound. Deep focus cinematography is a style in which a great deal of space is not only visible within a shot but also clearly in focus. This differs from the traditional Hollywood practice of focusing only on the foreground of the action and keeping the rear of the frame out of focus so as to direct the viewer's attention toward the area of primary importance. A variation on this is to actually shift the focus within a shot when there is a shift of importance in the dramatic action. When someone or something else becomes important, however, Hollywood films generally cut to that new area, a technique that once again refocuses our attention. Shots do not typically run for a long period of time within this style, since it tends to cut back and forth between significant characters and actions. Renoir, however, requires us to watch multiple planes of action within the frame simultaneously and frequently for long periods of time. Sometimes the characters come and go while the camera remains stationary, and at other times the camera follows them, constantly reframing a deep space in which multiple characters and actions are visible. This style can be demanding, since it asks us to watch for and listen to many things at once.

Fig. 3.19

A comparatively simple example of this style occurs near the beginning of the film when Andre and Octave arrive at the chateau. Tension is in the air due to the troubled affair between Andre and Christine, an element of which became public knowledge when he told a radio reporter that the woman for whom he undertook the flight is not even at the landing to greet him. As the guests enter the chateau, Christine announces to everyone present that she has something to tell them about her relationship with Andre. Rather than reveal the affair, she talks of her friendship with Andre and offers it as the explanation of why he dedicated his flight to her. We see Andre and Christine in the foreground of the frame as she gives her explanation (figure 3.19). Standing behind the couple in the rear of the frame we also see Robert and Octave. Thus, we simultaneously watch the announcement and the effect of the announcement on Robert and Octave. We do not see a typical Hollywood **shot/reaction-shot** structure whereby we would first see a close-up of Christine and then a series of reaction shots; here, we see it all at once in deep focus in a manner that requires us to divide our attention between different parts of the frame.

Fig. 3.20

But that is only the beginning of the complexity of the shot. After Christine finishes speaking, the camera pulls back and pans to reveal other guests, and then pans back again. Still within the same shot, the camera then moves to follow the group as they disperse. Octave walks off with Genevieve, Robert's mistress, and, as others talk and walk away, we see the two talking together in the rear of the frame (figure 3.20). Finally, after the others have left, they approach the camera and the shot ends (figure 3.21). A typical pattern of cutting on action would have simply shown Octave and Genevieve in the foreground as they walk to the stairs where they stand and talk.

Fig. 3.21

Renoir, however, requires us to watch them in the rear of the frame and, if we do not, we will miss noting their presence until the shot is almost over and they approach the camera.

A much more complex example occurs later in the film during a scene of the servants eating dinner in the kitchen. The shot in question begins with Schumacher at the top of the stairs at the left of the **frame** with several servants seated at a table in the lower foreground (figure 3.22). Someone asks him a question, and the camera follows him as he walks down the stairs but then continues moving to frame a chef, who approaches the table from the rear. The chef stands in the middle of the composition between two seated men (figure 3.23). As he talks, we see Schumacher pass behind him and exit offscreen right (figure 3.24). The chef finishes talking and leaves, and the camera quickly pans right where Schumacher stands talking to his wife, Lisette, at the end of the table (figure 3.25). The camera then moves back to its previous position as the chef returns to the table to once again enter the conversation (figure 3.26).

As he speaks, we once again see Schumacher enter the frame, this time walking far into the rear to another table, where he momentarily pauses before walking offscreen left (figure 3.27). The camera

Fig. 3.22

Fig. 3.23

Fig. 3.24

Fig. 3.25

Fig. 3.26

Fig. 3.27

Fig. 3.28

Fig. 3.29

Fig. 3.30

Fig. 3.31

Fig. 3.32

pans left and we see Schumacher walk up the stairs we saw him on at the beginning of the shot (figure 3.28). Rather than ending there, however, the shot continues by panning right to follow Marceau, who passes Schumacher on the stairs on his way to the kitchen for dinner (figure 3.29). Marceau approaches the table and introduces himself as the new servant. The chef is now visible working in the right rear of the frame (figure 3.30). At one point, he even walks further back into another room at the extreme rear of the frame (figure 3.31). The camera pans right as one of the servants gets up to go on duty. As he leaves, Marceau approaches his seat, which is at the end of the table where Lisette sits. As Lisette introduces herself as Mrs Schumacher, the wife of the groundskeeper with whom Marceau is already in trouble, he starts to leave, walking into the rear of the frame. She, however, invites him to sit by her and he returns and sits down (figure 3.32). The chef is once again visible in the far rear of the frame. As we watch Marceau, Lisette, and the chef, we hear an offscreen conversation. Finally, we cut to one of the participants in that conversation.

In conventional cutting on dialogue, action, and reaction, this single, extraordinarily long shot with deep focus and moving camera would have been broken down into many shots of the various characters with little visible space behind them. A final example of Renoir's long takes with deep focus occurs in the hallway of the chateau as the guests prepare for bed on the first evening of their visit. In this variation, however, the camera is stationary; the complexity derives from the manner in which the characters come and go from nearly every direction of offscreen space. The long hallway is lined with doorways into the many guest rooms on both the right and left sides. Throughout the scene characters come and go into and from their rooms, but we never see the rooms, which remain offscreen (figure 3.33). As if this were not enough, characters also enter the hallway from behind the camera. When the camera finally reverses position and shows the other end of the hallway, the space is even further complicated by an offscreen stairway at the left. Characters who have just mounted the stairs appear in the hallway along with those coming from and going to their rooms.

Non-dialogue Use of Sound

Along with this complex visual field, Renoir creates a complex aural field: *Rules of the Game* is a film with many sounds other than dialogue that have a significant place within its thematic development. During the long hunting sequence, we constantly hear the sound of offscreen gunshots. We do not just hear the gunshots while we

Fig. 3.33

see people shoot. Many dramatic interactions take place while we hear the shots, which lend an ominous tone to the proceedings and the romantic games of intrigue in which the characters engage. Not surprisingly, when the tragedy actually occurs at the end of the film, it takes place in the form of a shooting, and Christine, who is inside at the time, even remarks that she has heard a gunshot. The "gaming" has suddenly turned deadly serious.

Robert's mechanical musical instruments supply another source of important sound. After the skits and performances are over, he introduces his latest machine to the guests, an elaborate contraption with many lights, moving figures and, of course, musical sounds. During the ensuing chaos that develops among the guests, the machine breaks down and we hear noises instead of the music. The sounds of the broken machine here become a metaphor for the social breakdown occurring at the party. Nothing is orderly, nothing works – even the mechanical rules of the game no longer work. Breakdown is everywhere.

The Sixth Sense (1999)

We now turn to *The Sixth Sense*, a formally complex film that engages the Hollywood style in an unusual way. Like *The Crying Game* (see chapter 8) and *Psycho* (see chapter 6), *The Sixth Sense* is a movie with a secret so important that, once we have learned it, we must reinterpret what we have already seen. With *The Sixth Sense*, however, the secret is not hidden but, rather, is before our eyes throughout the film. This remarkable film can be read in two entirely different ways, depending on whether or not the viewer knows the secret. Its director, M. Night Shyamalan, uses a number of formal strategies to manipulate our expectations in such a way that most viewers do not get the secret on the first viewing and yet do not feel that they have been cheated when they see the film again. When we learn the secret, we suddenly understand the movie in an entirely new way, and this is encapsulated in the opening shot. It shows a dark screen with a few, faint points of light and appears to be an unreadable shot. Then we realize that we have been looking at an unlit bulb when it suddenly lights up (plate 7). A light bulb turning on has long been a popular image for someone suddenly understanding something confusing, suddenly "getting it," and that is what this film is about.

Story and Theme

The Sixth Sense was an unexpected and spectacular success when it opened in August 1999. Haley Joel Osment's line, "I see dead people," became a popular buzz-word, joked about on places like *The Tonight Show*, and many viewers saw this supernatural thriller more than once.

The movie begins with Dr Malcolm Crowe (Bruce Willis) and his wife, Anna (Olivia Williams), celebrating his receipt of an award for outstanding work as a child psychologist. Abruptly, however, he is confronted with a crazed former patient who berates Malcolm for not having helped him, then shoots him and commits suicide (plate 8). The screen goes black as Malcolm's wife rushes to comfort him.

The story jumps ahead to the following fall when we see Malcolm's first meeting with a new patient, Cole (Haley Joel Osment). Cole is deeply fearful, socially isolated, and has developed a number of half-effective strategies to appear "normal" and thereby prevent people from patronizing him for his odd behavior. When Malcolm learns Cole's secret, that he sees dead people all the time, Malcolm considers having Cole hospitalized. Gradually, however, Malcolm comes to respect Cole's belief and gives him a strategy for survival – not to fear the dead people he sees, but to listen to and help them. It cures Cole, enabling him to function without fear. Then at the end, Malcolm realizes that he, himself, has been dead from the time he was shot, and that is the film's secret.

But how can this be credible to a viewer for virtually the length of an entire film? On a first viewing, it appears as if Malcolm is alive throughout and interacts with numerous people. Is the ending simply a cheap trick on the part of the filmmaker? Not at all. But before we discuss the movie's formal workings, we must look more closely at its central theme.

In an important scene, Cole's mother Lynn asks him how his grandmother's pendant wound up in his dresser drawer. Cole says he didn't place it there, that sometimes things just get moved. This upsets Lynn, who feels that Cole is refusing to admit that he took it. Close to a breakdown with the stress of raising Cole as a single mother, she tells him she needs help. She says that she has been praying and, implying that she needs honesty from him, tells him that they need to answer each other's prayers.

Eventually they do, but not in the way she foresaw. After a breakthrough with Malcolm, Cole summons up the courage to tell his mother his secret, that he sees dead people. She is deeply upset and fearful for his sanity, until he reveals something his grandmother (whose spirit moved the pendant) told him, something only Lynn and her deceased mother would know. This revelation resolves not only her anxieties about her troubled relationship with her mother but also about Cole's strange behavior. Each has answered the other's prayer. Cole has always wanted to share his secret with his mother and be believed, not patronized. Lynn has always loved Cole and wanted to understand his disturbing behavior. Now both are happy. This meshes with two other revelations, two other light bulbs going off.

Malcolm listens repeatedly to a tape of a therapy session with the boy who shot him and suddenly realizes that he hears sounds of other people on the tape, dead people, apparent at the time only to his patient. Malcolm realizes that his patient was terrified because, like Cole, he also had the gift, and curse, of seeing dead people. Malcolm's inability to understand and help with this led to the boy's growing psychosis until, a decade later, he shot Malcolm and killed himself. Now Malcolm realizes that Cole is also telling the truth. He advises Cole to listen to the people, that they simply want help and do not want to hurt him. Cole does listen to a murdered girl and is able to uncover her murderer; he thereby saves her younger sister from the same fate. Here, Cole and Malcolm have answered one another's prayers – Malcolm feels he has atoned for having failed with the earlier boy and Cole is no longer afraid of the spirits he sees.

After Cole reveals his secret to Malcolm, Cole asks why Malcolm is sad. In parable form, Malcolm reveals that he and his wife have grown apart and that his greatest desire is to be able to communicate with her again. Cole later tells him to talk to her while she is sleeping – that it will enable her to hear him without knowing it. Malcolm returns home, finds his wife asleep and talks to her. When she drops a wedding ring on to the floor, he realizes it is not hers but his, and soon understands that they have not been communicating because he has been dead. He then tells her things that will enable her to overcome her grief and he also accepts his own death.

The central point is that these people find relief from profound anxiety by opening themselves up to what has been before their eyes all along. Cole has been trying to reveal his gift/curse to his mother but, since it defied common sense, she was blind to the clues. Cole, not wanting to be treated as a freak, tried adaptive strategies to look normal that only drove him more deeply into himself and his fears. The psychotic patient, like Cole, had repeatedly told Malcolm that he wanted to stop being afraid all of the time. Malcolm, limited by the presumptions of his profession, could not move beyond interpreting the boy's fears as the result of his parents' divorce. Not being understood drove the boy deeper into his terrors until he became suicidal, as it is likely Cole would have become without Malcolm's eventual help. Malcolm begins in the same inadequate way with Cole, asking if his fears began after his father left. Only after Malcolm re-examines the evidence that he had all along about the first patient does he believe Cole, and only then is he able to help him. Only then is Cole able to help Malcolm communicate with his wife and come to terms with his own death. Only after Cole, his mother, and Malcolm learn to look in a different way at what they have seen all along does the light bulb turn on.

Formal Strategies

The audience has also been fooled, although the evidence has similarly been before our eyes all along. But we have been fooled by the director's manipulations of our expectations even though at the same time he has given us any number of clues as to the secret. Some of the clues include the use of color as well as indications of inappropriate drops in temperature. Some of the manipulations involve stylistic norms of framing, staging, and editing.

Color

In our discussion of *Scarface* in chapter 1, we outlined the way in which that film used an X motif to develop its theme of violence. *The Sixth Sense* uses the color red in a similar way. The color red consistently appears when the real and spirit world interact.

The first time we see Malcolm enter his home after his death, he loudly calls, "I'm home," but there is no answer. As he passes through the kitchen, we see a single place setting with a bright red cloth napkin on the table. When he goes upstairs, we see his wife apparently asleep, facing the camera (plate 9). He sits pensively on the bed behind her. She reaches up to pull a red coverlet over her low-cut nightgown. He leaves.

An initial reading of the sequence is that he has come home too late, she has eaten and gone to bed. When he sits behind her on the bed, he cannot see her eyes. When she covers herself up, he takes it as a sign that she is awake but not interested in either conversation or in appearing sexual to him. Even though there is no direct communication between them, it appears as if she has expressed her annoyance with him by not answering his "I'm home" call and by not responding when he comes into their room.

A second reading, of course, works entirely differently. The red napkin and coverlet indicate an interaction of the living and the dead. The fact that the table has been set for only one person cues us to the fact that there is only one, that Malcolm is dead. Anna does not respond to his call because she can not hear it. She pulls the coverlet over herself involuntarily while sleeping, although his positioning behind her in the frame makes it impossible for him to see that she is actually sleeping. Furthermore, the film establishes that, when spirits of the dead are agitated, the temperature gets cold. At times of particular agitation, we see the breath of living people become frosted. In this scene, Anna may have sensed that cold in her sleep and covered herself accordingly.

Shyamalan uses red in a similar manner throughout the film. Anna wears a red dress in a scene when she eats alone in a restaurant and Malcolm tries to talk with her. Cole wears a red sweater to a party where cruel boys lock him in a closet that contains a ghost – and at that moment we see a bright red balloon burst. When Cole sees three ghosts who were hanged over a century ago in his school building, the lower portion of the dead woman's dress is red. When Cole gives a grieving father proof (a videotape in a box with a red stripe) that his wife murdered their daughter, the wife is wearing a bright red dress and lipstick. When Cole reveals his secret to his mother, she is wearing a red sweater. There are dozens of other examples.

Framing and editing

A major strategy by which Shyamalan maintains the movie's secret, and also renders the movie credible upon a second viewing, is by manipulating our expectations formed by the stylistic norms of classical Hollywood framing and editing. Two adjacent scenes illustrate this in different ways. In the first, we see Malcolm and Lynn greet Cole upon his return from school. All three appear to interact. In the second, Malcolm appears to talk with his wife in a restaurant. Lynn and Malcolm never directly interact, neither do Anna and Malcolm, but in both cases they initially appear to.

The first scene opens with a wide, long shot showing Lynn and Malcolm sitting and facing one another in Lynn's living room. The front door is between them in the rear of the frame (plate 10). Soon the door opens and Cole enters. He and his mother hug and talk affectionately as Malcolm watches. When Lynn goes into the kitchen to make Cole some pancakes, Cole looks suspiciously at Malcolm, who tries to gain Cole's confidence with a game. He tells Cole that he will make statements about Cole's situation. If he is correct, Cole will take one step toward him; if incorrect, Cole will take one step back and, if he reaches the door, he can leave and thereby cancel the session. After some initial success, Malcolm's questions go astray. Cole says that he thinks Malcolm is nice, but that he can't help him, and leaves the room. The scene ends.

When the scene opens, the placement of Lynn and Malcolm across from one another and alone in the room implies that they have been having a conversation. An initial interpretation might be that their silence is simply a lull. Malcolm looks directly at her, but their **eyelines** do not match. She looks in his direction but off to the side and slightly down. When Cole enters, both turn in unison to observe him, once more reinforcing the implication that they have been in conversation (plate 11). When Cole runs to his mother first, it is expected, and we even see Malcolm benignly looking on. When Lynn goes into the kitchen and Cole looks suspiciously at Malcolm, it seems as if this is their first formal session and his anxiety is understandable. Malcolm's game and Cole's participation reinforce this impression. When the scene ends with Cole's leaving, it is traditional for viewers to presume that Malcolm said farewell to Lynn but that it was simply elided.

The second reading, of course, is entirely different. Lynn and Malcolm do not talk because Lynn does not know Malcolm is there. Their eyelines do not match not because she is momentarily pensive, but because she feels she is alone. There is also no shot/reverse-shot editing between them. They turn their heads in unison simply because both see Cole. When Cole runs to his mother first, he knows she cannot see Malcolm. Shyamalan edits this part of the scene with alternating **two-shots** of Lynn and Cole together and single shots of Malcolm, clearly separating them (plates 12 and 13). We then get shot/reverse-shot editing between Cole and Malcolm (plates 14 and 15). Cole's fear when alone with Malcolm is not anxiety about a therapeutic session but rather because he knows Malcolm is dead and does not know what Malcolm wants from him. Ghosts have physically hurt him in the past.

The following scene is a single long take that begins with a long shot inside a large restaurant. As the camera moves toward a table, we see Malcolm approach it. Anna, wearing a red dress, sits with her back to the camera (plate 16). As Malcolm sits down, he jokes that he thought she meant the "other Italian restaurant I asked you to marry me in," indicating that he is late because he went to the wrong place. She seems to nod her head. He then begins an intense monologue about his difficulties with Cole's case. He says that he just can't seem to keep track of time lately, and that he didn't have a good session today. He says that Cole and the boy who shot him have the same patterns and that he fears that perhaps Cole is being abused.

As he speaks obsessively, the camera continues to move in to a close-up of him, then keeps moving to his side and turns to include Anna's tense face for the first time in the shot (plates 17 and 18). The waiter places the bill on the table and, as Malcolm's hand reaches for it, she abruptly takes and pays it (plate 19). Malcolm begins to apologize, saying he knows that he has been distant lately but it is because he feels he has been given a second chance. Tensely, she stands up, quietly mutters, "Happy Anniversary," and walks out, leaving Malcolm alone at the table (plate 20).

Again, the shot can be read in two ways. Initially it appears that he is late for their anniversary dinner and that she is furious. We cannot see her face for most of the scene but small movements of her head seem to correspond to tense responses. When we do see her, Malcolm is in the middle of his intense monologue. She says nothing, won't let him take the bill, and leaves him there. Her "Happy Anniversary" sounds like an ironic insult. On a second viewing, of course, we know that she does not see him. Her red dress signals this. When Malcolm sits, he sits without moving his chair. Her table is set for one all along and she is drinking coffee. Her "Happy Anniversary" is simply a sad, private comment on the occasion.

Another aspect of Hollywood **editing** is that, while it conspires to make spectators feel as if we are watching real events unfold before us in real time, it also allows for gaps in time. If a character, for example, says she is going across town to meet a friend, we may see her walk to her door and then, after a cut, we see her arrive at her friend's place. We do not consider it a violation of realism when we realize that she did not cross town in a second. The Hollywood style accepts that we are shown events necessary to the narrative, and not irrelevant ones – so we do not need to see her take the elevator to the street, walk out, catch a bus, leave the bus, and so on.

Thus, on an initial viewing of these scenes, we do not question why we do not see Malcolm say goodbye to Lynn in the kitchen as she makes pancakes – the total lack of interaction between them is subsumed under presumptions about the classical style of filmmaking. We are trained to presume that he did say goodbye, just as he earlier said hello, but that it was not shown because it was unnecessary to the narrative. Only on a second viewing do we realize that Shyamalan did not show us these things because they could never have happened, and relied upon our presumptions of the Hollywood norm to maintain the secret for him. In fact, much of the pleasure of repeated viewings of the film comes in seeing how skillfully Shyamalan used the formal properties of film style to both conceal and reveal his secret.

Our very ability to read this film in dual ways is only one indication that should make it clear that movies are about their formal elements as much as and, at times, even more than about their stories. Indeed this film draws a profound connection between the dilemma of the central character and its spectators: just as Malcolm cannot see the truth in front of his eyes, that he is dead, the spectators of the film cannot see the truth in front of their eyes. After years and years of assumptions about the classical style of filmmaking, we have been so lulled into seeing things in a certain way that our vision is "dead." As we have indicated, much of Hollywood cinema depends upon shot/reverse-shot editing and cutting on action, reaction, and dialogue. Yet most spectators of *The Sixth Sense* never notice that, with the exception of Cole, there are no shot/reverse-shot sequences of Malcolm interacting with people and no cuts of such interaction that take place on action, reaction, or dialogue. That more than anything, perhaps, is the main clue we fail to see. The formal brilliance of *The Sixth Sense* metaphorically opens our eyes to what we have been blind to – just as it turns on light bulbs.

SELECTED READINGS

Noël Burch analyzes film in terms of formal parameters, including cutting patterns and patterns of offscreen space, and discusses the Hollywood invisible style in *Theory of Film Practice* (Princeton, NJ: Princeton University Press, 1981 [1969]). Edward Branigan discusses shot scale (establishing, long, medium, close-up, and so on) in the Hollywood cinema and contrasts it with that of Yasujiro Ozu in "The Space of Equinox Flower," in *Close Viewings: An Anthology of New Film Criticism*, edited by Peter Lehman (Tallahassee: Florida State University Press, 1990). David Bordwell, Janet Staiger, and Kristin Thompson analyze space and cutting patterns as they developed in Hollywood in *The Classical Hollywood Cinema: Film Style and Mode of Production to 1960* (New York: Columbia University Press, 1985). Various brief, introductory essays on *Rules of the Game* can be found in the *Classic Film Scripts* edition of the screenplay by Jean Renoir (New York: Simon and Schuster, 1970). M. Night Shyamalan talks about the use of the color red and formal elements in *The Sixth Sense* on the "Special Features" section of the Collector's Edition Series DVD of the film, released by DVD Video for Buena Vista Home Entertainment in 2000.

4
AUTHORSHIP

The Searchers and *Jungle Fever*

The Ahistorical Author

In this chapter we turn our attention to what we can learn about movies by considering their **directors** to be authors of one kind or another. We begin, however, with a caution. The concept of an author as a genius outside history, who possesses profound, universal insights, though once a dominant notion, is now an outdated and dangerous one. As the remainder of this book will illustrate, all films are part of a complex cultural and historical context. No filmmaker, no matter how great, escapes that context or rises above it. Some early versions of authorship study (called the *auteur* theory) ignored this and discussed *auteurs* as if they were unique and independent geniuses; consequently, such studies are now limited and dated.

There are versions of what is sometimes called the "great man" theory of history, which presumes that a few select (nearly always male) individuals exert an influence that shapes and controls events. If we understand them we can understand why things happened or, in the case of films, what they mean. Such a model also commonly focuses on the director as a living biographical figure, implying that if we understand his or her life, we can better understand the films. Thus, if Steven Spielberg's films frequently feature single-parent homes and divorced families, it is because his parents divorced when he was young. Such a notion of the author is reductionist and simplistically fixes meanings precisely where, instead, they should be opened up and explored. Comparably, we cannot describe Spielberg's films as great just because they affirm the importance of timeless family values. As we shall see, Spielberg's films exhibit an anxiety about the family, but that anxiety is part of a pervasive cultural context of family crisis over which he has no control and into which he has no magical, gifted insight. Like all mortals, he is part of something that he doesn't fully control or understand.

Such a notion of a director does not deny the existence of major artistic talents who produce works of great importance. Those filmmakers, however, are part of both film and social history and cannot be understood outside it. They neither innovate film techniques in a vacuum nor possess godlike insights into either their times or history itself. We should not study their films to identify and valorize a pure vision that is all theirs or to attribute that vision to their lives.

What is an Author?

Who is the author of *A Tale of Two Cities*? Anyone familiar with the novel will immediately respond with the name of Charles Dickens. Who is the author of the successful film *The Fugitive* (1993)? Many people who have seen the movie will not as readily be able to produce a name to answer that question. Even if they knew the names of the principal "behind the camera" creative participants in the making of the film, they might not know whom to choose or they might choose a number of the participants, since filmmaking, unlike novel writing, is a collaborative effort. At first glance, the situation seems clear cut: novels have an easily identifiable author, while films are collaborative ventures involving many people, including the author of the screenplay, the director, the cinematographer, the editor, and the set designer, to name just a few.

The situation in either case may not be as simple as it seems. The term **author** is usually used to describe someone who writes a book, though it sometimes means the person or persons responsible for creating a work of art. When we think about Charles Dickens as the author of *A Tale of Two Cities*, we may be employing many different notions of authorship. Some may think of him as a genius who was fully in control of all the implications of every word that he wrote, while others may think of him as someone driven by unconscious fears and desires that he neither controlled nor understood. Some may think of him as a product of specific social and economic circumstances that he neither controlled nor transcended and that explain the novel's assumption that England is the center of the world as well as its sympathetic portrayal of the upper class in comparison with its less-appealing representation of the working class.

Dickens does, however, fit the traditional authorial image common to novelists and poets of an individual human being working in solitude to produce a work of art. The situation in cinema, however, seems more complex at first glance since it is a collaborative art form. The collaborative process, however, does not prevent an individual from exerting enough control over the process to shape a film in a manner similar to that in which novelists or painters shape their respective works. We will return to these thorny but fascinating questions in chapter 9 when we discuss film in relation to the other arts.

Plate 1

Plate 2

Plate 3

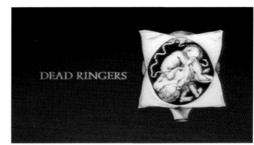

Plate 4

Plate 5

Plate 6

Plate 7

Plate 8

Plate 9

Plate 10

Plate 11

Plate 12

Plate 13

Plate 14

Plate 15

Plate 16

Plate 17

Plate 18

Plate 19

Plate 20

Plate 21

Plate 22

Plate 23

Plate 24

Plate 25

Plate 26

Plate 27

Plate 28

Plate 29

Plate 30

Plate 31

Plate 32

Plate 33

Plate 34

Plate 35

Plate 36

Plate 37

Plate 38

Plate 39

Plate 40

Plate 41

Plate 42

Plate 43

Plate 44

Plate 45

Plate 46

Plate 47

Plate 48

Plate 49

Plate 50

Plate 51

Plate 52

Plate 53

Plate 54

Plate 55

Plate 56

Plate 57

Plate 58

Plate 59

Plate 60

Plate 61

Plate 62

Plate 63

Plate 64

Arguing by analogy is always dangerous, and a film director can be compared with a literary author only within a full consideration of aesthetic issues involving both forms. At this point we have a much simpler goal. We have shown how narrative films are shaped by a complex development of story elements into a plot composed of free and bound visual and aural motifs. The characters and motifs of such films are represented within a system of formal elements composed of such things as camera position and movement, cutting patterns, and spatial relationships such as on- as well as offscreen space. While a screenwriter might provide a script giving dialogue and overall narrative direction, such scripts seldom provide more than an outline for the complex process of organizing an aesthetically integrated film. This complex process is usually overseen by the director, and an important trend in film criticism has developed built upon the premise that directors are the authors of films and that studying the entire body of works (or *oeuvre*, as it is frequently called) of individual directors can yield fruitful insights into their films. This school of criticism considers directors the author of a film even when they have not written or "authored" the screenplay. In this chapter, then, we are using the word author in its broadest sense.

Why do we care who, if anyone, is the author of a film? Some people have an economic interest in this question, since the author of the work may have certain rights that other participants in its creation do not have. They may receive income from the film that others do not receive. In this chapter, however, we are concerned with different issues. Regardless of the fact that Steven Spielberg has become rich from being perceived as the author of the films he has directed, what, if anything, can we learn by analyzing those films as being his rather than those of the studios that produced them or the screenwriters who wrote them?

In chapter 5 we will ask related questions about grouping films not by director but by genre. *The Lost World: Jurassic Park* (1997) or *AI: Artificial Intelligence* (2001), for example, can be examined as science-fiction films and compared with other such films just as easily as they can be considered Spielberg films and similarly compared with his other movies. No critical approach can tell us everything about a film but, rather, different approaches (such as formal, authorial, or genre) can teach us different things about a film. Critical methods are not mutually exclusive and may even be complementary at times.

Director's Worldview

Determining a director's worldview and filmmaking style is a starting-point for raising further questions about film style and cultural issues. Directors may become preoccupied with certain themes, ideas, narrative situations, and characters. At times this is obvious. Many who have seen the films of Steven Spielberg notice that he is attracted to adventures that frequently involve

Fig. 4.1

Fig. 4.2

Fig. 4.3

elements of the fantastic intertwined with family dramas of divorce, single-parent homes, and the precarious formation of romantic couples. Penny Marshall's films usually turn on a central character or characters who suddenly find themselves totally transformed: in *Big* (1988), a twelve-year-old boy's body instantly turns into that of a thirty-year-old man (figure 4.1); in *Awakenings* (1990), a patient who has been in a coma since childhood regains consciousness after thirty years; in *A League of their Own* (1992), women suddenly find themselves transformed from amateur to professional baseball players when men are called away to war (figure 4.2); in *Renaissance Man* (1994), an unemployed advertising executive becomes a military instructor (figure 4.3); and in *Riding in Cars with Boys* (2001) a teenage girl who unexpectedly becomes pregnant has to abandon her dreams of being a writer in order to raise her son.

Such an approach finds common elements behind apparently dissimilar films: *Sugarland Express* (1974), Spielberg's first theatrical feature, is a drama about a woman who escapes from jail and with her husband tries to reclaim her child from a foster home. Much of the film is structured around a dramatic chase as the police try to capture the fugitive parents. *Close Encounters of the Third Kind* (1977) is a science-fiction film about aliens who visit earth. At first glance, the two movies seem unrelated: the former is a modestly budgeted film premised upon plausible characters and believable events and the latter is a high-budget, special-effects extravaganza structured around fantastic events. In *Close Encounters*, however, the aliens abduct a boy from a single-parent home and take him in their spaceship. The fact that the boy comes from a divorced family and that his abduction further threatens the unity of his family clearly relates to the central dramatic premise of *Sugarland Express*. In *ET: The Extra-Terrestrial* (1982), the extra-terrestrial visits a single-parent home; in *Hook* (1991), children are abducted from their home, and their father, who has often ignored them due to professional obligations, searches for them in a wonderland; and in *Jurassic Park* (1993), a central male character learns to like children, a sign that his relationship with the central female character is likely to work out. In *The Lost World: Jurassic Park* (1997), the daughter of a single and often distracted scientist father stows away when he travels to a dinosaur-infested island, and the danger they share brings them closer together. In *AI: Artificial Intelligence*, a couple depressed over the comatose state of their child seeks to compensate for that depression by adopting a robotic child who is capable of feeling love. When their biological child comes out of his coma, however, they abandon the robotic child. For the rest of the film, the never-aging child sadly searches for the lost familial love that never was, finally finding a pathetic simulation in fantasy. These are all variations upon a central concern with the formation, break-up, and reconstitution of the nuclear family.

Director's Style

Directors may also become preoccupied with stylistic features of cinema. In such films as *Sisters* (1973) and *Carrie* (1976), Brian De Palma explores **split-screen** cinematography, but in such later films as *Dressed to Kill* (1980), *Scarface* (1983, figures 4.4 and 4.5), and *Mission: Impossible* (1996) he abandons the technique while developing the related one of using multiple images of television monitors and similar devices that comparably break up the traditional unity of the image.

Fig. 4.4

The Japanese director Yasujiro Ozu explored a style of filmmaking that, in such films as *Tokyo Story* (1953), used camera movements very sparingly, but rigorously explored the entire space of a scene by cutting between carefully determined camera positions in a unique manner that revealed 360-degree space. Most filmmakers confine their cutting to an area of 180 degrees or that on one side of an imaginary line drawn through the action (described in chapter 3).

Fig. 4.5

Shifts and changes in a director's work

Analyzing the works of a director, then, can help us to discover common threads among a diverse body of films; it can also show us changes in the styles and themes of that director's work over time. Not only, for example, can we discover similarities underlying both Howard Hawks's Westerns and comedies, but we can also see shifts in his Westerns from the 1940s to the 1970s. Such shifts are also evident in the career of Alfred Hitchcock, who throughout most of his career was identified with sophisticated, tasteful suspense films. Suddenly, in 1960, he made *Psycho* (see chapter 6), a graphic and bizarre shocker that initiated a cycle of horror films; in 1963 he made *The Birds* (figure 4.6), a more extreme horror film that abandoned all the plausibility of his previous thrillers by being premised upon unexplained bird attacks that, by the film's conclusion, seem to threaten the entire world.

Fig. 4.6

Fig. 4.7

Fig. 4.8

Such birds are a far cry from the Nazi villains of *Notorious* (1946, figure 4.7), the spies of *North by Northwest* (1959, figure 4.8), or the suspiciously behaving husband of *Suspicion* (1941).

Early, middle, and late periods

Sometimes it is possible to identify distinctive periods within a director's *oeuvre*. Such periods are usually divided into early, middle, and late periods. The early period introduces the director's pre-occupations in a simple manner, the middle period develops them in a complex manner, and the late period either extends them to an elaborate extreme or reduces them to a sparse simplicity that refers back to the previous work. Late-period works frequently have a reflective, sometimes even brooding, static tone that contrasts with a more energetic or even exuberant tone in the middle-period films. These periods are not necessarily clear cut in a director's *oeuvre*, and some films may have characteristics of two different periods. Nevertheless, significant tendencies can be observed from this perspective.

Charlie Chaplin's long career, which started during the silent era and extended well into the sound era, offers a clear example. He first appeared in what would become known as his tramp outfit in *Kid Auto Races at Venice*, a 1914 short that consisted largely of improvised gags. Although Chaplin did not direct it, the film introduced the character of the tramp, who would be the basis of nearly all the films he would direct. Within the year, Chaplin was, in fact, directing shorts in which he acted and developed his character and style of comedy. He achieved a mature middle period characterized by increasing complexity with such feature-length films as *The Gold Rush* (1925) and *City Lights* (1931). With *The Great Dictator* (1940), *Monsieur Verdoux* (1947), and *Limelight* (1952), he entered a characteristic late period premised upon referentiality to the early work and introspection. Both *The Great Dictator* and *Monsieur Verdoux* derive much of their meaning by reference to Chaplin's association with the lovable tramp character. In the former he plays a maniacal dictator who resembles Adolf Hitler, and in the latter he plays a serial murderer who marries and kills his wives for their money. *The Great Dictator* reduces Hitler to a comic buffoon, and *Monsieur Verdoux* puts the audience in the bizarre and unexpected position of switching their identification with Chaplin from that of the lovable tramp to that of a calculating mass murderer. These films are premised upon associations of Chaplin with the tramp that were widespread during his middle period. *Limelight*, an introspective film about an aging music-hall performer who is losing his ability to make audiences laugh, refers both to Chaplin's advancing age and his success during the early and middle periods as a popular comic entertainer.

Clint Eastwood, Blake Edwards, and Steven Spielberg are three directors whose work currently exhibits late-period characteristics. Eastwood's *Unfor-

Fig. 4.9

Fig. 4.10

given (1992) fits the model of a complex and elaborate development of a style rich in referentiality to earlier work, and *A Perfect World* (1993) is a scaled-back film of deceptive simplicity. *Unforgiven* is a Western with many references to the taciturn, violent character that Eastwood played throughout his early and middle periods, particularly the Westerns beginning with *A Fistful of Dollars* (1964) and continuing for decades with such films as *The Outlaw Josey Wales* (1976). By contrast, *A Perfect World*, the next film he directed after *Unforgiven*, was received by many critics as a minor piece and, although it is much less grand in scale, it is a reflective meditation on the very issues of masculinity and violence that have been so central to his career, this time with reference to his police films such as *Dirty Harry* (1971). Both films also acknowledge the physical aging of the Eastwood character: in *Unforgiven* he has trouble mounting and riding a horse (figure 4.9) and shooting straight, and in *A Perfect World* he is relegated to a minor role in the action where, in contrast to his normal romantic couplings, he is limited to a fatherly role with a young woman (figure 4.10).

From the mid-1960s to early 1980s, Blake Edwards developed a rich, personal *oeuvre* of largely comic films (the Pink Panther films, "*10*," and *Victor/Victoria*) that contained elaborate slapstick gags which frequently pervaded the films and, in *The Party* (1968), literally became the entire film. Simultaneously, these films were increasingly preoccupied with gender issues. In the 1980s, however, with such films as *The Man who Loved Women* (1983) and *Skin Deep* (1989), he began to make more static, scaled-back, introspective films with reduced amounts of slapstick; they characteristically devoted only a single scene to riotous development of gags. *The Man who Loved Women* contains only one such scene: when a husband unexpectedly returns home as his wife is having an affair and her lover inadvertently glues the couple's dog to his hand; somewhat similarly, in *Skin Deep*, a boyfriend unexpectedly returns home as his girlfriend is about to take a lover, and the ensuing confusion is structured around condoms that glow in the dark. Whereas Edwards's middle-period films were characterized by many such comic scenes, his late-period films are characterized by their reduced, sometimes even isolated, presence.

Steven Spielberg's career has clearly entered a late period with such films as *Schindler's List* (1993), *Amistad* (1997), *Saving Private Ryan* (1997), and *AI: Artificial Intelligence* (2001). All of these films deal with serious social issues such as, respectively, the Nazi holocaust, slavery in the United States, World

War II, and our culture's growing dependence upon artificial intelligence. As such, they provide a startling contrast to the previous emphasis on genre entertainment and even child-like fantasy. Nevertheless, there are connections with the early and middle-period work since all these films, for example, provide a white, male hero/father figure who saves something or someone, whether Jews, blacks, or even an entire nation in so far as *Saving Private Ryan* is really more about how Spielberg's father's generation saved American democracy than it is about how the title character is saved. *AI: Artificial Intelligence* is an even stranger example since it was a long-cherished project of Stanley Kubrick, an older director for whom Spielberg had great reverence. Kubrick died before he could make the film. By making the film himself, Spielberg, in a sense, saved it and allied himself with and carried the baton for the now dead cinematic hero/father figure who could no longer do it himself.

Structural versus Linear Analysis

The above-described model of authorship is based upon a linear analysis of a director's work. It charts shifts, progressions, and changes in both the world of the films and their style and gives much more weight to major or characteristic films than to minor or atypical ones. Hitchcock scholars, for example, typically do not pay much attention to his 1941 comedy *Mr and Mrs Smith*. Another view of authorship, however, examines the *oeuvre* from a structural rather than a linear perspective. In this approach all the films are considered to be part of a group wherein any film can be fully understood only in relation to the entire structure or *oeuvre*. Howard Hawks typically made male action films like *Rio Bravo* (1958) or comedies like *I Was a Male War Bride* (1949). The action films dramatically challenge and confirm a world of masculine values; in the comedies, that same world is turned topsy-turvy by feminine intrusion. Only by considering these two groups structurally in relation to each other does the full meaning of Hawks's vision of masculinity emerge; the action films in themselves seem to affirm a notion of masculinity that then becomes complicated when considered side by side with the comedies. Similarly, an uncharacteristic film like the musical comedy *Gentlemen Prefer Blondes* (1953) becomes pivotal rather than overlooked within this perspective, since it centers gender dynamics in a unique way within Hawks's *oeuvre*; a gangster film like *Scarface* (1932, discussed in chapter 1), which at first seems to belong with the male action films (like the Westerns), may revealingly be classified as a comedy of masculine failure. Such analyses reveal complex, deeply embedded structures within a director's work.

Another example comes from the films of John Ford, also recognized as a male action director. In 1956 Ford made *The Searchers*, a Western starring John Wayne. The following year he made *The Wings of Eagles*, an atypical film based upon a real-life military hero who was paralyzed after breaking his neck. Although the film starred John Wayne in the central role, it has been largely characterized by Ford scholars as a minor film. Yet, from a structural perspective, it bears a complex and integral relation to *The Searchers*. In that film, Wayne plays a character who has no home and is symbolically condemned to wander in the desert. In *The Wings of Eagles*, Wayne plays a man who has been gone from his home and returns only to suffer a paralyzing accident. Paralysis and its attendant stasis is, of course, structurally the opposite of movement and wandering, yet neither man has a place within the home. Thus there exists a deep structural relationship that the surface of the films may obscure and that has nothing to do with linear developmental patterns within Ford's career.

The Textual Author and the Unconscious

The primary focus of either a linear or structural authorship study is the films themselves, not the living persons who made them. We construct authors, in other words, from analyzing the works rather than studying the lives of the directors to explain the works. This is not to suggest that a biography of a director can be of no interest but, rather, that such a study helps us understand different things (for example, the studio system in which that director worked or the effect of budget on creative decisions). Implicit in the notion of this "textual author" is the assumption that the meanings that we can derive from studying their *oeuvre* are not entirely the conscious creation of the living filmmakers but rather that they emerge from the critical analysis of the works. Psychoanalytic theory can elucidate such aspects of films over which their directors had no conscious control.

Once again, Alfred Hitchcock supplies a wonderful example. He is known as a director who planned every shot well in advance of production; he knew exactly what he wanted. But did he know why he wanted it? An easy answer would be to create suspense. He was, after all, known as "the master of suspense." Using psychoanalytic theory as a method, however, we can uncover several unconscious patterns within his films.

Many of his films, like *Notorious, Psycho, The Birds*, and *Marnie* (1964), introduce central female characters who are in various ways out of the control of men and guilty of dangerous or criminal behavior. In the course of the films they are punished and brought under control. Many of the films also star beautiful, blonde actresses who are photographed in alluring and erotic ways. Such fetishism, which dwells upon one feature of a woman's beauty such as her hair color or an aspect of her figure, is another way in which men threatened by women make such women safe and pleasurable to look at. Finally, if one examines the patterns of violence toward men and women in Hitchcock's films, it is apparent that the deaths or punishing attacks on women (be they by knife-wielding murderers or attacking birds) are much more graphic and prolonged than those on men. Although it is unlikely that Hitchcock consciously thought of himself as a man who was afraid of women and therefore fetishized, controlled, and punished them in his films, a psychoanalytic notion of the author drawn from his *oeuvre* suggests such an unconscious component to his films. Although directors have some conscious control over the ideas they work with in a film, they are not aware of and do not control all the patterns of meaning they structure into a film. They might, therefore, be shocked and even angered at what psychoanalytic theory can uncover in their work.

To many people, Blake Edwards's slapstick Pink Panther films are a far cry from the sophisticated gender-bending comedy of *Victor/Victoria*. In the former, the bumbling Inspector Clouseau has countless accidents and pratfalls that appear to be sheer physical mayhem while, in the latter, a female performer pretending to be a man who is, in turn, pretending to be a woman, discovers much about the gender inequality of her society. Yet much of the physical comedy as well as the narrative predicaments in the Pink Panther films stem from Clouseau's inability to live up to his culture's standards of masculinity: he can't control his body, mind, wife, or girlfriends in the manner his culture expects. From this perspective, the Pink Panther films bear a close relationship to *Victor/Victoria*; beneath their slapstick veneer they somewhat unconsciously explore the same gender issues consciously articulated in the later film. Thus, what Edwards thought he was doing in the Pink Panther films and what he was actually doing may be two different things, and his conscious intentions should not be privileged. Whereas older methods of *auteur* studies frequently referred to interviews with directors to validate critical insight, current studies are much more circumspect and, in fact, frequently analyze and critique the interviews as well as the films.

A Director's Public Persona

This brings us to yet another useful way of studying directors. Many directors develop a "public persona" through public appearances, interviews, the media, studio publicity, and self-promotion. This persona circulates through society in a manner that affects the reception of the director's films. It is useful to study this "biographical legend" not because it tells us the true or preferred meanings the films may have but rather because it reveals how spectators and critics may be somewhat narrowly guided in their interpretation of and response to a director's work.

Once again, Steven Spielberg supplies an excellent example. He initially developed the persona of the innocent child who enjoys playing with movie magic as the result of attending too many Saturday matinees as a child; he exhibited a kind of "Gee whiz!" delight in making movies. Like his persona, most of his movies seemed like innocent fantasies that had more to do with the childlike wonder of the world of Hollywood entertainment than with serious issues in society. Such a persona, however, discourages critics and the public from taking certain disturbing elements of his movies seriously. If, for example, someone raises an objection about the sexist representation of women in *Indiana Jones and the Temple of Doom* (1984), many might dismiss it by saying the films should not be taken seriously and that the characters in them come from old genres that habitually represented relations between men and women in such a manner. Even if such a defense were true, it would obscure the relevance of asking about the cultural implications of recreating 1940s' images of women for the contemporary viewer. The image of the innocent child who fell in love with old movies can be a smokescreen that disarms rather than encourages criticism.

As we saw above, Spielberg later developed a new, mature persona. It included making such films as *Amistad*, *Schindler's List*, and *Saving Private Ryan*. Not surprisingly, his public persona also changed. Now, instead of talking like an awed, innocent child playing in the world of movies, he spoke and behaved like a socially responsible, reflective adult. He became interested, for example, in his Jewish heritage and involved himself in a number of Jewish-related social and cultural causes and projects. After turning down the opportunity to direct the highly anticipated first Harry Potter film, Spielberg indicated that he was no longer challenged by making yet another blockbuster based upon a children's book. But, as we stressed above, this new persona also has to be questioned. Perhaps Spielberg hasn't grown up or changed as much as he wants us to believe. Despite his admirable interest in and work for Judaism, for example, we have to remain critically alert to possible problems in his depiction of Jews and the Nazi holocaust in *Schindler's List*.

Hitchcock cultivated the label "the master of suspense" and took ghoulish delight in presenting himself as a macabre figure who enjoyed nothing so much as scaring people to death. He simultaneously cultivated the image of the technical wizard who knew just how to create the effects that would accomplish his goals. Such a persona makes light of the sadistic pleasure the director gets from frightening people; he often chuckles with wry humor as he introduces a film in a theatrical preview or a television episode. Yet, as we have suggested in our discussion of the usefulness of psychoanalytic approaches to a director's work, there is a more disturbing side to this sadism when it is directed at punishing out-of-control women. As with Spielberg, it may not all be the innocent fun that he presents it as. During interviews, Hitchcock loved to talk about the technical aspects of exciting scenes in his films. Such a persona encourages us to marvel at the shower murder in *Psycho* as a *tour de force* of editing. Although the scene seems graphic and protracted, it is actually composed of many brief shots of a knife wielded in a stabbing motion that almost never pierces the victim's skin. But discussing it in this way does not encourage us to wonder why a naked woman is killed in this manner in contrast to the rather swift manner in which a male private detective is later dispatched by a similar knife attack.

The Biographical Author

Finally, yet another current form of authorship studies actually returns to the living, biographical figure who made the films but does so with radically new intentions. Gay and lesbian scholars have shown that knowledge of the sexual orientation of a filmmaker can significantly affect how his or her films are received. Knowing that Dorothy Arzner was a lesbian, for example, opens up new meaning in a film such as *Christopher Strong* (1933), which stars Katharine Hepburn as a daredevil aviator who falls in love with a married man that she cannot have. Such films, while made at a time that did not allow direct acknowledgment of Arzner's sexuality, dealt with issues such as independent women, female bonding, and forbidden love that enables lesbian spectators to view the film as addressed to them by a fellow lesbian. This notion of the author centers primarily on the reception context of films and relates to chapter 8.

It can be useful, then, to consider directors as the authors of their films as long as we think of authorship as a shaping force within a collaborative, industrial process rather than analogous to the single author of a novel; and as long as we resist making authors godlike figures and instead explore different ways in which grouping their films together can shed light on important social and aesthetic issues. We turn now to a consideration of John Ford and Spike Lee, two quite different American directors who worked in different time periods. Ford is a major director of the classical Hollywood period and the studio system, and Lee the most prominent figure in a newly emergent African American film movement that developed after the demise of the old studio system. In both cases, much can be learned by considering them as the authors of their films.

The Searchers (1956)

For the generation of film directors who came to prominence during the 1970s and 1980s, *The Searchers* is a legendary film. Steven Spielberg, George Lucas, Paul Schrader, and Martin Scorsese are just a few who have praised the film in interviews and/or alluded to it in their films. While there are undoubtedly many reasons for the film's cult status, among them Ford's image as an eminent Hollywood *auteur*, its unusual visual sophistication is certainly a partial explanation. Perhaps more than with any other Hollywood film, the key to comprehending the most basic actions and behaviors of its characters is tied to a set of free motifs.

The Story

The story seems simple. In 1868, Ethan Edwards returns to his brother Aaron's home after an absence of some years. During an Indian attack, his brother, sister-in-law Martha, and nephew are killed and his nieces are kidnapped. Ethan sets out to find the kidnapped girls, one of whom is discovered dead. He spends years searching for Debbie, the other, whom he finally finds and returns home to a neighboring family.

Ethan's behavior seems puzzling for several reasons. After his initial attempt to find the little girl fails, he continues to search for Debbie, who is now a young woman, in order to kill her since she has become an Indian wife. He also seeks vengeance on her abductor, Chief Scar. He is deeply and at times maniacally driven in these pursuits and yet, when he finally catches up with her, instead of killing her, he sweeps her up in his arms and takes her home. Although to many this seems like a silly and clichéd Hollywood happy ending, it is anything but.

Visual Motifs

Ethan's decision to save Debbie rather than kill her is explained by the coming together of two **visual motifs**. When he enters his brother's home after years of absence, he lifts little Debbie high in the air (plate 21). When he approaches her at the end of the film, he repeats the same gesture (plate 22). But before he performs this action, an unusual **cut** takes place. Debbie runs into the desert to escape Ethan's seemingly murderous impulses; he pursues her on his horse. Suddenly, Ford cuts to a shot from within a dark cave; we see the action framed by the mouth of the cave (plate 23). Although Debbie runs toward the cave, before she gets there Ford cuts back to exterior views of the action. Debbie stops outside the cave where Ethan catches up with her (plate 24). Why does Ford cut to that unusual shot within the cave since that space is never used in the scene?

At the simplest level, the shot recalls one like it that occurred earlier in the film when Ethan and his companion Marty flee an Indian attack and seek shelter in a cave. As they approach, they are momentarily framed by the dark mouth of that cave (plate 25). Now, at the film's end, Ethan is in the reverse position of pursuing someone who seeks shelter in a cave. But this in itself does little to explain his behavior. The shots framing the action through the mouths of the caves, however, are part of a much larger visual motif involving doorways. Only by placing the final cave shot within that entire sequence can we begin to make sense of it.

The film begins with an image of darkness. A doorway opens and we see Martha looking out as Ethan approaches from a distance (plate 26). The final shot of the film shows the family to whom Ethan returns Debbie, and others, all entering the home. Once again, Ethan is framed through the dark doorway but, instead of joining the others within, he turns and walks away (plate 27). The door closes and we are again left in darkness. One of the film's themes concerns Ethan's inability to fit in with the family. This theme is articulated through a series of shots framing Ethan through doorways where he appears an outsider, even within his own brother's home. Or, perhaps we should say, especially within his own brother's home since other motifs of glances and caresses hint at a romantic relationship between Ethan and Martha.

When Ethan first arrives, he exchanges a long, intense look with Martha as they prepare to enter the house (plate 28). Once inside, he stares at her after she has taken his coat (plate 29). They sit together at dinner, and when Aaron says he is puzzled as to why Ethan stayed around as long as he did years earlier, Martha and Ethan exchange anxious glances, implying fear that Aaron will guess the real reason (plate 30). The most extreme visual clue, however, comes the next day when Ethan prepares to leave with a posse of Texas Rangers. As the Ranger captain drinks coffee, he glances off (plate 31) and sees Martha, standing in the bedroom, fondly stroking Ethan's coat (plate 32). She brings the coat out to Ethan and, in a remarkable shot, we see the captain in the left foreground of the frame with a troubled look on his face as Martha and Ethan express looks of intense emotion for each other as she slowly passes him his coat in the right rear of the frame (plate 33). In one shot we see both the nature of the hidden relationship between the two and the disturbing effect the knowledge of it has on the man who has unintentionally witnessed it.

Now Ethan's behavior begins to make sense. His incestuous desires for Martha threaten the sanctity of her family unit. This potential for destroying his brother's family makes Ethan resemble Chief Scar, who literally destroys that family. Ethan's maniacal, racist hatred of Scar results from a displacement of something within himself on to the racial other; rather than hating himself, he hates the Indian. His forbidden love of Martha motivates his vengeful search and his racist desire to kill Debbie. But why does he save her?

The image of the cave, combined with the gesture of lifting her high up in the air, together give a powerful explanation. The lifting gesture implies that, at some deep, perhaps unconscious level, he remembers having similarly lifted her years earlier in his brother's house in front of the fireplace. The cave, framed and darkly lit like the doorway of the home, shows the shocking distance Ethan has traveled from civilization to the barbaric wilderness. He cannot carry out his murderous intentions because, just in the nick of time, he becomes aware of their monstrous nature.

One of the things that makes *The Searchers* such a "director's" film is that much of its dynamics can be understood only by paying close attention to its visual style; there is not a word spoken in the dialogue that hints at either the relationship between Martha and Ethan or the reasons for Ethan's sudden reversal of his intentions at the end of the film. It is rare that, in the classical Hollywood cinema, so much of central importance should never be verbalized.

The Doorway Motif in Other Ford Films

In 1962, John Ford made *The Man who Shot Liberty Valance*, another Western starring John Wayne, who had also starred in a number of previous Ford Westerns. A brief contextualization of *The Searchers* with reference to those films shows how authorship studies can extend beyond consideration of an individual film. In *The Man who Shot Liberty Valance*, Wayne plays a once-powerful character who dies an old, forgotten man. His fall from power is chronicled by the use of a complex doorway motif. He is constantly framed as excluded from or interrupting what goes on within. One example occurs when he stands in a doorway and turns away into the night after discovering his girlfriend with the man she now loves (figure 4.11). Another occurs when he stands in a schoolroom doorway after disrupting an adult-education class. The West is changing and he no longer fits in.

Fig. 4.11

In 1949, seven years before *The Searchers*, Ford directed Wayne in *She Wore a Yellow Ribbon*, a film in which Wayne plays an aging cavalry officer forced into retirement. After returning from his last mission and being denied a request to continue as commanding officer, we see him walk into the night. A young woman who admires him stands in the doorway of the office, which is brightly lit behind her. An exterior shot shows the darkness into which the Wayne character has walked as well as a central female character standing in the doorway of the lit interiors from which he is excluded (figure 4.12). The shot is similar to one in which Wayne's girlfriend looks out after him in *The Man who Shot Liberty Valance* (figure 4.13). In all three films, the Wayne character's exclusion from home and community is represented compositionally through the careful use of doorways. Yet, all three films were made over more than a decade at three different studios with three different scriptwriters based on stories by three different authors and shot by three different cinematographers! John Ford is the only constant among the major behind-the-camera creative participants. Furthermore, none of the stories and novels upon which these films are based employs a doorway motif; the motif is, however, central to Ford's vision as a way of visually representing someone as isolated from his own community.

Fig. 4.12

Fig. 4.13

Changing Representations of American Indians

Other relationships emerge between these and other Ford Westerns starring John Wayne. In *Stagecoach* (1939), American Indians are represented primarily as savages swooping out of the wilderness to attack the coach. There are no scenes of their life or community, and they are not even granted language; they never even speak. The only sounds we hear them make are savage war cries. There is no motivation given for their attack except for the fact that they are represented as savages. Ten years later, when he made *She Wore a Yellow Ribbon*, Ford included scenes, however brief, of village life, and the Indians were granted speaking parts. One of them even plays a sympathetic old man. By the time he made *The Searchers*, Ford not only gave a motive to Chief Scar's actions (the cavalry had killed his family members), but he also represented the cavalry as reprehensible in their slaughter of an Indian village, including women and children. The films, in other words, show a progressive development of the Indians as more than mere savages and a concomitant questioning of the manner in which whites treat them. This reached an extreme in Ford's career when he made *Cheyenne Autumn* (1964), his last Western, which is told from the Indian point of view with the cavalry represented as the barbarians.

This shift in the representation of Indians in Ford's films exemplifies both how directors as authors have to be situated within history and how unconscious elements may be of great importance in understanding their work. No doubt, when he made *Stagecoach*, Ford was not consciously attempting to portray Indians in a demeaning or racist manner. He may, in other words, simply not have been fully aware of the implications involved in representing Indians solely as screaming, attacking savages. Such representations were common at that time. The fact that he may not have been aware of the harmful effects of perpetuating such stereotypes doesn't make them any less important or real. Clearly, however, Ford later became aware of these issues, though this also should not be viewed as a simple sign of his "genius." The historical period in which he was living and working was changing with regard to issues of racial sensitivity. Injustices against African Americans, Native Americans, and other minorities were receiving national attention. Thus, profound as it was, Ford's shifting representation of genre Indians was not an isolated, personal insight. From this perspective, it is revealing that *Cheyenne Autumn* was an adaptation of a novel that chronicled the abuse of Native Americans at the hands of whites.

Ford's Early, Middle, and Late Periods

Finally, these films reveal period distinctions within Ford's career. *The Searchers* is a prime example of a middle-period film that is extremely complex and fully developed. It is also full of the genre elements one expects in a Western: it has fight scenes, Indian battles, and beautiful scenery. *The Man who Shot Liberty Valance*, on the other hand, is a somewhat static, introspective film that, while uncharacteristic of Westerns, is characteristic of late-period work: it has very little action, takes place mostly indoors with no scenic shots of the landscape, and refers back both to earlier Ford films and to a nostalgic, mythic Western past. Like *Stagecoach*, it is even shot in black and white, unusual for a major studio production in the early 1960s. The choice of black and white is itself a nostalgic reference to the world of past Western filmmaking, a looking back by an older artist upon a genre to which he was a major contributor.

Jungle Fever (1991)

In contrast to the full career of John Ford, Spike Lee, to whom we turn next, is a comparatively young filmmaker who has entered a rich middle period with such films as *Jungle Fever* (1991), *Malcolm X* (1992), *Crooklyn* (1994), *Clockers* (1995), *Summer of Sam* (1999), and *Bamboozled* (2000). His career, while relatively recent and still in flux, shows how an authorship perspective can help us appreciate and better understand current films.

Near the end of *Jungle Fever*, Flipper and Angie playfully spar with one another in a mock argument. It is all in fun until police arrive, shove Flipper against a wall and hold a gun to his head. Outraged, Angie tells them to leave him alone, that he is her boyfriend. Flipper screams that he is not her boyfriend, but just a friend taking her home. The police leave, muttering, "What a waste." The incident casts a heavy pall over Angie and Flipper's relationship, which soon ends.

Flipper is a black man; Angie a white woman. The sight of the two having close physical contact led someone in the neighborhood to presume that he was assaulting her and call the police. Angie thinks she is helping Flipper when she tells the police that he is her lover; Flipper knows better, since even consensual interracial sex could get him in serious trouble with the white police. It is bad for a black man to be perceived as a rapist of a white woman, but it is even dangerous for him to be perceived as her lover, since such a situation implicitly threatens white manhood. Flipper, more than Angie, realizes that deep and dangerous social myths are being touched upon.

The first image of *Jungle Fever* is a snapshot of a young black man, Yusuf Hawkins, to whom the movie is dedicated. The sixteen-year-old Hawkins was murdered in 1989 in Bensonhurst (part of Brooklyn, New York) by a white mob that mistakenly believed he had come there pursuing a white girl. Spike Lee has claimed that Hawkins's murder, and the social ferment it revealed, inspired the movie. Both the real-life Hawkins murder and the *Jungle Fever* scene touch upon the often-tabooed issue of sex between blacks and whites.

Lee as Controversial Director

The issue is so volatile that, prior to *Jungle Fever*'s release, there was concern that it might stir up urban unrest. This echoed concerns two years earlier when Lee's *Do the Right Thing* was released in the summer of 1989. Both movies had received critical accolades at the Cannes Film Festival and soon after went into US release. They were considered so accomplished and so directly engaging of turbulent racial issues as not only to provide a trenchant social commentary but also to actually pose a danger of summer riots in American inner cities. Lee did not shy away from such implications. He ended *Do the Right Thing*, which climaxes with a racially fueled riot, with two quotations: one, from Martin Luther King, Jr, preaching non-violence; the other, from Malcolm X, refusing to eschew violence as a social tool. After *Jungle Fever*, Lee made *Malcolm X* (1992), a controversial movie on the life of the title character.

It is not only the fact that *Jungle Fever* deals with interracial sex and that *Malcolm X* deals with the controversial leader that generated controversy around the films, but also the fact that they were made by Spike Lee. Lee is the first African American to become a commercially successful, mainstream US filmmaker. He is not a star performer, like Sidney Poitier or Ossie Davis, who have directed occasional films, but rather a black filmmaker of widely acknowledged talent who has made commercially viable movies released by major studios, films that foreground black characters and contemporary black social issues. The extent of his success has made him a spokesperson for the African American community at large, although he has been criticized bitterly from within that community as well as from elements of the white community for his representations of both blacks and whites. Such controversial representations are immediately visible in *Jungle Fever*.

The Representation of Harlem

After the credits, *Jungle Fever* begins with a street map of Harlem. Then a newsboy hurls *The New York Times* on to a stoop. The camera tilts up to a second-floor window. Inside, we see Flipper and his wife, Drew, making love, with Drew moaning loudly and Flipper cautioning, "Don't wake the baby." Lee cuts to another room to show their daughter sitting up in bed listening and smiling. At breakfast, she reveals her knowledge of what went on, mildly embarrassing her parents.

This is not a standard image of Harlem in contemporary American movies. Harlem is generally represented as a wasteland of urban blight, with burned-out buildings, grinding poverty, single-parent households, and drug warfare. Here, the street is tree-lined and well kept, Flipper is a respected architect, and Drew a buyer for Bloomingdale's; they read *The New York Times*. They are a loving, upper-middle-class family.

Spike Lee's movies consistently present non-traditional images of African Americans – from the sexually independent woman of *She's Gotta Have It* (1986) to the college students of *School Daze* (1988) to the obsessive jazz musicians who are not drug or alcohol abusers in *Mo' Better Blues* (1990) and *Crooklyn* (1994). Here, the images of Harlem and of upper-middle-class black professional life are consistent with that profile. But Lee, also here and for the first time in his career, engages some culturally dominant and negative images of urban black life, something to which he returned in *Clockers*.

Later in *Jungle Fever*, Flipper is cheerfully walking his daughter to school when a prostitute propositions him (plate 34). He is outraged on two accounts. The woman is a drug addict, and we have earlier seen that Flipper is deeply troubled by the fact that his older brother, Gator, is a hopeless junkie. We have also seen the devastation that drugs are wreaking on the black community, and Flipper knows that they are turning many black women into prostitutes. He inappropriately seizes his daughter and screams that, if he ever catches her using drugs, he will kill her. The issues, then, are drugs and sex, but the sexual aspect implicates Flipper. He is at this time living out of his home, having left his wife and moved in with Angie. He cannot answer his daughter's questions as to why he has not come back home, but clearly a contributing element to his outburst is his guilt over leaving his daughter in a single-parent household, often cited as a breeding ground for drug abuse. The very last shot of the movie rhymes with this scene. Flipper, close to a reconciliation with Drew, is again confronted in the same way by a prostitute, but this time younger and requesting less money (plate 35). In a paternalistic gesture, he clutches the girl to his chest and screams a despairing "No" as the film ends in freeze frame (plate 36).

Jungle Fever opens with an idyllic image of a nuclear family that is subsequently ravaged by a cluster of social forces. The main one is racial conflict, which is a central concern of Lee's career, whether represented by means of the concern among blacks with skin color in *School Daze* or the race riot in *Do the Right Thing* or the social mission of *Malcolm X*. Flipper's affair is not really about sex. Lee presents Flipper as having an active and satisfying sex life with Drew. His attraction to Angie, and hers to him, is developed as an outcome not of sexual frustration but of the mutual fascination of different racial mythologies. Both characters live in racially segregated communities. In the street-sign credit motif that opens the film, a sign that categorizes the mainly working-class, Italian community of Bensonhurst is the international "forbidden" symbol with the word "Niggers" in the center (plate 37); the sign that characterizes Harlem is "a Guinea-free zone" (plate 38).

Jungle Fever was the most ambitious movie of Lee's career to this point. Its structure is a comparative one that parallels Flipper's black world with Angie's white one. When Flipper, in Harlem, tells his best friend, Cyrus, of his affair, Lee cuts to Angie in Bensonhurst telling her girlfriends of it. The combined responses of outrage and support, as well as the ensuing domestic convulsions, are similar in each case. Both Flipper and Angie become outcasts.

Social Context

Lee's films reveal a deep social anxiety, a terror of a bad situation getting worse. They have recently been ending with the death of a significant black character, deaths that have sad and widespread repercussions – the riot in *Do the Right Thing*, Gator in *Jungle Fever*, Malcolm X's assassination, even the mother's death in *Crooklyn*.

Flipper and Angie's affair occurs not in isolation but as part of a dense social fabric. Flipper's father is a half-mad, defrocked Baptist minister who disowns and kills his drug-addicted son. Flipper's half-white wife is profoundly traumatized by her pigmentation. Angie's father and brothers are controlling and patriarchal. Her boyfriend, Pauli, is a gentle soul, himself oppressively controlled by his father. Pauli later becomes attracted to a black woman. On each side, Lee provides a kind of Greek chorus that extends the significance of individual situations. Pauli must deal with a group of malcontented Italian loafers who congregate at his candy store and vocalize their dyspeptic opinions of his situation; Drew's female friends hold a kind of encounter session bemoaning the social position of African American women. *Do the Right Thing* has a comparable group of streetcorner philosophers whose presence gives the specific incidents of the movie a wider social extension.

Lee's Style

Lee's films also have recurring stylistic features. At two points in *Jungle Fever* we see central characters walking down the street exchanging dialogue – first Angie and Pauli as they go on a date (plate 39) and, later, Flipper and Cyrus as they discuss Drew's expulsion of Flipper from their house (plate 40). Generally, Lee adheres to a classical style and develops viewer expectations of an homogeneous "realism" throughout his movies, but in each of these cases he photographs both characters with a low-angle **tracking shot** that makes them appear to be floating down the street; the bodies do not move as if they were walking. It is simply a brief, fantasy-like break with realist expectations.

In *Crooklyn* we have similar breaks. Two characters are established as the neighborhood glue sniffers and are nearly always stoned. In one shot we see them both apparently upside-down and floating down the street. In another extended sequence, a little girl leaves Brooklyn for a vacation in suburban Maryland with relatives. The whole sequence is photographed to look squeezed and distorted. The upside-down shot apparently represents the characters' stoned state, and the squeezed and distorted sequence signifies a different environment. These kinds of scenes, one of which also appears in *Clockers*, characterize Lee's periodic departures from "realist" norms.

African Americans and Whites

A central theme of *The Searchers*, and much of John Ford's career, is culture clash. Ford generally made his movies from the perspective of the dominant social group, white culture, and *The Searchers* shows evidence of a shift in Ford's career in his posture toward the marginal social group, the American Indians. Lee's films are also often about culture clash but are made from the point of view of a marginalized social group. *Jungle Fever* may signify a shift comparable to Ford's in that it gives a partially sympathetic view of the white community. Lee's following film has as a central moment the shift in Malcolm X's career toward reconciliation with elements of white culture, and in *Clockers* a sympathetic white police detective is a main character.

Such observations are tentative, since it is notoriously difficult to categorize an artist in mid-career. While it is fairly easy to posit a line of development in explicit concern with the effects of racial conflict on society, from *Do the Right Thing* to *Jungle Fever* to *Malcolm X*, that line of development is not so obvious between *Do the Right Thing* and *Mo' Better Blues*, or even among *Malcolm X*, *Crooklyn*, and *Girl 6* (1996). The title of *Summer of Sam* (1999) refers to David Berkowitz, a real-life, white, serial killer who terrorized New York City, and the film deals centrally with whites living in New York. Lee seems increasingly interested in making films that do not focus primarily on African Americans.

The Biographical Lee and his Persona

In contrast to John Ford, who functioned primarily as a director on his films, Lee generally serves as the highly visible director, writer, producer, and actor on most of his. Ford spent most of his career working within the Hollywood studio system; Lee came along after the studio system's demise and defines himself in opposition to the Hollywood system even though he uses some of its financing and distribution structures. He is widely seen as the breakthrough African American filmmaker, and many younger black filmmakers view him as their model, just as he openly acknowledges his debt to predecessors such as Ossie Davis, who has appeared in some of his films.

Although Lee often presents himself as an extremely independent, almost self-created filmmaker, he readily admits that he is a product of his times, that social conditions were different twenty years ago and would not have allowed him to achieve the prominence he has. His persona thus balances an image of himself as strongly independent while simultaneously being a product of his times. Reviews of his early films often compared him with Woody Allen, partly as a writer–producer–director who also acts in his films, but also as a visibly ethnic, New York-based filmmaker whose work, due to shifting social conditions, would play for the first time west of the Hackensack River.

Authorship, then, studies individual filmmaker's careers with definable thematic and formal concerns within historically specific cultural and social conditions. In the next chapter, we will explore the possibilities of grouping films by genre rather than director.

SELECTED READINGS

Andrew Sarris originally applied the *auteur* theory to US cinema in *The American Cinema: Directors and Directions 1929–1968* (New York: Dutton, 1968). Peter Wollen offers a structuralist account of the theory that considers the author a construct of the text rather than a living person in *Signs and Meaning in the Cinema* (Bloomington, IN: Indiana University Press, 1972). David Bordwell formulates the notion of the author as a biographical legend in *The Films of Carl-Theodor Dreyer* (Berkeley, CA: University of California Press, 1981).

Joseph McBride and Michael Wilmington analyze *The Searchers* and discuss Chief Scar's relationship to Ethan and the shifting representation of American Indians within Ford's work in *John Ford* (New York: Da Capo, 1974). For a discussion of Spike Lee's films, see "Spike Lee at the Movies" by Amiri Baraka and "Spike Lee and the Commerce of Culture" by Houston A. Baker, Jr, in *Black American Cinema*, edited by Manthia Diawara (New York: Routledge, 1993).

5

GENRES

Murder, My Sweet and *Gunfight at the OK Corral*

When we go to the movies, we almost always have expectations about what kind of movie we are going to see. With *Geronimo* (1993), *Posse* (1993), *Tombstone* (1993), and *Wyatt Earp* (1994), the titles alone mark the films as Westerns. *Bad Girls* (1994) was advertised with an image of young women dressed as "cowboys" and carrying guns. Clearly that image, combined with the film's title, prepares the viewer for a Western with a twist – women will be in the parts where we normally expect men. That is precisely what the movie delivers. We expect Westerns to have certain features: as their name implies, they are set in the American West, typically between the end of the Civil War and the beginning of the twentieth century, and involve battles with either outlaws and/or American Indians. All four of the above-cited Westerns meet these criteria. Films that conform to a specific set of expectations are called **genre** films, and most Hollywood films belong to identifiable genres such as science fiction, musicals, action and adventure, horror, comedy, or mystery.

Genre Entertainment

Since the word simply means "type," all films will fall into one genre or another. In this chapter, however, we are going to be more specific and examine Hollywood entertainment genres, such as those listed above, as opposed to what is commonly referred to as serious drama. Dramas about serious social problems such as drug and alcohol addiction are just as generic as musicals or Westerns, but critics and public alike frequently assume that recognizable social ills are inherently a more serious topic for a film than, for example, singing and dancing. The word entertainment is not neutral: it connotes fun as opposed to seriousness, escapism as opposed to reality, and formula as opposed to creativity. Although such a notion is simplistic and mistaken, it pervades our society. Even the industry itself helps to perpetuate these notions, since Academy Awards are seldom, if ever, awarded to films in certain entertainment genres such as slapstick comedy or horror. The implicit message is that such genres are unworthy of serious attention.

Once again, Steven Spielberg's career is illustrative. After years of success so immense that he was frequently characterized as the most successful filmmaker in the world, he finally won an Academy Award for Best Director in 1993. Ironically, *Schindler's List*, the film for which he won that and other prestigious Academy Awards, did not typify the kind of genre filmmaking that had made him successful. Indeed, it is a serious drama that does not fit any of the Hollywood entertainment genres. He also made *Jurassic Park* in 1993 and, although it also won a number of Academy Awards, they were all minor awards that recognize technical excellence. The implicit message is that, no matter how well made a dinosaur film is, it is no match for a film about the Nazi Holocaust; it might be well-made entertainment, but it isn't profound.

What is Entertainment?

But what is entertainment? Is it just fun? Is having fun doing something with no socially redeeming value? Is watching a Western comparable to playing miniature golf? Are some films "mere" entertainment? It is true that certain kinds of films are likely to make us leave the theater in different states of mind than others. After viewing *Schindler's List*, people are likely to wonder how something as horrible as the Holocaust could occur and if it could happen again; or they might feel grateful for the existence of a man like Schindler who, in coming to the aid of condemned Jews, affirmed that even in the darkest of times some human beings will rise to an unexpected level of ethical behavior. Few if any spectators will have anything lofty on their minds after leaving *Jurassic Park*. They are likely to remember a scary scene like that of the ferocious Velociraptors stalking the children in the kitchen or a breathtaking special effect such as the first sighting of a herd of dinosaurs. Although

some spectators might become motivated to learn more about dinosaurs after watching the film, the situation seems clear cut: *Schindler's List* is a serious film and *Jurassic Park* is just entertainment. Where's the ambiguity?

As outrageous as it may seem at first, let us momentarily reverse the situation. What if genre films are the more serious form of filmmaking and socially serious dramas are a limited form? How can this be? The contemporary horror film supplies an excellent example with which to explore these questions. In the 1970s such films as *The Hills Have Eyes* (1977), *The Texas Chainsaw Massacre* (1974, figure 5.1) and *It's Alive!* (1974) initiated a new cycle of horror

Fig. 5.1

films. Influenced by Alfred Hitchcock's *Psycho* (1960, see chapter 6), these films located horror at the center of the family, the very place that had been a haven in previous horror films. *The Hills Have Eyes* includes a mutant family of savages that lives in the hills and terrorizes a seemingly normal family on vacation; *The Texas Chainsaw Massacre* includes a bizarre family of cannibals who kill people and then sell their flesh as barbecue. The plot in *The Texas Chainsaw Massacre* centers on a group of young people, one of whom is returning to his childhood home when the horror begins. In *It's Alive!*, a seemingly normal couple creates a monster that suddenly appears during a birthing scene. In *Psycho*, a boy has killed his mother after discovering her having intercourse with another man after the death of his father. He has preserved her body and, years later as a young man, he adopts her persona when he engages in murderous attacks.

All of these films were made to scare people, not to make them contemplate the shortcomings and failings of the contemporary nuclear family. But all of them share a vision of the nuclear family that implies all is not well. In *Psycho*, the "monster" is symbolically born within the family as a result of the trauma the boy has suffered from discovering his mother's sexual activities; in *It's Alive!*, the monster is literally born into the family; and in *The Hills Have Eyes* and *The Texas Chainsaw Massacre*, entire families are literally monstrous. These patterns of family representation are typical of countless other horror films that followed them. Among other things, the contemporary horror film gives genre filmmakers the opportunity to explore family issues and to suggest that things are not rosy in that most venerable of institutions.

Explorations of crises within the family sound like the stuff of which socially serious dramas are made and, sure enough, during the same time period that the family horror film flourished, Hollywood produced such acclaimed dramas as *Ordinary People* (1980) and *Kramer vs Kramer* (1979), two films that deal with the break-up of the family. Now it seems as if "mere" genre entertainment has something in common with "serious" drama. But doesn't serious drama provide a more profound treatment of this most urgent of social problems? Perhaps not. Socially serious dramas usually supply a liberal critique that implies an unquestioned commitment to the value of our most basic cultural institutions. *Ordinary People* and *Kramer vs Kramer*, for example, tell us that serious problems threaten marriage and the family, but they never suggest that the institutions themselves are breeding grounds for oppression, repression, and revolution. There is, in other words, nothing fundamentally wrong with the family that can't be fixed up if we come to our senses and change our ways. Family values are fundamentally affirmed even if it means, as in *Ordinary People*, that the mother disappears from the narrative so that father–son bonding can take place, a bonding with which the audience is asked to identify. The contemporary horror film not only implies that it may be too late to fix the family, but it also makes us wonder who in their right mind would want to save the family. How is it possible that such a dismal appraisal lies at the center of our fun when we are being scared to death?

Creativity, Spectatorship, and the Unconscious

There are two related though quite different answers to the question: one involves a conscious manipulation of genre entertainment by directors and the other involves unconscious creative activity. Let's begin with the latter. Many genre directors talk of their pleasure in making such films as horror films that scare us, comedies that make us laugh, or adventure films that thrill us. When they speak this way, they are talking about producing pleasurable effects, not about making us think about serious issues, and herein lies the clue to the answer to our question. Genre entertainment provides both the filmmaker and the audience with a pleasurable veneer or smokescreen that enables filmmakers to explore and audiences to enjoy deeply disturbing material – material so disturbing that an unflinching and non-generic look at it would require backing off from and toning down the grimmest aspects. As such, a genre might become a playground for both the filmmaker and the audience, but a playground that lets us all examine what truly scares us. Genre filmmakers themselves frequently discover along with the audience the substantive material that lies at the heart of their entertainment.

Blake Edwards created many side-splitting slapstick gags with Peter Sellers as Inspector Clouseau in the Pink Panther films. Yet, he remarked in retrospect that he was only then becoming aware of how those gags rested upon the premise that Clouseau's masculinity and sexuality were being questioned constantly. He did not, in other words, start with a notion of critiquing conventional masculinity and then devise gags that would embody that critique but, rather, he wanted to create funny gags that increasingly led him to explore failed masculinity. His initial intentions were simply to make himself and us laugh, just as many horror filmmakers want to explore what scares them and us.

It is unlikely that the makers of *The Hills Have Eyes*, *The Texas Chainsaw Massacre*, and *It's Alive!* all consciously decided in the 1970s that the family was a nightmare and then turned to horror films as the genre to embody that horror. More likely, they explored their nightmares in the genre suited to such explorations and discovered along with their audiences that at the center of the nightmares lay the good old nuclear family. Much to everyone's surprise, something had happened to the happy families of such popular television shows of the 1950s as *Father Knows Best* and *Leave it to Beaver*.

Genre Periods

From this perspective it is not surprising that genres, like directors (see chapter 4), go through developmental periods. A genre cycle will typically end with a reflective, introspective late period or with one that is highly referential, which is precisely what has happened to the horror film in recent years. Genre filmmakers themselves have become more aware of what their work is about. The highly successful *Scream* films (1996, 1997, and 2000) typify late period referentiality in the humorous manner in which they rely upon the spectator's knowledge of the rules of the genre, such as what happens when one picks up the phone, or has sex, or gets separated from friends. Such other horror films as *The Stepfather* (1986) and *The People Under the Stairs* (1991) articulate a critique of cultural institutions in a manner that goes beyond the critique buried within the earlier films of the cycle. In *The Stepfather*, a serial murderer marries into a single-parent family (figure 5.2). He then murders his new family when it fails to live up to his ideal of what family life should be, an ideal that the film implies is

Fig. 5.2

long gone, if it ever existed. In *The People Under the Stairs* (see chapter 14), a slum landlord and his sister barricade themselves within their house from the alleged dangers without. But what goes on within their house (incest, murder, and torture) is the true horror. The film explicitly indicts capitalism, the family, and patriarchy as the outmoded sources of racial and sexual oppression that breed psychotic behavior and revolution.

Convention and Invention

Like the works of individual directors, genres have a developmental history from which we can learn much. All genres are a mix of **convention** and **invention**, and this mixture explains how some genre directors consciously manipulate their entertainment form for the purposes of social commentary and critique. It is fairly easy to learn what the conventions of any genre are. Contemporary urban action/adventure films like the *Lethal Weapon* series, for example, typically include car chases, explosions, shoot-outs, and male-dominated narratives with beautiful women in supportive roles that focus on romantic encounters with the hero. Conventions of the Western include the fact that men carry six-guns at their side and that, in the course of the film, they use their guns to resolve disputes. The genre also divides its men into good guys and bad guys and often pits white civilization against American Indians. Nearly all Westerns will include two of these three conventions and some, like *Stagecoach* (1939), include all three.

The formulaic nature of genres enables writers and directors to approach their material with the attitude that, if they put in enough of the expected elements, they can do whatever they please with the rest of the film. From this perspective, genres provide a trade-off: filmmakers include, for example, a certain amount of sex and violence in some genres, which they feel will fulfill their audience's expectations, in exchange for which they have the opportunity to present them with serious food for thought. In *Victor/Victoria* (1982), Blake Edwards gives the audience the expected amount of scenes of bedroom farce, slapstick gags, and lavish musical numbers for a musical comedy. This entertainment format allows him to explicitly critique homophobia and male domination of women, material that would offend many in his audience if it were presented to them in a socially serious drama. Indeed, many people who love *Victor/Victoria* probably wouldn't even attend a socially serious drama on those topics or, confronted with them, might walk out of the theater.

Critics and public alike sometimes overestimate the formulaic nature of genre entertainment, frequently presuming that genre films are little more than their predictable formulas. Yet only the most mediocre of genre films rely entirely on conventions, while the best of them include a great deal of inventiveness. Some Westerns, like *The Man who Shot Liberty Valance* (1962), blur the distinction between the good guy and the bad guy by making both men so much like each other that they emerge as being two sides of the same coin rather than two different coins. Similarly, *The Searchers* (1956, see chapter 4) shows the cavalry's brutality toward the Indians in a manner that motivates the Indian attacks and even creates some sympathy for them. Even though it has a likely candidate in the star presence of Henry Fonda, *The Ox-bow Incident* (1943) does not have a typical Western hero who accomplishes his goals and with whom we identify throughout the movie. When he is finally moved into action, the Fonda character fails to prevent a lynching and, throughout much of the film, he doesn't even exhibit enough moral character to be

Fig. 5.3

Fig. 5.4

disturbed by the impending miscarriage of justice. Finally, although his former girlfriend makes a brief appearance in the film, she is newly married and never seen again, thus denying the expected romantic subplot. The film doesn't even include the expected Western action sequences. When a fight breaks out near the beginning, it is quickly over rather than developing into the usual bar-room brawl.

The creative tension between genre convention and invention appears in all the high-visibility Westerns that have been made in recent years. *Dances with Wolves* (1990, figure 5.3) foregrounds the Indian perspective, which is usually a backdrop; *Posse* (1993) foregrounds the presence of African Americans in the West rather than marginalizing or ignoring them (figure 5.4); *Geronimo* (1993) makes the title character an heroic figure who has been wronged rather than a savage (figure 5.5); *Tombstone* (1993) recognizes homosexuality in

Fig. 5.5

Fig. 5.6

the West (figure 5.6); and *Bad Girls* (1994, figure 5.7) gives the usually passive, marginalized women of Westerns the action roles normally reserved for men. *Unforgiven*, directed by and starring Clint Eastwood (1992), examines disturbing elements of the mythology of the Western hero, specifically Eastwood's incarnation of that hero in the countless previous Westerns that made him a star. Most of these are somewhat extreme examples of genre invention, but they point to an ever-present element of genre entertainment: genre formulas are open to constant revision. Studying genres includes charting those changes and examining their significance.

Fig. 5.7

All of the recent Westerns cited clearly respond to both the formula of previous Westerns and to the times in which they were made. On the one hand, these films address the past of their genre and attempt to be different from those films and, on the other hand, they respond to contemporary awareness of cultural diversity in the form of the women's movement, Native American and African American movements, and the gay rights movement. Stated simply, in today's climate, women, Native Americans, African Americans, and homosexuals are likely to be granted more prominent and different representations within the genre than they had in the past. This does not mean that these films are better than their predecessors or even that they are good films but rather that genre critics must take note of these changes and of what they mean.

Genre Cycles

In a related manner, genre criticism must chart the popularity cycles of different genres. The Western enjoyed varying degrees of popularity from the 1950s to the mid-1970s, but it virtually disappeared in the 1980s. It made a comeback in the early 1990s. Similarly, films like *Fatal Attraction* (1987) and *Basic Instinct* (1992) are part of a current wave of erotic thrillers. The family horror film and such related subgenres as the slasher film (for example, the *Friday the 13th* series), which enjoyed such popularity during the 1970s and 1980s, are waning. Indeed, as noted above, the popularity of *Scream* (1996) and its sequels (1997 and 2000) owes much to the manner in which they playfully, even nostalgically, invoke this once vital genre. The genre is in some ways transforming, as evidenced by prestigious remakes and variations on older classics: *Dracula* (1931) provides a source, or at least a point of reference, for *Bram Stoker's Dracula* (1992), *Frankenstein* (1931) for *Mary Shelley's Frankenstein* (1994), and *The Wolf Man* (1941) for *Wolf* (1994, figure 5.8).

Genres have always functioned in this way. The 1940s, for example, saw the proliferation of a number of subgenres of women's films. As their name implies, women's films are made for and addressed to female spectators. Traditionally, melodrama has been the most dominant women's genre. Melodramas typically deal with issues of

Fig. 5.8

Fig. 5.9

romance, family, and career and include domestic crises such as affairs, divorce, child–parent difficulties, illness, and conflicts between career and family. As opposed to the pattern with action films, for example, women play central, frequently leading roles in this genre. During the 1940s women were represented in a number of films as having serious physical illnesses (e.g., a brain tumor that causes blindness and then death in *Dark Victory*, 1939), possessing a defect (e.g., muteness in *Johnny Belinda*, 1948), or being psychologically disturbed (e.g., obsessiveness and an absence of marital sexual desire or activity in *The Cat People*, 1942). In these films, doctors and psychiatrists are frequently called in to diagnose what is "wrong" with the women and to prescribe a "cure." These male doctors represent a voice of patriarchal authority as they attempt to bring the female characters into line with their culture's expectations of proper female behavior.

Love stories were also very popular in the 1940s (for example, *Humoresque*, 1946, and *Letter from an Unknown Woman*, 1948). In these films women fall in love with romantic men, but the romance leads only to suffering as their desires remain unfulfilled. Women are frequently put in positions of watching their lovers depart and then waiting interminably for their return. The women, who frequently gaze intensely on the men they desire, are repaid by being forgotten – sometimes literally as in *Letter from an Unknown Woman*, in which the central male character does not even recognize the central female character with whom he has, years earlier, had an affair (figure 5.9). In both *Letter from an Unknown Woman* and *Humoresque*, the female lovers die unfulfilled.

Reputable and Disreputable Genres

Melodramas reveal a number of important genre issues. During the 1940s and 1950s, they were referred to as "women's weepies," a derogatory term implying that they were inferior entertainment meant for overly emotional women. Men, who presumably were not subject to such hysteria, were thought to keep their emotions in check and have more important things on their minds.

At the beginning of this chapter, we pointed out that genre films are generally devalued in comparison with socially serious drama, but that tells only part of the story. Within the world of genre cinema, certain genres are devalued with relation to other genres. Many have dismissed the contemporary horror film as particularly disreputable, as nothing more than an extremely misogynist form in which males take great pleasure in seeing sexually active women slashed to death. It is important to note here that horror films are made and marketed for adolescent males, not a prestigious target audience. At best, the heavily teenage audience for horror films is considered immature and at worst a social threat. In this regard the contemporary horror film has something in common with melodrama: neither genre is primarily made for middle-class men. Melodramas were long looked down upon precisely for that reason, and melodrama directors like John Stahl and Douglas Sirk were frequently recognized belatedly and with less acclaim than such male-action filmmakers of the time as John Ford and Howard Hawks.

Melodrama

During the 1950s, Douglas Sirk made a number of melodramas (for example, *All that Heaven Allows*, 1953, *Magnificent Obsession*, 1954, and *Written on the Wind*, 1956) in which he developed a social critique of women's places within American society. In *All that Heaven Allows*, for example, a wealthy, middle-aged widow falls in love with her younger gardener. Everyone from her friends to her grown children are shocked at her improper behavior. Her desires violate two cultural laws: one is gender based and the other class based. Countless films glorify romances between middle-aged men and younger women, and our culture approves of such relationships. The reverse, however, is not true. Middle-aged women are presumed to be non-sexual, and their proper role is that of caretaker. Similarly, the upper middle class, to which the central character belongs, considers a lowly gardener beneath her station in life.

All that Heaven Allows critiques both of these widely held cultural assumptions, but it does so within the conventions of full-blown melodrama. The woman's children, for example, give her a television for a Christmas present, implying that she should spend her time in front of it rather than pursue an active life of romance. But rather than aligning itself with the children, the film represents them as petty, narrow minded, and prejudiced and even compares the ancient Egyptian custom of burying a widow with her husband with the contemporary treatment of widows. The widow ignores her children and friends and acts on her desires. Although the couple is happy with the time they spend together, the societal pressures lead to conventional melodramatic illnesses: she develops severe headaches and her lover suffers a serious accident near the end of the film. She goes to his side to nurse him and the final scene shows the couple, happy together.

Happy endings

The melodrama, then, manages to make the audience sympathetic to the forbidden sexual desires of a middle-aged woman, in the process critiquing the manner in which "proper" society brutally denies any legitimate sexual and romantic desires for such a woman. Rather than condemning her unconventional desires, the film condemns society for its repressive, unjust ways. This is no small accomplishment, even for a "serious" film. But what about the happy ending? Happy endings are, of course, common in Hollywood films, but their presence in melodrama is frequently noted as a sign of how silly the form is: by definition, melodrama deals with an excess of pain and misery pointing toward anything but happiness. The ending of *All that Heaven Allows* is indeed unbelievable. After nothing but trouble and illness, suddenly the dark clouds have passed and the couple looks to a happy future. Similarly, in *Magnificent Obsession*, the central male character's irresponsible behavior causes a woman's blindness. He goes from being a playboy to becoming a renowned doctor so that he may restore her eyesight and, near the end of the film, that is precisely what he does during a dramatic operation.

The unbelievable endings frequently feel like nothing more than tacked-on endings that fulfill a requirement of the genre formula; they are not convincing, and that is precisely the point. If they were believable, such endings would imply that society is capable of acknowledging and allowing the fulfillment of such things as the sexual desires of middle-aged widows. If she can be happy in society, then society can't be all that bad. But since the endings are unbelievable and do not carry conviction, much of the social criticism that runs through the film retains its force and validity; we take that criticism seriously in a way we do not take the endings. Thus, although the happy ending is a convention in melodrama, it does not mean that all melodramas mindlessly affirm that everything will work out fine. The happy ending is one of the pleasures that enables the exploration of disturbing material.

Condemning Genres

We have to be wary of condemning genres because of their supposed audience, since such judgments frequently betray a prejudice against certain groups. The world of pop music offers some interesting examples of this dilemma. Many have condemned all rap music, in the process implying that this African American form of music that speaks to economically disadvantaged, young minorities is inferior to other forms of rock 'n' roll. While it might seem that way to middle-class whites, it denies the validity of the genre for those for whom it is made. We will return to these crucial issues in chapter 13 on race and chapter 14 on class.

It is worth recalling the well-known critic who once remarked that, just when he had drawn the line at "spaghetti Westerns," along came Sergio Leone. He was referring to the director of such now highly acclaimed films as *A Fistful of Dollars* (1964, figure 5.10), *For a Few Dollars More* (1965), *The Good, the Bad, and the Ugly* (1966), and *Once upon a Time in the West* (1968). "Spaghetti Westerns" was the derogatory term applied to Westerns cheaply and quickly made by Italian production companies due to favorable economic conditions. Although the movies were popular at the time, nearly all critics dismissed them as unworthy. Most critics and scholars now, however, acknowledge Leone as among the finest of Italian directors and his films among the best Westerns ever made. The moral is

Fig. 5.10

simple: we cannot draw the line at any genre. Film history has shown time and time again that very important works emerge in the most despised of genres; whether women cry while watching them or teenage boys shout obscenities shows only that these films speak in a meaningful way to these groups. As with all kinds of films, some speak in profoundly inventive ways and others in mediocre, conventional ways. Genre criticism, however, cannot afford to prejudge any genre.

We turn now to an analysis of *Murder, My Sweet*, a detective film typical of 1940s' *film noir*, and *Gunfight at the OK Corral*, one typical of 1950s' Westerns. These two films, made in quite different genres during decades in which each genre was immensely popular, enable us to illustrate many aspects of genre entertainment.

Murder, My Sweet (1944)

Fig. 5.11

In *Murder, My Sweet*, private eye Philip Marlowe (Dick Powell), after having been kidnapped, beaten, and drugged, stumbles into the home of a friend for refuge. She tells him: "You go barging around without a very clear idea of what you're doing. Everybody bats you down – smacks you over the head and fills you full of stuff, and you keep on hitting between tackle and end. I don't think you even know which side you're on." Exhausted and depressed, Marlowe replies, "I don't know which side anybody's on. I don't even know who's playing today."

A Confused Detective

This is not the kind of confident and analytical talk that we would expect from Sherlock Holmes, and the differences between *Murder, My Sweet* and most detective movies that came before it will show us a great deal about the relationship between convention and invention in genres and ways in which genres change over time.

Fig. 5.12

The first shot of *Murder, My Sweet* sets up different kinds of confusion that pervade the movie. Under the credits, we see an image that looks unrecognizable and maybe abstract (figure 5.11); the camera slowly pulls back and we eventually learn that it is the reflection of a lamp on a table in an interrogation room (figure 5.12). This image is shot in such a way that, at first, we have no idea of what we are looking at. This confusion extends to the characters in the movie. Marlowe is being interrogated by the police and his eyes are bandaged (figure 5.13). He asks a detective, "The boys tell me I did a couple of murders. Anything in it?" The detective gives him no answer, but advises him to tell his story from the beginning. As

Fig. 5.13

Marlowe begins, the camera moves past him and out the window to shots of Los Angeles at night. We then see Marlowe in flashback in his office at night, without bandages on his eyes but lonely and depressed. A flashing light outside illuminates his office in an eerie way. Suddenly a giant of a man appears hulking over Marlowe's desk. Trying to conceal his shock and nervousness, Marlowe leaves with this intimidating man, called Moose, to search for Moose's lost girlfriend.

This opening gives us a good sense of what to expect from the movie. Most of it takes place at night and in darkness. We do not even know what we are looking at in the first shot. Marlowe is worse off; he is literally blinded and blindfolded, does not know if he is to be indicted for murder, and does not know who has been killed. He begins to tell a troubling story whose outcome he does not know. Not only are the narrative events puzzling and the main character confused and blinded, but the look of the movie is mysterious and often disorienting.

Opening a movie with confusing events is not unusual for a Hollywood film. In fact, it is common, as we have seen with *Jurassic Park* (see chapter 2), and standard in detective movies. After all, what is a detective movie without a mystery? What makes *Murder, My Sweet* helpful for our purposes is that it was part of a new trend in the detective genre in the 1940s, and a look at it within its context shows genre transformation.

Genre Transformation

The movie is very much in keeping with Hollywood styles of narration; it is no *Rashomon* (1950, see chapter 2). Although much of the story, which contains a hallucination scene, is told in flashback with extensive voice-over narration, and although the viewer, like the narrator, is forced to puzzle out the significance of events, this movie, unlike *Rashomon*, clarifies everything by the end. While it is a Hollywood movie, *Murder, My Sweet* nevertheless differs from many detective movies that went before it. We all know what to expect from a detective movie: we generally get a private detective in a modern city who solves a difficult crime that the police cannot solve. We are generally impressed by the intelligence and daring of the hero in deciphering the clues and identifying the villains.

Viewers before the 1940s went to detective movies expecting a certain kind of detective, a certain kind of mystery, and a certain kind of mood. *Murder, My Sweet* and movies like it changed those expectations. Compared with its predecessors, it is more disorienting to the viewer, its hero more degraded and confused, its characters more perverse and sexually compromised, and it makes more extensive use of flashbacks and voice-over narration. Its whole look and mood is shadowy and sinister, uncommon in detective movies up to that time. It was part of a new trend in American movies called *film noir* (a French term meaning "black film," with "black" referring to both the look of the movies and their mood). The history of the detective film is intertwined with the development of the *film-noir* style. *Film noir* has been considered both as a genre and a style. We are defining it here as a style, and what is important for our purposes is how that style changed the detective genre.

Murder, My Sweet was based upon a famous detective novel, *Farewell, My Lovely* by Raymond Chandler, which had already been used as the basis of a detective movie that conformed to earlier expectations of the genre. The two movies, made only two years apart by the same studio, start with the same basic story but are entirely different. A comparison of them will show the specific ways in which the genre was changing.

Detective movies are nearly as old as movies themselves, going back at least as far as American Biograph's *Sherlock Holmes Baffled* of 1903. They did not become a major form, however, until the sound era, partly because speech and elaborate verbal reasoning are so important to them and partly because they were strongly influenced by detective fiction, which was still a new literary form. In fact, many of the major literary detectives, like Hercule Poirot, Philo Vance, Ellery Queen, Charlie Chan, the "Saint," Sam Spade, and Philip Marlowe, did not even appear until after 1925. In the 1930s detective movies became popular. Many were complicated mysteries that the charming hero would investigate while making jokes. The heroes were often sophisticated, or two-fisted, or both, but they were seldom personally affected by the ugly crimes they so readily solved. They often appeared in a series of movies, and *Farewell, My Lovely* was first used by Hollywood in the Falcon series.

In *The Falcon Takes Over* (1942), the detective is not Marlowe, as in the source novel, but Gay Lawrence, "The Falcon," a rich socialite whom we first see, not blinded in an interrogation room, but wearing a tuxedo in a fashionable New York nightclub. He becomes involved in the case not because he is broke and depressed like Marlowe but simply because he happens to be in a nightclub when the giant of a man who is looking for his lost sweetheart kills someone. The Falcon takes the case on as a lark. He has a goofy sidekick whose working-class origins and Brooklyn accent provide comic contrast with the debonair Falcon. Marlowe, by contrast, in both the novel and *Murder, My Sweet*, has no one. He is alone and depressed. The Falcon has a genially antagonistic relationship with the police. When Detective O'Hara arrives on the crime scene, he quips, "Oh, the great Falcon. Haven't seen you around for about a half dozen murders." The movie does not take its crimes seriously; they are mainly excuses to show off the Falcon's cleverness, and much of the film is comic in tone. Its style is set by its opening credits, which appear over a silhouette of an elegant man in top hat, overcoat, and walking stick. This is a far cry from the opening shots of *Murder, My Sweet*, which are confusing and anything but elegant.

Edward Dmytryk directed *Murder, My Sweet*. Only a year earlier, he had directed a film in the Falcon series, *The Falcon Strikes Back*, for the same studio, RKO, but the styles of these two films were completely different. It is unlikely that the studio would have used Raymond Chandler's novel as the basis for two films only two years apart, but a new way to make detective films was emerging, and these two films seem to have virtually nothing in common beyond a similar story.

One way to look at these changes is to look at differences in the heroes. Detective heroes from the 1930s nearly always succeeded; their manly prowess was seldom questioned. The films left issues of failed masculinity to minor characters, such as bumbling police detectives, comic sidekicks, or number one sons whose ineptness provided running comedy. The hero, by contrast, was generally in control and, by the end, whether Sherlock Holmes, Philo Vance, Bulldog Drummond, or Nick Charles, smugly wrapped things up.

In *film noir*, the hero does not so readily wrap things up. At times he becomes so involved with the seductive and degrading world of his case that he fails or it destroys him. In *The Maltese Falcon* (1941), the detective never finds the famous Maltese Falcon and sends the woman he loves, a murderer, off to prison. In *Out of the Past* (1947), Robert Mitchum's detective is hired by a gangster to find his girlfriend, who shot and robbed him. The Mitchum character finds her but they fall in love and run off. This detective, then, betrays his employer and is ultimately killed by his lover. We do not expect this kind of behavior, nor such a fate, from Sherlock Holmes. Holmes's ethics were always impeccable and he generally kept his sexual desires tightly under control. Threats to his moral and sexual integrity are rarely evident.

The Marlowe of *Murder, My Sweet* is often on the verge of losing control. This movie places him in a perverse and highly manipulative sexual world that is fraught with danger. It is a world, new to this genre in the 1940s, in which people are often driven by consuming desires. The lost girlfriend that Moose Malloy is pathetically looking for turns out to be the wife of a rich old man as well as a brutal murderer. She is the link between the two cases that Marlowe investigates, that of Moose's lost girlfriend and that of jewels stolen from the wealthy Grayle family. She is also a character type common to *film noir*: a "black widow" who exploits and then kills her sexual partners.

Women in *Film Noir*

Film noir often presents women as profoundly dangerous and evil. Much of Marlowe's integrity lies in his ability to resist women. This contrasts boldly with the behavior of the Falcon, who, in a running gag of the series, is engaged to be married but constantly assumes false names to pursue other women. These multiple involvements are presented as the sign of a tireless bon vivant rather than as a profoundly dangerous character flaw.

A similar transformation in the genre is evident in different versions of *The Maltese Falcon*. Perhaps the most popular detective movie ever made and often called one of the first *films noirs*, the 1941 film shows its hero, Sam Spade (Humphrey Bogart) involved with two dangerous women, his partner's wife and Brigid O'Shaughnessy. The two earlier movies based on Dashiell

Hammett's novel (*The Maltese Falcon*, 1931, and *Satan Met a Lady*, 1936) present the detective as a compulsive womanizer. As with the Falcon, the trait is established as part of the character's charm, not a dangerous character flaw. Humphrey Bogart's Sam Spade and Dick Powell's Philip Marlowe are more troubled and compromised than their predecessors. No longer ever-grinning ladies' men, they have much to fear from women.

This sense of women as dangerous is central to *film noir*, which became an important American film style by the mid-1940s. It was a style whose look, with its sinister night-time shadows and high-contrast lighting, recalled the look of German Expressionist films of the 1920s (e.g., *The Cabinet of Dr Caligari*, 1919) as well as American horror films of the 1930s (e.g., *The Bride of Frankenstein*, 1935). This is also the look of *Citizen Kane* (1941). Many other elements converged in the 1940s to give birth to *film noir*: a relaxation of censorship laws accompanied by a willingness of studio filmmakers to explore dark sexual material, a fascination with moral depravity, the influence of psychoanalysis as an explanation for character motivation (particularly in creating characters driven to their fates by uncontrollable and unconscious drives), and a sense of dangerously stronger women and dangerously weaker men as a threat to the social order.

The Grayle family in *Murder, My Sweet* provides a good illustration of some concerns of the new style. The father is enthralled and degraded by his attractive young wife. The wife is the black widow who is also Moose's lost girlfriend. Devastatingly attractive, she has nearly all of the men in the movie in her thrall and causes most of their deaths. Clearly rejecting the traditional maternal role, she is the sexual rival of her stepdaughter, Ann, for Marlowe. Ann hates her bitterly as she watches her stepmother humiliate her father by pursuing not only Marlowe but also other men, even leading to the father's suicide attempt. Ann lives in a Freudian nightmare without parallel in both Chandler's novel and *The Falcon Takes Over*. This is most evident in the climax when she sees her stepmother shot dead by her father, then her father and stepmother's former lover kill each other, and the man she loves is blinded. All of this is the direct outcome of her stepmother's sexual manipulations.

Film noir provided a new image of women for the detective genre, and concern with reformulating women's images was not confined to this genre in the 1940s; it was also a time when many women's melodramas appeared. However, where the black widows in *film noir* were frequently seductresses with guns who were manipulative and destructive of traditional families, the women in 1940s' melodramas were often victimized by social pressures, illness, or their dysfunctional families, as in *Mildred Pierce* (1945). The fact that these two genres presented radically different views of women at the same time can be seen as an indication that there were significant changes in the social roles of women at the time and that different genres complexly mediated these changes in different ways. During World War II, for example, women left the home to play important roles in the war effort both by joining the civilian workforce and the military. Many assumed that, once the war was over, these

Fig. 5.14

women would return to their traditional roles as homemakers, but the social reality was more complex. The contradictions within and between these genres were different ways of responding to real contradictions and tensions within a changing society.

Men in *Film Noir*

Shifts in the roles of women obviously affected the roles of men. In 1940s' detective films like *Murder, My Sweet*, we see comparable reformulations of notions of American masculinity, the questioning of previous certainties, and the making of the strength of the detective highly suspect. This is clear in the movie's climax, where most of the characters meet in a beach house. A standard scene in many 1930s' detective movies had the detective gathering all the suspects together and then flamboyantly exposing the guilty party. Here, although Marlowe sets up the final confrontation, he quickly loses control of it. He is seconds away from being shot by Mrs Grayle (figure 5.14) when her husband shoots her, and in the ensuing shoot-out he is blinded by gunfire and passes out without even knowing how things turned out.

In detective movies of the 1940s, the nature of the crime and the nature of the detectives had changed greatly from those of the 1930s, revealing a good deal about shifts in American culture and the creative manner in which genres respond. Genre formulas and conventions are continually being reinvented. Nowhere is this more evident than in the Western.

Gunfight at the OK Corral (1956)

The Western has been a staple of American movies since *The Great Train Robbery* of 1903 and is often considered the genre most representative of American values. It has been characterized as epic in scope, bearing the cultural significance of the drama of a nation being formed. Its conflicts are fundamental ones, of civilization against savagery and of good versus evil. The form has always appealed to notions of rugged male individualism, and its battles, while generally occurring in the isolated wilderness, assume the significance of building the foundations for the American nation to come.

Good Guys and Bad Guys

Gunfight at the OK Corral (1956) takes its title from the most famous gunfight in the history of the American West, that between the Earp brothers and

Doc Holliday on one side and the Clanton and McLaury brothers and their friends on the other on October 26, 1881, in Tombstone, Arizona. Although the actual battle took less than a minute, and the morality and motivations of its participants are still being debated, the movie stretches the fight out significantly and leaves no question about who was right and who deserved to die.

Fig. 5.15

The movie was a prestige Western starring Burt Lancaster and Kirk Douglas at the height of their careers. Douglas, who the previous year had won accolades playing Vincent Van Gogh in *Lust for Life*, now played Doc Holliday. Lancaster's Wyatt Earp is a figure of mature and powerful masculinity (figure 5.15). The movie does not begin with the gunfight nor even the events leading up to it but rather with the beginning of the Earp–Holliday relationship, which remains the center of the film. It has a rambling narrative, with Earp saving Holliday from hanging, Holliday helping Earp catch bank robbers, and the locales shifting from Fort Griffin to Dodge City, all before anyone gets to Tombstone.

Fig. 5.16

Earp is a strong and morally righteous man, clear-sighted in his goals and austere in his behavior. He is often shown without a gun. In one scene in a saloon when a man pulls a gun on him, Earp holds his coat open to show that he is unarmed (figure 5.16). He then disarms the man with the sheer power of his presence. His power is enhanced by contrast with many characters in the movie, starting with Sheriff Cotton Wilson at the beginning. Earp is dismayed to learn that Wilson has not detained Ike Clanton for him as he had requested. He tells him that, ten years ago, Wilson was the toughest marshal on the frontier and Earp admired him; now Earp sees him as a coward. By the end Wilson has fallen so far that he is on the Clanton side in the OK Corral fight, but he even tries to run away from that. He is shot in the back by Ike for cowardice. Wilson represents the kind of moral laxity and accommodationism that Earp's austerity will not allow. Doc even calls Earp "Preacher," and a major sign of his moral strength comes in his dealings with women.

Men and Women

From its nineteenth-century origins in pulp fiction, the Western has constructed reality as a masculine enterprise. Women are impeding to it or peripheral. This is made explicit in Owen Wister's 1900 novel *The Virginian* in which the Virginian's betrothed demands that he choose between her or meeting his enemy in the street. Wyatt faces the same decision. He falls in love with Laura and they speak of marriage (figure 5.17). When he is called to Tombstone, she demands that he not go. He refuses to stay, and we never see her in the film again. Only at the end, after he has cleaned Tomb-

Fig. 5.17

Fig. 5.18

Fig. 5.19

Fig. 5.20

stone up and thrown his badge to the ground, does he speak of returning to her.

The movie makes it clear that women and a lawman's duty do not mix, never questioning the rectitude of the lawman's duty. It establishes Wyatt's ability to renounce women as part of his strength. All of his brothers in Tombstone are married or about to be married, and they are presented as the weaker for it. That is why they have called Wyatt, the only single man in the family, to help them clean up the town. One admits that his wife has been asking him to quit marshaling for a year because "You know how women are." The movie presents women as emasculating to different degrees. The worst is Kate (figure 5.18), with whom Doc has a degrading, sadomasochistic relationship. She often humiliates him, or is humiliated by him, and runs off with a rival.

The real relationship is between Wyatt and Doc, who are polar opposites: Wyatt is all simple integrity, plainly dressed, deliberate in his movements (figure 5.19); Doc is all urban flash, flashily attired, quirky and often manic in his movements, frequently drunk, and subject to outbursts of coughing and violence (figure 5.20). Both are impeded by women, but Wyatt is able to leave his while he attends to his duties. Doc lives with his, and she resembles another one of his debilities, like his tubercular coughing and his drunkenness. Wyatt leaves at the end with a future before him; Doc always seems on the verge of death.

The Cultural Climate

The movie never questions the value of the title gunfight. The Earps are good, the Clantons are bad. It is that simple. This reflects the moral structure of a popular television series, *The Life and Legend of Wyatt Earp*, which was part of an unrivaled boom in television Westerns in the late 1950s. These were characterized at the time as "adult" Westerns, a way of asserting that they were not simple adolescent or working-class entertainment, which was the main way the genre was perceived at the time, but worthy dramas for "mature" people. President Dwight Eisenhower was widely known as a lover of Westerns and a champion of their values. The Western heroes of the 1950s, like the Earps of the movie and the television series, tended to be white men with conservative values. This was not a time in which movies like *Posse* or *Bad Girls* were being made.

The cultural trauma of the 1960s led to a reconfiguration of the Western and of the figure of Earp. Some of the investment our culture had in conservative values had unraveled by the 1970s, challenged by the rise of feminism, the anti-Vietnam War movement, and the coming of age of the post-war generation with its profound critique of the values of its elders. One of the most obvious sites for discontent became the favored genres and heroes of the previous generation. The values of the strong, righteous men of the 1950s now came under question, and Wyatt Earp was no exception.

Doc (1971) presents Earp as a pompous, power-hungry, shifty-eyed, corrupt, and homicidal politician. The television series and the 1957 movie presented the OK Corral gunfight as a triumph of the forces of justice over the forces of evil; *Doc* presents it as Wyatt's premeditated murder of political rivals. The earlier works presented Wyatt as a man of great physical courage and power; this one has him beaten and humiliated in a fair fight by Ike Clanton.

Wyatt Earp is still presented as a figure of controlling masculinity, but that masculinity is unattractive and corrupt. Unlike the Earps of the 1950s, this man is no model for young boys. His activities involve neither moral righteousness nor the building of a new nation but, instead, personal gain. The cultural climate had changed substantially from the 1950s to the 1970s, and part of that climate involved not only a shift of values in many Westerns but also a decline in popular interest in the form so that by 1980 what had been one of the most powerful of genres had virtually ceased to exist. The 1990s brought about a revival of interest in the Western, with the genre changed yet again. This revival included two big-budget Earp movies: *Tombstone* (1993) and *Wyatt Earp* (1994). For the remainder of this chapter, however, we will look at two representations of Earp in the work of John Ford, the director most associated with the Western.

Ford's *My Darling Clementine* (1946) presents Earp as a hero but, in 1964, Ford's last Western, *Cheyenne Autumn*, depicts him as corrupt. This shift reflects changes in Ford's personal vision of American history as well as changes within the Western genre and within American culture. A look at the opposition in these two Ford films casts light on the Earps of other directors because Ford both influenced and was influenced by them.

My Darling Clementine

My Darling Clementine presents Earp as a strong man of the land who becomes marshal of Tombstone only to avenge his brother's murder. He gives his reasons in a private talk at his brother's grave, "Maybe when we leave this country, young kids like you will be able to grow up and live safe." He is a noble man making the West safe for progress.

When he enters the town only to get a shave, it is lawless. Wild shots crash through the barbershop, fired by the drunken "Indian Charlie," who is shooting up a brothel. When the cowardly sheriff refuses to stop it, Earp goes in and drags Charlie out. He yells, "Indian, get out of town and stay out" and kicks him in the pants.

Having removed one form of perceived threat to the town, that from a different race, he then accepts the job of marshal and, over time, proceeds to remove another threat, the murdering, white-trash Clanton family. The town is prime for civilization when he leaves, with a church and a schoolmarm. Earp is presented as a town tamer, as someone who literally casts out forces of savagery and corruption and allows unproblematized progress and domesticity to prosper.

Cheyenne Autumn

As Ford neared the end of his career, however, his view of American historical progress and white heroism grew more complicated and jaded. He returned to the character of Earp in his last Western, *Cheyenne Autumn*, but here Earp is not a pure man of the earth but a cynical dandy in a white suit. He has no evident interest in family or in making the West safe for progress; rather, he is obsessed with gambling and gets 10 percent of all the action in town. He is not part of the solution, he is part of the problem. He shoots a cowboy in the foot with a hidden Derringer and recognizes a whore from Wichita by looking up her thighs. He is much closer to the Earp of *Doc* than to that of *My Darling Clementine*.

The different representations of Earp have less to do with fidelity to or deviation from "historical truth" than with a complex mix of factors, including the ways in which genres change over time. John Ford, in fact, claimed to have known the real Wyatt Earp, and yet represented him in very different ways at different points in his career. Furthermore, those representations differ significantly from the ones in *Doc*, the 1950s' television series *The Life and Legend of Wyatt Earp*, *Gunfight at the OK Corral*, *Tombstone*, and *Wyatt Earp*, among many other Earp Westerns. This does not mean that one of these representations is true and the others are false, but rather that each of them, although belonging to the same genre, creates a different set of meanings around the same historical figure. Part of the vitality of genre art results from the tension between convention and invention. From this perspective, it is not surprising that two major films about Wyatt Earp and the gunfight at the OK Corral appeared within half a year of each other in 1993. There are, after all, an infinite number of ways to represent Earp and part of the desire to do so stems from the internal dynamics of the genre (to do something different from how it has been done before) and part of the impetus relates to cultural changes (to represent something in a manner that speaks to contemporary concerns). Far from being entirely fixed and formulaic, genres are in a constant state of flux, and we can learn much from studying their vitality.

SELECTED READINGS

Robin Wood argues for the value of genre entertainment, including the modern horror film, in relation to films of serious social criticism in *Hollywood from Vietnam to Reagan* (New York: Columbia University Press, 1986). John Cawelti analyzes genres in terms of convention and invention as well as formula in *The Six-gun Mystique* (Bowling Green: Bowling Green University Popular Press, 1971) and *Adventure, Mystery and Romance: Formula Stories as Art and Popular Culture* (Chicago: University of Chicago Press, 1976). In *The Desire to Desire: The Woman's Film of the 1940s* (Bloomington, IN: Indiana University Press, 1987), Mary Ann Doane analyzes the cultural significance of that genre addressed primarily to women, including melodramatic love stories and films involving illness. Carol J. Clover analyzes the cultural significance of horror films targeted primarily at teenage boys in *Men, Women, and Chainsaws: Gender in the Modern Horror Film* (Princeton, NJ: Princeton University Press, 1992). Philip French supplies an introduction to the Western genre in *Westerns* (New York: Oxford University Press, 1977), and E. Ann Kaplan's anthology *Women in Film Noir* (London: British Film Institute, 1979) focuses on the representation of women in the *noir* detective film.

6

SERIES, SEQUELS, AND REMAKES

Goldfinger and *Psycho* (1960 and 1998)

Why have movies with numbers at the end of their titles, such as *Friday the 13th, Part VI: Jason Lives* (1986), *Rocky V* (1990), and *Home Alone 3* (1997), become so popular in recent years? Today's generation has grown up with this phenomenon and, particularly during the summer rush of major studio releases, can expect the arrival of new movies with an overt relationship to films that they have already seen. Not all sequels are numbered, like *The Mummy Returns* (2001) or *The Lost World: Jurassic Park* (1997). These films, none the less, refer to the earlier films in their titles and *Jurassic Park III* (2001) returns to the numbering system. Some are not sequels or series films but remakes of older movies, such as *Scarface* (1983), *The Three Musketeers* (1993), *Psycho* (1998), or *The Man in the Iron Mask* (1998). And some, like *Superman* (1978), have gone on to become the basis of series or sequels of their own. We have all looked forward to a "new" James Bond movie, or a new Indiana Jones, Terminator, Rocky, Dirty Harry, Pink Panther, Rambo, Karate Kid, Ghostbusters, Star Trek, Alien, Halloween, or Batman. And a few years after having seen that "new" movie, we await another "new" installment.

These movies are generally major studio productions with large budgets, wide distribution, and saturation advertising. They constitute a significant part of today's filmgoing experience. Some are very similar to the movies they recall, particularly recent horror movies like the *Friday the 13th* and *Halloween* series in which some installments seem more like remakes than sequels. Others, like the Pink Panther series, differ in important ways from the earlier films. In *The Pink Panther* (1963, figure 6.1), for

Fig. 6.1

example, Inspector Clouseau is married, but in the following five films he is single and no explanation is given for what happened to his wife.

As audiences, we often approach series, sequels, and remakes expecting to see "more of the same." In many cases we do, but we also, often without being aware of it, sometimes have different expectations of the new film. These resemble the expectations we have for genres, where we presume we will see a gunfight when we go to a Western, song and dance numbers when we see a musical, and gory death when we see a horror film. Because of the pervasive nature of series, sequels, and remakes since the 1960s, it is important to understand how they function.

What are Series and Sequels?

In 1911, D. W. Griffith made *Enoch Arden*, Parts 1 and 2. Although the two parts of roughly ten minutes each were later combined into one movie, they can be seen as an early movie with a sequel. The two parts were also remakes of his 1908 movie, *After Many Years*, since both were based upon the same Tennyson poem. These are not the earliest examples. Series, sequels, and remakes have existed almost since the beginning of movies. All three capitalize on the success of an earlier movie and offer the audience the promise of revisiting parts of the experience that they had with the first film.

A **series** is a number of movies that usually employ the same basic characters, situations, and style as the original movie. The James Bond series is a good example. In each film, Bond, a suave international spy, upsets an international criminal organization that threatens global chaos. Along the way he uses high-tech equipment and has affairs with beautiful women. It is a series because each episode is self-contained; no knowledge of the events of an earlier film is necessary to an understanding of any other one. In fact, with minor exceptions, it is impossible to figure out the order of the episodes in Bond's career, and, when it is possible, it is irrelevant.

A **sequel** starts after a prior film left off. A good example would be the Godfather movies. *The Godfather* (1972), deals with the transfer of power from Michael Corleone's father to Michael; *The Godfather, Part II* (1974) deals mostly with Michael consolidating that power in his middle age; *The Godfather, Part III* (1990) deals with Michael as an older man trying to divest himself of his power and atone for his sins. While it is irrelevant whether the events of *Thunderball* (1965) came before or after the events of *Goldfinger* (1964) in the fictional life of James Bond, that is not the case with *Godfather* and *Godfather III*. Both series films and sequels, however, clearly attempt in some way to revive elements of earlier films; in this they share a strong similarity with remakes.

Why Remake a Film?

Remakes are attempts to "make again" an earlier film, often using similar characters and storylines. An obvious question would be: "Why not just re-release the earlier movie?" The answer often has to do with the notion that the earlier film is in some way obsolete. Sometimes this presumption is the result of technological change, so *The Hunchback of Notre Dame* (1923), while a successful silent movie, was remade in 1939 as a sound movie. That movie was photographed, as was standard for the time, in black and white. In 1957, when color dominated "A" feature film production, a color remake appeared; in 1982 a remake was made for television; and in 1996 there was an animated Disney remake.

There are many other reasons aside from technological ones behind remakes, but some are also related to the notion of obsolescence. *The Three Musketeers* (1921) was remade a number of times in black and white after the silent era (in 1935 and 1939), and color versions exist from 1948 and from 1974, but Keifer Sutherland and Charlie Sheen are current stars with appeal to a new generation, so they appear in a 1993 version. A color 1991 remake of the black-and-white 1962 *Cape Fear* appeared with a muscular Robert DeNiro in the role of the savage criminal originated by Robert Mitchum; Mitchum, visibly embodying one reason for the remake, appears notably older in a minor role in the 1991 film. Sometimes a remake is made not because the earlier film was a success, but because it was a failure and the filmmaker thinks that he or she can improve upon it. Sometimes a recent foreign film is remade because it received limited or no distribution in the United States and producers consider it relatively unknown to American audiences; examples are the 1993 Hollywood *Point of No Return*, which remade the 1991 French *La Femme Nikita*, and the 1987 Hollywood *Three Men and a Baby*, which remade the 1985 French *Three Men and a Cradle*.

Sometimes the relaxation of censorship codes inspires a more "daring" remake, as with the 1981 *The Postman Always Rings Twice*, which was much more sexually graphic than the 1946 Hollywood version. Sometimes a new approach to a recent film inspires a remake, as with *The Man who Loved Women* (1983), which changes the occupation of the central character from a writer to a sculptor and adds a psychoanalyst to the basic concept of the 1977 film.

Remakes cross national borders for reasons of generational differences, presumptions of audience unfamiliarity, and a new approach to the original film. The first *The Man who Loved Women* was a French film, the second a Hollywood one. *Cyrano de Bergerac* demonstrates all three reasons: it was a big budget 1923 Italian film, a 1946 French film, a prestige 1950 Hollywood film, and a big budget 1990 French film, as well as the basis for the updated 1987 Steve Martin Hollywood comedy, *Roxanne*.

Recent Trends I: Big Budgets

Some critics talk of the past twenty years in a disparaging way as an age of series, sequels, and remakes. They cite the trend as a sign that filmmakers have run out of ideas and must simply recycle old ones. This reveals a number of assumptions, the most obvious being that an "original" work is necessarily more creative and, therefore, superior to a derivative work. The second is that derivative works are of necessity creatively exhausted, that "it" was all said and said better the first time around. Both of these assumptions are questionable.

The film industry often finds series, sequels, and remakes attractive projects for economic reasons. If an audience paid for something once, the logic goes, their interest is whetted and they will do so again, and the wisdom of such thinking has been demonstrated repeatedly throughout film history. Early in the twentieth century, for example, theater owners sometimes placed a cardboard cut-out of Charlie Chaplin as "The tramp" with a sign saying "I am here today" outside their theaters when they had a new "tramp" movie. They knew that audiences had loved the "tramp" in earlier movies and would pay to see him again. Conforming to a related logic, the box-office success of *Lethal Weapon* (1987, figure 6.2) made the studio eager to produce three sequels (1989, figure 6.3; 1992, figure 6.4; and 1998). This pattern can also involve different media and include both sequel and series formats as well as remakes. *Planet of the Apes* (1968) not only inspired four sequels (1970, 1971, 1972, and 1973) and two television series (an hour-long, live-action one on CBS in 1974 and an animated one on NBC in 1975), but also a 2001 remake (in which Charlton Heston, who starred in the 1968 film and played a small role in the 1970 one, again played a small role, this time as an ape).

Series, sequels, and remakes have functioned in different ways at different times in film history. The current wave has greater prestige and is more central to the industry than at any other time. It is only during this period that films have blatantly advertised their status as series films or sequels with numbers in the titles such as *Lethal Weapon 2*, *3*, and *4*. Earlier, series and sequels generally used the titles to indicate that something was significantly different about this film, so *Dracula* (1931) was followed not by *Dracula 2* but by *Dracula's*   Fig. 6.2

Fig. 6.3

Fig. 6.4

Fig. 6.5

Daughter (1936); *Frankenstein* (1931) by *The Bride of Frankenstein* (1935) and *Son of Frankenstein* (1939); *Tarzan the Ape Man* (1932) by *Tarzan's New York Adventure* (1942); *King Kong* (1933) by *Son of Kong* (1933). This pattern of indicating that each film does something new still functions with serial films like the *Star Wars* or Indiana Jones films and series like the James Bond movies. But it is dropped with the successors to *Psycho*, *Rocky*, and *Halloween* or is present only in a subtitle.

Not only do recent films take pride in their series or sequel status, but they are also often "A" productions, frequently with larger budgets than their predecessors. After the $14 million horror film *Scream* (1996) became an unexpected box-office hit, Miramax, the film's studio, increased the budget of *Scream 2* (1997) to $23 million and quickly followed that with *Scream 3* (2000). Many sequels are among the most expensive movies made that year and some, like *Terminator 2: Judgment Day* (1991, figure 6.5) are among the most expensive movies ever made. Furthermore, unlike the situation in the past when actors like George Raft would turn down *The Maltese Falcon* on the grounds that his contract forbade him to do remakes, many of today's highest-paid actors not only gladly do remakes but also frequently appear in series and sequel films, and some in more than one. The stigma of connection with an earlier film has largely disappeared. Sylvester Stallone, for example, has appeared in the Rocky and Rambo films; Harrison Ford in the Indiana Jones, *Star Wars*, and Jack Ryan series; Clint Eastwood in the "Man with No Name" and Dirty Harry series; Mel Gibson in the *Road Warrior* and *Lethal Weapon* movies; Eddie Murphy in the Nutty Professor and Dr Doolittle movies; and Arnold Schwarzenegger in the Terminator films and *Batman and Robin* (1997).

This mega-budget market is different from the situation in the 1930s to the 1950s, when series films and sequels were generally "B" films. During this time, "B" films were generally considered inferior to "A" films, which were seen as prestigious and/or popular by studios and often given major personnel, budgets of a million dollars or more, and extensive publicity. "B" films had smaller budgets, less prestigious personnel, and shorter shooting schedules. They were commonly presumed to be not only financially but also artistically inferior. Series films and sequels were not only widely seen as "B" films but also usually had dwindling budgets as the series went on and used second- or third-tier actors. This does not discount, however, the extraordinary popularity and longevity of some of them. The character Bulldog Drummond, for example, appeared in different series in at least twenty-five movies from 1922 to 1968 and was played by at least thirteen actors. And that does not begin to compare with Sherlock Holmes, who, beginning in 1903, has appeared in close to a hundred movies and half a dozen television series. Examples of other movie series are Buck Rogers, Flash Gordon, Mr Moto, The Three Mesquiteers, Hopalong Cassidy, The Saint, The Cisco Kid, Mike Shayne, Tarzan, The Falcon, Ma and Pa Kettle, and Andy Hardy. Sometimes, as with the Basil Rathbone Sherlock Holmes series, "A" films slipped to "B" status as a series went on: the Holmes series went from two films at a "major" studio (Twentieth-century Fox) to twelve at a "minor" one (Universal).

In the 1950s most "B" series disappeared or shifted to television in half-hour formats. Examples include Hopalong Cassidy, Roy Rogers, Superman, Sherlock Holmes, The Cisco Kid, and The Thin Man. In the 1960s and 1970s things changed again when the first hugely successful series films appeared with the James Bond, Pink Panther, and Clint Eastwood "Man with No Name" series. All three were released by the same studio, United Artists, and demonstrated to the major Hollywood studios that series could be a lucrative market.

Recent Trends II: Allusionism

In the 1970s a new pattern of dealing with series, sequels, and remakes emerged in Hollywood. The generation of filmmakers that rose to prominence in the 1970s was the first to learn its craft not within the industry but in film schools. This includes filmmakers like Martin Scorsese (*Cape Fear*, 1991), Steven Spielberg (*Raiders of the Lost Ark*, 1981), George Lucas (*Star Wars*, 1977), Francis Ford Coppola (*Bram Stoker's Dracula*, 1992), Walter Hill (*48 Hours*, 1982), Brian De Palma (*Scarface*, 1983), Paul Schrader (*The Cat People*, 1982), and John Milius (*Dillinger*, 1973). These directors are deeply immersed in film history, which has affected the way in which they make films and even the films they choose to make. Every film just cited, for example, is either a remake of an individual film (*Cape Fear*, 1962, *Dracula*, 1931, *Scarface*, 1932, *The Cat People*, 1942, *Dillinger*, 1945) or a film with at least one sequel (*Raiders of the Lost Ark*, *48 Hours*, *Star Wars*). Most are also films that explicitly and nostalgically invoke old genres.

George Lucas and Steven Spielberg, for example, have great affection for the space and adventure serials and series, such as Flash Gordon or Jungle Jim, that were popular Saturday matinee children's shows in the 1930s and 1940s. The two directors made the *Star Wars* and Indiana Jones movies largely to recapture for today's generation the excitement that the early movies generated. At times they even copied actual shots from earlier movies as a way of attempting to duplicate the effects. Lucas, for example, used airplane attack sequences from World War II battle movies as models for the staging and editing of his spaceship attacks in *Star Wars*. In the same film, he copied the look of *Triumph of the Will* (1935) for the formal heroes' award ceremony at the end of the film, and refers to *The Searchers* (1956) in the scene in which Luke Skywalker returns to find his aunt and uncle murdered and their home burned, much as Marty does in the earlier film (see chapter 4). This generation of filmmakers draws upon the kinds of movies shown in film schools and **canonized** by film critics and scholars, and they have a great range of reference to old, foreign, and often obscure films. In order to fully appreciate and

Fig. 6.6

comprehend the **allusionism** in their films, audiences need to have an awareness of these films.

Parody and satire are other ways of referring to older films, but they function differently. When we see the Pink Panther in a dress racing across a grassy hilltop with its arms spread during the credits of *The Pink Panther Strikes Again* (1976, figure 6.6), we immediately recognize it as a comic reference to Julie Andrews in *The Sound of Music* (1965), a reference further heightened by the highly publicized fact that its director, Blake Edwards, is married to Julie Andrews. Similarly, when we see a submarine rising from the water in *1941* (1979) and hear the music from *Jaws* (1975), we know that Steven Spielberg, director of both movies, is making fun of his earlier work. These are brief invocations of popular movies as jokes, which is a very different strategy from that of Brian De Palma's *Obsession* (1976), which has extensive story elements and even uses camera shots resembling those in Alfred Hitchcock's *Vertigo* (1958) as well as similar music by Bernard Herrmann, who wrote the music for *Vertigo* and other Hitchcock films.

Some sequel and series movies become so much a part of popular knowledge that other films refer to them. In *The Last Action Hero* (1993), for example, Arnold Schwarzenegger walks past the actor who played the villain in *Terminator 2: Judgment Day* (figure 6.7), and *True Lies* (1994) opens with a sequence in which Schwarzenegger (playing a different character) is on a spy mission. He rises from underwater and removes a scuba outfit to reveal formal clothing underneath (figure 6.8), just as James Bond did at the beginning of *Goldfinger* (1964, figure 6.9). Such references resemble the scene in

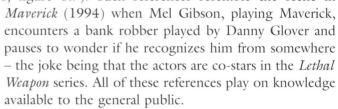

Maverick (1994) when Mel Gibson, playing Maverick, encounters a bank robber played by Danny Glover and pauses to wonder if he recognizes him from somewhere – the joke being that the actors are co-stars in the *Lethal Weapon* series. All of these references play on knowledge available to the general public.

The kinds of sources upon which series, sequels, and remakes draw clearly affect the kinds of movies they become. The most traditional way, whether with *Son of the*

Fig. 6.7

Fig. 6.8

Fig. 6.9

Sheik in 1926 or *Terminator 2: Judgment Day* in 1991, is to draw upon films widely known to the general public of the day. The film-school generation at times draws on more specialized sources. A recent trend is to draw not upon old movies but upon popular television series, as with *Maverick*, *The Fugitive* (1993, figure 6.10), *Mission: Impossible* (1996) and *Mission: Impossible 2* (2000), *The Untouchables* (1987), *The Flintstones* (1994), *Dennis the Menace* (1993), and *Leave it to Beaver* (1997). This gets further compli-

Fig. 6.10

cated since, in some cases, the television series were preceded by movies and movie serials, as with Batman and Superman and, before that, by comic books. At times it is difficult to decide what, exactly, is being remade.

How Do Remakes Differ from the Original?

A remake is never the "same" as the original. This goes beyond the obvious fact of different technologies, actors, and story variations. In the 1932 *Dr Jekyll and Mr Hyde*, Jekyll is a good man who rebels against unjust Victorian moral conventions. Those unjust conventions are ultimately responsible for his turning into the monster Hyde and the ensuing tragedy. In the 1941 remake, however, society's conventions are not unjust, but just, and Jekyll is an evil man for defying them. In both cases, the story is similar: a scientist finds a way to split man's moral personalities and create two people from within himself, and he dies in the end. But the world of the 1932 film was closer to the lingering effects of Victorian morality and was built on a need to criticize it. The 1941 world was more distanced from Victorian culture but was engaged in war, and unquestioned faith in one's society had become an important value.

Comparably, the vampire in *Dracula* (1931) is a threat to pure women in a world of traditional moral values; the vampire in *Andy Warhol's Dracula* (1974), however, laments that he needs the blood of virgins to survive and that he is having trouble finding a virgin in the modern world. In the earlier film, then, the central character is a threat to traditional sexual values; in the remake, made during the sexual revolution of the 1960s and 1970s, he is a defender of them.

Series, sequels, and remakes reveal many different strategies for approaching their source material. Some, like the *Friday the 13th* series, virtually duplicate the structure and iconography of the original; the films are structured around teenagers being methodically terrorized and killed – in the original by Jason's mother and in the rest of the series by Jason, who always wears a hockey mask. Some sequels, however, explore areas that the original did not attempt. *Frankenstein* presents an uncivilized and brutal monster, but *The Bride of Frankenstein* civilizes him by giving him speech, table manners, a friend, and hopes for a mate.

Sometimes remakes court the audience's memory of their famous predecessors, as with the 1978 *Invasion of the Body Snatchers*, in which the star and

Fig. 6.11

Fig. 6.12

director of the original 1956 movie make cameo appearances; other remakes have virtually unknown predecessors for current audiences, as with *Victor/Victoria* (1982), which remakes the 1933 German film *Viktor und Viktoria*, and *True Lies* (1994), which remakes the 1991 French film *La Totale*. In such cases the first film may supply little more than inspiration or an idea for a quite different film. *La Totale* is a small farce, whereas *True Lies* is an action film with elaborate special effects sequences and one of the biggest budgets in the history of cinema. Sometimes remakes even try to erase a relationship with an earlier film and acknowledge instead that film's literary source, as with *Bram Stoker's Dracula* (1992) and *Mary Shelley's Frankenstein* (1994). Similarly, *Greystoke: The Legend of Tarzan, Lord of the Apes* (1983) evokes Edgar Rice Burroughs's novel, *Tarzan of the Apes*, rather than the 1932 film, *Tarzan the Apeman* and the "B" films that followed it.

Certain directors seek not so much to remake an earlier film, start to finish, as to recreate the circumstances that gave that film its vitality and then move in a new direction. Howard Hawks took similar characters, actors, and situations in *Rio Bravo* (1958, figure 6.11), *El Dorado* (1967), and *Rio Lobo* (1970, figure 6.12) but moved them in different directions. All three Westerns star John Wayne and include a close-knit group of men of varying ages, a woman who threatens the all-male group, and a narrative structure whereby the protagonists seek shelter in jails. Other recurring story elements and motifs include the exchange of hostages and the wounding and scarring of the body. Hawks saw *Rio Bravo*, the first of the trilogy, as a remake of a film he despised, *High Noon* (1952). In that film no one in the town is willing to help the sheriff against gunmen. In the Hawks film, the sheriff has the strong support of a group of men.

Robert Rodriquez's *Desperado* (1995) illustrates just how complicated all these patterns and strategies have become. Although it appears rather like a sequel to his 1992 film, *El Mariachi* (figure 6.13), it so closely resembles its predecessor that many critics understandably called it a remake. Both films involve a central male character who is a stranger in town and either carries weapons in a guitar case or is mistaken for someone who does. Both also have a similar romantic subplot and even use the same bar as a set. *Desperado*, however, is a much higher-budgeted film starring Antonio Banderas, an international star, than was *El Mariachi*, an independent film that won notoriety for being shot in two weeks with no stars, for $7,000. In this case, the different budgets and production schedules and values, including the star system, were the major differences between the two films rather than the passage of a long period of time or technological innovation.

Regardless of varying aesthetic strategies, series, sequels, and remakes significantly shape the perceptions and expectations of contemporary

Fig. 6.13

film viewers. We can now turn to an examination of *Goldfinger*, which is part of the extraordinarily popular James Bond series, and Alfred Hitchcock's *Psycho* (1960) and its 1998 remake by Gus Van Sant. We have chosen these films because *Goldfinger* perfectly illustrates central features of the Bond series and the *Psycho* remake raises questions about remake strategies.

Goldfinger (1964) and the James Bond Series

Among James Bond enthusiasts, 1983 is famous for its "battle of the Bonds." Three "new" Bond adventures came out that year. Roger Moore played Bond in *Octopussy*; Sean Connery was Bond in *Never Say Never Again*; and a new Bond novel, *License Renewed*, appeared. What was going on? The Eon Company, which had produced most of the Bond films, made *Octopussy*, but not with Connery, who had established the Bond role on screen. Connery, who had not played the role since 1971, appeared as Bond for a different company. And *License Renewed* was written not by Ian Fleming, the author of the original Bond novels, but by John Gardner, who continued the series after Fleming's death. Which one, then, was the "real" Bond?

The answer, of course, is all of them, and it points to some of the issues that arise when dealing with series, sequels, and remakes. The James Bond series is probably the most successful series in movie history, with nearly twenty films since 1963 in which five actors (Sean Connery, George Lazenby, Roger Moore, Timothy Dalton, and Pierce Brosnan) play Bond. More will likely come. While the first two movies in the series (*Dr No*, 1963, and *From Russia with Love*, 1964) were successes, *Goldfinger*'s (1964) runaway popularity made future Bond movies a virtual certainty. At that point, each film had been made by the same production company, each starred Connery as Bond, and each was based upon a novel by Ian Fleming. Eventually, all of that would change.

The Bond Formula

Goldfinger solidified the Bond series "formula," the basic set of characters, circumstances, and styles that each film would revive. At the center is Bond himself, a suave, rugged, British spy with great sexual appeal, gourmet tastes, and skill at using high-tech equipment in dangerous situations. His mission takes him to exotic locales where he thwarts international plots and meets beautiful but dangerous women. The sound track includes John Barry's distinctive theme music.

Like all series episodes, *Goldfinger* begins and ends at the same place, with Bond unchanged, unattached, and available for the next assignment from his superior, "M." The order of the episodes, even when it can be determined, has no special relevance. *From Russia with Love*, for example, contains a single line in which a character refers resentfully to the fact that Bond killed Dr No, the villain of the first film, thus placing *Russia* after that first film. But it is a throwaway line, and nothing in the movie builds upon events in *Dr No*. Similarly, at one point in *Goldfinger*, Bond inquires about his attaché case and is told that it was damaged in transit, a wry reference to the exploding case he received in *Russia*. While these could place those installments in chronological order, the references are so slight and the continuity with other components of those episodes so minor that the order has no relevance. *Goldfinger* could as readily precede *Russia* or *Dr No* as follow them. Bond is no older, and neither his career nor his associates have changed.

This is further emphasized by *Goldfinger*'s precredit sequence, which introduced a new element into the formula. From this point on, most Bond films would have exciting precredit sequences unrelated to the rest of the story; they show Bond triumph in a dangerous situation that has nothing to do with the narrative of prior films and nothing to do with the narrative of the film in which they appear. They almost become a little series of their own.

The *Goldfinger* sequence shows a Latin American industrial installation at night. A seagull swims to shore in a nearby harbor. Bond suddenly arises from the water in a scuba suit, the seagull attached to his headgear for camouflage. He discards the headgear, eludes armed guards, and plants explosives in the installation. He then removes the scuba suit to reveal a perfectly tailored and unwrinkled white-jacketed tuxedo underneath. He places a red carnation in the lapel and is in a nightclub when the explosives go off (plate 41). He goes to the room of the club's exotic dancer and finds her naked in a bathtub. As they kiss, he sees the reflection of an approaching assailant in her eye, turns and uses her as a shield, then hurls the attacker into the bathtub. When the assailant reaches for a gun, Bond flips an electrical appliance into the tub and electrocutes the man, archly commenting, "Shocking . . . positively shocking."

In narrative terms, the sequence is irrelevant to the rest of the film, which, after the credits, begins anew with the story of the villain Goldfinger's scheme to blow up Fort Knox. But, stylistically, the sequence tells us what the film, and the series, is about: Bond will ingeniously accomplish his mission in an exotic place, encounter beautiful but dangerous women, and handle dangerous situations with an amusing excess of style. The sequence comically foregrounds absurd or near-impossible things such as the unwrinkled white jacket topped off with the red carnation, the ability to see an approaching assailant in the eye of the naked woman he is kissing, even the seagull on the headgear. All of this is capped by Bond's unflappable suavity and his pun on the word "shocking."

After the credits we see the staples of the series. Bond reports to "M" (plate 42) in England for his next mission and, while doing so, engages in sexual banter with "M"'s secretary, Miss Moneypenny (plate 43). He also receives dazzling, high-tech equipment from the strained bureaucrat "Q" (plate 44). Then the mission begins, taking him to picturesque parts of the world and forcing him to outwit and outfight at least two villains: a perverse, megalomaniacal mastermind, here Goldfinger (plate 45) and a deadly henchman, here Oddjob (plate 46). The mastermind sets a plot in motion that would result in international chaos, and Bond thwarts it with little time to spare. He also kills the henchman in a brutal fight. He ends the film in an erotic encounter with a woman, here Pussy Galore (plate 47), whom he has met along the way.

The Bond Formula II: Sexuality

Bond's appeal to women is so powerful that many change their allegiances for him. Often the women are employed by the villain, and it is against their best interests to succumb to Bond's overtures. No sooner has he thwarted Jill Masterson, Goldfinger's bikini-clad accomplice, in a card-cheating scheme, than she is passionately kissing him and making plans to meet in his room. Later, Goldfinger's pilot, Pussy Galore, resists Bond's overtures. Her resistance even leads to a half-playful ju-jitsu fight which ends with Bond landing between her legs and kissing her. We see no more, but later learn that she had informed US authorities and thwarted Goldfinger's plot to blow up Fort Knox, thus changing sides and destroying her livelihood, all to save Bond, and all after one kiss.

The series presumes Bond to be irresistible to women and thus presents any resistance as coyness or an inability on the woman's part to recognize what is "good for her." These presumptions are used to justify extremely sexist behavior on Bond's part. In the scene in which they are alone in Goldfinger's barn, he even forcibly seizes Pussy in an attempt to kiss her. She resists and he seizes her again, and they fight. Bond overcomes her physical and sexual resistance, and this enables him to overcome Goldfinger.

Sexuality is central to the series. The credits are often shown over images of a naked woman's undulating body, and a common image used to advertise the films is that of Bond framed by the legs of a woman. Frequently, Bond is endangered by the woman or the woman's presence; he then turns the tables and gains control over the woman. This happens four times in *Goldfinger*. The first is with the woman in the precredit sequence, who clearly has set Bond up to be murdered. Secondly, he quickly seduces Jill Masterson away from Goldfinger, only to have Oddjob enter his bedroom, knock him unconscious, and murder Jill. Thirdly, in Europe, Jill's sister seems to have him in the sights of her rifle, but she fires and misses him. She was, in fact, aiming at Goldfinger, who was situated beyond Bond. Her resistance to Bond seems to be melting when she is killed. Finally, Pussy is Goldfinger's pilot, who takes the imprisoned Bond to the United States. All of the women pose a danger to Bond, yet he never doubts his power over any of them. They are also eminently discardable and, in this way, resemble the various gadgets Bond enjoys. None of these women come from earlier films, none appears in later ones, and two are killed in this one. Bond is briefly upset, but not much; the series implies that there will always be others.

In addition to the actual sexual encounters, the movie develops a pervasive atmosphere of sexual anticipation and by-play. It revels in barely veiled *double entendres*. The slang connotation of Pussy Galore's name is a good example, and even Bond is amusingly shocked when he hears it. It was so extreme for its time that the filmmakers expected the censors to delete it, and even had a back-up name, Kitty, for the character. Another example occurs when he is in bed with Jill Masterson. He answers the phone and declines a meeting on the grounds that "something big's come up," an obvious sexual pun.

The movie also jokes with pop-psychology references to weapons as male sexual symbols. When the exotic dancer asks Bond why he always wears his gun, he jokes, "I have a slight inferiority complex," although he clearly does not. He is skilled with guns and also with the high-tech equipment that "Q" gives him, such as the sports car equipped with everything from radar to machine guns to an ejector seat. But Bond does not need weapons to be powerful; he also functions ingeniously without them, so when the precredit assailant grabs Bond's gun, Bond uses an electrical appliance to defeat him.

The sexual symbol joke is on Goldfinger. He has large and expensive weapons, but they do not ultimately help him. When he captures Bond, he has him tied to a table and aims a large industrial laser between his legs (plate 48). Bond prevents his own castration by outwitting Goldfinger and getting him to turn the laser off. Goldfinger has the guns, but Bond has the power. Later, when the attack on Fort Knox is thwarted, Goldfinger pulls out a golden pistol. He eventually kills himself by stupidly firing his golden gun during a fight with Bond and getting sucked out of his own plane.

Variations in the Series

By *Goldfinger*, the continuity of the series was sufficiently ensured that the traditional closing title, "The End," was followed by "of *Goldfinger*. But James Bond will be back in *Thunderball*." The promise, then, is endless variations on the same formula. After *Thunderball* (1965) will come *You Only Live Twice* (1967), and so on. But series are not that simple, and the practicalities of long-term production lead in strange directions.

The Bond series contains extensive variations, including a remake. *Never Say Never Again* is a remake of *Thunderball*, both of which are based upon the same Fleming novel (a situation made possible by legal technicalities allowing a rival company to make a Bond film). The most obvious variations are in Bond himself. Five actors have played Bond. And the actors themselves change. Not only did Connery and Moore grow noticeably older in the part, but they also had different acting styles and skills. Timothy Dalton's Bond, as opposed to the promiscuous Bonds of Connery and Moore, had limited sexual encounters in the late 1980s' age of AIDS awareness; Pierce Brosnan has described himself as a "Bond for the '90s."

While different actors play Bond, they are all given significant star status as driving forces behind the series, as are the producers Harry Salzman and Cubby Broccoli. The directors are not. The Eon films have had a number of directors, such as Guy Hamilton, Terence Young, and John Glen, without its style being attached to any one of them, which is the case with many long-lived series such as the Tarzan, Sherlock Holmes, or *Star Wars* films. This is different from the situation with the two other major series started at United Artists in the 1960s. Both the "Man with No Name" and Pink Panther series are widely perceived as driven not only by the star (Clint Eastwood, Peter Sellers) but also by the director (Sergio Leone, Blake Edwards), as are the Indiana Jones films of the 1980s (Harrison Ford, Steven Spielberg).

The Bond series also reflects cultural and political changes over time. The first films presume a Cold War mentality, which dissipates in later films with the collapse of the Soviet Union. Bond's masculinity also changes: his sexist physical aggression on Pussy becomes unacceptable by the 1980s, and both Timothy Dalton's and Pierce Brosnan's Bonds have more involved relations with women. The series also shows an awareness of its own history. In *On Her Majesty's Secret Service* (1969), George Lazenby made references to the viewer about "the other fellow," meaning Connery, in the role. By *Moonraker* (1979), with its outer-space plot, the series was using a good deal of self-parody. A preview for *Tomorrow Never Dies* (1997) even jokes about audience familiarity with tropes of the series by having Pierce Brosnan, after adopting a traditional Bond stance, face the camera and say, "Bond. . . ." After a pause, indicating that it is no longer necessary to finish the famous line, he says, "You know the rest," referring to the tagline "Bond, James Bond," which has been part of the series since *Dr No*.

How Does the Bond Series Keep Going?

The Bond series has been going on for so long and has undergone so many changes that there is a debate as to what the **canon** of Bond films is. Is it just those seventeen films produced by Eon, which owns the rights to most of Ian Fleming's novels, even though they star five actors as Bond? Could it just be the seven films starring Connery as Bond, even though *Never Say Never Again* was not an Eon production? What about *Casino Royale* (1967), which has a number of Bond characters and was based upon Fleming's first Bond novel, but did not star Connery and was not produced by Eon? And if source novels are the issue, even Eon, by the time of *Octopussy*, no longer based the movies upon Fleming's novels but used short stories or original scripts with little but Fleming's titles on them.

Such variety can become bewildering until we refocus on the nature of series. Like sequels, they are closely related to remakes in attempting to reactivate something familiar in ways that are both repetitious and innovative – something old, something new. They set a cluster of elements into motion, hoping that the overall pattern remains similar from episode to episode even though individual components change. Generally, the characters of Bond, "M," "Q," and Moneypenny remain similar from episode to episode and are played by the same actors, although the original actors were replaced in the 1990s. The villains and the "Bond girls" are all different characters and actors, but they fit similar patterns. The villains, whether Dr No or Goldfinger, are perverse and megalomaniacal and unconcerned about mass killing; the "girls" are attractive and dangerous. The same theme music is used from film to film, but each film also has a distinctive theme song, such as Paul McCartney's "Live and Let Die" or Shirley Bassey's "Goldfinger." The overall assumption is that, even if the Bond actor or the "M" actor is replaced, the series can carry on by continuing the cluster of other components and finding replacements that fit the overall pattern. Another suave, tuxedo-clad actor will identify himself as "Bond, James Bond."

The audience also changes over time. What appealed to a 1963 audience might seem outdated or even offensive to a 2003 one. The trick to maintaining a series, then, is to adapt some of the cluster of its components not only to provide variations in each installment but also to keep up with shifting audience tastes and beliefs. Most series die after a few films because they cannot reconfigure themselves in this complex way. Such activations of differential elements of the formula make a "battle of the Bonds" possible. They also account for differences in meaning among installments, since it is not one element that is carried over, but a cluster, and changes always affect the whole. This also happens with remakes, even a remake with an unprecedented degree of similarity to its source as Gus Van Sant's *Psycho*.

Psycho (1960)

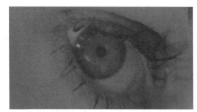

Fig. 6.14

Fig. 6.15

Halfway through Alfred Hitchcock's *Psycho* (1960), we see a profoundly disturbing **close-up** of Marion Crane's (Janet Leigh) dead eye (figure 6.14). She has just been slashed to death in the film's famous shower scene; her body has partially fallen out of the shower and her head lies awkwardly on the floor. We then see a slowly whirling close-up of her motionless eye. This follows two graphically matching shots, one of the spraying, circular shower head, and one of the circular shower drain with water and Marion's blood swirling into it (figure 6.15). The camera slowly moves back from Marion's eye, out of the bathroom and into her motel room, pausing on the newspaper containing the stolen money that brought her to this motel in the first place, and then continues on to a window showing the haunted-looking home of Norman Bates, her killer.

Narrative and Formal Elements

The **shot** is disturbing on many levels beyond the fact that it abruptly confronts us with the eye of a dead woman who, moments before, had been young, vital, and planning her future. Within *Psycho*'s narrative, the shot indicates a development almost unheard of in mainstream cinema: the narrative's central character and its primary goal have been obliterated in the middle of the film (see chapter 2 on narrative structure). According to traditional logic, the film has nowhere to go! Up to this point, *Psycho* has revolved almost exclusively around Marion. At its opening, we see that she is unhappy because her lover considers himself too debt-ridden to marry her. On an impulse, she steals $40,000 in cash from her job and drives from Phoenix to California to surprise him. Caught in a rainstorm, she stops at the motel to rest. Just prior to entering the shower, she decides to return the money. Now, abruptly, she is dead and her killer unknowingly disposes of the money with her body. Up to this point and conforming with classical Hollywood practice, the narrative had given us a clearly defined central character, Marion, and a clear goal, getting the money to enable her and her lover to be together. But both the main character and the money are suddenly gone, leaving the narrative to begin anew, to pick up the pieces, in the middle. The middle of what?

The shot of the eye works on another level, the thematic one of perception. Thus far, the film has been about Marion's perception, what she sees and thinks. The camerawork stresses this. As she drives to her boyfriend, we see many **close shots** of her pensive face (figure 6.16). The shots are frequently accompanied by voice-overs of what she thinks. We also see her responding anxiously to the gazes of others: the man who deposits the $40,000 leers at her and tries to engage her in sexual banter; soon after she steals the money, her boss sees her driving out of town after she had told him that she was going home to rest; a highway patrolman looks intimidatingly at her through mirrored sunglasses and then follows her; a used car salesman looks suspiciously at her when she does not haggle over the price of a car she wants to buy, and then again, when she almost drives off forgetting her luggage. Furthermore, we see her watched when she is unaware – Norman Bates (Anthony Perkins), the proprietor of the motel, watches through a secret peephole as she disrobes. Much of the film is about the implications of seeing and being seen (and its second half centers on Norman's profoundly disordered perceptions, ending with him staring directly into the camera: figure 6.17). Particularly within this context, the abrupt cessation of Marion's ability to see, signified by her apparently staring dead eye, is profoundly disturbing.

Fig. 6.16

On a formal level, the shot of her eye not only graphically matches the shot of the circular shower head but it also graphically matches the one of the circular shower drain as water and Marion's blood swirl into it.

Fig. 6.17

We have just watched her life's blood swirling away and now we see her eye and it is the camera that swirls.

Reception Context

The shot also involves things that would have affected audiences in 1960 differently from those of today. The film was made near the end of the three-decade period during which Hollywood films hoping for broad distribution needed the Production Code Seal of Approval. That approval required conformity to detailed censorship stipulations concerning what could and could not be shown. This scene included potentially censurable images, which gave the film a disturbing, and titillating, tone for contemporary audiences. The scene is set in a bathroom, shows a toilet, and implies nudity. Few films released under the Production Code showed bathrooms, and virtually none showed either toilet bowls or nudity. The shot moves from Marion's eye past the toilet, in which a clue is hidden. The framing and rapid **editing** of the shots in the shower scene employ a peek-a-boo strategy that makes us think we see her nude body, although in fact we do not. Even earlier shots of Marion in brassière and slip were "daring" for the time (figure 6.18). After the Production Code was discarded in the late 1960s, things such as implied or actual nudity, undergarments, and toilets became commonplace. Such images do not carry the same implications of the "forbidden" for today's audiences. In fact, people seeing the same film today might not consider anything "daring" about the images at all.

The film closes as Norman looks directly at us, the camera. Entirely mad at this point, he believes himself to be the mother he murdered ten years before. In Norman's disordered mind, his body is her body, his voice is her

Fig. 6.18

voice, and his eyes are her eyes. A **match dissolve** superimposes his mother's mummified, eyeless skull upon Norman's staring face (figure 6.19), and both shots dissolve into the film's closing shot of Marion's car, with her body in the trunk, being retrieved by a large chain from a swamp. Marion can longer see, as in a way Norman no longer can because his personality has been erased by that of his mother within him. But the fact that Norman/Norman's mother stares directly at us engages our perception in a disturbing way. The shot vio-lates traditional "invisible-style" practice by having the actor stare directly into the camera and implicates our own voyeurism in watching the film.

Fig. 6.19

Psycho opens with long, panning shots of Phoenix, Arizona. The camera finally moves into a hotel bedroom to show Marion and her lover. As it enters the window, it introduces the film's voyeuristic strategy as it passes one of the film's many bathrooms on its way to the bed and the illicit lovers. This scene shows Marion in her undergarments; later, we see what Norman sees as he watches her disrobe through the peephole, and, soon after, we see her die. Then something very unusual happens. Norman places her body and belongings in the trunk of her car (the image of which later closes the film) and drives the car into a nearby swamp. It sinks part way but then stops. Hitchcock **cuts** repeatedly to shots of Norman watching from the shore and becoming distressed. If the car does not sink, the body will be discovered. As he seems close to panic, the car sinks and we see him relieved.

This sequence engages spectators in a very perverse manner. Hitchcock has constructed the film to this point around viewer sympathy with Marion. But here, minutes after her brutal murder, he radically shifts our point of view and invites us to identify with the man attempting to dispose of her body. The relief in Norman's face when the car sinks invites a parallel relief in us. But if we share Norman's relief, as many do, the scene has disturbing implications. The film is about watching, and shows us that watching can not only lead to frightening revelations about a character's interior life but also to horrible consequences. What are we doing watching it? Furthermore, if in fact we are disturbed by the shot of Marion's dead eye, how can we so quickly shift our allegiance to her killer?

Psycho's Legacy

Psycho was remarkably successful upon its release and has remained one of the most influential movies in history. In June 2001, the American Film Institute placed it in the number one position on their list of the one hundred top thrillers of all time. It has inspired two sequels (*Psycho II*, 1983 and *Psycho III*, 1986), a made-for-TV prequel (*Psycho IV: The Beginning*, 1990 – all films mentioned up to this point involved Anthony Perkins), a made-for-TV movie (*Bates Motel*, 1987) and, as we will discuss below, a remake (*Psycho*, 1998). Furthermore, it is widely acknowledged as inaugurating the era of the modern horror movie, both in its graphic use of violence, often cited as the inspiration for "slasher" movies such as *The Texas Chainsaw Massacre* (1974), and in its placing the source of its horror within the traditional family unit (see chapter 1).

Psycho and Hitchcock's Authorship

Alfred Hitchcock was a singularly successful director whose career, beginning in the silent era, spanned more than half a century. He was one of the few directors whose style was so popular with the general public that his name was used in marketing his films. *Psycho* marked a daring and radical shift in his career. Unlike anything he had done before, it brought to the surface sinister implications of earlier films. By the late 1950s his style had become associated with glamorous thrillers, exciting chase scenes, macabre comedy, and sexual *double entendres.* His previous film, *North by Northwest* (1959), for example, followed the stylish Cary Grant and Eva Marie Saint characters through a number of attractive locales across the United States, from the United Nations Building in New York to Mount Rushmore. It closed implying that they were about to make love in the cabin of a moving train. The film's last shot, comically implying sexual intercourse, shows the train in long shot zooming into a tunnel.

Psycho was nothing like this. Shot in black and white on a small budget in only thirty-seven days, it is stark, unglamorous, seemingly humorless (although Hitchcock called it a comedy), and graphically horrifying. It deals with perverse material and employs a radical narrative structure. However, this harshness was ameliorated at the time by Hitchcock's authorial image. By 1960 he had become a widely recognized celebrity as a result of his popular television show (*Alfred Hitchcock Presents,* which began in 1955, went from a half-hour to an hour show in 1962, and continued until 1965), in which he appeared as a witty host who delighted in the macabre. He used this image to promote *Psycho,* and the trailer showed him escorting the viewer through the film's various sets and ending at the shower. The trailer implies a style of humor entirely absent from the film but, with contemporary audiences, linked his cherubic image to the film.

Hitchcock had long toyed with censorship restrictions, often cleverly implying things that could not be shown, and he pushed it one step further in his television series. Fully aware that the shows had to abide by current censorship restrictions, such as the requirement that all crimes must be punished, he often presented shows in which that did not happen. At the end, however, he would appear and tell the audience a preposterous resolution that conformed to censorship codes. It was his way of winking with the audience at the censors, of showing his audience a story whose logical conclusion violated censorship norms, but then verbally adding an ending as an epilogue that, while satisfying the letter of censorship constraints, underscored by its very absurdity the silliness of such constraints.

Such comically tacked-on justifications relate to a career-long indifference to certain narrative continuities in his films. When he worked with Raymond Chandler a decade earlier, Chandler complained that Hitchcock would always come up with an idea for a spectacular shot that had no relation to narrative logic, and then want his screenwriter to invent a justification for it. The closing of *Psycho* relates to this. It, almost desperately, presents a psychologist's long and complicated explanation of Norman's disorder to justify the behavior we have witnessed.

This strange movie has shown us some odd things. Not only has it changed its narrative direction in mid-film but it has also built the body of its story on a "secret." We learn that Mrs Bates – whom we think we have seen and heard repeatedly, whom we heard arguing repeatedly with Norman, whom we saw attack Marion, whom we saw Norman physically carry downstairs while they loudly argued – in fact does not exist but has been dead for ten years!

We get shocking evidence of this when Marion's horrified sister Lila (Vera Miles) discovers Mrs Bates's mummified body (figure 6.20), followed immediately by the image of Norman wearing a dress and wig and brandishing a large knife (figure 6.21). But those images so joltingly contradict what we have seen earlier that it takes a long expository scene at the end by a psychologist to lull us into the impression that it all actually does make sense. We are told that Norman was

Fig. 6.20

psychologically split. After murdering his mother out of jealousy, his guilt impelled him to deny his action and recreate her within himself. He mummified and cared for her body, dressed up as her and at times even spoke in her voice, sometimes arguing in two voices with himself. On one level, it seems a desperate narrative logic. On a deeper level (somewhat primed for audiences by national interest in the notorious Ed Gein case of the late 1950s, the inspiration for the novel on which the film was based), however, it conforms to the film's logic. Norman is a split character with a secret; so also is Marion at the time of her death. These appear in a film with a narrative that is split in two, a film with a secret.

Fig. 6.21

Hitchcock's biographical image inflects the film in many ways. He clearly used the image he cultivated with his television show to promote the film as just good, scary fun. The well-known French director François Truffaut, in his book on Hitchcock, discusses elements of the film, such as the shower scene, to celebrate Hitchcock's technical skill as a filmmaker. More recently, however, feminist scholars have pointed to the film as not "just good fun" but as revealing a darker side of Hitchcock, and part of a career-long pattern of placing attractive women in situations of embarrassment and danger and often brutally punishing them.

Psycho (1998)

Gus Van Sant's *Psycho* is one of the most extreme remakes in history, and an examination of it underscores much of the logic behind remakes. On the one hand, it conforms to some of the traditional patterns for remakes: it is in color where the original was in black and white; it uses actors popular in the late 1990s, many of whom were not even born when Hitchcock's film appeared; its music and sound were recorded in multi-track stereo where the original sound was in mono; on the other hand, however, it follows the earlier film to an almost unheard of degree. As Van Sant publicized during the making and release of the movie, it follows Hitchcock's film almost shot by shot, line of dialogue by line of dialogue. Joseph Stefano, who wrote Hitchcock's film, wrote this one, and the scene structure and dialogue are almost identical. Comparably, Bernard Hermann's music from Hitchcock's film is used, as is Saul Bass's credit design.

Fig. 6.22

Although the movie is set in the 1990s and items like furniture, automobiles, hairstyles, and clothing are of the 1990s and not the 1950s, the film does not foreground the temporal difference. Van Sant used Hitchcock's floorplans for many of the sets, such as the Bates Motel, so that, although the furniture may be different, the blocking is similar. He even filmed according to Hitchcock's thirty-seven-day shooting schedule and invited Hitchcock's daughter, Pat, to the set when he shot a scene that paralleled one in which she had acted nearly forty years earlier. More extremely, he showed some scenes from the Hitchcock film on the set to the actors and crew just prior to shooting the comparable scenes in this film. In many cases, not only do the camerawork and blocking of scenes in the two movies match, so also do the line readings of the actors.

This extends to visual and thematic **motifs**. In both films, when Norman serves supper to Marion in the parlor behind the motel office, he discusses his interest in taxidermy. The framing of the shots in the scene associates him with birds he has stuffed, which are displayed around the room. When Norman begins to discuss the tensions of his relationship with his mother, the camera on him shifts from a frontal shot to a low angle, side perspective, placing him in the same frame with birds in predatory attack positions, with wings outspread, on the wall (figure 6.22; plate 49). They visually imply a menace behind Norman's shy manner. Marion is also associated with birds, but generally gentle songbirds. In this scene we see small, non-menacing birds near her. Only when she stands to leave do we see a larger, beaked, more sinister-looking stuffed bird to her left, poised as if menacing her. Pictures of docile looking birds hang on the wall in her room. This fits into the larger pattern of bird imagery in the films: Marion's last name is Crane, Norman tells her she eats "like a bird" and that his mother is as harmless as one of his stuffed birds; the film even begins in Phoenix.

Comparably, both movies develop a central theme of dysfunctional or non-supportive families. Norman's murder of his mother and psychotic reincarnation of her is the most dramatic instance, but we also learn that his father died when he was young and that he murdered a lover of his mother. Marion's parents are dead and she lives with her sister. Her desire to be married is thwarted because of her lover's draining familial entanglements – his dead father's debts and alimony he pays to his ex-wife. The only family resembling a traditional one is that of late-middle-aged deputy sheriff Al Chambers, and he appears only briefly.

Extreme similarities of shots, camera movements, dialogue, sets, sound and music, character relations, visual motifs and themes – what is going on? This far exceeds the traditional pattern of remakes which use a good deal of material from the original, but also develop in new ways, often ways adapted to the difference in times. One example is *A Perfect Murder*, a remake of Hitchcock's own *Dial M for Murder* (1954 – also remade in a 1981 made-for-TV movie), which appeared in 1998, the same year as *Psycho*. Another example is Brian De Palma's 1983 remake of Howard Hawks's *Scarface* (1932; see chapter 1). Like the Hawks film, it deals with a gangster from an ethnic minority in the United States who rises to the top of a criminal empire only to die violently. As with *Psycho*, different actors are involved (Al Pacino instead of Paul Muni) and the film is in color instead of black and white, but, unlike *Psycho*, no attempt is made for shot-by-shot parallels, and substantial changes of locale and history give it an entirely different cultural and thematic structure. Al Pacino's gangster is a Cuban émigré involved in drug trafficking in the Miami of the 1980s, whereas Paul Muni's Scarface was ethnically Italian and involved in bootleg liquor in the Chicago of the 1920s. And, aside from *Dial M for Murder*, a number of Hitchcock films have been conventionally remade, including one by Hitchcock himself. In 1956 he released a remake of his 1935 *The Man who Knew Too Much*. His 1935 *The Thirty Nine Steps* was remade in 1959 and again in 1978; *The Lady Vanishes* (1938) was remade in 1979; *Strangers on a Train* (1951) was remade as *Once You Kiss a Stranger* in 1969; and *Rear Window* (1954) as a made-for-TV movie in 1998.

Psycho also exceeds the pattern mentioned above in the *Friday the 13th* and *Halloween* films, in which successive films pattern themselves upon preceding ones in a highly formulaic way. Although audiences of those films expect "the same" experience, it does not involve shot-by-shot parallels. However, there are certain precedents for different movies that are identical in many ways. As a strategy for international **distribution** in the early sound era, some movies were shot simultaneously in different languages, using the same sets and sometimes the same actors. Josef von Sternberg shot *The Blue Angel* (1930) in both German and English at the same time. When Universal made *Dracula* (1931) with Bela Lugosi, a Spanish language version was shot at the same time using the same sets but different actors and production crew for the Mexican market. One might term this a process producing simultaneous remakes.

A closer, stranger, and more germane precedent involves Hitchcock. In 1985, five years after his death, NBC (and in 1987–8, USA Cable Network) ran a "new" Alfred Hitchcock television series in color, introduced by Hitchcock himself! His black-and-white introductions from the original television series were colorized and used in newly made episodes. In some cases the episodes were color remakes of the original ones; in others, new scripts were used. Here, we have the actual footage of Hitchcock reprocessed and used as if it were shot for the new show.

The extremes of similarity in the 1998 *Psycho*, however, should not blind us to the differences. It is, after all, a film in color; it uses a different cast; some scenes are constructed differently; some shots have no parallels whatsoever in the earlier film. Furthermore, however closely the movie approximates the earlier one, we are, in fact, looking at images and listening to sounds that are entirely new to this film. But before discussing things unique to this film, we will address what Van Sant was up to in the first place.

Van Sant knew full well that his remake deviated from traditional film practice and that it would outrage many Hitchcock lovers. However, as precedents for his rationale, he cited the multiple film versions of *Hamlet*, which confine themselves to Shakespeare's dialogue and scene structure. One might also look for parallels in other art forms, such as ballet, music, and theater, where close recreations of earlier productions are often valued. Of course, one might argue that those forms generally involve live performance, and much of the value of close recreations comes from the fact that the earlier performances are no longer available to audiences. Films that are remade, however, are generally available to audiences. But even when they are, their reception context, as discussed above, changes over time. Van Sant's remake strategy, while unusual in movie history, is neither without precedent nor parallel.

Van Sant's other films (including *Drugstore Cowboy*, 1989, *My Own Private Idaho*, 1991, *To Die For*, 1995, *Good Will Hunting*, 1997, and *Finding Forrester*, 2000) are noted for their diversity of ambition and creativity. *Psycho*, however, made within a critical climate that often values originality, virtually defies that notion. Many directors, when required to work within a formula, such as that of a series, have complained that the limitations of the formula hampered their creativity. Here, Van Sant actively chose such limitation. In this, he resembles Hitchcock, who took great pleasure in surmounting, and publicizing, self-imposed formal constraints. His feature-length *Rope* (1948), for example, appears to be a single, uninterrupted shot; *Lifeboat* (1944) and *Rear Window* (1954) largely confine themselves to single sets throughout the entire film. Clearly, limitations that would drive some directors mad provide welcome artistic challenges to others.

A further aspect of the reception context for the two films is that the 1960 *Psycho* was a Hitchcock film with a "secret." The 1998 one did not have Hitchcock and the "secret" had an entirely different status. *Psycho*'s fame is extensive (not only through recirculations of Hitchcock's film but also through sequels, the prequel, and other activations), and "Norman Bates" and "Bates Motel" have become popular terms for demented, murderous people and dangerous places. There was even a *Saturday Night Live* skit about the Norman Bates School of Hotel and Motel Management. The *Psycho* house is part of the Universal Studio tour, and the shower scene, with Bernard Hermann's music, is one of the most parodied in history. It is hard to expect audiences to be fooled by a secret contained in one of the most popular movies ever made, so by 1998 the secret was hardly a secret at all. In fact, along with the shower scene, knowledge of the secret may be the piece of information audiences could be most counted upon to bring to their first watching of the new film.

The cultural climate also changed considerably between 1960 and 1998. Shots such as those of the toilet and of Marion in her undergarments no longer have the same "daring" connotations of comparable shots in Hitchcock's film. In implicit acknowledgment of this, the opening hotel-room scene shows Sam (Viggo Mortensen), Marion's naked lover, walk to a window and we see him naked from behind. Such a shot would have been impossible to show in 1960; in 1998 it had very little shock value. Comparably, at the end of the murder scene when she has fallen partially out of the shower, we also see Marion's (Anne Heche) naked rear end. Audiences in 1998, who have just witnessed her brutal murder, are hardly likely to see anything transgressive about that shot. A more complex instance, since it affects characterization, occurs with the 1998 shot in which Norman secretly watches Marion disrobe. Although framed similarly, this shot lasts much longer than the 1960 one and indicates, through sound effects and body motion, that Norman (Vince Vaughn) masturbates as he watches. This could never have been shown in 1960 and there was no hint of masturbatory activity in Hitchcock's film. While Norman's actions are disgusting, the showing of such things within the current movie climate is neither uncommon nor particularly shocking.

A number of things are entirely new to this film. We see brief, interpolated shots as Marion and, later, the detective Arbogast (William H. Macy) are killed. The shots most likely signify visions of what goes through their minds as they die. As Marion dies, we see shots of clouds; as the mortally wounded Arbogast falls backwards down a staircase, we see, first, a shot of a nearly naked woman, then a shot of a steer through the rain-soaked windshield of an approaching car, then a fuzzy shot of a knife-wielding Norman (dressed as his mother) approaching. These images acquire a startling power in their unexpected departure from the logic of the rest of the film.

Unique to this film, for obvious reasons, is its color scheme. The movie's colors are largely unsaturated until the shower scene, when Marion's bright red blood appears on the starkly white bathroom with dramatic visual potency. Counterpointing the intensity of the deep red on bright white of the shower scene, much of the rest of the movie develops an orange motif. We first see Marion in an orange bra and slip; at the used car lot she uses an orange parasol; her dress is mostly orange. When she arrives at the Bates Motel in the rain, Norman greets her with an orange umbrella. The walls of her room often appear orange, as do those of Norman's office. Her sister, Lila (Julianne Moore), and Arbogast have red hair that sometimes looks orange, and the color often appears in clothing, in the polished wood surfaces in the Bates house, and elsewhere.

One major scene is shot and edited in a manner substantially different from its counterpart in the 1960 film. In both, Lila goes down into the fruit cellar and discovers the mummified corpse of Mrs Bates, is then attacked by Norman, who is then subdued. But in this film Lila finds the body in a separate section of the cellar, facing a small aviary of live birds, rather than alone (plate 50). Sam stops the attacking Norman, but unlike Anthony Perkins's character, this Norman is about to get away (plate 51) and retrieve his knife until Lila rushes up and kicks him in the face (plates 52 and 53). This film makes her a much more aggressive woman than her more passive 1960 counterpart.

There are other differences, but they are much less important than the simple fact that, by its radical approach to remaking, this film makes us consider important issues concerning the very process of remaking. Like series and sequels, remakes engage and evoke earlier films. But even when a remake is as unusually similar to its source as the 1998 *Psycho*, it is far from a simple repetition of what has already been done. These increasingly pervasive forms of filmmaking acknowledge complex relationships between the new film and previous films and the times in which they were made.

SELECTED READINGS

Noël Carroll discusses how much and in what way 1970s and 1980s films directed by film-school graduates refer to and remake older films in "The Future of Allusion: Hollywood in the 70s (and Beyond)," *October 20* (Spring 1982), pp. 51–81. Our discussion of the shifts in the figure of James Bond as well as in the series over time, and especially our analysis of the precredit sequence of *Goldfinger*, draw upon Tony Bennett and Janet Woollacott's *Bond and Beyond* (New York: Methuen, 1987). The laser disk of *Goldfinger* provides the information on censorship concerns about Pussy Galore's name. François Truffaut's *Hitchcock* (New York: Simon and Schuster, 1984) discusses the direction of the shower scene in *Psycho*. Tania Modleski's *The Women who Knew Too Much: Hitchcock and Feminist Theory* (New York: Routledge, 1998) discusses feminist perspectives on Hitchcock's work. The Special Features section of the 1999 Universal DVD Video, Collector's Edition, of Gus Van Sant's *Psycho* includes interviews with Van Sant about his rationale for the remake, as well as footage of his screening scenes from Hitchcock's film on the set as he shot his remake.

7

ACTORS AND STARS

Morocco and *Dirty Harry*

We have all argued over favorite movie actors. Who is the sexiest, smartest, coolest, funniest, toughest, best looking, most talented? While we have certainly cited roles in specific movies as proof, we were really talking about something beyond individual films, an image of the actor that comes not only from acting roles but also from a sense of the actor's personality, talent, private and public life, work habits, sense of style, and love interests. Few people speak of these things with reference to the actor who played the President of the United States in *Clear and Present Danger* (1994), and yet many people bring such issues up when talking about Harrison Ford. Both are actors in the same film, but Ford is a movie star. What is the difference?

The actor who is someone's favorite – say, Julia Roberts, Tom Cruise, Cameron Diaz, or Jackie Chan – may not have been their favorite five years ago, or may not be five years from now. It is likely that one's parents and grandparents had different favorites whose appeal may not even make sense to that person now. Some of the reasons for this are discussed in chapter 8. Stars come and go and stars change over time, but they are an important and often misunderstood aspect of film.

Why are Stars Important?

Some fans will see their favorite stars in a movie regardless of what it is about or how it has been reviewed, and they will see it repeatedly. Stars receive the highest salaries in a movie's budget, some, like Arnold Schwarzenegger (figure 7.1) or Jim Carrey or Mel Gibson, earning in the tens of millions of dollars for a single

Fig. 7.1

movie. Several have entered the $20 million–plus category. Harrison Ford earned $20 million for playing the President of the United States in *Air Force One* (1997), which is a hundred times the salary of the real President of the United States! Why do stars earn so much? Why much more than the director or writer?

The most obvious answer is that the stars are the most visible people involved in the movie and that audiences will pay to see them. They are often a major component of a movie's narrative image, which is the "hook," or the implicit promise that advertising makes about what the viewer will experience when he or she sees the movie. Generally the name and image of the star overshadows the image of the character or role in the movie. Clark Gable's first movie after military service in World War II was *Adventure* (1945), co-starring Greer Garson. The ads screamed "Gable's Back and Garson's Got Him," as if the movie recorded a real-life romance between the actors rather than the characters they played. And the fact that Gable was "back" had nothing to do with the story of the movie but with the actor's personal life, as fans of the time knew.

What is a star, how does this interweaving of acting roles and personal life work, and why is it so important? In this chapter we first discuss some of the differences between movie and stage acting. Then we look at the difference between movie actors and movie stars. Finally, we discuss the history of the star system and show how a star's "image" is created over time.

Film and Stage Acting

In *The Last Action Hero* (1993), shots of Arnold Schwarzenegger (figure 7.2) are **intercut** with scenes from Laurence Olivier's *Hamlet* (1948). The Schwarzenegger scenes are shot in black and white, and the costuming, sets, even the skull Schwarzenegger contemplates, seem at first to blend in with Olivier's movie, but then he brutally flings the skull at the head of an approaching enemy. The character of Hamlet is known for self-doubt and inaction, but when threatening men appear, Schwarzenegger mows them down with an automatic weapon. The joke, of course, is that not only would this not happen in *Hamlet* but also that Schwarzenegger has a star image of power and decisive action that would make him unlikely to play Hamlet credibly. Hamlet may be the most famous dramatic role ever written, but that character is no action hero.

Laurence Olivier played Hamlet many times on stage before he made the Academy Award–winning movie. He was one of the most respected stage actors of the twentieth century and had a certain disdain for movie acting. From his perspective such disdain is understandable, since stage acting and movie acting are very different, even when the same role – Hamlet – is involved.

Fig. 7.2

Movie and theatrical stardom are also different. Renowned stage actors seldom have the international visibility that film stars do, nor do their personal lives become confused with their roles on stage. Furthermore, the career-building challenges of major stage actors to play roles in which other actors have excelled, like Hamlet or Lady Macbeth or Hedda Gabler or King Lear, in order to test their skills, does not exist with film stars. Film stars achieve success with individual roles and then move on to others. There is no such thing as a circulating repertory of film roles as there is on stage.

Furthermore, theater actors often pride themselves on the variety of roles they have mastered, demonstrating not only their skill but also their versatility. At times, for example, well-known actors performing *Othello* have exchanged the major roles of Othello and Iago on successive nights, showing their skill in one major role, then in another. This taking on of diverse roles, even roles with which other actors have become famous, is not a major part of film stardom, with the relatively minor exceptions of stars doing film versions of famous plays, such as Mel Gibson in *Hamlet* (1990), or some frequently revived roles, such as Christopher Plummer playing Sherlock Holmes in *Murder by Decree* (1979) or Robert De Niro as the monster in *Mary Shelley's Frankenstein* (1994).

This model of versatile stage acting has influenced film criticism. Some reviewers prize actors known for a wide range of roles (such as Marlon Brando, Denzel Washington, Meryl Streep, Dustin Hoffman, Robert De Niro, or James Earl Jones) over actors known for a more limited range (such as Doris Day, Kevin Costner, Clint Eastwood, Robert Mitchum, and John Wayne). In fact, the second type, those with a more unified star persona, have been disparaged for "playing themselves," which does their skills a disservice. Such disparagement reinforces popular presumptions that movie actors are inferior to stage actors.

A movie actor does not create his or her role in the same way a stage actor does (see chapter 9). Both perform as a character based upon a script, but those performances are neither constructed by the actor nor received by the audience in the same way. A stage actor creates the full performance in one space and time before a live audience. He or she performs the entire play with great intensity for two or three hours and is responsible for the timing, the continuity, the modulation, and the shaping of the whole performance. He or she can also vary the performance from night to night to keep it "fresh" and to adapt to the moods of different audiences.

A movie actor seldom performs for more than a few minutes at a time, and the average is much less. He or she acts not before an audience but before a camera, and has little ability to control the overall modulation of the performance. The actor's performance occurs in short bits over a roughly three-month period, and the entire work is shot and pieced together by other people.

But more than that, even when performing, a movie actor does not control the performance in the way a stage actor does. A stage actor performs before an audience that sees his or her whole body on a stage from slightly different perspectives. With relatively minor help from lighting, stage and sound effects, and music, it is the actor's voice and gestures that affect the audience. That is not the case with a movie. A movie actor does not know exactly what part of his or her body the camera is photographing (in many instances, there are several cameras shooting the action from different positions, and even the director doesn't know which footage, if any, will be used) or what the difference in effect on the audience will be from a close-up or a medium or long shot. He or she cannot know how a long speech will be edited. Will it be shown performed in its entirety, or will other actors' responses be cut in? What else will be on the sound track? Furthermore, a movie audience sees the actor in a different way from the way in which the stage audience sees its actor – not a full body in a confined, actual space, but a constantly changing array of perspectives on that body in an ever-changing photographic space.

A classic example of the relation of other components to an actor's film performance was reportedly demonstrated by the founder of the world's first film school, Lev Kuleshov, who was also a famous Russian director of silent movies. He took a shot of an actor with a blank expression on his face and intercut it with shots of a bowl of soup, a girl, and a child's coffin. He claimed that those who viewed it were deeply impressed by the actor's subtle and moving "performance" – his look of hunger for the soup, kindly affection for the girl, and sorrow at the coffin. Then Kuleshov told them that it was the same shot; the man had not varied his expression at all. The impressions of hunger, affection, and sorrow seemingly created by the actor's "performance" of his character's emotions toward what he saw were, in fact, created by the editing and were projections of those emotions by the audience on to the actor.

This experiment is sometimes cited to claim that movie actors have little talent or, to use Alfred Hitchcock's term, are like "cattle." It would support the disdain that stage actors like Olivier sometimes felt about film acting, but such disdain does not really show an awareness of the difference between the two activities or the areas in which the true talents of some movie actors lie.

Fig. 7.3

A powerful moment in *The Searchers* (1956, see chapter 4) comes when John Wayne's tortured character looks in vain for his kidnapped niece among rescued Indian captives. He is about to leave when one girl, driven insane by her captivity, screams. As he turns to glare in fury at her (figure 7.3), the camera **dollies** in for a close-up of his tormented face (figure 7.4). It is a haunting moment that could never be performed on a stage. Its power comes partly from Wayne's movement and facial expression, but also from the camera angle from which he is shot and from the camera movement, which changes what we see and soon fills the screen with Wayne's face. The **dolly shot** is particularly noticeable since there is only one other like it in the movie. The enlarged face, its beard stubble, and the dark shadow his hat brim casts on his eye become significant parts of the way in which the image affects us. Wayne's performance in this shot

Fig. 7.4

cannot be separated from the way in which it is photographed, from its relationship with the prior shots of the girl, and the powerful effect of the camera movement.

This fact does not diminish Wayne's strengths as a movie actor but shows that stage and film acting are different things. A performance of a play occurs when its actors perform it. A performance of a movie occurs long after the actor has performed, when the finished film is projected before an audience. A stage actor's death makes future stage performances impossible; in the case of movies, however, we are constantly entertained by recorded performances of deceased actors such as Marilyn Monroe, John Belushi, James Dean, Greta Garbo, Cary Grant, Robert Mitchum, and James Stewart.

A stage actor has a much more dominant role in the creation of a stage performance than a movie actor has in that of a film. This does not diminish the talents of movie actors; rather, it makes them people with different types of talents. Most successful film actors understand this and often make it their business to become knowledgeable about things like lighting and camera placement. If they rise in stature in the industry, they may seek script approval and choice of directors and co-stars in an attempt to increase their control over the construction of their performances.

Actors and Stars

Many talented actors never become stars, and some stars have minimal acting talent. A movie star is not only a featured player in a film but also someone who has been able to create an "image" that generates popular interest outside individual films. Such an image circulates through profiles and interviews, gossip columns, fan clubs and magazines, television talk and tabloid shows, and parody and imitation. It has been suggested that Clark Gable became an important star after the 1934 movie *It Happened One Night* not because he won an Academy Award but because in one scene he removed his shirt and was not wearing an undershirt (figure 7.5). This reputedly caused undershirt sales to drop in the United States because men wanted to imitate Clark Gable, which indicates that he was seen as something beyond the role he played in the movie. That "something" could also be used to market future films, as the "Gable's Back and Garson's Got Him" slogan shows. During the Vietnam War era, a popular bumper sticker read "John Wayne for Secretary of Defense," placing the star's image of powerful, decisive masculinity into the political arena.

In both of these cases there is a slippage of meaning between the actor in the role, the actor in real life, and the actor's image. It is quite common in talking about what a character does in a movie to use the actor's and not the character's name ("Wasn't Wesley Snipes vicious in *Demolition Man*?"), and even to complain that something the movie's character does is inappropriate for the actor's image.

Fig. 7.5

Some people, for example, felt it unlikely that a Robert Redford character would ever have to pay to have sex with a woman, as one does in *Indecent Proposal* (1993). Movie performances are always mediated connections between the actors and the audience, and most fans never see their movie idols in person. This, in a way, makes actors always as "alive" as they ever were in film performances and has led to the phenomenon of some stars, such as Marilyn Monroe or James Dean, being adored and reputedly receiving fan mail dozens of years after their deaths. People do not as much admire the star as they do the star image. But what is a star image?

A **star image** is a set of characteristics that has great popular appeal and that makes the actor a known and desired quantity. These characteristics do not necessarily remain constant and are often adjusted to suit changing audience tastes, industry trends, and the physical aging of the actors. Some stars have an almost rigidly fixed image that makes people think that they are not acting at all but are "playing themselves." Male action stars, such as John Wayne, Robert Mitchum, and Clint Eastwood, have been seen in this way. Sometimes a star's image becomes so fixed that even when he or she tries to break it by doing roles directly opposed to that image, the public ignores such deviations and continues to support the original image. Julie Andrews is a good example. Her image as a virginal, high-spirited innocent in G-rated films was established with her first film, *Mary Poppins* (1964) and immediately reinforced by *The Sound of Music* (1965). Her appearance in a more sexually sophisticated role in *The Americanization of Emily* (1964) at around the same time had no effect on the image, nor, over a decade later, did her topless appearance in *SOB* (1981) or another topless appearance in *Duet for One* (1987). People seem to want to see Julie Andrews as Mary Poppins, regardless of what else she does. Indeed, when she returned to that type of role in *The Princess Diaries* (2001), widespread critical response hailed her as the ultimate family actress, as if the other roles had never existed.

Some stars have no fixed images and are prized for the variety of roles they play. Examples are Kevin Spacey, Dustin Hoffman, Meryl Streep, and Jimmy Smits. But stars rise and fall, and the star system has a history.

The Star System

For its first fifteen years, cinema had no stars at all. Individual actors were not even named in most films or used to advertise them. After 1910, that changed. Stars first became visible and then began to wield great economic power. Part of the reason for the change was the awareness on the part of some **producers** that audiences would pay to see stars and would choose films on that basis. They opposed the policies of other producers to keep actors anonymous as a means of controlling the money actors could demand. By the mid-1910s, the **star system** was taking hold and actors like Charlie Chaplin were making over a million dollars a year. By the 1930s, the major studios placed a number of stars under exclusive contract and even created stars by means of carefully assigned film roles and publicity campaigns. When the **studio system** declined in the 1950s, many stars formed their own production companies and often participated directly in the production of their films, which is currently the situation.

Fig. 7.6

During this time, dominant cultural values and industry restrictions determined what kinds of people became stars. In classical Hollywood, virtually all stars were white. Actors of other races who achieved visibility did so in minor and highly stereotyped roles (see chapter 13). Hattie McDaniel, a black actress, achieved a certain stardom and even an Academy Award in secondary roles as mammies and maids in such films as *Gone with the Wind* (1939, figure 7.6). Stepin Fetchit became so famous as a shuffling, incompetent, servile character that his name has become a byword for negative black stereotypes.

In the 1960s, when the civil rights movement opened up some opportunities for minorities in the United States, Sidney Poitier received not peripheral but starring roles. He established a star persona as a wise, black man with seething restraint and dignity in a racist society. Subsequently, the limitations on Poitier's mostly heroic range for blacks have diminished and now actors like Wesley Snipes are able to play brutal villains in films like *Demolition Man* (1993) without feeling that they are demeaning their race.

A Star's Image

Hugh O'Brian, an actor known for playing Wyatt Earp in the popular 1950s' television series, recently described the course of an actor's career as reflected in five statements by a hypothetical producer. First, "Who's Hugh O'Brian?"; then "Get me Hugh O'Brian!"; then "Get me a Hugh O'Brian type!"; then "Get me a young Hugh O'Brian!"; and, finally, "Who's Hugh O'Brian?" This progression, from an unknown actor to one who gets work, to a popular "type" that producers want when they can no longer afford the original, to a younger version of the actor who has aged beyond the range of the type he created, to an unknown again, points to the fact that not only do actors and their images rise to and fall from popularity, but that they also change over time.

Let us look at the development of the **star image** of a major current star, Bruce Willis, and of a star of the studio era, James Cagney. Willis became extremely popular in the television series *Moonlighting* which began in 1985 and ran for four successful seasons. Before then, he had no star presence at all. Thus, before he ever made a movie, Bruce Willis was strongly fixed in the public's mind as a certain type of character – a wise-cracking, romantic, detective hero. Given the weekly exposure in the same role, it is inevitable that a TV actor will get typed in a show, especially if he is new, as Willis was, and the show is a long-running hit, as *Moonlighting* was. Those reasons may help account for the fact that many successful TV actors like David Caruso have had problems becoming successful film actors.

Willis's first film, *Blind Date* (1987), was a moderate success that played against type by having him cast in a slapstick comedy as a somewhat nerdy character who has to go on a blind date in order to meet a woman. The film appeared in the midst of his TV success. He followed this with *Sunset* (1988), a mixture of Western, comedy, action, and historical genres, in which he plays the legendary Hollywood cowboy star Tom Mix. These two films have had little or no lasting impact on Willis's star image, though they show him as an actor willing to take risks and expand his repertoire. These films, however, were followed by *Die Hard* (1988) and *Die Hard 2* (1990) and suddenly Willis had a whole new star image as a muscular action hero more closely related to an Arnold Schwarzenegger character than to the one he had played on *Moonlighting*. Even his body looked virtually unrecognizable from that in the TV series or the previous two films. It appeared as if he had been working out non-stop at the gym, creating a highly muscular, buff, body-builder physique. In place of the suits, shirts, and ties that covered his body in *Moonlighting*, in the *Die Hard* films he displayed his biceps and chest in clothing that exposed much of his torso.

Although Willis became a huge box-office success and continued to play muscular action heroes, he did two things that were very unusual for his kind of star at that historical moment. Perhaps most surprisingly, he took minor roles in small, independent films or even in films with a well-known established star. The most successful instance of the former was in Quentin Tarantino's *Pulp Fiction* (1994). Although it became an unexpected hit upon its release and then quickly became a cult classic, at the time it was a risky project. Willis had a comparatively small role in a film with an elaborately experimental narrative structure. Shortly thereafter, at the other end of the spectrum, he played a small supporting role in *Nobody's Fool* (1995), a Paul Newman star vehicle. Newman was a legend at the time the film was made and it was advertised as a Newman star vehicle.

Why would any star accept such roles? These were neither cameos, an old tradition for stars, nor leading roles but, rather, small supporting serious roles with diverse characterizations in quite different films. It had several effects on Willis's career. First, it complicated his star image more than that of any other action hero. It also gave him a reputation as an actor who wanted to do "serious" work rather than just genre "entertainment" (see chapter 5). This undoubtedly related to the wide range of roles that directors were willing to offer him. Brian De Palma, for example, cast Willis as a newspaper reporter in his adaptation of the best-seller, *Bonfire of the Vanities* (1990), and Alan Rudolph cast him as a car salesman in *Breakfast of Champions* (1999). Most importantly, M. Night Shyamalan cast Willis as a psychologist in his formally complex and hugely successful film, *The Sixth Sense* (1999, see chapter 3). Most action heroes would simply not have demonstrated the range of roles and acting skills necessary to be cast as a psychologist in a supernatural thriller.

Willis's major roles were now so broad that it is no exaggeration to say that, aside from skillful acting, his characters in *Moonlighting*, *Die Hard*, and *The Sixth Sense* have little in common. Willis has accomplished something that very few television actors do – he has not only built an extremely successful film career but he has done so in a manner that has all but obliterated any fixed association between him and his first major television role.

Throughout this successful career, Willis's private life has inflected his star persona in various ways. When he first rose to fame as a film actor, he was associated with wild bachelor-style living, rowdy parties, rock 'n' roll, fights, women, and so on. After marrying Demi Moore, his popular image changed to that of a responsible family man, a good husband and father. In 1998, however, he and Moore got divorced and visibility about Willis's family life lessened. These shifting images correlate in some ways with the shift in emphasis in his roles, his rowdy bachelor days coinciding with the predominance of the action star image and, despite his then very recent divorce from Demi Moore, the responsible family man who has settled down coinciding with *The Sixth Sense*.

Fig. 7.7

James Cagney provides quite a contrast to Willis. His first movie, *Sinner's Holiday* (1930), is almost unknown today. It was based on a Broadway play, *Penny Arcade*, in which he played the same role. What is surprising in the film today is that the whining and cowardly role Cagney plays has little resemblance to the star persona he later developed. His first major success was in *The Public Enemy* (1931), which was part of an early 1930s' trend for violent gangster movies that also included *Scarface* (1932, discussed in chapter 1). The aggressive, brutal, hyperkinetic, gangster Cagney played became the prototype for his image (figure 7.7). Throughout his career he generally played a man whose whole body seethed with repressed energy and tension which often exploded. Whether the film required him to gracefully and energetically tap dance, smash a grapefruit in a woman's face (figure 7.8), or explode into a demented rampage in a prison dining hall (figure 7.9), he radiated the charm and pathology of a modern, urban man filled with barely containable and unpredictable energy. These qualities contributed to his rise to stardom in gangster roles.

Fig. 7.8

By the mid-1930s strong social pressure forced the studios to ban gangster films due to their violent content, so Warner Brothers, the studio to which Cagney was under contract, starred him in *G Men* (1935), in which he played not a tough, hyperkinetic gangster, but a tough, hyperkinetic FBI agent fighting gangsters.

In the 1930s, Cagney not only went on strike against his studio over wages and supported the emerging Screen Actors Guild, but also as a private citizen was accused of having communist sympathies. Partly to counter the potential career damage of those accusations, he made *Yankee Doodle Dandy* in 1942, a patriotic film

Fig. 7.9

biography of George M. Cohan in which Cagney did a good deal of singing and dancing. It became the most successful film of his career and may have helped shield him from the legal and career problems many left-wing Hollywood people suffered in the late 1940s and 1950s during the McCarthy period. In the late 1940s, when his career was sagging and he was becoming visibly older and heavier, he returned to the gangster form and made *White Heat* (1949) about a psychotic gangster. While he personally disliked the gangster form by this time, he realized that his star image was indelibly associated with it, and it could be used to revive his career.

Cagney's image remained a powerful one for nearly half a century. It provides a good example of not only a popular star image, but also of a number of variations on that image for reasons of popular genres (the gangster film) as well as the fall from fashion of those genres (see chapter 5), personal image problems with little direct relation to film roles (left-wing accusations), and career revival. Some of these roles, and others in his long career, differ extremely. What relation does a patriotic song-and-dance man have with a demented gangster who sits in his mother's lap, and what connection do both have with an FBI agent? They have James Cagney. The sense of a unified star image remained powerful throughout his life and continues today, long after his death, when his image is still used by impersonators and in commercials.

We will now look at two stars in roles that helped define their images, Marlene Dietrich in *Morocco* and Clint Eastwood in *Dirty Harry*, and examine the relationship between individual films and star images. *Morocco* helped establish Dietrich as a star with an image of exotic and erotic femininity, and she maintained her image by making major adjustments to her exotic, national, and feminine identity over her long career. *Dirty Harry* built upon Eastwood's images as both a Western hero and a modern police detective to establish him as an icon of powerful American masculinity, an image he complicated and developed over the next three decades.

Fig. 7.10

Morocco (1930) and Marlene Dietrich

Marlene Dietrich's first musical number in her first American film, *Morocco* (1930), helped solidify her star image. Her character, Amy Jolly, is booed when she appears before an unruly audience in a Moroccan nightclub dressed in men's formal clothes. She responds by staring in a half-indifferent way at the audience, calmly smoking a cigarette, and waiting (figure 7.10). Tom Brown (Gary Cooper), a Foreign Legionnaire in the audience, is taken with her beauty and calms the crowd (figure 7.11). She then sings in French and wins over the audience. After the song, she enters the crowd, stopping at one table to ask a woman for a flower and, receiving it, kissing

Fig. 7.11

Fig. 7.12

Fig. 7.13

Fig. 7.14

her on the mouth (figure 7.12). Again she is cheered. She soon tosses the flower to Tom, who wears it behind his ear (figure 7.13). After a second song, she secretly gives him her room key.

Kennington (Adolphe Menjou), a wealthy artist who has fallen desperately in love with Amy (figure 7.14), observes the action. He has asked to see her after the show and has been refused. The sight of her obvious infatuation with Tom pains him. Similar romantic pain pervades the film. Kennington is seated at a table with Adjutant Caesar, who is Tom's embittered commanding officer, and Mme Caesar. Not only is it implied that Kennington has had an affair with Mme Caesar, but Tom boldly waves at her and it is evident from her expression that she is desperately in love with him. Her husband seems bitterly aware of all of this. The public flirtation of Amy and Tom, then, occurs within a complicated erotic context. Later that night, Mme Caesar, tormented with jealousy, will try to have Tom murdered; later in the film, her husband will also try to murder him. Kennington pursues Amy with great intensity, dignity, and repressed agony, fully realizing all along that she loves Tom. *Morocco* is an exotic-looking movie about decadent people in a foreign place who experience great passion, cruelty, and pain; these associations became central to Dietrich's star image.

In this scene, Dietrich's character controls all. She fascinates Tom and Kennington, infuriates Mme Caesar and a woman sitting with Tom, and wins over the unruly audience with the sheer power of her presence. That presence would also make Dietrich a star unique in Hollywood history.

Dietrich's Star Presence

What kind of presence creates such a star? Most obviously it is a highly erotic presence. Dietrich is a beautiful woman, but her presentation here involves more than that. The movie was directed by Josef von Sternberg, known for his creative cinematography and lighting, and photographed by Lee Garmes, one of the most talented cinematographers in Hollywood history. Dietrich is

Fig. 7.15

Fig. 7.16

frequently shot in diffused light, through obscuring smoke and shadows in a manner that creates an appealing but mysterious and often contradictory presence. The intricate shadows that often partially obscure her face were an unusual departure from the full lighting characteristic for actresses of the time. Much of what she does as an actress is to quietly look and be looked at, as when she greets the unruly audience. She moves slowly, even while performing on stage, and holds herself very still while interacting with other characters. Such nearly static moments allow the viewer unusually long periods to contemplate her beauty and the beauty of the manner in which she is photographed. Furthermore, there is often great ambiguity in her expressions.

Later in her career, while making a film without von Sternberg, Dietrich became upset because she felt the new director was simply making her look like any other pretty woman. She realized that her appeal lay not simply in her physical attractiveness, but also in the way in which she was photographed. She made it her business to learn a great deal about lighting and cinematography in order to protect her screen image.

The film presents her in a number of boldly contrasting ways, not only visually, but also in character behavior, setting, and narrative situation. We first see her on a foggy night on a ship, wearing a veil, and looking weak and depressed (figure 7.15). An officer describes her as a "suicide ticket," a type of woman who comes to Morocco on a one-way fare, never to return. Kennington approaches her but is rebuffed on the grounds of her wearied suspicion of all men's motives. Her melancholic reserve in this scene contrasts with the arrogant sexuality of her performance in the musical number but, in both instances, the narrative presents her as a woman with a "past."

The pattern of her life becomes evident when, in her dressing room, Tom notices a picture of her in an expensive sable coat and asks if she still has it. She replies that, if she still had it, she would not be where she is. Tom also notices pictures of a man. She has clearly had romantic ups and downs, and this pattern repeats itself. She later becomes engaged to the wealthy and loving Kennington, only to throw it all away to run off into the desert after Tom's regiment as a desperate and degraded "camp follower" (figure 7.16).

Dietrich's Exotic Sexuality

The image of a jaded but passionate woman became part of Dietrich's star persona. This was reinforced at the time by the fact that American audiences knew her to be German, which in the early 1930s carried with it associations of exotic sexual daring and decadence. The movie reinforces these associations not only by making her a woman with a past, but also by showing her dressed in men's clothing and kissing a woman on the mouth. She is a character who knows a lot about different modes of sexual experience and who knows how to exploit that knowledge. A Dietrich character in another von Sternberg film (*Shanghai Express*, 1932) further plays upon this star image when she says that it took a lot of men "to change my name to Shanghai Lily."

Fig. 7.17

Deitrich's foreign origins had connotations not only of sexuality but also of exotic places and ways of life. Here, the exotic quality of her European background is both muted and enhanced by placing her in a setting like Morocco. It was muted because, while Germany was somewhat exotic to Americans in the 1930s, Africa was much more so and, in a sense, she seems less foreign than the polyglot Moroccan environment. On the other hand, she was repeatedly associated with what were, for Americans, exotic foreign environments in her films: Germany in *The Blue Angel* (1930), Shanghai in *Shanghai Express* (figure 7.17), Russia in *The Scarlet Empress* (1934), Spain in *The Devil is a Woman* (1935), and Morocco.

For Dietrich's character in this film, love is a compulsive descent into a cesspool of pain and degradation. It begins when we see her as a "suicide ticket" on the boat and ends with her as a "camp follower." When she falls in love with Tom, she is constantly and degradingly reminded of or exposed to the many other women in his life. In an important scene, she comes to see him off on a mission and finds him unashamedly surrounded by adoring Moroccan women. Kennington has driven her there and, paralleling her degradation, the situation is obviously troubling to him. After she wishes Tom off, she describes the camp followers, the women who leave everything to follow the men into the desert, as mad. But at the end of the movie, again with the devoted and wretched Kennington watching, she becomes one of them, and disappears into the desert holding on to a goat.

Adjustments to Dietrich's Star Image

Between 1930 and 1935, Dietrich made seven films with von Sternberg, all highly exotic in look and often in locale, and all emphasizing the destructive aspects of love. They established her image, but that image also became a kind of trap for her and, like Bruce Willis and James Cagney, she made a number of adjustments to her star persona that kept it strong for decades.

In the 1920s she had appeared in German films with little success. Von Sternberg "discovered" her and starred her in *The Blue Angel* (1930), a German film about degrading passion (figure 7.18). Before it was released in the United States, she made *Morocco*. To prepare for shooting *Morocco*, she lost weight and improved her English to appeal to American audiences. In *The Blue Angel* she

Fig. 7.18

plays an attractive but unsympathetic nightclub performer who is coldly indifferent to the fact that her husband sacrifices all for her, is horribly degraded by the manner in which she treats him, and dies from the anguish she causes him. In *Morocco*, while she again causes others pain, she also sacrifices herself to romantic love at the end.

The seven films Dietrich made with von Sternberg not only established her star image but also linked the two as one of the most famous director–star teams in film history. Some have seen her stardom as totally his creation, others consider it a more symbiotic relationship; whatever the actuality, both careers declined after they ended their work together. She was, however, able to maintain a significant star presence for the rest of her life.

In 1937, two years after her last film with von Sternberg, an association of theater owners took out a famous ad in the industry trade journals labeling her and four other major actresses "box office poison." Some felt that her image, which had been established in the more liberal early 1930s, had become outdated or even morally repugnant to mainstream American audiences. Her success in *Destry Rides Again* (1939) helped alter that image by presenting her as a brawling dance-hall girl. She seemed much less exotic, much more "American" in a film set not in far-off lands but in that most American of places, the American West of the late nineteenth century. This, combined with a number of other activities, served to diminish the exotic and now career-endangering aspect of her image.

The most visible German actress in Hollywood, Dietrich became an American citizen in the late 1930s and publicly denounced Hitler's regime. By this time, Germany had come less to signify decadent sexuality and more to signify its Nazi regime. Furthermore, during World War II she entertained US soldiers overseas and was often photographed not in the exotic costumes of the von Sternberg movies, but in military clothing. This was a time when American women were encouraged to enter the military to support the war effort. Dietrich's slacks and military garb did not have the decadent cross-dressing associations of her costumes in *Morocco* and other films but rather those of a woman happy to discard traditional female frills in order to be "just one of the boys" while engaged in patriotic activity.

After the war, her major film roles diminished, although her star power was still sufficiently strong to garner her important roles with major directors, such as Billy Wilder (*A Foreign Affair*, 1948, and *Witness for the Prosecution*, 1958), Alfred Hitchcock (*Stage Fright*, 1950), Fritz Lang (*Rancho Notorious*, 1952), and Orson Welles (*Touch of Evil*, 1958). While Dietrich often received praise for these roles, they did little to affect her star image, which remained largely that established in the seven films she made with von Sternberg in the early 1930s. In fact, during this time she launched an internationally successful career as a Las Vegas and theatrical performer with a one-woman show that was built around her image as an ageless beauty with great style and nostalgic appeal. No longer perceived as decadent and potentially threatening to dominant values, she was now a cultural icon.

Contradictions and Ambiguity

Both foreign and patriotic, exotic and one of the guys, decadently sexual and a fun-loving chum, Dietrich's persona contained many contradictions. She appeared both accessible in her public persona, particularly while entertaining troops during the war, and also remote, inaccessible, and enigmatic. The general public knew little of her private life; even the fact that she had a husband and daughter was virtually unknown. At the end of her life she became a recluse, never leaving her Paris apartment; this isolation, linked with the mysterious appeal of her early screen roles and star persona, became the subject of the documentary *Marlene* (1984).

It is often difficult in *Morocco* to "read" what her looks mean. The very stillness of her demeanor encourages viewers to read many things into her face, and it is clear that her knowing characters sometimes encourage and calculate such ambiguity. Near the end of *Morocco*, Dietrich's character, thinking Tom has been wounded, races to a distant city. To do so, she must leave her engagement party, causing Kennington profound embarrassment and pain. When she arrives at the hospital, she desperately runs from bed to bed but cannot find Tom; then she learns he is not badly wounded but nearby at a nightclub with an attractive woman.

She approaches him entirely composed and smiling (figure 7.19). He asks if she has got married and she says no; then he asks if she is going to marry Kennington. She smiles and tells him, of course, that "I don't change my mind." It is a remarkable and complex moment. The last time Amy saw Tom they were to run off together but he walked out, leaving a message saying that he had changed his mind. Her statement clearly recalls his and the pain it caused her. Furthermore, the viewer has just seen her change her mind, having promised to marry Kennington but then hysterically running off. But here her composure is perfect. There is clearly a great difference between what she says and what the audience has just seen, and between her desperate emotional tensions and the geniality of her smile and manner, but the very impenetrability of her look and demeanor gives the scene its ambiguous strength. It points to her character's ability to perform, not only on stage but also in life.

Fig. 7.19

It is further made credible and given contrast by the scenes in which Amy loses all composure, as at her engagement party when she breaks down and says in front of all that she must go to Tom (figure 7.20), or the following morning when, seeing Tom going into the desert, she loses composure and marches after him. In these scenes, the pain in her face becomes entirely readable.

After she loses control at the party and races through the line of troops looking in vain for Tom, she returns to the stunned party. She enters an outside room and is all alone and in darkness. She

Fig. 7.20

Fig. 7.21

careens around and clutches at her hair, virtually out of control in an unusual private moment. Then she re-enters the party to say she must go. The movie allows us to see her out of control and sometimes in control when in a troubled state, but there are times when we have no idea of what is behind her face. Before she goes on stage for the first time, the club owner comes to her dressing room. We see her quietly smoking a cigarette and humming a song (figure 7.21). The comic hysteria of the owner's nervous movements boldly contrasts with the unreadable interiority of her behavior. We know from the earlier boat scene that her situation is desperate and that this is her opening night and may be her last chance, but we see a beautiful woman in a man's outfit casually smoking a cigarette, apparently without a care in the world. We know what we see contains all kinds of contradictions, but it is visually compelling and somehow appropriate. Such an image lies at the center of Dietrich's stardom.

Dirty Harry (1971) and Clint Eastwood

The "Dirty Harry" Character

"Go ahead. Make my day!" "Dirty Harry" Callahan, a San Francisco police detective played by Clint Eastwood, says this while holding a gun on an armed criminal in *Sudden Impact* (1983). He is taunting the man to shoot him and is confident that, if he tries, it will be the criminal's last move. The line was widely quoted in the 1980s – it was even used by President Ronald Reagan in a 1985 news conference – and seemed to sum up a character, an actor, a film series, and conservative American politics. Here was a charismatic white man wielding righteous power and not afraid to use it.

Sudden Impact was the fourth film in the Dirty Harry series, which contains many similar situations (see chapter 6). Their prototype came in *Dirty Harry* (1971), in which Harry similarly held a gun on two armed criminals, one at the beginning (figure 7.22) and one at the end of the film (figure 7.23). He tells each "punk" to ask himself, "Do I feel lucky?" and confrontationally adds, "Well, do you, punk?" Harry is not a man to fool with.

The last thing he does in the movie, after killing the second criminal, who was foolish enough to "feel lucky," is to throw away his inspector's star (figure

Fig. 7.22

Fig. 7.23

Fig. 7.24

Fig. 7.25

7.24). The film opens with an image of a plaque honoring San Francisco police officers who have died in the line of duty, and we see a similar star on the plaque, which dissolves into the image of a murderer's gun barrel. During the film, Harry becomes disgusted with the bureaucratic, permissive society that constrains his ability as a police officer to bring the murderer to justice. He finally disobeys orders, follows a higher morality, and kills the murderer (figure 7.25), while saving the lives of a busload of children. Then he throws away his badge. This gesture directly recalls Gary Cooper's character throwing away his star at the end of *High Noon* (1952); he was also disgusted with the refusal of his society to back him up.

Indictment of the Contemporary Justice System

Dirty Harry added a major component to Eastwood's star image, which, like that of Dietrich, Wayne, and Cooper, was established relatively early in his career. In the film, Harry pursues Scorpio, a crazed serial killer who tries to blackmail the city of San Francisco with threats of more murders. Four connected scenes sum up many of the tensions in the film. In the first, Harry wounds and captures Scorpio (figure 7.26), who has buried a girl alive with only a limited amount of air. Scorpio refuses to give the girl's location, instead screaming that he has rights and wants to see an attorney. Fearing the girl will soon die, Harry sadistically steps on the man's open leg wound to get him to speak (figure 7.27). The second scene has no dialogue. It simply shows Harry silently watching as the now dead girl is pulled from the pit where Scorpio buried her (figure 7.28).

Fig. 7.26

Fig. 7.27

Fig. 7.28

Fig. 7.29

In the third scene, Harry is called into the district attorney's office. The DA, reading Harry's arrest report, comments, "Really amazing!" Harry replies, "I had some luck." The DA replies that Harry's "luck" is that he isn't indicting Harry for assault with intent to commit murder. While Harry sits aghast with repressed fury, the DA tells him that he has violated Scorpio's civil rights, that nothing Harry found can be used as evidence, and that Scorpio will be set free. He also tells Harry not to pursue Scorpio. In the fourth scene we see a "peace" symbol spray-painted on a wall. The camera pans left to show Scorpio with a similar symbol on his belt. He goes to a playground to look at children, his next intended victims, but Harry has ignored the DA's order and is watching him.

These scenes present Harry as extremely competent, morally outraged, painfully frustrated, and hopelessly hamstrung by a world gone "crazy," as he describes the legal system. The film strongly justifies virtually everything Harry does. He tortures Scorpio because he knows the kidnapped girl could soon die and no other method will induce Scorpio to reveal her location. The scene following the torture shows that Harry had obviously learned the location, but that the girl was already dead. Furthermore, in an earlier scene in which Harry gives Scorpio the ransom money he had demanded for the girl's release, Scorpio not only beats and kicks Harry mercilessly (figure 7.29) but also tells him that he is going to let the girl die anyway and that he is going to kill Harry too. He is prevented only when Harry's hidden partner shoots at him and, even then, Harry tells the partner not to kill Scorpio. Even at the film's end, when Harry has Scorpio in his sights, he gives him a chance to surrender. He maintains his own strict moral code and shoots only when Scorpio feels "lucky" and goes for his gun. The movie creates an extreme disjunction between the sadistic evil the viewer and Harry see, and the way the legal and political system deals with that evil. In contrast to Harry, the "system" is represented as morally bankrupt.

Social Issues

More than most movies of its era, *Dirty Harry* became a rallying point for a cluster of social issues. Some critics called it a fascist film; others found it a stinging indictment of all that was wrong in American society. Harry became a rallying image for notions of white male heroism of the kinds embodied in Gary Cooper and John Wayne for earlier generations, but that were now beleaguered by the erosive onslaughts of the anti-Vietnam War movement, the civil rights movement, the rise of feminism, and general disdain for the police (at the time, commonly called "pigs") and the military.

Eastwood's Star Image

By association, Eastwood became an embodiment of conservative heroism, and this played a major role in his star career, which is currently one of the most powerful in Hollywood. By the time of *Dirty Harry*'s appearance, the three major components of his image had been established: his Western persona, his police persona, and his behind-the-camera presence as a producer and director.

Eastwood first became widely known as a Western actor in the *Rawhide* television series, which ran from 1959 to 1966, but the likable cowboy he played in that series had virtually nothing in common with his character in the three Italian-made "Man with No Name" movies directed by the remarkably talented Sergio Leone: *A Fistful of Dollars* (1964), *For a Few Dollars More* (1965), and *The Good, the Bad, and the Ugly* (1966, figure 7.30). These films were part of the then-disreputable "spaghetti Western" genre, a term referring to Westerns made not in Hollywood but in Italy. They established Eastwood's image as a poncho-draped, flinty-eyed, largely silent and extremely brutal killer. They were also renowned for Leone's bold and often unusual camera angles and movements, as well as his elaborately choreographed, virtually operatic scenes of violence. The great popularity and cult status of these Westerns soon made Eastwood an international star.

Eastwood's first starring film on his return to the United States, *Hang 'Em High* (1968), capitalized on the image established in Leone's Westerns and, in that same year, he made a movie that would lead to another dimension of his image. It was *Coogan's Bluff* (1968, figure 7.31), his first film directed by Don Siegel, who would become a mentor and direct four more Eastwood films, including *Dirty Harry*.

Fig. 7.30

Coogan's Bluff was Eastwood's first modern-day starring role and in some ways a precursor to *Dirty Harry*. In it, he plays an Arizona lawman who goes to New York. Much of the movie deals with the conflict between the frontier methods of justice, embodied in Eastwood's character, and the problems of urban crime fighting, embodied in Lee J. Cobb's world-weary, New York City detective.

Eastwood does not wear Western garb or live in Arizona in *Dirty Harry*, but many of the conflicts are similar. At this point in his career, he did not need the garb, since he had already established a strong Western persona to his star image and carried it with him. Frank Sinatra was originally cast as Harry, but withdrew after an injury. It is useful to consider what the difference would have been between his and Eastwood's image in the role. Sinatra was much older than Eastwood, and his non-musical acting image rather involved a world-weary, urban type than a transformed cowboy. His presence in the role would not likely have carried with it the sense of urban conflict with traditional Western genre values but rather

Fig. 7.31

the sense of an older man regretting the lost promise of the society in which he was raised, probably like the Lee J. Cobb character in *Coogan's Bluff*. There is, in fact, a long tradition of urban police dramas in which an older, cynical officer deals with crime, as Sinatra did in *The Detective* (1968). Eastwood, however, is a young Harry. His lieutenant even jokingly tells him to "get a haircut." Indeed, Harry's hairstyle contradictorily aligns him not with the conservative establishment but with the rebellious youth movement of the time. Except for his assistant, he is the youngest police character featured in the film. Harry's cynicism does not evoke the older urban tradition in which he presumably grew up but rather the old West of Leone's films.

Actors and Directors

The end of *Unforgiven* (1992) has a dedication to "Sergio and Don," which is revealing about Eastwood's career. Many star actors have important associations with directors, such as Dietrich with von Sternberg, John Wayne with John Ford and Howard Hawks, and Peter Sellers with Stanley Kubrick and Blake Edwards. The major components of Eastwood's star image come directly from his work with Sergio Leone and Don Siegel. Each developed Eastwood's relationship with a genre – Leone the Western and Siegel the urban police drama – and such genre associations are also often part of major star images. Both genres are centrally concerned with issues of American masculinity. In fact, it was precisely Eastwood's Western associations that gave his appearance in *Dirty Harry* its individuality. Furthermore, the 1960s' linkage of many traditional Western stars such as John Wayne with conservative politics fueled some of the debate around *Dirty Harry*'s politics.

Both Leone and Siegel had extensive experience in their film industries and, as directors, worked efficiently and without budget overruns. Eastwood used them as models when he established the third component of his image, that of producer and director. In 1971, the same year as *Dirty Harry*, he directed his first film, *Play Misty for Me*, in which he plays a disk jockey terrorized by a woman with whom he had a brief affair. Don Siegel played a minor role in it and also became involved with Eastwood's production company, Malpaso, which has produced most of his subsequent films. Around this time Eastwood also developed a long-term relationship with Warner Brothers, which has distributed most of his films, starting with *Dirty Harry*.

Like Siegel and Leone, Eastwood has also become known for efficient directing and producing. He disdains blockbuster films and makes his often wildly popular films cheaply by industry norms. His "family" of actors and production people follows him from film to film, and he is known in the industry for running a comfortable set, even waiting in line with the crew for meals. When he appears on talk shows to promote his films, he appears unfailingly unpretentious and self-effacing, an all-around "nice guy." He has also in recent years achieved visibility as a genial presence at prestigious film events such as the

Cannes Film Festival and the New York Film Festival. He even served a term as mayor of his town of Carmel, California. It is virtually impossible to conceive of the Eastwood of the talk shows or the film festivals or the Carmel mayor snarling, "Go ahead. Make my day!" These images of Eastwood the industry figure contrast boldly with and serve to soften and distance the hard-bitten and often violent edge of the killers he plays in many of his films, but, as we indicated before, such disparate components are quite common in star images.

Part of Eastwood's unpretentious image relates to the limited range of his acting ambitions. Unlike actors such as Gene Hackman, Dustin Hoffman, or Jack Nicholson, he has never been considered as having much of a range as an actor and has often seemed to play the same character repeatedly. His work behind the camera has certainly given him power and won him respectability in the industry, and his star image has proved to be a highly marketable commodity over three decades, but it is significant that, when nominated for producer, director, and acting awards, he won for producing and directing but not for acting.

After *Dirty Harry*, Eastwood played mostly variations on his star image in four more Dirty Harry films including *Sudden Impact* (1983, figure 7.32) and a number of Westerns including *The Outlaw Josey Wales* (1976, figure 7.33). He has also played in a number of non-Harry police films, such as *The Gauntlet* (1977), *The Rookie* (1990), and *A Perfect World* (1993), and one, *Tightrope* (1984), that explicitly probes the sexual problems of Eastwood's hero figure. He has also made comedic action films such as *Every Which Way but Loose* (1978) and military movies such as *Heartbreak Ridge* (1986). His career provides an interesting investigation of issues of embattled white American masculinity over the past forty years. He has made attempts to stretch his range as both director and actor, including three films in which he does not appear. *Breezy* (1973) deals with a romantic relationship between a conservative older man played by William Holden and a young, hippie-type woman. *Bird* (1988), about the black jazz musician, Charlie Parker, clearly encroached on territory that at first seems antithetical to Eastwood's embattled white male persona. Comparably, *Midnight in the Garden of Good and Evil* (1997) is based upon historical events and its central gay male character, as well as its exploration of the gay subculture of Savannah, Georgia, engage areas not previously associated with Eastwood's persona. As an actor, he veered considerably from his customary style, diction, and mannerisms when he directed himself in a thinly veiled impersonation of director John Huston in *White Hunter, Black Heart* (1990).

Fig. 7.32

While doing such films, he constantly returns to his star image by doing Westerns and police films. He provides a

Fig. 7.33

perfect example of a film star who has no pretensions to a versatile or a wide acting range but who has developed a star image and then worked systematically not only to maintain and adapt that image but also to control the industry conditions in which it is produced. Because of his longevity as a star, Eastwood's career shows how age can change a star's image over time. Beginning with *The Bridges of Madison County* (1995), Eastwood played characters who showed their age. In that film, he plays a photographer who has an affair with a married woman. In one scene that could easily have been cut from the film or never shot at all, we see Eastwood taking off his shirt and washing himself outside. Despite the good shape he is in, this is the body of man in his sixties, not that of a youthful star. Many actors would have chosen to keep their shirt on to protect their more idealized, youthful body image. Eastwood, however, goes even further and makes his aging persona the explicit subject matter of *Space Cowboys* (2000). Eastwood had long wanted to make this movie about aging fliers who become astronauts for an important mission but he could not get funding for it since the studios considered the subject unrealistic and unappealing. After John Glenn became a national hero for the second time when he went back into space as an astronaut in his late seventies, however, suddenly Eastwood's story was both plausible and appealing. Eastwood cast the film with other aging actors such as James Garner. The title itself refers back to Eastwood's old cowboy persona, though now this modern-day version is also aged. Eastwood and his fellow older stars huff and puff their way through the film wearing glasses and even jokingly getting Ensure, a nutritional supplement primarily associated with the elderly, served to them for lunch.

The long-lived star images of both Dietrich and Eastwood resulted from their ability to maintain their appeal to a great variety of audiences over changing times and under changing social conditions.

SELECTED READINGS

Star Texts: Image and Performance in Film and Television, edited by Jeremy G. Butler (Detroit: Wayne State University Press, 1991), introduces important essays that define different acting styles and star images. These essays make a number of important distinctions between film, stage, and television acting. John Ellis's *Visible Fictions: Cinema, Television, Video* (London: Routledge and Kegan Paul, 1982) explores the incoherence of a star image and the fact that a star's image often remains unchanged by films that depart from it. Robert Sklar's *City Boys: Cagney, Bogart, Garfield* (Princeton, NJ: Princeton University Press, 1992) describes the development of and various shifts in the star image of James Cagney. James Naremore's *Acting in the Cinema* (Berkeley, CA: University of California Press, 1988) analyzes Dietrich's acting style in her first two sequences in *Morocco*, concentrating on the use of diffused light, her decadent associations, and the tableau quality of her poses. Paul Smith's *Clint Eastwood: A Cultural Production* (Minneapolis: University of Minnesota Press, 1993) gives detailed information on Clint Eastwood's production strategies, especially in relation to Malpaso, and the development of his star persona. Dennis Bingham concentrates on issues of masculinity in Eastwood's films in *Acting Male: Masculinities in the Films of James Stewart, Jack Nicholson, and Clint Eastwood* (New Brunswick: Rutgers University Press, 1994).

8

AUDIENCES AND RECEPTION

A Woman of Paris and *The Crying Game*

In 1993, Henry Louis Gates, Jr took his young daughters to spend Christmas in the West Virginia village where he grew up. He wanted to pass the spirit of his own childhood on to them. Since the big Christmas Eve event of his youth had always been the *Amos 'n' Andy* television episode "Andy Plays Santa Claus," Gates gleefully played a videotape of it for his daughters. While he found it as charming and hilarious as he had as a child, his daughters were bored and annoyed, wanting instead to see *Ernest Saves Christmas* (1988).

For Gates, who had grown up as an African American in a racially mixed rural area, part of the show's appeal had been the wonder of seeing its all-black, urban world of Harlem, where department stores even had black dolls. Furthermore, he had found Kingfish's malapropisms and Andy's gullibility hilarious, and he was deeply moved when Amos taught his daughter the Lord's Prayer. Gates's daughters, however, found all of this contrived and corny.

They were watching the same show, but they were not having the same experience. Why? They had different responses to the show based upon what they brought to their watching of it. To an extent, the same show became two different shows in the experiences it gave these viewers. While Gates associated it with warm memories of his youth, his daughters had grown up in a different world. The sight of an all-black community on television was nothing new to them, and dramatic devices like the use of the Lord's Prayer to evoke reverence and deep emotion did not have the same appeal for their generation as they had for that of their father. They found all of this old-fashioned and tedious.

Compare this situation with the scene we discussed in chapter 1 from the film *Dragon: The Bruce Lee Story* (1992) in which Bruce Lee watches *Break-*

fast at Tiffany's (1961) in a theater with a primarily white audience. While the majority of the audience laughs uproariously at the antics of a stereotyped Asian buffoon, Lee becomes deeply troubled and leaves the theater. He is disturbed by demeaning racial implications that the rest of the audience does not even notice. As with Gates and his daughters, a single film can have different meanings for different viewers.

When we disagree with friends about the meaning of a film, we might accuse them of not "getting it," of misunderstanding the film. While this happens, it is not the case with the examples above. In those instances, all of the viewers got "it," but they got different "its." While the Gates family would probably agree that the Lord's Prayer scene showed Andy's love for his daughter, and Bruce Lee would probably have agreed with the rest of the audience that the buffoon was a comic character in the film, the significance of these things was different for them all. Those differences underline an important consideration for our understanding of movies.

The meaning of a movie is not simply contained within it. No movie has one "right" meaning that every viewer can "get" by approaching it "correctly." Rather, the meanings of a film are produced by viewers in their interactions with it. Many things influence these interactions, such as the background, desires, and biases of the viewer, the way the film is made and marketed, how other people respond to it, and the cultural climate. The same film can mean different things to different viewers at the same time; it can also have different meanings even for the same viewer at different times. Gates, for example, an African American scholar, would certainly know that the *Amos 'n' Andy* show has been considered racist. When not involved in family nostalgia, he might very well have a more troubled reaction to the show than he did as a child or during Christmas 1993.

What is Reception Study?

In recent years, film and other cultural scholars have incorporated elements of **reception study** into their work. What exactly does it do? Reception study explores the variety of ways in which historically specific audiences have responded to films and other works of art as well as the reasons for those responses. It teaches us that all the meanings of a film are never fixed but rather are in part shaped by the viewing context and can shift, as audiences shift, over time. We have seen in chapters 2 and 3 that films have narrative (e.g., the arrangement of plot elements) and formal (e.g., space) structures. In everyday language, we would say that the meanings and significance of those structures are *in* the film. But, as reception study shows us, this is only part of the story. Audiences are not passive receivers of the significance of a movie but rather active participants in the production of that significance; meaning is not simply text based, but the result of a process of interaction of text and context. Reception is one important part of that context and includes such things as

Fig. 8.1

what kind of theater the film is screened in, how the film is advertised, and how it relates to current events.

Reception study can also help us avoid simplistic generalities about the single meaning of a film, or presumptions that only one meaning is credible. It can enable us to understand the complex ways in which movies are understood at different times by people belonging to different races, classes, ethnicities, genders, and sexual orientations. Reception study is not based on what a film's self-contained, formal meanings are, nor on what the filmmakers wanted to say, nor on what some reviewers said, but on what the film actually has meant to different audiences.

Basic Instinct (1992, figure 8.1) was a controversial film at the time of its release, in part because of the manner in which it represented lesbians. Outcries arose even while the film was in production, and members of the gay and lesbian community demanded changes based upon their reading of the script as well as upon reports about the production. Before the finished film was even seen, spokespersons for the gay and lesbian community condemned it and, on opening day, there were organized protesters and picket lines at theaters in such major cities as New York. The allegations of homophobia as well as the responses of the film's makers and stars were widely covered in the news media. Such a reception context positions viewers to respond strongly to that aspect of the film. The protesters, who wanted spectators to stay away or at least to see the film as an offensive example of Hollywood's homophobia, created a context for viewing beyond that of either the film itself or what its distributors wanted to promote. The film was not made and distributed as an example of Hollywood homophobia but, for some, that is what it became.

The situation became even more complex. Although the protesters claimed to speak for the entire gay and lesbian community, this was far from true. Some lesbians, for example, while admitting that the film's treatment of lesbians was disturbing, saw that disturbance as reflecting a deep-seated fear and insecurity on the part of heterosexual male filmmakers who openly acknowledged their fear of lesbianism as a different and threatening form of sexuality. They felt, in other words, that while some films have embraced gay and lesbian sexuality with the assumption that all people are fundamentally alike, the makers of *Basic Instinct* acknowledged real differences between some heterosexual and some homosexual people and thereby acknowledged that those differences can be threatening to straight people. Such an approach reads the film as symptomatic of a problem but not necessarily in a way that asks people to condemn the movie out of hand; rather, it invites them to learn from it. Even within particular groups, audience responses are varied and multifaceted.

If none of this highly publicized aspect of the film had been part of its reception context, audiences would have been positioned to view it as just another erotic thriller, and it may never have crossed the minds of many to pay particular attention to the representation of lesbians as knife-wielding murderers.

And, in fact, if the film is shown in twenty years as part of a retrospective of the work of its director, Paul Verhoeven, that representation may not even be part of the context; rather, such a retrospective will create an entirely new context that will position that audience to see connections with other films made by Verhoeven such as *Soldier of Orange* (1977), *Robocop* (1987), *Total Recall* (1990), *Starship Troopers* (1997), and *Hollow Man* (2000). Although the initial reception context of *Basic Instinct* may have been more dramatic than that surrounding most films, the issues of diversity in reception are always operative.

How Can a Meaning Change?

In early 1995, a freshly struck **35 mm** print of Russ Meyer's *Faster Pussycat! Kill! Kill!* (1962) was released in a number of **art-house cinemas**. Many critics reviewed it with respect and even talked about Russ Meyer as an important American filmmaker. Furthermore, a major feminist critic praised it for its strong and aggressive female characters, admitting that, had she reviewed the film twenty years earlier, she would have dismissed it as sexist trash. Viewers attending an art-house screening after reading a serious review are positioned to respond differently to a film than those surreptitiously ducking into a porn theater. Thus, art-house distribution and respectable reviews promote and encourage a certain kind of response to the film.

Such a reception in 1962 would have been virtually unthinkable. Meyer was then considered an unregenerate pornographer and *Faster Pussycat! Kill! Kill!* an example of sleazy exploitation of women and violence. It was shown in porn houses and disreputable theaters in the United States, and serious reviewers ignored it. In Germany, however, Meyer has long been considered an important American filmmaker and was even honored at the prestigious Berlin Film Festival at a time when such recognition would have been unthinkable in America. In this case, nationhood supplies an important aspect of the reception context. Furthermore, those attending a major international film festival are, like Americans going to art houses in 1995, positioned to see the films shown there as worthy examples of film art. The movie has not changed; the reception contexts have.

Meyer's growing international reputation, shifts in the feminist movement that have made some more receptive to genres that were once condemned out of hand, and greater tolerance for sexually explicit material in films have contributed to a shift in reception that has given this film meanings unimaginable to most Americans in 1962. In fact, a guide for movies on video comments that the film was perceived as hard-core in its day but today could be shown on late-night television. And, of course, people seeing *Faster Pussycat! Kill! Kill!* as just another late-night television movie are positioned within a quite different reception context than people sneaking into a porn theater to see something forbidden.

Fig. 8.2

We have all had the experience of loving a film but then seeing it again and being disappointed that it did not live up to our memory of it. We have also been surprised to find films "about" things different from what we had remembered. The film has not changed; we have, and the context in which we see it has, and these changes give it a different meaning for us.

Sometimes a shift in meaning is caused by a cultural event. Winston Groom, the author of the novel *Forrest Gump*, responded to the huge spurt in sales of his book after the 1994 release of the popular film based upon it (figure 8.2) by wondering where all of the eager new readers had been eight years earlier when the book was published, saying, "It's the same damn book."

It is and it isn't. The spurt of sales resulted from the success of the film. Many people read the novel after seeing the film, placing the book in the shadow of the film. The popularity of the film became a factor in the reading of the book, and it is virtually impossible for a 2002 reader of the novel to experience it in the same way that he or she would have experienced it a decade earlier. This includes a reader who has not even seen the film. The cover of the fifteenth paperback edition of the novel proclaims in large letters, "Tom Hanks is Forrest Gump." The character in the novel, however, looks nothing like the lean Hanks and is described as being 6 foot 6 inches tall and weighing 240 pounds. Groom, in fact, envisioned John Goodman in the role, an actor radically different in appearance from Hanks. But it is altogether likely that readers of the novel will envision Hanks in at least some aspects of the main character.

Shifts in meaning do not necessarily result from broad cultural or historical events; they can also result from how changes in the world of cinema have impacted upon audiences. A film such as *The Phantom of the Opera*, which was considered terrifying in 1925 when it was originally released, is often now perceived as quaintly old-fashioned and even unintentionally funny. The current reception context includes so many graphic horror films with disturbing and previously taboo subject matter that much older films like *Phantom of the Opera* now seem tame.

How is our Impression of a Film Formed?

Most movies quickly acquire a popular image of having a limited number of dominant meanings; many things influence this. At the earliest stage, filmmakers try to shape a film so that it will be received in the way they desire. When they complete the film, they often hold preview screenings at which audiences are asked to record their responses to the film. Often, directors or studios make changes in the film based upon such test screenings. If the film is perceived as too long, they might shorten it; if the film is considered confusing, they will try to clarify its major issues; if the film is perceived as "needing" something, like greater punishment for a character (for example, Alex in *Fatal Attraction* as discussed in chapter 1), they will try to add it.

When the film is finished, its marketers take over and attempt to influence the film's reception. They want to whet public interest in it to maximize its box-office potential. The producer/director William Castle was famous for publicity stunts that tantalized and even dared the public with the prospect of a terrifying movie. These included sensational advertising campaigns and even physical changes in theaters. He would claim to have taken out an insurance policy on the life of anyone who would die of fright during a horror film, or have nurses visibly present at screenings, implying that the film was so scary that viewers might faint or have a heart attack. For *House on Haunted Hill* (1959) he installed devices in some theaters that would send a skeleton flying over the heads of the audience at appropriate moments in the film and, for *The Tingler* (1959), he wired the seats in some theaters to "tingle" at appropriate moments.

Castle's antics may seem outrageous, but they are simply an exaggerated form of widespread attempts to influence the reception context of films. If we see medical professionals standing by as we file into a theater, we expect to have a strong physiological response to the film we are about to see and, indeed, the very anticipation of having such a response primes us. It may be the reason we attended the film in the first place. We have all become accustomed to phrases like "It's a four-hankie movie" or "another laff riot" or "Get set for the ride of your life." Such ads similarly prime our expectations for the film and indicate the response its makers intend us to have. Soon after a film's release, ads often quote from reviews to reinforce the notion that the film creates its desired response.

A film's makers are not the only ones who affect its reception. As we saw with *Basic Instinct*, at times people not involved in the making or marketing of a movie will try to influence its popular image at an early stage. Some fundamentalist Christian groups considered *The Last Temptation of Christ* (1988) blasphemous and mounted a campaign that included pickets outside theaters and media coverage to protest against its showing. They wanted to promote a popular image of the movie as offensive and decadent, obliterating the thoughtful image that the producers sought to convey. All of these instances – from the making of the film, to its marketing, to protests against it – are examples of attempts to shape audience response and to make certain readings available and even likely.

Differences in Audience

A group of parents looking at a home movie of a school play might all see the same movie but, for each, it is really "about" their child's performance. They will watch that child's performance with intensity and perhaps ignore those of other children. They might each remember it as a film about *their* child's play, and each parent will remember the film in a different way. Film marketers have long been aware of this phenomenon in a way that relates to reception context beyond such limited individual responses. *Imitation of Life* (1934), which deals with the mother–daughter relationships of two mothers, one white (played by Claudette Colbert) and one black (played by Louise Beavers), was released in the Atlanta area with two different ad campaigns. For white areas, it was advertised as primarily *about* Claudette Colbert with hints of a romance with the white actor, Warren William. Louise Beavers was hardly mentioned. For black areas, however, it was advertised as a Louise Beavers film and prominently featured images of Fredi Washington, the actress playing Beavers's daughter. In these ads, Claudette Colbert and Warren William appear to be minor players. The ads give the impression of two totally different films.

This way of selling the same film to two different audiences indicates that those audiences, like the parents watching the home movie, are likely to respond to the film in entirely different ways and go away with different memories of it.

Unanticipated Responses

Sometimes films have evoked responses entirely unexpected by their makers and marketers. Reactions of professional film critics often fall into this category. *Heaven's Gate* (1980) was an extremely expensive film that went over budget and was not finished until the eleventh hour before its release. Led by prestigious reviewers from such newspapers as *The New York Times*, national critics joined a kind of feeding frenzy to proclaim the film an epic disaster and colossal waste of money. The film was withdrawn and then drastically cut and re-edited for US distribution; not surprisingly, it nevertheless failed abysmally at the box office. In a case like this, the unusually shrill and nearly unanimous critical outcry positioned the public to consider the film not as a serious epic but, rather, as a self-indulgent flop and one they should avoid.

The critics themselves, however, were also positioned by historical circumstances that shaped their reaction. Specifically, the film's director, Michael Cimino, was part of a new, young group of film *auteurs* who viewed themselves as serious artists and fought for total control over their films. Not only did they frequently have little regard for production schedules and cost overruns, but they also produced films that many in the industry considered pretentious and even hard to understand. Their films were often heavily influenced by the European art cinema and contained references to old and sometimes obscure movies. The critical reaction to Cimino's film may in large part have resulted from a desire within the American critical establishment to make an example of one of these young filmmakers and bring him and his peers into line. Thus, many critics may have been responding to something much larger which, for them, the film stood for. Later audiences who have had a chance to see Cimino's original cut of the movie are often puzzled as to what provoked such a strong critical reaction, since nothing about the film itself seems to warrant condemning it as one of the worst movies ever made. Indeed, when the original version of the film opened in Paris, it met with critical praise and box-office success.

During the spring of 1995, the media began to circulate stories about the production of *Waterworld* (1995), another film that not only went way over budget but also, with reported costs of $175 million, was called the most expensive film ever made. Since the film was produced by its star, Kevin Costner, there was, once again, a larger context involving Costner's presumed ego. The media went so far as to circulate jokes about the film, such as calling it "Kevin's Gate" and "Fishtar." The former, of course, puns on *Heaven's Gate* and the latter on *Ishtar* (1987), another big-budget box-office failure that had been panned by the critics. The punning references back to the earlier films reveal that their original receptions have remained part of their meaning to this day. Those references also worked to create a particular reception context for *Waterworld* by linking it with a string of infamous, egotistical mega-budget flops, thus positioning viewers to perceive the film in a way that had nothing to do with the film's narrative, formal design, or marketing plan.

Another kind of unexpected response has little to do with either critics or filmmakers and comes directly from audiences. *Fantasia* (1940, figure 8.3) was made and marketed by Disney as a film linking animation with classical music and making classical music accessible to mainstream audiences. Leopold Stokowski, a famous conductor, even makes a brief appearance in the beginning. *2001: A Space Odyssey* (1968) was released as an innovative science-fiction film about space exploration, investigating its philosophical implications rather than simply providing a genre adventure with robots and death rays. In the 1970s, however, both movies assumed entirely different dimensions when young people, while high on drugs, viewed them as films enhancing hallucinogenic or marijuana experiences. The smell of marijuana was commonplace in theaters screening the films, and attending them stoned became part of a cult experience. Regardless of the combined intentions of filmmakers, producers, distributors, and exhibitors, movies acquire meanings beyond their control. *Reefer Madness* (1936), made to warn people about the dangers of using marijuana, ironically became a cult movie in the 1960s and 1970s for those very users who enjoyed what they perceived as its unintentionally absurd depiction of the effects of marijuana.

The Rocky Horror Picture Show (1975) was released as a musical spoof of horror films but, in a way that its makers, distributors, exhibitors, and reviewers neither intended nor foresaw, it became a cult "midnight movie." Audiences repeatedly attended midnight screenings at certain theaters and treated the film as a kind of interactive performance. They dressed up as characters in the film and loudly interacted with it in ways that deviated dramatically from traditional viewing behavior. They shouted out warnings to characters

Fig. 8.3

in dangerous situations and danced and sang during musical numbers; when a character in the film proposes a "toast," audience members threw toasted bread at the screen. This cult reception of the film continues to this day. The same kind of interactive response is part of the reception context of a 2001 print of *The Sound of Music* (1965) which includes the lyrics to the songs at the bottom of the screen in follow-the-bouncing-ball sing-along style. Audience members attend such screenings attired in costumes like those of the characters in the film and sing along with the musical numbers.

Unforeseen historical events can affect a work's meaning. *Outbreak* (1995) is particularly interesting since its makers exploited widespread anxiety about deadly viral epidemics in the mid-1990s. The anxiety was fueled by global awareness of the AIDS epidemic; Richard Preston's best-selling non-fiction book, *The Hot Zone*, which describes the horrors of the deadly Ebola virus; and a general media frenzy about the manner in which new bacterial strains were proving resistant to antibiotics. What no one involved in the making, marketing, and exhibiting of the film foresaw was that, while the movie was still in theaters, an outbreak of the Ebola virus would occur in Africa and become worldwide front-page news. In fact, when *Newsweek* did a cover story on the epidemic, it reproduced a still from *Outbreak* and created a highly specific context for a current film. As a result, the film became part of a discourse about a news story that did not even exist when the film was released; that news story, in turn, helped shape the responses of those seeing the film.

Brandon Lee was accidentally killed during the shooting of *The Crow* (1994, figure 8.4), and this sad event strongly affected the reception context for the film. During production, the film had been touted as the beginning of a promising career for Lee, who was the son of Bruce Lee, the hugely successful international star of kung-fu movies. Suddenly, however, Brandon Lee's career was no longer beginning; it had abruptly ended. News stories at the time of his death even mentioned that the film had not been completed, so the public was aware that some scenes in the completed film would be affected by these circumstances. In addition, Bruce Lee's legend had become infused with the notion of a family curse since, among other things, the famed actor himself died unexpectedly at the height of his career. In fact, *Dragon: The Bruce Lee Story* had the previous year dramatized this curse. Consequently, the public was already positioned to view Brandon Lee's death as the most recent instance of the curse. This grim reception context, however, may be considerably altered ten years from now. Someone watching the movie then might have no awareness of Lee's death during the making of the film, and even those spectators who know of it will, due to the passage of time, be positioned differently from those in 1994 who were responding to recent, emotionally charged events. The intensity of our responses to such things as tragic death diminishes with time, since part of their original impact comes from the unexpectedness of the events.

Fig. 8.4

Two months before *Die Hard with a Vengeance* (1995) was scheduled to be released, the terrorist bombing of a building in

Oklahoma City that killed 168 people caused a national trauma. Although the filmmakers did not know of the bombing until the movie was almost completed, they were profoundly concerned that the film, which concerns urban terrorist bombings, would upset its audiences rather than entertain them. The studio considered delaying the film's release but decided against it since the film was made and marketed as that studio's entry in the summer sweepstakes. (Summer is when certain kinds of blockbuster hopefuls must be released to cash in on the youth market. Had the film delayed its prime May opening date, it may have lost much of its market due to competition with other blockbuster films.)

Comparably, the September 11, 2001 simultaneous destruction of the World Trade Center towers in New York City and assault on the Pentagon, the most devastating act of terrorism in US history, caused considerable reshuffling in the film world. A number of completed films dealing with terrorist violence that were about to be released, such as *Collateral Damage* (scheduled for an October 5 release) starring Arnold Schwarzenegger as a fireman whose wife and child are killed when a terrorist blows up a Los Angeles skyscraper, and the comedy *Big Trouble* (scheduled for a September 21 release), containing a scene in which a nuclear device is smuggled past Miami airport security, had their release dates delayed. *Swordfish* (2001) in which John Travolta plays an urban terrorist, although already released in the US, was pulled from some theaters in Europe. Even films about mass destruction scheduled for television showings, like *Independence Day* (1996), were withdrawn for fear of seeming insensitive or even of attempting to profit from the horrible disaster. All of these films were completed before the incident, but the distributors were well aware that the reception context for them had abruptly changed.

Even the way in which films were being advertised, an important part of their reception context, was affected by the terrorist attacks of September 11, 2001. Posters in theaters advertising the forthcoming release of *Spider Man* (2002), a highly anticipated, big-budget studio adaptation of the famous comic book, featured the reflection of the twin towers of the World Trade Center in the eye of the title character. The studio immediately pulled all the posters.

Fig. 8.5

A Film's Reputation over Time

A film's reputation, even when unintended and unforeseen, can influence the ways in which people experience it. Neither *The Wizard of Oz* (1939, figure 8.5) nor *It's a Wonderful Life* (1946, figure 8.6) were spectacular hits upon their release. Over the years, however, they have taken on the aura of "family" films and are often shown on television during holiday seasons like Christmas and Easter. People often approach them as national holiday institutions.

Fig. 8.6

Fig. 8.7

Examples of audience response affecting the meanings of films should show us that any categorization of a film's meaning is limited and, of necessity, incomplete. We can learn a great deal by researching reviews of a film, but we must also realize that they give the film's meaning for a specific reviewer at a specific time, not necessarily others at that time and certainly not its meaning for all time. We must examine all reviews with a critical eye and try to understand what the reviewers might not have understood or what they may have avoided talking about. In addition, we must realize that the opinions of many types of peoples such as racial, ethnic and religious minorities, or gays and lesbians, have often gone unrecorded in or ignored by the mainstream media. At times, however, as we saw with *Basic Instinct* (1992), controversy has brought out differences in response that in other situations would have remained silent or unnoticed.

The Birth of a Nation (1915, figure 8.7) is one of the most controversial films ever made. Widely considered a deeply racist film, it also has a reputation as a breakthrough in film style. Its director, D. W. Griffith, is often called the "father" of American cinema. When *Birth of a Nation* was released it drew both extravagant praise, even from President Woodrow Wilson, and outraged condemnation, particularly from the newly formed National Association for the Advancement of Colored People (NAACP), which organized a nationwide protest against the film. Violence broke out at some showings and, indeed, it still does. One instance occurred at an August 1978 exhibition of the film by the Ku Klux Klan in Oxnard, California. Protests organized by the Progressive Labor Party, a militant communist splinter group, and by local Mexican American and African American associations who objected to both the Klan and the communist group, erupted into violence. Over the years, the movie has also been described as promoting international capitalism, as promoting race warfare, as an historically accurate representation of the Civil War and Reconstruction period, as hopelessly biased and fabricated "history," and as a cinematic "classic."

When the film was initially released, the protests of the NAACP positioned people to be critical of the film's representation of blacks similarly to the way in which the gay and lesbian protests about *Basic Instinct* positioned viewers to be critical of that film's representation of lesbians, or the manner in which religious protests against *The Last Temptation of Christ* asked viewers to be critical of that film's representation of Christ. These initial reception contexts are important, but the case of *The Birth of a Nation* illustrates how complicated a film's reception contexts can be. How do all these historically specific and varied contexts for *Birth of a Nation* contribute to the context in which we watch the film today?

Most obviously, we watch it as a kind of historical document, something from the past with a history of inciting controversy. The debated issues help shape our viewing of it today, and we are likely to ask ourselves whether or not we consider it racist or capitalist or masterfully crafted or historically accurate or whatever. We are also likely to ask ourselves why it has been so potent, and what we think of the hotly debated perspectives of others, then and now. The film's contradictory meanings over the years reveal much not only about it but also about our society. All of these meanings cannot help but influence our understanding of the film.

We cannot presume that everyone sees a film in the same way, or that if they disagree with us they are wrong. We must realize that people have many different responses to films and that those responses are, in part, formed by specific reception contexts that change over time. Indeed, taking an introduction to film course with screenings in college is one such context. Students may now seriously examine a film that they saw a year ago on a Friday-night date and which, at the time, they had simply dismissed as entertainment. Within the context of the course, they might be "looking for" specific elements based upon the lectures, readings, and discussions. In the remaining part of this chapter, we will look at ways in which the meanings of two films, *A Woman of Paris* (1923) and *The Crying Game* (1992), were shaped by their initial reception contexts and how those have shifted.

We have chosen *A Woman of Paris* because it was made by Charlie Chaplin at the height of his popularity as a great clown of the silent cinema. The film's original reception context was shaped by the fact that it is not a comedy and that he doesn't even act in it. Furthermore, Chaplin's career was marked by particularly severe shifts in the public's perception of him, and the same film that, at the height of his popularity, was seen as evidence of his artistic growth could, during his fall from grace, be seen as evidence of degeneracy. If we have chosen *A Woman of Paris* because its reception contexts changed dramatically over decades as part of the *oeuvre* of an extremely famous star/director, we have chosen *The Crying Game* because of the dramatic manner in which its original reception context was shaped and then quickly reshaped within a year; the film's distributor, critics, and segments of the general population all played roles in creating these diverse and quickly shifting reception contexts.

Fig. 8.8

A Woman of Paris (1923)

Few film figures have had as polarized a relationship with their audiences as Charles Chaplin, and no film reveals as much about that polarization as *A Woman of Paris*. Affectionately known as Charlie Chaplin, he became the most successful actor/director of his time soon after his first film appeared in 1914. By 1923, he had made dozens of successful comic shorts such as *The Tramp* (1915), *The Pawnshop* (1916), *The Rink* (1916, figure 8.8), *Easy Street* (1917, figure 8.9), *The Immigrant* (1917, figure 8.10), and

Fig. 8.9

Fig. 8.10

Fig. 8.11

Sunnyside (1919), as well as his first comic feature, *The Kid* (1921). These films featured his lovable tramp persona, a mustachioed little man invariably dressed in baggy pants, a tight jacket, a bowler hat, two oversized shoes worn on the wrong feet, and a bamboo cane, which he twirled regularly. In the mid-1940s, however, Chaplin lost his audience; the public's rejection of him was so intense that he was hounded out of the United States in 1952 and spent the remainder of his life in Europe.

A Woman of Paris was a radical departure from the films Chaplin was making at the time and yet quite typical of the kind of film he would make a quarter of a century later. From *Monsieur Verdoux* (1947) to *A King in New York* (1957, figure 8.11), Chaplin's films were greeted with open hostility in the United States and were called anti-American, decadent, and cynical. Both the content of the films and scandals in Chaplin's personal life were cited as evidence of his depravity and unsuitability for mass audiences.

A Woman of Paris, curiously, contains much material that could similarly be interpreted as anti-American, decadent, and cynical, and it appeared amid events in Chaplin's personal life that could also readily be seen as scandalous, yet these perceptions did not dominate its reception context. Audiences and critics of the early 1920s treated it with a sympathy and tolerance that they did not extend to similar works from the mid-1940s on. It was initially seen as a noble artistic experiment and later as a significant influence upon young filmmakers.

When *A Woman of Paris* appeared, Chaplin's phenomenal popularity was still growing, and yet the film avoided virtually all of the ingredients upon which his fame was built. Although he had become famous playing his "little tramp" character in slapstick comedies, this film is not a slapstick comedy and he does not act in it (excepting a cameo appearance in which he is barely recognizable). Where the tramp films had generally been set among social outcasts in the United States, this film is set in Parisian high society.

While the public viewed Chaplin more as an actor than as a director, this film was critically perceived as a directorial triumph. Finally, where his tramp films tended to be sexually innocent, this concerns itself in serious ways with adult sexual issues and reveals a "continental" or sophisticated moral perspective. One reviewer wrote that any fifteen-year-old who appreciated it should be taken home and spanked.

The movie indicated Chaplin's desire to move his career in new directions, toward more "serious" art. While it received respectful reviews and influenced many filmmakers, it did not have the box-office success Chaplin expected. In response, he withdrew it from circulation for about fifty years and returned to making tramp comedies for nearly two decades. He dropped the tramp in the 1940s and, for the rest of his career, made films more similar to *A Woman of Paris* than to the tramp films.

The Shift in Chaplin's Audience

For nearly thirty years, it seemed as if Chaplin could do no wrong. The actor was associated with his endlessly charming, inventive, and innocent tramp character, attuned to the heartstrings of mainstream America. To his audiences, it did not really matter that he had two marriages to teenagers that ended in messy divorces; it did not really matter that the British-born actor never became a United States citizen and did not serve in World War I; it did not really matter that he spoke sympathetically of Bolshevik Russia during the anti-communist agitation of the early 1920s.

In the 1940s, however, it seemed as if he could do no right. Chaplin, now in his fifties, wed the much younger (by over thirty years) Oona O'Neill and was also accused by the young actress Joan Barry of fathering her child. He was widely denounced as a dirty old man, a despoiler of young women. He was also branded as a communist sympathizer and as unpatriotic. Many people resented his support of unpopular alliances with the Soviet Union in World War II and his refusal to become a US citizen. In 1947, Congressman John Rankin demanded his deportation; the Catholic War Veterans urged the Justice and State Departments to investigate Chaplin. After World War II, his movies had strong European affinities and adult points of view. In *Monsieur Verdoux*, for example, he plays a Frenchman who seduces and then murders women for their money. At his trial he defends himself as insignificant when compared with global mass murder. The film ends as he is about to be beheaded. It was a far cry from the tramp movies, and the films did poor business. In 1952, popular resentment against him was so intense that he left the United States for good. In the 1970s, however, the reception climate for his work and image changed again. The anti-communist climate faded, and he was again honored as a giant of early cinema.

The Place of *A Woman of Paris*

A Woman of Paris fits the profile of the later Chaplin, the one alienated from mainstream American values and tastes. It is not set in the working-class United States, but rather in upper-class Paris; it is not a slapstick comedy but a serious drama of manners; it is not sexually naïve but rather concerned with mature sexual relations and, what is worse, defies middle-class values. It shows the nuclear family as constraining and often destructive while the libertine life of its decadent upper class is not harmful but fun and rewarding. It contains virtually everything for which Chaplin would later be driven from the United States (Europhilia, anti-middle-class values, adult sexuality). Furthermore, events in Chaplin's private life in the early 1920s could readily have fueled condemnation of him and the film, but it simply did not happen. In fact, the

Fig. 8.12

film appeared at a time of great sensitivity about the private lives of film figures, following such scandals as the "Fatty" Arbuckle case, in which the star was accused of raping a woman and causing her death during an alleged Hollywood orgy; the William Desmond Taylor murder case, in which the slain director was linked to a scandalous private life; and the revelation of the morphine addiction of the popular star Wallace Reid. To compound all of this, three months after the movie's release, its star, Edna Purviance (figure 8.12), was involved in a highly publicized scandal concerning the shooting of Courtland Dines, an oil magnate. Some cities banned *A Woman of Paris* as a result of the publicity, but the situation did not escalate into an assault on Chaplin.

A Woman of Paris could easily have been interpreted as an amoral film dealing with decadent foreigners and deriding traditional family values made by a man of questionable moral behavior and political views, but audiences were not yet disposed toward such a characterization. They did not see Chaplin and his work in 1923 in the way they would see it in 1952. The reception climate was different. Different social contexts bred different interpretations of Chaplin.

Instead, the film was praised in 1923 by critics as a sign of artistic maturity, international breadth, and innovation. It was strongly influential upon other filmmakers. Ernst Lubitsch was overwhelmed by it; it is often credited with changing the course of his important directorial career, giving birth to the

Fig. 8.13

famous "Lubitsch touch," a sly and often risqué way of dealing with "sophisticated" comedy in such films as *Trouble in Paradise* (1932). *A Woman of Paris* was not shown in the 1940s but, given the censorship climate and the popular rejection of Chaplin, it probably could not even have been made then. Film censorship became more rigorous in the early 1930s and in *A Woman of Paris* transgressions against mainstream sexual mores go largely unpunished and the characters who embody traditional family values are destructive.

The Film's Plot

Fig. 8.14

The movie begins as Marie St Clair's (Edna Purviance) brutally stern father locks her out of her house (figure 8.13) after she has planned an elopement to Paris with her boyfriend, Jean Millet (Carl Miller). She goes with Jean to his house for shelter, but his comparably stern father refuses to allow her to spend the night (figure 8.14). She and Jean determine to leave for Paris that night, but his father's abrupt death, unknown to her, leads to a misunderstanding and she leaves for Paris alone. The film jumps ahead a year to find her the mistress of the elegant playboy Pierre Revel (Adolphe Menjou, figure 8.15) and traveling in libertine high-society circles. She accidentally meets Jean, who has come to Paris with his mother

Fig. 8.15

Fig. 8.16

to eke out a living as an artist. They tentatively maneuver to resume a relationship, but Jean cannot overcome his mother's possessiveness as well as his revulsion at Marie's lifestyle. Slobbering in self-pity, he commits suicide after confronting Marie and Pierre in a nightclub (figure 8.16). At the film's end, Marie and Jean's mother have set up a rural home for orphans, and she and Pierre, now worlds apart, unknowingly pass one another on a country road ninety kilometers from Paris (figure 8.17).

Fig. 8.17

Questioning of Conventional Morality

The three central characters are developed in opposition to what conventional morality would suggest. Although Jean is a home-town, struggling artist, faithful to Marie and devoted to his mother, he is largely unsympathetic; Pierre, a rich playboy engaged to another woman, is charming, non-possessive, and generous; and Marie, a fallen woman and not the blushing virgin Edna Purviance traditionally played in Chaplin's films, is sympathetic.

Both Pierre and Marie seem reasonably contented at the film's end; neither seems to have suffered permanently for their moral turpitude. Indeed, much of the film revels in its sexual playfulness, with many scenes containing risqué sexual behavior presented as benign, merely the witty hijinks of the wild set. In one, Marie is being massaged and gossips about sexual intrigues with a friend (figure 8.18); in another, a woman is disrobed at a drunken party in front of the revelers. In both scenes, Chaplin's peek-a-boo camerawork and editing tease the spectator by keeping the actresses' naked bodies just out of sight. None of these scenes results in tormented guilt or the significant punishment of the participants.

Family life is presented as mean-spirited and limited; in fact, a central theme is the inadequacy of traditional family life. The one complete nuclear family that we see, Jean's, is divided and non-supportive. Both parents fail him; either one could have saved him from the suicidal spiral his life takes after his separation from Marie.

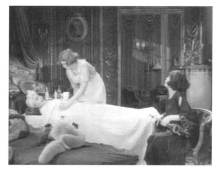

Fig. 8.18

Fig. 8.19

His father refuses to sanction his relationship with Marie or even to shelter her for a night. Had he done either, the film implies, Jean would have both had the relationship that he desired and avoided despair. The stress of the conflict with his son kills the father. Furthermore, a year later in Paris, Jean's mother's possessiveness pollutes the possibility of his marrying Marie, leading to his demise. The film's one nuclear family, then, is devastated by narrow-mindedness and selfishness and comes to a tragic end. Marie's father is no better as a parent.

Pierre, on the other hand, despite his engagement to a wealthy woman, openly consorts with Marie to little evident harm. When Marie laments to him that she wants "a real home, babies, and a man's respect," he points out the window, cynically indicating his view of family life. We see a poor family struggling miserably across the street, the father burdened with packages and the mother with three unruly children in tow (figure 8.19).

The 1923 Reception

The context in which Chaplin's artistic experimentation was received in 1923 was not what it would be in 1947. Although Chaplin was beloved for his tramp films, he was beginning to tire of the character. Many important critics were declaring him a genius and suggesting that he try more "serious" things. His determination to do just that is evident in the film's preface, which reads "TO THE PUBLIC: In order to avoid any misunderstanding, I wish to announce that I do not appear in this picture. It is the first serious drama written and directed by myself. CHARLES CHAPLIN." Many critics at the time loved the film, proclaiming it to be evidence of a new maturing of the cinema itself, and a very important film.

A Woman of Paris shows Chaplin discarding the tramp and capable of writing and directing sophisticated "adult" drama, of being interested in sophisticated, upper-class European society, of questioning traditional American values, particularly those of the nuclear family. In the 1940s, these things were signs of the decline of an anti-American, morally degenerate artist who had alienated his audience; in the 1920s, however, the same things had revealed a maturing and influential artist, respected on an international scale, who was taking risks to broaden the vision of his art.

The Crying Game (1992)

Entertainment Weekly cleverly summed up the early reception context for *The Crying Game* (1992) as "The Movie Everyone's Not Talking About," meaning not that the British film was being ignored but that it was very popular and contained a secret that everyone was keeping. The basis for this secrecy was laid in September 1992 when Miramax, the US distributor, asked reviewers not to reveal the movie's secret; when the movie opened in November 1992, all major reviewers complied.

This in itself is not an unusual strategy. Most reviewers observe an unwritten journalistic law not to reveal surprise plot twists or unexpected outcomes of films. When we read reviews, we expect this and become annoyed if they "spoil" the film for us by revealing plot surprises. What is unusual in this case is the widespread cooperation of critics with the plan devised by the distributor for emphasizing the film as one with a special secret and, in turn, the enthusiasm for this categorization by the media and the public at large. By the time most Americans saw the film, they saw it within a reception context that created a unique expectation that they would be surprised in an astonishing manner.

Part of the reason for this may be that, with *The Crying Game*, the "secret" goes much deeper than the usual unanticipated plot turn, like a revelation about who committed a murder; it crosses into transgressive areas that hold the potential of not only surprising but also of distressing and even outraging some viewers. A look at the reception of the movie will show how it avoided becoming an outrage and instead became an outrageous success. Although initially marketed and exhibited as an art-house film, *The Crying Game* crossed over into the much larger mainstream, commercial market and ended up being by far the largest grossing art film in American history up to that time. *The Crying Game* is a particularly interesting film to study from the perspective of reception because, with this expanded market and popularization, the film's reception context quickly shifted to include three major phases: preferred readings, negotiated readings, and contested readings. Before defining and illustrating those types of readings, it is important to briefly analyze the film.

Jody, a black British soldier stationed in Northern Ireland, is kidnapped and held hostage by the Irish Republican Army (figure 8.20). Fergus becomes sympathetic with Jody while guarding him (figure 8.21) and agrees to look up Dil, Jody's girlfriend (figure 8.22), if things go badly. Jody is killed while trying to escape and Fergus flees to England. He falls in love with Dil, is sickened when he learns Dil is a male transvestite but, regardless, the two develop a deep personal bond. Jude and her

Fig. 8.20

Fig. 8.21

Fig. 8.22

Fig. 8.23

Fig. 8.24

Fig. 8.25

Fig. 8.26

Fig. 8.27

IRA compatriots track Fergus down and threaten Dil (figure 8.23). Dil eventually shoots Jude, who had not only been Fergus's lover but had also enticed Jody into his kidnapping. Fergus, however, assumes responsibility for Jude's death and goes to prison. Dil faithfully awaits his release.

As we have stressed throughout this book, all issues of cinematic representation require careful attention to formal issues, and the gender surprise in *The Crying Game* is no exception. The opening scene of *The Crying Game* contains a conventional reference to male genitals when Jody urinates at a fair. He stands in such a manner that any view of his genitals is blocked by a tent (figure 8.24). A similar scene occurs during his captivity when he has to urinate. The camera is positioned in such a manner that his genitals are off-screen at the bottom of the frame. Yet the unusual circumstances of the scene bring extraordinary attention to them. Since he is hand-cuffed, he asks Fergus, his guard, to unzip his pants, take out his penis, and hold it while he urinates. Fergus eventually does so, but only with great discomfort (figure 8.25). These scenes lull the audience into a false sense of conventional expectations. The way in which they are shot implies that, as in most films, no matter how much attention is given to the penis, the organ will not be shown. This further heightens what would under any circumstances be the shockingly unexpected representation of the organ in the revelation scene. In a film that positions us not to expect to see a penis even when we hear about one, we are hardly prepared to see one in a scene where we do not even know a character has one. Not surprisingly, that scene is one of intense melodrama.

At Dil's apartment, Fergus lies on the bed as Dil goes into the bathroom preparatory to love-making. Dil re-emerges, comes over to the bed, and Fergus rises, kisses her (figure 8.26), and begins to remove her dress. As he slides it down he sits on the edge of the bed. With the camera placed behind him, we simultaneously see both him looking and the sight of Dil's male genitals (figure 8.27); Fergus's stunned reaction coincides with the spectator's. This camera positioning doubly heightens what is already a dramatic moment. The director, Neil Jordan, could easily have shot the scene in a conventional manner, in which the spectator would have learned that

Dil is a man without seeing his genitals or, in a less conventional scenario, at least have learned that information before seeing the genitals. Jordan's strategy maximizes the shock value of the moment by making it a perceptual experience for the spectator. This in turn is heightened by keeping Fergus in the frame, since the spectator's shock is intensified through character identification with the heterosexual man who actually finds himself in this distressing situation.

The Preferred Reading: The "Secret" of *The Crying Game*

Thus, the "secret" that everyone was not talking about existed on a number of levels. In terms of plot, the surprise is the revelation that Dil, the hairdresser with whom Fergus falls in love, is not a woman but a male transvestite. Since most of the audience, like Fergus, has been deceived by Dil, who is represented as an attractive, erotic woman, the audience's own perceptions and desires may be called into question. Heterosexual men, for example, who find Dil attractive may have a fearful response. Furthermore, the film continues to represent Dil as an attractive character after the revelation. Had he been represented as despicable or revolting, the audience could have hated him for having tricked them. Instead, however, the previously heterosexual Fergus remains involved with this attractive man and even goes to jail for him at the end (figure 8.28), thus indicating the potential for heterosexuals to change their sexual orientation. Most provocatively, however, the film's audience sees Dil's genitals at the same moment that Fergus does and this single shot is really the "secret" of the film. If the audience had simply learned that Dil was a man without seeing his genitals or even if they had learned of it before seeing them, the effect would have been much less shocking.

Most initial reviews were highly respectful of the film and took their cue from Miramax in not revealing the "secret," although many did mention that there was a secret. Thus, the movie's initial image, created by advertising and reviews, was of one containing a major and tantalizing surprise. This is what reception scholars call a **preferred reading**, since the responses are those encouraged by the filmmakers, distributors, and exhibitors. The fact that *The Crying Game* is a low-budget, British art film, written and directed by Neil Jordan, who, with such films as *Mona Lisa* (1986), had already established a strong critical reputation, may help account for the initial critical reception. Furthermore, in addition to sexuality, the film addresses socially significant topics such as racism and terrorism. Had a similar surprise been at the center of a despised slasher film in the teen horror genre, the critics might have been less willing to play along.

Fig. 8.28

The Negotiated Reading: "Outing" Jaye Davidson

A cartoon by Warren Miller in the March 15, 1993, issue of *The New Yorker* shows an office in the "Jaye Edgar Hoover Building." Understanding the cartoon requires knowledge, both that Jaye Davidson is the actor playing the gay transvestite Dil and that J. Edgar Hoover had recently been described in the national media as having a secret life as a gay transvestite. This revelation about Hoover, furthermore, relates to the current practice of "outing" famous homosexuals who have chosen not to make their sexual orientation a matter of public record. Some gay and lesbian organizations believe there is political value in the controversial practice of outing famous people, since it brings attention to how widespread homosexuality is. They feel that many Americans presume that their leaders as well as sports and media stars are naturally heterosexual. Outing can, thus, make a dramatic point about that heterosexist assumption.

Outing is an historically specific way of speaking about homosexuality in our culture, and the manner in which *The Crying Game* became part of the discourse of outing illustrates a **negotiated reading** of the film. Negotiated readings, like preferred readings, accept much of the **dominant meaning** that the filmmakers and publicists want, but they inflect the film further with meanings of particular value for certain segments of the population, for example, men, women, homosexuals, working-class people. Nothing within the film thematically, narratively, or formally is about outing, nor did the advertising for the film allude to it. A segment of the population, nevertheless, placed the film within such a context. This discourse of outing even applied to the Academy Awards when Jaye Davidson was nominated for best supporting actor and a prominent critic noted that Davidson had "been 'outed' by the Academy of Motion Picture Arts and Sciences." Davidson was known as a straight man in his hometown of London. Gossip and speculation occurred about whether he would show up as a man or a woman at the awards ceremony.

Although not technically an "outing," another related event that occurred in conjunction with *The Crying Game* involved Boy George, the well-known pop singer who recorded a new version of the film's title song. The star used the occasion of the film to publicly declare himself gay. In a sense, then, the "truth" of the gender and sexuality of the character of Dil, Jaye Davidson the actor, and Boy George the singer were all outed, though none of these outings was part of the original critical reception context.

Oppositional Readings: The Critique of Liberalism

An **oppositional reading** of a film is one that opposes the preferred reading. Critics and spectators who view films oppositionally do so with knowledge of what the filmmakers and the producers want them to accept but reject those readings and choose quite different ones. Neither *The Crying Game*'s writer/director nor Miramax, the distributor, wanted the film to be read as racist and sexist nor, obviously, did they advertise it as such. As we have seen, the film seems to challenge the audience in its sexual perceptions and assumptions and, furthermore, positions audiences to sympathize with the relationship of a transvestite gay man and a previously heterosexual man. Furthermore, since this relationship involves a black man and a white man, the film also seems to promote racial harmony. Yet one group of vocal critics outside the mainstream rejected all these seemingly positive readings and read it as racist, sexist, and homophobic.

How could this be? First of all, for these critics, the film privileges white male heterosexuality since it centers upon the white heterosexual's point of view. Put simply, Fergus is the main character and the film concerns itself with his moral dilemmas and growth. We care about Jody, the black man, primarily through his relationship with Fergus. Furthermore, with its heavy emphasis on sexuality, the film characterizes blacks and gays as oversexed and exotic. And who is the villain? It is Jude, an IRA member who is represented throughout as a manipulative, cruel, and frustrated woman. She is eventually killed by Dil in a brutally graphic manner (figure 8.29). One critic compared her character to that of Glenn Close in *Fatal Attraction* (1987, see chapter 1). In both films, the woman is represented as being so hideous and evil that many audiences delight in her graphic death, which strikes them as just punishment. From this perspective, the serious art film, which supposedly supplies an alternative to Hollywood, suddenly sounds just like Hollywood.

But there is an added dimension here since it is a man who dresses as a woman who kills the real woman and since we are asked to like him just as clearly as we are asked to dislike her. The film, then, affirms a male version of femininity over the real thing: in other words, a man impersonating a woman is more attractive than a woman.

All of these oppositional readings share something: they accuse the film of having a false, "liberal" conscience, one that seems to embrace multiculturalism and sexual diversity but that really wants to keep white heterosexual men at the center of things. Audiences can come away feeling good about their acceptance of homosexuality and transvestism as well as their acceptance of blacks, but their entrenched social beliefs have not really been threatened. Homosexuality can easily be tolerated if it does not require one to rethink heterosexuality. One of the strategies the film uses (for these critics, a strategy resembling those of mainstream Hollywood) is to collapse the personal and the political. It introduces profound political issues involving the IRA, race relations, and sexual orientation and never addresses them beyond resolving the character conflicts. We are happy that

Fig. 8.29

Fergus and Dil are united and that Jude is killed, and we are not encouraged to think beyond that. The larger social issues become forgotten.

Another way of stating this critique of an easy liberalism is that it denies difference and affirms that all people of differing races and sexual orientations are really very much like one another. Oppositional critics feel that the real challenge would be to acknowledge and accept difference, in the process decentering the white male heterosexual norm. Those critics who played along with Miramax's advertising campaign for *The Crying Game* not only prepared the public to accept the preferred reading but also helped block oppositional readings, since offering such readings would require revealing "the secret." Obviously, one cannot fully explore the disturbing significance of the film's sexual ideology in a public forum if one does not mention what lies at the very center of that aspect of the film.

Thus, within a brief time after its release, *The Crying Game* was part of a number of differing reception contexts. Like *A Woman of Paris*, though in a much shorter period of time, it has been perceived in many ways. And both films will undoubtedly be received in currently unimaginable contexts in the future, since reception studies show us how changing historical circumstances and historically specific audiences contribute new and quite differing meanings to them.

SELECTED READINGS

Henry Louis Gates, Jr discusses his family's response to "Andy Plays Santa Claus," in "An 'Amos 'n' Andy' Christmas," *New York Times,* December 23 (1994), p. A35. *Faster Pussycat! Kill! Kill!* is reviewed in Mick Martin and Marsha Porter, *Video Movie Guide 1991* (New York: Ballantine Books, 1990), p. 43, and the 1995 reception context of the film's re-release, including feminist praise, is reported by Hal Hinton in "Russ Meyer, Porn in the USA," *Washington Post*, April 12 (1995), p. B1. Winston Groom's reaction to the film *Forrest Gump* is reported in William Grimes, "Following the Star of a Winsome Idiot," *New York Times*, September 1 (1994), p. C13. Janet Staiger traces the sources of a variety of responses to *The Birth of a Nation* from its release in 1915, when the NAACP and the Ku Klux Klan provided the highly visible poles of reaction to the film, through the 1930s, when the film's reputation became linked with various left-wing debates, and into the 1970s, when it still inspired political and social controversy, in *Interpreting Films: Studies in the Historical Reception of American Cinema* (Princeton, NJ: Princeton University Press, 1992). K. A. Burke analyzes the advertising campaign for *Imitation of Life* in Atlanta in "Imitation of Promotion: Race as a Factor of Discourse in the Promotion of *Imitation of Life*," a paper delivered at the Society for Cinema Studies Conference, Syracuse, New York, 1994. In "The Reception of *The Crying Game*," a paper presented at the same conference, Robert T. Eberwein analyzes the preferred, negotiated, and oppositional readings of that film. Mark Simpson compares *The Crying Game* with *Fatal Attraction* in *Male Impersonators: Men Performing Masculinity* (New York: Routledge, 1994).

9

FILM AND THE OTHER ARTS

Dr Jekyll and Mr Hyde and *Nosferatu*

How often have we heard someone say, "I didn't read the book but I saw the movie"? Or, "I liked the ending in the book better than the one in the movie"? Such statements betray the presumption of a close linkage between novels and movies based upon them, a sense that they are virtually two versions of the same thing. Recently, John Grisham's novels and the films based upon them (*The Firm*, 1993, *The Pelican Brief*, 1994, *The Chamber*, 1996, *A Time to Kill*, 1996, and *The Rainmaker*, 1997) have been talked about in such a manner. The interest surrounding the publication of a new novel by such popular writers as Grisham or Michael Crichton (*Jurassic Park*, 1993, and *The Lost World*, 1995) often hinges as much upon the anticipated movie adaptation as it does upon the novel itself.

   Even when adaptation is not an issue, movies resemble novels in having characters and telling stories. We tend to speak of them in similar ways, and the *auteur* theory, which we discussed in chapter 4, takes its name from the analogy between an author and a film director. But movies are also like theater. They have actors, scripts, and sets, and we use much of the same language when talking about the two forms: the term "screenplay" implies a play written for the screen as opposed to one written for the stage. At other times, we speak about movies as resembling photography or painting as, for example, when we praise the composition, lighting, or color of a particular shot. People in the industry even refer to movies as "pictures." And at still other times, movies have been compared with music. We discuss in chapter 16 how Mike Figgis conceived of *Timecode* (2000) along musical terms. A number of *avant-garde* European filmmakers of the 1920s, such as Walter Ruttmann in *Berlin: Symphony of a Great City* (1927), used musical concepts to construct their films. In Hollywood, Walt Disney called an animated series the *Silly Symphonies*.

As all of these ways of talking about movies indicate, films are often compared with many other art forms. When we talk about film directors as being the "authors" of their movies, however, we must be careful because such a claim is based upon analogy and arguing from analogy is notoriously dangerous. When we draw an analogy between one art form and another, we may notice the similarities but overlook the differences.

We classify the arts in different ways such as narrative and non-narrative and performing and non-performing. Even here there are gray areas. We think of music as non-narrative but some forms of classical music contain narrative elements. Thunderstorms are musically represented, for example, in Beethoven's Sixth Symphony and Grofe's *Grand Canyon Suite*. Similarly, we think of literature as being a narrative, non-performing art form, but some novels contain such ambiguous and oblique narratives that readers can follow little or no story. There is currently a boom in audiocassette recordings of famous actors reading novels, which in effect makes the cassettes performances of those novels.

In this chapter, we explore the relationships between film and theater and between film and literature. We focus on these art forms because they illuminate issues with which we are centrally concerned in this book. The relationship between film and theater helps us to understand film acting (discussed in chapter 7) and authorship (discussed in chapter 4). It is, however, the connection between film and literature that most centrally shapes common assumptions about movies, and in the second part of the chapter we examine two films that are adaptations of well-known novels. In doing so, we question common assumptions about adaptation, including notions of "faithfulness" and cinematic "equivalents" of literary techniques; we also reveal deep affinities between the form of the nineteenth-century novel, its popular twentieth-century counterparts, and the **classical Hollywood film**. Although individual novels and films based upon them are less closely related than is commonly thought, the forms of the nineteenth-century novel and twentieth-century popular fiction are in fact significantly linked to feature filmmaking. Furthermore, at times, works in multiple forms can establish a tradition of influence. We will see that the 1932 film *Dr Jekyll and Mr Hyde* is influenced not only by Robert Louis Stevenson's 1886 novel but also by a number of plays based upon that novel as well as earlier films.

Theater and Film

In the dominant Western theatrical tradition, language creates the fictional world. If we read a play without ever seeing it performed, we know what the play is about, what motivates the characters, what the themes are, and so on. We can judge how complex and well developed it is and determine whether it is a good or bad play. We can do all of this without paying attention to the stage directions or even seeing a production of it in which the characters may or may not do what we think is generally indicated in the directions. It is for this reason that sometimes play readings are staged in which the actors simply sit in chairs and read their parts, and at other times stage directions, including period and setting, are entirely changed. A well-known example of the latter is Peter Brooks's production of Shakespeare's *A Midsummer Night's Dream* performed on playground gymnastic equipment! Not only did Shakespeare not write the play for such a setting, but such equipment did not even exist at the time.

Since the identity of the work lies in the words spoken by the actors, what they are doing or not doing when they speak their lines is infinitely variable. A famous Shakespearean actor reportedly changed something in his performance every night during a production of *Hamlet*. On Tuesday night he might have delivered a line standing on the floor with his right hand raised and on Wednesday night he might have leapt on to a table and delivered the same line. It is precisely because the language creates the fictional world of the play that it can sustain such different interpretations. Interpretations concerning fundamental aspects of character can also vary. Richard Burton interpreted Hamlet as virile and athletic, Peter O'Toole saw him as homosexual, and Laurence Olivier portrayed him as having an Oedipal crisis. The dialogue creates enough of the character, his fictional world, and the predicament he is in to sustain these and other interpretations of *Hamlet* much like written characters in novels are reinterpreted by readers and critics of different generations. Indeed, plays are frequently read, enjoyed, and even taught as literature.

Though cinema may seem like theater, in this regard it is nearly a polar opposite. Language in the cinema is a part, and sometimes a small one, of a fictional world that is created and sustained by images and sounds. Language in cinema does not create a continuous fictional world, nor does it frequently speak about fundamental issues within that world; indeed, much can remain entirely unspoken in the cinema. Jacques Tati used little dialogue in his famous comedy, *M. Hulot's Holiday* (1953), and what little dialogue he did use – snippets of everyday language – had no thematic or psychological importance. However, the non-verbal sounds of the movie are critical; in one scene, for example, we see a puzzled hotel official trying to discover who has tracked up his lobby with wet footprints. We do not see Tati's character at all. However, as the official investigates the footprints, we hear the off-screen thumps that we later learn are made by a boat oar Tati's character had been carrying (figure 9.1) but then dropped as he attempted to sneak away from the embarrassing situation.

Fig. 9.1

Similarly, consider the example in *The Searchers* (1956, see chapter 4) when, at the end of the film, Ethan reverses his stated intention and saves rather than kills Debbie. Nothing in the dialogue hints at why he has acted in this way, but the complex visuals, cutting patterns, and gestures combine to explain the action. Similarly, nothing in the dialogue hints at the relationship between Ethan and Martha; it is all established through glances, gestures, compositions, even the use of music. Not one word about it is ever spoken by any character. Nothing comparable to that can happen in the theater. If Hamlet is indecisive, he or other characters must remark on that indecision.

The end of *The Searchers* supplies an excellent example for distilling this essential difference between film and theater. Let us compare the gesture of Ethan lifting Debbie high in the air when he catches up with her outside the mouth of the cave (see plate 22) with the hypothetical gesture of the raised arm of the stage actor playing Hamlet. As he cradles her in his arms, Ethan says, "Let's go home, Debbie." Imagine if, during the shooting of the film, John Wayne had told director John Ford that, instead of lifting Debbie up in the air, he only wanted to pull her up from the ground to a standing position. While such a change would be perfectly sensible and acceptable in the theater, in this movie it would compromise the entire meaning of the scene, since the lifting gesture rhymes with the earlier scene when Ethan lifted the younger Debbie high in his arms in his brother's home (see plate 21). The gesture here counts for everything, the spoken line for very little. If Wayne said, "C'mon, Debbie, let's go home," or "I'm taking you home," or even if he said nothing, it would make little difference. The situation is the opposite of that with *Hamlet* in which the spoken line contains so much meaning that it can sustain an infinite number of gestures accompanying it. You cannot change Hamlet's "To be or not to be" speech without changing the identity of the work or its fundamental meaning, but because that meaning is verbally articulated, it can be performed and interpreted in a wide variety of ways.

The Searchers' example is admittedly extreme, and dialogue does play a significant role throughout the film. For example, it is important that we hear about Ethan's mysterious absence since the end of the Civil War. And certainly different kinds of movies use language in different ways. Yet even character-driven movies with a great deal of dialogue are fundamentally different from plays. The status and nature of dialogue rather than the amount of dialogue is really at issue. No matter how much a character talks in a film, that character is part of a fictional world created and sustained by the image in which he or she appears.

Although screenplays appear to resemble stage plays in that they contain both general directions and spoken dialogue, they are in reality profoundly different. The role of the dialogue in constituting the work of art is entirely different: in the theater, the dialogue is the primary means of creating and maintaining the fictional world, but in the cinema it is a small and frequently discontinuous part of that world. The shot of Ethan chasing Debbie framed through the mouth of the dark cave followed by the shot of Ethan lifting Debbie constitutes the fictional world. For this reason, a staged reading of the screenplay of *The Searchers* would be an exercise in futility and a version of it on gymnastic equipment would be a totally unrecognizable thing. Screenplays, as opposed to stage plays, are seldom read for enjoyment or taught separately from the films that were made using them.

There are, of course, different kinds of plays. We have thus far been speaking of "straight" or "dramatic" plays, plays largely driven by spoken language and narrative. These comprise the dominant and most critically respected tradition of Western drama, but if we look at Broadway plays in recent years, many of them are musicals. Unlike the case with traditional drama, very few people would think of reading the book of a musical or, having done so, would feel they had experienced the play. With musicals, the music and songs are of central importance, and people wanting to get a sense of a musical do not buy the book but rather listen to the CD of the music.

There is a long tradition of relationships between films and musicals, even pre-dating the sound era. Most instances involve films based upon popular musicals, such as *Show Boat* (1936 and 1951), *My Fair Lady* (1964), or *The King and I* (1956) but there is a growing tradition of musicals based upon films, such as Mel Brooks's *The Producers* (2001, based upon his 1967 film). We will look briefly at another example, *Victor/Victoria*. The musical, based upon Blake Edwards's 1982 film, opened on Broadway in 1995 and was, to the best of our knowledge, the first time a Hollywood film director wrote and directed a Broadway production of his film. As we discuss in chapter 10 on radio, television, and film, Edwards has worked creatively in a number of mass media, and adapted his work to the demands, strengths, and industrial traditions of each of them. Although he had directed and written the 1982 movie, in writing and directing the play, he produced a substantially different work. This resulted from creative decisions attuned to the demands of musical theater as opposed to film. One indication of such demands is that, unlike the film, the credits for the play give as much status to the writers of the music (Henry Mancini) and lyrics (Leslie Bricusse, with additional musical material by Frank Wildhorn) as they do to Edwards as writer of the book. Furthermore, the play has roughly twice the amount of musical numbers as the film and substantially less narrative development than the film. This results in part from the decision to transform the film from a comedy about a performer into a complete musical where most of the characters sing and dance. In the film, in other words, all the singing and dancing is part of a performance for an audience within the movie; the characters do not break into song and dance when, for example, they are at home alone. Yet, that is precisely what they do in the Broadway play.

Some of the characterization in the play that is done through action and dialogue in the film is done through song, such as "King's Dilemma," a song, new to the play, that develops King's gender confusion. Although Rodgers and Hammerstein's 1943 musical *Oklahoma* is legendary in Broadway history for integrating its musical numbers with its narrative, the dominant appeal of many musicals still lies in the performance of the songs. In fact, some musicals appear to be little more than songs linked together by minimal narrative, and often what narrative there is seems to do little more than set the stage for the next song. Henry Mancini, whose reputation largely rests on the music he composed for films, realized that film audiences seldom notice film music, which generally takes a back seat to the narrative. He even self-deprecatingly entitled his autobiography, *Did They Mention the Music?* But this is certainly not the case with traditional musicals, in which audiences might forget the narrative but remember the songs. Most musicals, like *Victor/Victoria*, begin with an orchestral overture, introducing the audience to the main melodies of the show and establishing an aural environment for the evening. Only when that aural environment is established do the actors appear. In the film, the music appears with the opening credits and has a much less foregrounded role.

Although Julie Andrews starred in both film and play, her performance style is very different in each. In the movie, she acts in a highly "dramatic" manner – grand gestures, dramatic poses, full oratorical voice – whenever she is on stage as the title character performing before audiences. Andrews employs a more muted, intimate manner when interacting with other actors in private moments when no audience is present. In the play, the difference in acting style between her "performance" life and "private" life is much less than that in the film. Even her "private" moments appear highly performative in the play because she is always performing before the live audience in the theater, including those seated in the back rows.

The play has a great deal of physical comedy and some hilarious bedroom farce which involves dividing up the space in the elaborate sets, but the kind of complex cutting in the film is impossible. The film's hallway scene using **offscreen space** that we discuss in chapter 10 has no parallel in the play but could conceivably have been adapted because it involves a single-audience perspective. Other scenes, such as the cockroach in the restaurant or King sneaking into Victoria's bathroom to see her naked (again without parallel in the play) rely on different camera perspectives and movement and would have had to be entirely reconceived. Some scenes in the play without parallel in the movie, however, like Victoria's tango with Norma, are well suited to the traditional strengths (single-audience perspective, music, carefully choreographed dance and movement, dramatic production values) of the musical stage.

Film and Performance

But let us return to the dominant tradition of dramatic theater. An old cliché calls theater a writer's medium and film a director's medium, and from this perspective it has validity. Since the aesthetic identity of a play is contained in the dialogue, that identity can be attributed to the writer and not the director. When Arthur Miller wrote *Death of a Salesman*, he created the characters and themes that were later performed and interpreted by those who staged productions of it. Since the dialogue in cinema is only a small part of the fictional world, however, it is the director rather than the writer who gives the work its aesthetic identity. The shots of doorways, caves, and lifting gestures as well as the dialogue constitute the aesthetic identity of *The Searchers*.

The fact that movies are neither written nor performed like plays does not mean that screenplays and screenwriters are unimportant. Screenplays are extremely useful in the making of most feature films, but there is a crucial difference between being useful in the creation of the work and actually creating the work. An example from painting can be helpful in clarifying this distinction. An artist may use a photograph or a sketch in the creation of an oil painting, but that photograph or sketch does not determine the aesthetic features of the finished painting. A great artist and an untrained amateur could easily base an oil painting upon the same sketch, but the former might produce a complex, beautiful masterpiece while the latter might produce an unsightly mess. Screenplays, even character-driven ones with a great deal of dialogue, rather resemble preliminary sketches or photographs used to create a painting than they do the finished works. Sometimes, in fact, screenplays are used as the basis for the preliminary step of storyboards, which add sketches of shots to the written script. The role of both, however, is subordinate to the photographed film.

If the same screenplay were given to ten directors, we would end up with ten different movies, some good, some bad, and some mediocre. If we give *Hamlet* to ten theater directors, however, we would have ten productions of the same brilliant play. Although some of the productions might be good, some bad, and some mediocre, all ten would still be Shakespeare's play even if, as in the case of Brooks's *A Midsummer Night's Dream*, some might border on the outrageous. It is precisely for this reason that, as we discussed in chapter 4, film studies has a rich tradition of critical works analyzing the films of individual directors but no such comparable tradition with the works of screenwriters. It may also explain why, when well-known playwrights such as Harold Pinter (*The Go-Between*, 1971), Tom Stoppard (*Despair*, 1977), and David Mamet (*The Untouchables*, 1987, figure 9.2) write screenplays, critics usually minimize the significance of those screenplays within the playwright's *oeuvre*. Ultimately, the screenplays and their authors are overshadowed by the films and their directors (respectively, Joseph Losey, Rainer Werner Fassbinder, and Brian De Palma in the above examples).

The independent cinema may on occasion enable an unusually close and even unorthodox relationship to blur the boundaries between a writer and a **director**. Such is the case in the collaboration between the acclaimed novelist Paul Auster (*New York Trilogy*) and the equally acclaimed filmmaker Wayne Wang (*Chan is Missing*, 1982). Their collaboration on *Smoke* (1995) and *Blue in the Face* (1995) was so unusually close that they shot the second film immediately after the first and didn't even distinguish between Auster and Wang as writer and director; they are equally credited in creating the film. Here a novelist/screenwriter has developed such a close working relationship with a director that they collaborated in a manner that destroys the usual distinction between a writer and a director and a screenplay and a film.

Fig. 9.2

Such blurring of the writing and directing roles is much less likely to occur within the Hollywood industry. If the relationship between screenplays and films and writers and directors is generally so tenuous, what kind of relationship exits between a film and a novel upon which the screenplay was based?

Film and Literature

The most extreme answer would be "None at all!" We have seen how the severely limited role that language plays in cinema makes it a substantially different form from drama, in which language plays a dominant role. The gap is much greater with literature in which language plays not only the dominant role, but also the only role. Literature is not performed; it has no actors or interpreters, stage settings, lights, or music. Literature is read.

The perception of film as a director's medium and theater as a writer's medium results from a consensus about the dominance of those roles over competing creative roles. Literature allows little debate; the author has the only creative role except in situations in which an editor changes or helps shape a manuscript. From this standpoint, literature is light years away from cinema, in which language plays a limited role. Why, then, do people constantly mix the two together? Why also will movie production companies pay millions of dollars for the rights to make a movie based upon popular novels like John Grisham's *The Firm* or return repeatedly to classic novels such as *The Three Musketeers*? One answer to the question is economics, since films adapted from best-selling or famous novels have frequently enjoyed box-office success. But this raises the question as to why people who loved a novel want to see a movie adaptation of it and why many even feel the two forms are so closely linked as to be virtually interchangeable.

Part of the answer lies in our culture's emphasis upon story over form in narrative works. As we discussed in chapter 2, most people, when asked what a movie is "about," will respond by talking about its story. Yet, as we demonstrated, a story achieves its aesthetic effect and complexity when it is woven into a plot including **free motifs**. In chapter 3, we saw that the formal properties of film, such as the representation of space, are as important and at times more important than narrative elements. Such formal properties of film, however, are not properties of stories. Furthermore, the manner in which our culture values story ideas extends from the aesthetic realm into the legal realm. Appropriation of story material has a legal history, including such highly publicized cases as that in which Art Buchwald successfully sued the Paramount studio claiming plagiarism of his story idea in the Eddie Murphy movie *Coming to America* (1988). Although the history of cinema includes many remakes of films (see chapter 6) and a great deal of litigation over rights to use story material, there is no tradition of filmmakers having been sued for copying the visual style of the earlier film.

Studios pay millions of dollars for the rights to best-selling novels because they recognize that readers of those novels value the stories, rather than the style or the manner in which the stories are told. Furthermore, once they have paid for the rights they cannot be sued for plagiarism. After the publication of the novel *Jurassic Park* (see chapter 2), any filmmakers who wanted to make a movie about rampaging dinosaurs re-created in the modern world from DNA, without buying the rights to Crichton's novel, would be likely to face serious legal consequences. Studios have at times paid for and acknowledged source material simply to protect themselves from lawsuits because of the similarity of their subject and story to a prior literary publication.

Despite the fact that they can both share the same stories and sources, film and literature are radically different creative forms. They require quite different skills and mental activities (for example, linguistic as opposed to visual) from audiences and readers. There have been major painters who were also major sculptors (Michelangelo) and major novelists who were also major poets (Thomas Hardy), but there has never been a major novelist who was also a major movie director, although some, such as Alain Robbe-Grillet and Norman Mailer, have directed films. Similarly, some major film directors such as Samuel Fuller have written novels but they are not recognized as being significant from a literary point of view.

While the forms are aesthetically more different than alike, they do, however, share important narrative and cultural traditions. As a form the novel reached its zenith in the nineteenth century. While some twentieth-century novels, such as James Joyce's *Finnegan's Wake*, have explored new directions, twentieth-century popular novels have largely drawn upon literary traditions established in the nineteenth century, particularly those of the realist novel. The classical film has drawn on these same traditions, and this accounts for the cultural affinity between the two forms.

Differences between Novels and Films

Consider the novel *Wuthering Heights* and the 1939 movie based upon it. The novel is a sequence of pages with words upon them; the movie is a number of reels of celluloid with images and a sound track on it. The activity of spending an hour with the novel is to read words at your own pace; some will read ten pages, some fifty. The activity of spending an hour with the movie in a theater is to watch images and listen to sounds at exactly the same pace as everyone else in the theater.

The novel was written by Emily Brontë working alone; the movie was created by many performers, writers, business people, and technicians guided by its director, William Wyler. Brontë wrote words on paper and, when she was done, she had her finished work. Wyler took words written by Ben Hecht and Charles MacArthur, based upon Brontë's novel, worked with producer Samuel Goldwyn, set designers, costumers, actors, cinematographers, and editors. Many hands participated in the finished work.

This in no way implies that either Brontë or Wyler is the greater artist. They are different artists with different skills who worked in different media. These fundamental differences invalidate many of the assumptions underlying traditional ways of talking about film and literature such as "what was left in and what was taken out" of the novel and what was "changed." A reader of the novel *Jurassic Park*, for example, might claim that the exciting river raft chase did not appear in the movie (see chapter 1), or that the Tyrannosaur's attack on the Velociraptors did not appear in the book. A reader of *The Big Sleep* might complain that the gangster Eddie Mars remains alive and the detective Marlowe has no romantic partner in the novel, but that the 1946 movie ends with Mars being gunned down by his own men and with Marlowe in a budding romantic relationship. These are differences in two parallel narratives, not variations on one.

It is fine to talk about such differences in the narrative structures of two works. The problem comes with the assumption that, if there were not such differences, the works would be essentially "the same," which is absurd. Even if every narrative event were the same, the works would be more dissimilar than similar.

If one walks into an art museum and looks at medieval and Renaissance paintings, one will find many scenes from the life of Christ, inspired by the Bible. A whole tradition in art history has developed around these paintings, discussing them not only in terms of their sources but also in terms of the careers of the artists, their formal properties, and their social contexts. An art critic discussing Leonardo da Vinci's *Last Supper* in terms of its "faithfulness" to the biblical account would miss much of what the painting is about, yet that is virtually what is often done with some discussions of films based upon novels.

Another way of talking about differences between novels and films is to justify narrative elements of the novel without parallel in the film on the grounds that films are shorter and have to "leave something out" of novels. While it is true that the average feature film cannot contain as much narrative information as the typical novel, this should not obscure the fact that the narrative elements they do share are embedded in fundamentally different works.

If we look at a few brief examples, we will see the inadequacies of using the notion of equivalency in any but the most general terms. It makes little sense to speak of what from a novel was "put in" or "left out" of a movie, since it implies that something identical or at least very similar is either in or out. At one point in Raymond Chandler's novel *Farewell, My Lovely*, the narrator awakes after having been beaten. "Cold sweat stood out in lumps on my forehead, but I shivered just the same. I got up on one foot, then on both feet, straightened up, wobbling a little. I felt like an amputated leg" (p. 55). Later, he describes a woman's expression. "Anne Riordan took her lower lip between her teeth and held it there for a moment as if making up her mind whether to bite it off and spit it out or leave it on a while longer" (p. 106). In another

Chandler novel, *The Long Goodbye*, a character appears: "He had short red hair and a face like a collapsed lung" (p. 147). All of these are brief sentences, but their literary texture involves the precise use of the words that create a brutal physical image. Thinking of their filmic "equivalents" is ludicrous. Would a shot of an exhausted man arising intercut with a shot of an amputated leg be "the same"? What of a shot of a woman chewing her lip intercut with a "fantasy" shot of her biting it off and spitting it out? And although it is easy to have a character with short red hair, how can we even begin to imagine, let alone represent, what a collapsed lung looks like? Thus, even if the story events in these passages are included in a film, it makes no sense to speak of them as simply being "in" the movie. What is "in" is something very different from what was in the novel. When Dashiell Hammett in *The Maltese Falcon* writes, "The ashes on the desk twitched and crawled in the current" (p. 4), he gives an image of cigarette ashes moving in a breeze, but he also gives connotations of writhing agony that a simple picture of ashes could not convey.

Oscar Wilde's *The Picture of Dorian Gray* opens with "The studio was filled with the rich odor of roses, and when the light summer wind stirred amid the trees of the garden, there came through the open door the heavy scent of the lilac, or the more delicate perfume of the pink-flowering thorn" (p. 35). This establishes the environment of the painter's studio as suffused with an atmosphere of strong and subtle floral odors, prized by aesthetes, but it ends with a reminder of the thorn, the dangers underlying beautiful things. Nothing a movie shows us could be equivalent.

Finally, Dickens's *A Tale of Two Cities* has one of the most famous openings in literature. "It was the best of times, it was the worst of times, it was the age of wisdom, it was the age of foolishness, it was the epoch of belief, it was the epoch of incredulity, it was the season of Light, it was the season of Darkness, it was the spring of hope, it was the winter of despair, we had everything before us, we had nothing before us, we were all going directly to Heaven, we were all going direct the other way – in short, the period was so far like the present period, that some of its noisiest authorities insisted on its being received, for good or evil, in the superlative degree of comparison only" (p. 35).

This remarkable sentence is built upon broad generalizations that are compared with their opposites, such as best/worst and light/darkness, but in general ways to suggest a time of great intensity and confusion. Film can certainly contrast things, but not in the same way. Yet *A Tale of Two Cities* has been filmed a number of times. How? Largely by appropriating the overall narrative structure and character conceptions of the novel.

Common Properties of Literature and Film

Both film and novels are predominantly narrative forms, which are forms that tell a story (see chapter 2). While it cannot be said that the forms share visual, aural, acting, design, or rhetorical traditions, they do share narrative traditions. They tell certain kinds of stories that follow certain kinds of characters in action through time. In these areas there are many similarities between the two forms.

During cinema's first twenty years, movies developed from shorts of 10 minutes or less to films of over an hour, and to sustain the greater length they developed more sophisticated storytelling techniques. They learned some of those techniques from the dominant narrative tradition of the day, that of the nineteenth-century novel. Those techniques cannot be separated from their historical context and their audience. The novel itself was a relatively new form, with its beginnings in the early eighteenth century. The period of its greatest popularity in the nineteenth century related to new institutions such as serial publication and lending libraries which catered to the rapidly growing middle class. It was also a period of European, and especially British, world dominance, a fact evident in the topics and characters of the novels.

Plots and characters can be constructed in many ways, but they are not unchangeable things. Before the eighteenth century, for example, especially in medieval and Renaissance narratives, it was common to develop characters along allegorical or totally symbolic lines. In the seventeenth-century religious narrative *The Pilgrim's Progress*, the characters have no psychological complexity but rather stand for moral attributes. The main character is called Christian and other characters are called Mr Worldly Wiseman, Hopeful, Giant Despair, and Faithful. Comparably, in the fifteenth-century play *Everyman*, the characters have names like Worldly Goods, Good Deeds, and Everyman. The rise of the novel brought psychologically individualized characters, more likely to be named Oliver Twist or Moll Flanders than Sloth or Pride.

Fig. 9.3

Similarly, medieval chronicles tend to give records of events over time. They often move from one set of characters and events to another. The kind of plot developed in the realist novel is less concerned with chronicling events through time than with setting up a core of characters, establishing a few goals for them, and then developing the novel around the fulfillment or non-fulfillment of those goals, rather than simply following the characters' lives from beginning to end. Early film developed its narrative complexity trying to appeal to a broad, largely middle-class audience, and in its appropriation of aspects of Victorian fiction included that form's topics and narrational style.

Fig. 9.4

In a scene in *Gone with the Wind*, a group of women await the return of their husbands and male friends (figure 9.3). To pass the time, one reads Dickens's *David Copperfield* aloud, starting with "Chapter One. I Am Born" (figure 9.4). The movie is a 1939 movie about the Civil War era; the novel is an 1850 novel about the early nineteenth century. The narratives of the two works have little obviously in common, less so, it would seem, than the novel and the 1935 movie *David Copperfield*. But in many ways, Dickens's novel and *Gone with the Wind* have a great deal in common. In narrative terms, both have a main plot (the story of David Copperfield, the story of Scarlett O'Hara) and a number of related subplots. Both begin by establishing the social environment of the main characters as a way of establishing their goals and the major questions that run through the works and are resolved at the end. As the works develop, major goals become success in "the world" and a heterosexual romance. The novel ends happily for David, the movie unhappily for Scarlett, but both endings are clear-cut resolutions of their main problems. That resolution is not simply death. Both characters are alive at the end, so in their "lives" more story could come (and did in the recent novel and television mini-series *Scarlett*), but these narratives are not so much constructed around their lives as around a specific set of narrative questions intertwined with their lives. When the questions are resolved, the narrative is resolved. Such similarities in character and narrative construction reveal a good deal about the relation between literature and film, and do not deal in notions of equivalency or "faithfulness." They respect the two forms as fundamentally different, but also as sharing traditions that can shed light on both.

We now take a closer look at two well-known adaptations of nineteenth-century novels, *Dr Jekyll and Mr Hyde* (1932) and *Nosferatu* (1922). The former is a classical Hollywood film, the latter a German silent film. We will examine these movies, which are part of quite different film styles and time periods, in relation to the novels upon which they were based. The comparisons show that works with a great many character and narrative aspects in common can also be fundamentally and complexly different. An understanding of this enables us to more fully appreciate the artistic vitality of the different forms.

Dr Jekyll and Mr Hyde (1932) and Stevenson's Novel

Everybody knows about Dr Jekyll and Mr Hyde. Robert Louis Stevenson's novel, *The Strange Case of Dr Jekyll and Mr Hyde*, has been popular since it appeared in 1886. People who have never read it feel that they know what it is about; it has also inspired many stage and film adaptations. The plays began only a year and a half after the novel appeared; the movies in 1908.

Discussion of adaptations of the novel often presume that, with obvious but largely superficial differences in actors and technology (from John Barrymore to Fredric March to Spencer Tracy; or silent to sound to color), the movies are fundamentally telling the "same" story and that all are to varying degrees "faithful" to the novel. Not only is this presumption untrue, but it also stands directly in the way of any real understanding or enjoyment of the novel and films.

Dr Jekyll and Mr Hyde is about a respected, nineteenth-century British physician who experiments with a drug that splits his personality: the immoral Hyde that the potion produces looks monstrously different from the virtuous

Jekyll. Hyde engages in various vices, culminating in murder, but he eludes discovery by transforming himself back into Jekyll. Eventually Jekyll cannot control the transformations, Hyde appears without the potion, and both soon die. This summary describes most of the Jekyll and Hyde works, so how can they be all that different? Let us look more closely at the novel and one of the movies.

Narrative Structure of the Novel

The novel was written at the height of the Victorian age (1837–1901) and has been seen as a commentary on its hypocrisy. England then dominated the world, and some attributed its power to its moral superiority over other nations. Some critics of the time saw a dark underside to this smugness, a feeling that England concealed moral hypocrisy under its proud surface. They felt that Stevenson's novel was about that hypocrisy. Jekyll was a publicly right-eous man who created Hyde in order to indulge in vices without tarnishing his image.

As Jekyll's story, however, the novel has a curious narrative structure. It begins not with the origins of his experiment but long after he has become Hyde. Furthermore, it does not end with Jekyll's death, which occurs three-fifths of the way through the novel. The death is followed by two chapters: long accounts by Dr Lanyon and, finally, Jekyll.

This narrative structure seems a peculiar way of telling Jekyll's story until we realize that it is not Jekyll's narrative; it is the narrative of Mr Utterson, Jekyll's attorney. The novel begins when Utterson is shocked to learn that the sinister Hyde had a connection with Jekyll. Fearing danger to Jekyll, he decides to investigate, thinking, "If he be Mr Hyde . . . I shall be Mr Seek" (p. 68). The narrative lurchings back and forth in Jekyll's story make sense when we realize that the novel is not so much Jekyll's story as it is the narrative of Utterson's discovery of Jekyll's plight.

The Role of Perception and Subjectivity in the Novel

Not only are the narrative events structured around Utterson's perceptions, but the workings of perception itself are central to the horror of the novel. Hyde is never described beyond being pale, dwarfish, and agitated. Utterson says that he had the impression of deformity and monstrosity in Hyde's appear-ance but that, looking at him, he could find nothing abnormal. Everyone who sees Hyde is revolted by his appearance, but we never get a description of him – his effect is subjective.

Subjectivity is important to the way Stevenson constructs the novel. Hyde holds legendary status as a villain but, aside from the killing of Sir Danvers

Carew and brief, non-lethal outbursts, we never learn of his evil deeds. Those deeds we do learn of are not admirable, but why have they made Hyde into a villain comparable with Dracula, Frankenstein, and Jack the Ripper? We must look beyond the actions and into the subjective perceptions of those who see him. This is what the novel focuses upon and where the legendary aspect of his evil emerges.

In one brief passage we see the killing of Carew through the eyes of a maid. She was watching him from her window and thinking what a wonderful-looking man he was. Then Carew encountered Hyde, who burst into a rage and beat Carew to death with his walking stick. Seeing this, the woman faints. Stevenson presents the event through the servant's point of view. Her idealization of Carew makes Hyde's actions doubly horrifying, and she loses consciousness. Later, we get the narrative of Jekyll's friend, Dr Lanyon, which closes with his horrified description of Hyde's transformation into Jekyll. The experience so traumatizes Lanyon that he soon dies. The servant girl fainted, Lanyon literally died from the shock to his perceptions. The novel, which follows Utterson throughout, does not tell us what happens after he reads Jekyll's narrative and learns the whole shocking truth about his friend. It has shown in others the destructive aspects of shocks to one's beliefs, but we never learn whether or not Utterson is able to bear it.

The Novel's Literary Style

Stevenson's literary style is justly famous for its precision and power. Not only is he interested in the idea of opposites being bonded together, but we see this interest worked into the way he forms his sentences and paragraphs. The novel begins: "Mr Utterson the lawyer was a man of rugged countenance that was never lighted by a smile; cold, scanty and embarrassed in discourse; backward in sentiment; lean, long, dusty, dreary and yet somehow loveable" (p. 61). The last word, loveable, does not seem to belong; it at first seems to contradict all of the unfriendly characteristics that precede it, but it opens up the character to greater depth by showing us something that makes us expand our sense of what he is about.

The next paragraph works in the same way by describing the Sunday walks of Utterson and Mr Enfield. The first two sentences describe how the men seemed to have nothing in common, said little, and seemed uncomfortable together. But the third sentence describes how it was the "chief jewel" of each man's week, important enough for them to put all else aside to hold the walks uninterrupted (pp. 61–2). Again, Stevenson begins by painting a clear and unified negative picture, but then he closes by shattering the unity with an observation that makes us look more deeply into what at first seemed obvious. Such techniques are particularly appropriate in this extraordinary story of a man who is not what he seems to be.

The Movie's Narrative Structure

The movie *Dr Jekyll and Mr Hyde* (1932, directed by Rouben Mamoulian) begins with a scene that has no parallel in the novel. We see hands playing an organ. A servant looks and speaks directly into the camera (figure 9.5). The camera moves through the house and stops at a mirror. Then we see Jekyll appear in the mirror as the servant gives him his coat. We know now that we are seeing things through Jekyll's eyes. He leaves the house for the university. Then, in the lecture hall, we get a reverse shot and for the first time we leave his point of view and see him as others see him (figure 9.6). He lectures about splitting the human mind in two. Later, in private, he performs the experiment that first turns him into Hyde.

Two things should be obvious. The first is that the movie is using the point-of-view shots to create Jekyll's subjectivity, to show us the world as Jekyll sees it. The movie also gives us him as an object, Jekyll as others see him. In the final shot of the movie we see the police staring down at Jekyll's dead body (figure 9.7). It is an exact opposite of the first shot: at the beginning, we saw things through his subjectivity and at the end we see him totally objectified.

One might be tempted to say that here the movie is giving us an "equivalent" of the novel's concern with subjective perception, but this is a good example of the danger of talking of literature/film "equivalencies." The novel

gives us verbal descriptions of what Utterson and others experience and think; the movie gives us images and sounds of what Jekyll and others see and hear. They are not equivalent at all. Furthermore, where a central concern of the novel is the devastating effect that shocks to one's subjective presumptions can have, that concern is absent from the movie. The movie develops as a central theme the ruinous effects of sexual repression, a theme that has no parallel in the novel.

The second striking point about the first scene is that the movie's narrative begins with Jekyll before he has taken the potion, not long after as in the novel. Also, unlike the novel, the movie follows

Fig. 9.5

Fig. 9.6

Fig. 9.7

Jekyll's story in linear fashion and ends with his death. Where the novel was Utterson's story, the movie is Jekyll's. Utterson is irrelevant as a character, only briefly appearing in one scene. The narrative of the movie, then, is developed in fundamentally different ways from that of the novel.

After Jekyll's lecture, he performs surgery on a charity patient that makes him late for a party at the home of Muriel, his fiancée. Hold it, what fiancée? There is no fiancée in the novel; in fact, there are no significant female characters. The movie has not one but two major female characters. They are part of the film's two romantic subplots that point to major differences between the narrative strategies of novel and film. Jekyll's fiancée, Muriel, represents a socially acceptable life; Hyde's kept woman, Ivy, represents his baser impulses.

Sexuality points to how causality functions differently in the two works. In the novel, Hyde emerges because Jekyll wants to conceal all but his most noble behavior from the public eye; in the film, Hyde is the result of Victorian sexual repression – he comes into being because Jekyll cannot have a reasonable wedding date. Finally, the movie's plot, which is built around Jekyll, integrates the characters in a much more organic way than that of the novel. Carew, for example, is not an isolated character used in one incident, as in the novel, but Muriel's father. He is attacked not because of a random encounter but because he tries to disrupt Hyde's attack on Muriel.

Theatrical and Film Traditions

These substantial changes in narrative strategy did not originate with the movie. As with many popular stories, Stevenson's novel has been adapted many times and for many different media. As mentioned above, the novel was adapted for the stage only a year and a half after it appeared, and substantial changes in narrative strategy begin with that stage production. We will briefly look at some of the alterations in the story structure in different forms that have influenced the popular notion of what Stevenson's novel is about.

The most basic change occurred immediately and has not yet been reversed. Stevenson's novel deals not so much with specific events as with the effect specific events have on the perceptions of the characters, especially Utterson. Utterson's point of view serves a dominant formal function in the novel: it provides a central focal point from which the reader may view Jekyll and his effects on the other characters; a moral focal point against which Jekyll's excesses may be measured. The novel begins when Utterson learns to his surprise of a connection of the horrid Hyde with his friend Jekyll; it ends with his discovery of Jekyll's secret. The last two-fifths of the book occur after Jekyll's death; the reader reads Lanyon's and then Jekyll's accounts just as Utterson reads them.

All of the plays and films drastically alter this structure. They make Jekyll the central character and the central sensibility. They drop Utterson altogether or make him a minor character. The plot, unlike that in the novel, becomes linear and chronological. The novel begins long after Jekyll has first become Hyde and makes huge jumps backward and forward in time. Hyde dies three-fifths of the way through the book; the remainder of it leads up to his death but ends before it. The films generally begin with the motives that lead Jekyll to become Hyde and end, in a linear progression of dramatically integrated events, with his death. The plays and films focus on Jekyll/Hyde's fate, and only peripherally on any filtering sensibility.

The plays and films, then, drop the perceptual outer layer of the story and give the events of the story quite different contexts. They all, however, follow similar patterns. Most obviously, they create a concrete dramatic context in which Jekyll and Hyde function. The first play based upon the novel, written by T. R. Sullivan (commissioned by and starring Richard Mansfield), gave Jekyll a fiancée and made her the daughter of Sir Danvers Carew, whom Hyde murders in the first act. This murder, a seemingly similar story event, serves wholly different functions in novel and play (as well as in many of the films). Hyde murders Sir Danvers Carew in both, an event leading, in the storylines of both, to his pursuit by the police and contributing to his self-inflicted death. The progression of events in which Hyde and Carew are involved seem quite similar in novel and play but the similarities are superficial.

The Carew of the novel appears only in the scene in which he is murdered and has no relation to any of the characters. His murder provides evidence of Hyde's evil but, more importantly, evidence of a sensibility (the servant girl's) other than Utterson's. The servant girl, like Carew, does not reappear in the book but the presentation of her romantic sensibility is central to the book's structure. The murder of Carew and the servant's observation of it have no direct story relation to other events or characters in the book but are important only in terms of the novel's development of the theme of perception.

Sullivan's play, by making Carew the father of Jekyll's fiancée, has Hyde destroy that which is dear to Jekyll. The murder becomes not an indiscriminate outburst having no direct effect on Jekyll as in the novel, but one by which Hyde begins to destroy things important to Jekyll. This is important to the play which, like the films, develops Jekyll's world, not Utterson's.

Sullivan's play, and other plays and films that followed, not only center the dramatic events causally around Jekyll and integrate them with one another, but they also introduce women into the story. Except for extremely minor characters, like the servant girl, the novel has no female characters. By the time the Mamoulian film appeared, it was common to have women in central roles. The Sullivan play gives Jekyll a fiancée, embodying his hopes for a romantic future and a proper Victorian life. Later works, like the 1920 John Robertson movie starring John Barrymore, also give Hyde a "bad" woman, commonly a prostitute. The Mamoulian film adopts this structure, with a "good" woman (Muriel) embodying Jekyll's aspirations and a "bad" woman (Ivy) embodying Hyde's depravity.

It is important for us to realize, then, that when we talk of relationships between film and other arts, the relationships may involve individual works, but they also may involve traditions that cross multiple art forms. We will now return to our discussion of the Mamoulian film.

Visual Style of the Film

Fig. 9.8

The elderly charity patient for whom Jekyll is late to Muriel's party is neither sexually attractive nor wealthy. Unlike the socially prominent Muriel, she has nothing to offer Jekyll. In a remarkable shot we see the patient as Jekyll comforts her (figure 9.8), then a wipe that appears to move the next shot, one of Muriel waiting for Jekyll, across the screen, pushing out the earlier shot of the patient. It is very slow, however, and stops in the middle, so it appears for a moment that the two women are in the same space (figure 9.9). They embody two of Jekyll's options: a pleasurable society party with his fiancée or charity work. His choice of charity work demonstrates his altruism. This sort of technique can only be done with images and transitional devices unique to film.

Fig. 9.9

In the novel, to give another example, Jekyll creates Hyde to act out his forbidden desires without taking responsibility for them. He is a hypocritical man who represents a hypocritical society. The movie's Jekyll is a good man who does not want to be a hypocrite. His society is hypocritical and wants him to repress his natural impulses. He wants to marry Muriel without a long wait but her stuffy father forbids it, saying "It isn't done," implying that sexual desire, even between two people in love who are eager to marry, is improper and should not be acknowledged.

The film uses two **dissolves** to show how this repression leads to Hyde. We see a shot of Muriel as Jekyll and Lanyon leave her house (figure 9.10). The next shot shows the two men walking together, but the dissolve is very slow, leaving the image of Muriel superimposed over them for a relatively long time (figure 9.11). Jekyll talks of his hatred of Muriel's father for keeping them apart, and her image still on the screen parallels her presence in his thoughts.

Fig. 9.10

Soon after, he saves Ivy, a prostitute, from being beaten. In her room she tries to seduce him. As he leaves with Lanyon she tells him to come back and provocatively dangles her leg over the bed (figure 9.12). The next shot shows the two men again walking, but Mamoulian holds the shot of Ivy's leg in an extremely slow dissolve (figure 9.13). Jekyll talks of his frustrated desire for Muriel, and the image of Ivy's leg shows how strong a presence she is for Jekyll. We see the image again as he becomes Hyde, and Hyde's first activity is to seek her out and begin a sadomasochistic relationship with her that ends in her murder.

Fig. 9.11

Fig. 9.12

Fig. 9.13

Fig. 9.14

Fig. 9.15

Once more, in a manner unrelated to the novel, Jekyll's options are established in women. He sought a "proper" relationship with Muriel but his repressive society would not allow it; the resulting frustration led him into a perverted relationship with Ivy. The ways in which the dissolved images represent the two women are telling. We see Muriel's face and body, implying a whole person. We only see Ivy's leg, however, implying not an individual to relate to as a person, but merely a fragmented, erotic object. Furthermore, the use of wipes and dissolves to show Jekyll's progression from pure to perverse demonstrates cinematic artistry just like the novel's use of language demonstrates literary artistry.

Motifs in the Film

Artistry is also evident in the **visual motifs** that run through the film. One example is the use of candles, a motif totally absent from the novel. When Hyde comes to Lanyon for the potion, Lanyon holds a pistol on him while he drinks it and is horrified at the transformation to Jekyll. Jekyll tells his story, but we do not hear it. Instead, we see a series of dissolves of a candle burning down. The whole scene has been visually structured around this candle, which is generally between the two men (figure 9.14). It is not an isolated example. Candles, lit and unlit, appear in carefully orchestrated ways throughout the film. Unlit candles generally signify things of which society does not approve, so when Jekyll first changes into Hyde, we see an unlit candelabrum in his laboratory (figure 9.15). Lit candles signify social approval, so when Jekyll thinks he has renounced Hyde, we see lit candelabra all over his house (figure 9.16). In the scene with Lanyon, the lit candle joins Lanyon's gun and the picture of Queen Victoria on the wall to symbolize the social structure that Jekyll has violated; the one that will destroy him.

In the movie, the villain is not so much Jekyll as it is that social structure and this affects the manner in which he dies. In the novel,

Fig. 9.16

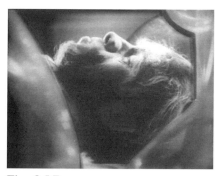

Fig. 9.17   Fig. 9.18

the hypocritical man kills himself; in the film, Jekyll is not a suicide but is shot by the police, the agents of the society that destroyed him. At his death in the film, he changes back from Hyde (figure 9.17) to Jekyll (figure 9.18) for the last time. These changes, using dissolves, lighting and make-up, are a major attraction of the film. They occur in extreme close-up yet, upon reflection, it is jolting to realize that the novel never even describes Hyde's face. Rather, it describes the perceptual effect that seeing him had on others.

In the novel, then, we do not have the horrifying face of Hyde or his transformation from the face of Jekyll, we do not have the central female characters, we do not have Hyde killed by the police, nor Jekyll's frustrated romance, nor Hyde's sadomasochistic relationship, nor wipes, nor dissolves, nor candle motifs, nor much more that is central to the film. These individual works that seem so much alike are fundamentally different. Not only are their forms different, but their narratives and themes and characters and descriptive emphases are also different in basic ways. The forms share many traditions, but the individual works here could hardly be more different.

Nosferatu (1922) and *Dracula*

Dracula and Stoker's Novel

Like *The Strange Case of Dr Jekyll and Mr Hyde*, Bram Stoker's *Dracula* is a Victorian novel that has inspired a number of plays and dozens of film adaptations. Most films based upon the two novels have had a good deal of sexual content, but where the sexual issues are deeply buried in the subtext and have no overt narrative manifestations in Stevenson's novel, they are present to a high degree in *Dracula*. No one at the time of the novel's publication acknowledged this due to Victorian cultural norms, which made the treatment of sexual issues, even if disguised, highly taboo.

The story of *Dracula* is of a centuries-old Eastern European nobleman who is a vampire. Because his primitive world is depleted of vitality, he goes to England for new blood. His vampirism threatens the society's very survival, but he is discovered and destroyed.

Victorian Domesticity and Sexuality

Where Stevenson's novel implicitly criticized Victorian England's vanity, Stoker's novel gloried in it. When Jonathan Harker travels to Eastern Europe to meet Count Dracula, Harker comments on the inferior nature of the people. He considers England the most civilized place on earth and feels that travel away from it is like going back to the primitive past. When Dracula travels to England, he threatens the center of civilization.

The particular form of Dracula's menace relates to the value Victorian culture placed on domestic life. Dracula's danger goes beyond the deaths of his victims; it imperils the bedrock of Victorian life, the family. He violates a central Victorian taboo, that against unrestrained sexuality, particularly female sexuality. Not only does Dracula mostly attack women, he attacks them in their own beds. They not only die, but they return from the dead as sexualized beings who seduce men into vampirism. He also makes the most desired woman drink his blood. Dracula's real threat is to the sexual restraint that the Victorians felt lay at the basis of their social structure.

Near the beginning of the novel, most major characters suffer a domestic loss: they lose a parent or a surrogate parent, or are separated from loved ones by a great distance. Consequently, Dracula arrives when everyone is vulnerable because the support they could expect from an intact family is diminished. Early on, three men propose marriage to Lucy, a desirable single woman. She accepts one, but Dracula secretly visits her repeatedly in her sleep and drinks her blood, bringing her near death. He threatens not only her life but also her coming marriage, the institution upon which the continuity of her society depends.

Dr Van Helsing is called in from Amsterdam and realizes that a vampire is involved. The men in love with Lucy give transfusions of blood to her, and each considers this a private, intimate act, further developing the novel's depiction of blood as a quasi-sexual fluid. Eventually Lucy dies, but Van Helsing shocks all by showing how she returns from the dead in a voluptuous form. The explicitness of her sexuality disgusts her formerly adoring fiancé and makes him eager to pound a stake into her heart and behead her corpse.

Dracula then attacks Mina, Jonathan's wife. He is found in her marriage bed, alongside her unconscious husband. He not only sucks her blood, but he also forces her to drink his blood in an act with strong sexual connotations. This outrage cuts to the center of Victorian taboos based upon notions of the inviolability of marriage, of the husband as the protector, and of female sexual restraint; the remainder of the novel becomes a desperate fight to save Mina from Dracula.

Mina is more than Jonathan's wife; she becomes a surrogate mother and sister to the good men of the novel. They gather around her, she gives them a sense of belonging to a domestic unit, and they thereby gain the strength to band together and defeat Dracula. After they do, she bears a child and gives it the names of those men. The ability to defeat Dracula, then, comes from the ability of the English to combine into a domestic unit and work together, reinforcing England's notion of itself as able to overcome all threats due to its moral strength.

Narrative Technique of the Novel

A reader of the novel cannot help but notice the almost bewildering variety of texts that tell the story. No one person narrates, nor do we have an omniscient narrator. We get a multitude of diary and journal entries from different characters, and diary and journal entries recorded in different ways: handwritten, written in shorthand, typewritten, spoken into a phonograph. We also get shipping invoices, newspaper stories, telegrams, letters. What is going on?

In his prefatory note, Stoker gives us a reason, that "a history almost at variance with latter-day belief may stand forth as simple fact" (p. xxi). In other words, while the supernatural nature of the events may stretch credulity, the way they are presented should not. All is presented as evidence would be presented in a court, so that the story will have the impression of "legal" evidence for the reader. The reader cannot question the narrator's credibility because there is no narrator; the reader will judge the "evidence" itself.

Stoker uses this legal model for the evidence in a sophisticated way, and chapter 14 of the book is an ideal illustration. In it, two characters read journal entries that we as readers have already read, and this affects the future behavior of those characters. Then, two other characters resume writing journals that they had earlier resolved to end. Finally, Van Helsing closes the chapter by announcing that Lucy has returned from the dead as a vampire.

The chapter develops a complex pattern of reintegration. First, texts we have already seen are used again to influence other characters. Where we as readers have been led to expect that those journals had served their function, they are now brought back for a new function. Secondly, the texts once declared ended are now reopened, so they are reintegrated into the body of the novel. Finally, Lucy, although dead, now walks. Now a vampire, she re-enters the action in an unexpected way. As a character says, "Everything is, however, now reopened" (p. 171).

Two chapters later, characters gather all the texts the reader has read and type them up; they "are knitting together in chronological order every scrap of evidence they have" (p. 201). In other words, they are reconstructing the novel exactly as the reader has witnessed it. At this point, all of the "good" characters read it, catching up with the reader. This unites them. Their texts are unified, they are unified, and they now have the strength to defeat Dracula. In this manner, then, we can see how Stoker's literary techniques parallel the themes of his remarkable novel.

Nosferatu as Adaptation

Nosferatu (1922, directed by F. W. Murnau) was created as an adaptation of *Dracula* because its producers thought *Dracula*'s dreamlike engagement of the world of the undead would be an ideal narrative for the popular Expressionistic trend in German cinema at the time. German Expressionism distorted the appearance of the external world, portraying a great deal of anxiety, terror, and horror. The producers of *Nosferatu* made no attempt to secure the rights to the novel, however, and, after the film was completed, Florence Stoker engaged them in a bitter legal battle over the rights to her husband's novel, and won. In 1925, all prints of the movie were ordered to be destroyed. Fortunately for film history, some survived.

The very fact of contention between different claimants to source materials poses important questions. Is an unauthorized adaptation still an adaptation? We touched upon this in chapter 6, with the question of what is an official James Bond movie: one with Sean Connery, one authorized by Eon Productions, one with Pierce Brosnan, or other possibilities? For our purposes, we will work within the widest possible range and consider *Nosferatu* an adaptation of *Dracula* because of narrative similarities between the works as well as the historical intentions and activities of its creators, being fully aware that the legal issues are a separate matter.

Different Social Contexts for Novel and Film

The overall narrative direction of *Nosferatu* resembles that of the novel, *Dracula*, with the major difference being that, instead of going to London, the vampire goes to Wisborg in Germany, but the subtextual implications are virtually opposed. *Nosferatu* was the first movie based upon Stoker's novel and remains the most artistically respected. Where *Dracula* supports the value system of a self-confident society, *Nosferatu* reflects the demoralized Germany after its devastating defeat in World War I. Characters in *Dracula* gather together in a domestic-type unit to actively fight the vampire, whose threat is sexual. Characters in *Nosferatu* are isolated and demoralized throughout, and the passive act that defeats the vampire is not one of public unity but a private and unknown one.

Where *Dracula*'s characters rose from depleted family units to a solid and fruitful one, *Nosferatu* begins with a happy marriage that is eroded and destroyed. None of the novel's sexual subtext has parallels in *Nosferatu*, and in fact sexuality is largely irrelevant to the movie. The threat presented by Count Orlock (the movie's parallel character to Dracula) is of death, pure and simple. His victims do not rise from the dead afterward and become vampires themselves; they simply die. Sacred paraphernalia such as crucifixes, holy wafers, and holy water are not established as having any effect on Orlock.

When he dies, it is due to a natural occurrence, the rising sun. In fact, his activities are not perceived as supernatural at all but are associated with a natural disaster, the plague.

Associations of the Vampire with Natural Forces

Orlock is constantly associated with rats, the traditional bearers of the plague. With his bald head, pointed ears, and long, pointed fingers, he looks like a rat (figure 9.19). He is also constantly surrounded by rats. When sailors open one of his boxes, rats swarm out (figure 9.20), and when sailors on the ship carrying him to Wisborg look in the hold for the cause of the deaths on the ship, they find rats. Reports of plague follow Orlock wherever he goes.

This associates vampirism more with natural forces than supernatural forces. In one scene, Professor Bulwer shows his students instances of vampire-type activities in nature (figure 9.21): a Venus flytrap (figure 9.22) and a polyp with tentacles. Furthermore, the people of Wisborg treat Orlock's activities not as a supernatural phenomenon but as a natural disaster. They never discover his real nature; they simply accept the deaths and proceed in an orderly way with disposing of the bodies (figure 9.23). Social institutions are useless. The police discover nothing, and the hospitals tell the people to stay at home. The society can neither identify nor deal with a threat to its existence.

Fig. 9.19

Fig. 9.20

Fig. 9.21

Fig. 9.22

Fig. 9.23

This is fundamentally different from the novel's presentation of Victorian English society's ability to band together and obliterate basic threats. Even the various documents that make up the novel are brought together to empower the characters. In *Nosferatu*, documents work in the opposite way. A preface to the film announces that only now, presumably 1922, has an historian discovered the real cause of the 1843 Great Plague of Wisborg, and the film reveals the story for the first time. The historian's document, then, does not help anyone defeat Orlock; it uselessly appears after everyone is dead.

A Society of Weak Men

As opposed to the powerful men in the novel, the men of the film are all weak and ineffective. When Orlock comes into Hutter's room, Hutter does not fight back (as his parallel Jonathan did in the novel) but childishly and hysterically pulls his sheet over his head to hide (figure 9.24); when a burly sailor later discovers Orlock on his ship, instead of attacking, he drops his hatchet and hysterically jumps overboard (figure 9.25).

Where Dracula is destroyed in the novel by a thundering band of heavily armed men, Orlock is killed by an isolated and passive woman. Ellen (Hutter's

Fig. 9.24

wife) finally destroys Orlock by inviting him into her bed and keeping him there drinking her blood until dawn, when the rays of the rising sun vaporize him (figure 9.26). It also causes her death. It is a strangely sexless act, since Orlock remains clothed throughout and the movie develops none of the novel's sexual subtext. The very naturalness of the sunrise once more links Orlock's activities with natural and not supernatural processes. The movie develops the sense that this is the way society works and that, even though Ellen has saved her society, the society was so ineffective it was hardly worth saving. As opposed to the novel, which ends on a note of renewal for a vital society, the movie ends on a note of loss and also of an heroic deed entirely unknown in its time.

Fig. 9.25

Fig. 9.26

Visual Motifs

In addition to Orlock's linkage with rats, another formal motif involves various portals. Orlock is associated with rounded or arched entrances, more linked with Eastern than Western Europe. We first see him in his castle framed by a number of entrance ways, all rounded (figure 9.27). When he first attacks Hutter, he enters Hutter's room framed by an arched doorway. But when he comes to Wisborg, we see the more rectangular portals the movie associates with Western Europe. Ellen summons him to her bedroom from its rectangular windows (figure 9.28) and he accepts, standing framed by rectangle within rectangle (figure 9.29). The rays of the sun that destroy him come through the rectangular bedroom window.

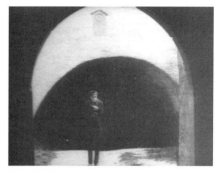

Fig. 9.27

The visual motifs linking Orlock's appearance with rats and with Eastern European architecture may have a disturbing ethnic dimension to them. Orlock's large nose, often emphasized in profile, his long, grasping fingers, and the fact that in some shots he wears a skullcap, conformed to stereotypes of Jewish physical features and dress at this time of growing anti-semitism and the rise of Hitler. Indeed, Jews in Germany were sometimes associated with rats and characterized as bearers of a plague of moral decay that demagogues like Hitler vowed to eradicate. Thus, the Eastern European motif combined with the stereotyped Jewish connotations may have functioned at the time to associate *Nosferatu* with a perceived ethnic threat to German racial purity. These possible meanings are entirely visual and have nothing to do with either the source novel or the use of language in the film.

Fig. 9.28

The study of the relationship of film with other art forms leads in many interesting directions. It is important, however, to respect each form for its unique qualities. We must understand how different the many forms are, as well as the traditions they share.

SELECTED READINGS

Fig. 9.29

Observations on the musical, *Victor/Victoria* are based upon the Broadway production as well as the 1995 DVD of that production distributed by Image Entertainment. David Bordwell, Janet Staiger, and Kristin Thompson discuss the influence of the nineteenth-century novel and short story upon early cinema narrative form in *The Classical Hollywood Cinema: Film Style and Mode of Production to 1960* (New York: Columbia University Press, 1985). David J. Skal discusses the legal battles over *Nosferatu* in *Hollywood Gothic: The Tangled Web of Dracula from Novel to Screen* (New York: Norton, 1990). Literary quotations used in this chapter are drawn from Raymond Chandler, *Farewell, My Lovely* (New York: Ballantine

Books, 1975) and Raymond Chandler, *The Long Goodbye* (New York: Ballantine Books, 1978); Charles Dickens, *A Tale of Two Cities* (Baltimore: Penguin Books, 1975); Dashiell Hammett, *The Maltese Falcon* (New York: Vintage Books, 1972); Robert Louis Stevenson, *The Strange Case of Dr Jekyll and Mr Hyde* in *Minor Classics of Nineteenth-century Fiction, Volume II*, edited by William E. Buckler (Boston: Houghton Mifflin, 1967); Bram Stoker, *Dracula* in *The Annotated Dracula*, edited by Leonard Wolf (New York: Ballantine Books, 1975); and Oscar Wilde, *The Picture of Dorian Gray* (New York: Dell, 1960).

10

FILM AND ITS RELATION TO RADIO AND TELEVISION

Richard Diamond, Private Detective,
Peter Gunn, and *Victor/Victoria*

Nearly all of us have had the experience of watching a favorite movie on television, whether a network broadcast, a premium channel cablecast (e.g., HBO), a rented videotape, a laser disc, or a DVD. Obviously there is some similarity between film and television. But, as we have seen with so many other "obvious" things throughout this book, the situation is much more complex than it first seems. The differences between film and television may be more significant than the similarities.

The mere fact that we are willing to rush out and see *Pearl Harbor* (2001) or *Lara Croft: Tomb Raider* (2001) in movie theaters, even though we know that they will almost certainly be available for video rental within a year, indicates that we value something about the theatrical experience over the home-viewing experience. Maybe we simply prefer to see the movies sooner in theaters while everyone is still talking about them. While that may undoubtedly be true, this chapter will offer many other explanations. We will explore not just the similarities and differences between film, television, and radio but also the interrelationships between these media. Although contemporary radio may seem far removed from the other two media, we will see that, historically, it holds an important place among them.

Film

It is important for us to understand the unique aspects of each medium, and a good place to begin is with differences in our experience of them. When we go to the movies, we go out to a public place, sit in a darkened auditorium, and watch a large projected image, usually in **35 mm** gauge. Additionally, we are likely to be listening to sophisticated stereo sound systems such as Dolby surround sound, DTS digital stereo, or THX stereo. Going out may include such social contexts as dates or getting together with friends.

The mere fact of going out to the movies indicates another important feature of that activity – deciding which movie to see. We seldom just wander aimlessly into a movie theater. We normally look through the paper to see what is showing, then choose a theater and check the start times. But the process of selecting a movie usually begins even prior to checking the paper to see what is on. In many cases, we have seen previews of coming attractions when attending other movies or on television. Sometimes we have seen the stars and/or director of the film on television talk shows or have read interviews with them in newspapers and magazines. Or we may have noticed the film's poster displayed outside the theater. In short, selecting a movie is a process that frequently extends over a period of time. It is not uncommon to see trailers at Christmas announcing big movies coming during the summer. Our experience with television, to the contrary, requires virtually no preparation and, traditionally, it involves less-focused attention.

Television

We watch television in the privacy of our homes, and in many American households we do so on more than one set in different rooms. Important changes are currently taking place with regard to television technology and these are related to the digital revolution that we discuss in chapter 16. The advent of HDTV (high-definition television) is here. Among other things this means that television images will have a new widescreen aspect ratio, a higher resolution image, and digital stereo sound. Larger screens may very well also become more common than they currently are. And some people will even watch television programs in home theaters equipped with large-screen video projectors. It is, however, too soon to speculate about what, if any, effect these technological changes in television will have upon viewing habits. For the remainder of this chapter, when we refer to "television," we use the term in its usual sense, referring to the technology that most of us have grown up with and which is commonplace in most American homes now.

Television sets – even large ones – are small in comparison to film screens. A small movie theater screen is many times larger than a 35-inch home television screen. We seldom watch television in a totally dark room and, in fact, the lights are frequently on at night and the drapes or blinds left open during the day. Furthermore, the image we see on a television screen has far less resolution (i.e., clarity, detail, and color nuance) than that of a projected 35 mm film image.

One reason we do not typically watch television in a darkened room is that other activities are occurring in the room simultaneously. It is not uncommon to be reading the paper, folding laundry or ironing, talking to family members or friends, cooking, or even talking on the phone while the television is on. When we are in a movie theater, we are pretty much focused on only one thing: the big screen at the front of the dark auditorium.

How do we decide when and what to watch on television? There are several patterns, and they all differ from the common patterns of deciding which movie to see. We might walk into a room and turn the television on simply because we have just come home or are taking a break from working at home. We have given it no special forethought. We flip through the channels, watch a while, and perhaps flip over to something else. At other times, we plan to watch a favorite show by making a point of being home on the evening that the program airs. Many of us have "our" shows on "our" nights that become part of our routine home life. Channel "surfing" or being home at certain times on certain days of the week (or even daily for programs such as soap operas) is quite different from determining when to go out, where to go, and whom to go with. Flipping through channels reveals a casual, "let's see what's on" attitude, and watching the same program at the same time of day or night on a certain day or days of the week reveals a commitment to a highly predetermined pattern – we don't bother to see what else is on because we already know what we want to watch.

Television producers encourage habitual watching because it is a way of maintaining a stable audience. This is one reason why the series format is so important to television: it not only draws an audience once, as movies do, but it keeps them coming back, ensuring good advertising revenues for the networks.

This desire to attract habitual viewers has also led to targeting and stereotyping particular audiences. At times television has been called a "woman's medium," not only because of its associations with a domestic environment, but also because producers have targeted particular time slots, such as much of daytime television, toward a largely female audience on the assumptions that homemakers will be the largest available audience. Such presumptions have determined the type of programming – soap operas, quiz shows, and so forth – presumed to appeal to women. Comparably, Saturday morning has often been considered a children's market dominated by cartoons.

Form and Style Differences between Film and Television

The differences in the nature of the image and the viewing contexts affect the form and content of both film and television. Even though we can watch movies on television, television programming is quite different from feature film presentation. Some of the differences are obvious: network television programming (for example, shows on CBS, NBC, ABC, Fox, and Warner) includes a wide variety of shows including news, talk shows, soap operas, and sitcoms. With the exception of the Public Broadcasting System and premium cable services such as HBO, television programming involves commercials that

Fig. 10.1

appear before, during, and after any program. Many television stations are on the air 24 hours a day. Thus, television involves a flow integrating any particular program with a number of other segments. In 2001, for example, Fox's prime-time Sunday night programming included *The Simpsons* and *Malcolm in the Middle*, followed by *The X Files*. But any viewer watching for the full two hours would also see, in addition to commercials, brief news updates and scenes from next week's episodes. The two-hour viewing experience involves a segmented flow of quite different types of material.

For our purposes, however, we will focus on the series format that occupies so much of prime-time programming. Although a television series narrates stories with characters like those in Hollywood feature films, there are significant differences between the formats. No matter what the genre or type of film, the feature film places a strong emphasis on resolving narrative questions. In a science-fiction film like *Village of the Damned* (1995, figure 10.1), we may wonder if the humans will succeed in ridding the planet of the alien children who are plotting to take over. We learn the answer at the end when all the children except one are blown up. The one child who is allowed to escape this fate shows signs of acquiring human emotions, and the film ends with his mother driving away with him as the camera lingers on his ambiguous facial expression. We are unsure whether he is one of "us" or one of "them." Such an ending is common in science fiction, where scaring the audience is a staple of the genre. It also allows for a sequel if the film is a success.

Interestingly, the main character, a doctor played by Christopher Reeve, is killed with the children. At the time of the film's release (before his disabling accident), Reeve was most known for his starring role in the series of Superman films years earlier. Similarly, Kirstie Alley, a well-known actress who plays the female lead, a scientist, is gruesomely killed when the children use their telepathic powers to make her commit suicide. Both of these central characters die near the end of the film. Michael Paré, another established actor, plays a man married to an ambitious career woman who has just become principal of her school. Tension exists in their marriage because he is frustrated that they have no children; the implicit message being that he thinks she is placing her career above having children. Yet near the beginning of the film, he is killed in a truck accident.

Let us imagine a television series *Village of the Damned*, not a far-fetched notion in this era of movies, even series of movies, based on television programs (for example, *The Fugitive*, 1993, *Mission: Impossible*, 1996, and *Mission: Impossible 2*, 2000) and television programs based on movies (for example, *M*A*S*H* and *Clueless*). Let us also assume that the series stars Christopher Reeve, Kirstie Alley, and Michael Paré. Perhaps the most obvious difference between our hypothetical series and the film would be that Reeve, Alley, and Paré would have to be left alive at the end of each episode. Imagine *Star Trek* if Captain Kirk and Mr Spock were killed during the fourth episode, or *Star Trek: The Next Generation* or *Star Trek: Voyager* or *Star Trek: Enterprise* if, respectively, Captain Picard and Captain Janeway and Captain Archer were similarly eliminated. Television series are structured around a recurring set of characters who, week after week, retain virtually identical relationships among themselves. Thus, in our series, we would expect the Paré character and his wife to be secondary characters whose relationship would be strained by the tensions between career and family. It would be unlikely in such a series that, in episode two, Paré's wife would suddenly decide to resign as principal and have a baby.

This is not to suggest that none of the characters or their interrelationships ever change on a television series. Indeed, Murphy Brown (Candice Bergen), in the show of the same name, had a baby after the show had been running for several seasons. Similarly, David Caruso left the popular *NYPD Blue* and his character was replaced by one played by Jimmy Smits, which in turn was replaced by one played by Rick Schroeder, who also left the show, which continued on. In *Picket Fences*, the small-town mayor who suffers from Alzheimer's disease dies after having been a presence in the show for many episodes.

Such changes notwithstanding, a television series tends to begin and end each episode with the same characters and relationships intact. In *Murphy Brown*, for example, we expect the same characters in the same newsroom to treat one another in essentially the same manner week after week: Miles, Murphy's boss, will typically be a nervous wreck who worries himself to death. We can hardly imagine the show were he to get therapy and emerge as a self-confident man. Similarly, it is hard to imagine *Star Trek*'s Mr Spock becoming an emotional man who values feelings over logic. Life in the small Wisconsin town in *Picket Fences* revolves around, in addition to the central Brock family, such minor characters as the stern Judge Bone and Wambaugh, the overly enterprising defense lawyer. Other characters come and go. During one episode in 1995, for example, James Coburn made a guest appearance as James Brock's estranged father. Although the father is a central character in that episode, he leaves at the end. Furthermore, even in that episode, we have the usual minor characters such as Bone and Wambaugh as well as two young deputies who are in love with each other. Next week, the father may be gone but we expect the Brocks, Bone, Wambaugh, and the young lovers to be back and essentially unchanged.

Television in many ways lacks suspense in comparison to cinema. When we watch *Village of the Damned*, we truly do not know the fates of the characters, and indeed the two central characters die. When we watch an episode of *Dark Angel*, however exciting the action may be, we never for a moment believe that the title character will be killed. When we watch a television show, we enjoy watching familiar characters; they are like old friends we expect to revisit week after week. With the variation found in a series such as the *Lethal Weapon* films (see chapter 6), films focus almost exclusively on answering a number of narrative questions posed at their beginning. Both individual

Fig. 10.2

characters and relationships among characters change profoundly along the way. This is true of nearly all films, even serious dramas far removed from genre entertainment. Much of *Driving Miss Daisy* (1989, figure 10.2) turns on the unusual relationship between a rich, elderly Jewish woman and her black chauffeur. The film traces the changing relationship from its beginning to its end. Indeed, Miss Daisy dies at the end of the film. Although films typically conclude with a resolution and sense of equilibrium, that equilibrium does not return us to where we started. In short, films are separate units that have to first arouse our interest so that we will go to see them and then fulfill those interests so that we leave satisfied. Television episodes, on the other hand, are structured around series components in which we are already interested and which we do not want to see fundamentally changed during any single episode.

Technology and Reception Contexts

Additional differences between these two media relate to their technologies and **reception contexts**. If we sit in a dark theater watching a highly defined image projected on a large screen, our attention will naturally be focused on that screen since, with the exception of momentary distractions, there is little else we can do. When we are at home watching a small, less-defined image amid many distractions, there are many things we can do besides watch the screen. These differences affect how stories are told in the two media.

Films typically rely upon their visual dimension to attract and maintain our attention. Filmmakers presume that the audience is nearly always watching the screen and convey important narrative, character, and thematic information primarily and, at times, even exclusively via the visual image. This is not to deny the importance of sound but to point out that the assumption in filmmaking is that sound accompanies the visual image. While listening, in other words, the audience is also watching.

Television producers, on the other hand, assume that their audience members are often distracted and are frequently only listening rather than listening and watching simultaneously. Unlike film spectators who gaze intently at an image, television viewers glance casually and intermittently at the image. Television producers are thus less likely to give important information exclusively in visual terms and more likely to incorporate that information into the dialogue. Television also uses various techniques such as increasing the sound level to attract a viewer's attention back to the screen. Sportscasters implicitly recognize this, often raising their voices with excitement when something important happens during a game. Sports fans who may be reading the paper or walking around the room are likely to quickly redirect their attention to the screen in time to see the home run or touchdown.

Narrative Patterns

The difference between the relative importance of the soundtrack and visual image is not the only one that affects how the two forms structure their narratives. Filmmakers presume that, once you are in the theater watching the film, they have your undivided attention. They structure their narratives on this assumption and typically build plots toward a climax followed by a brief denouement. Films generally begin with a stable situation, then introduce disruption and complications, and finally restore order. The restoration, however, usually differs from the situation found at the beginning of the film.

Sometimes the initial stability is brief. In *Village of the Damned*, we see people sleeping as an ominous cloud passes over their bodies (figure 10.3). They awaken and begin what appears to be a normal day that is interrupted when all the people and animals drop into a deathlike trance. When they awaken, everything seems fine until an inexplicable number of pregnancies occur, some of which involve virgins and women who have not had sexual relations for some time. The brief images of the people sleeping and their morning routines are the only "normal" images of their lives we see in the film.

Similarly, in *Jurassic Park* (1993, see chapter 1), after the ominous events of the prologue, we see scenes of comparative stability as scientists go about their work and as an entrepreneur prepares to create his dinosaur park. Like the mysterious cloud in *Village of the Damned*, the mysterious accident occurring when men transport a large animal cage (figure 10.4) is an ominous foreboding of things to come. But then there is relative stability until the dinosaurs escape and go on a rampage. Just as we wonder if, and how, the dinosaurs will be brought under control in *Jurassic Park*, we wonder if and how the children will be brought under control in *Village of the Damned*.

Unlike filmmakers, who assume our undivided attention from beginning to end, television producers assume not only distractions but necessary interruptions such as commercials and the ever-present temptation to flip channels. Television shows thus typically build up to a particular moment of suspense or plot complication immediately before a commercial so that viewer interest will be maintained. Just as they do not assume that spectators are always focused on the image, television producers do not assume that the spectator

Fig. 10.3

Fig. 10.4

will watch the show through to the end. They structure their narratives, therefore, in ways that will entice the viewer to stick with or return to the program.
As such, television narratives are more segmented than film narratives and
contain mini-climaxes that occur before a commercial.

Radio

When we think of radio today, we are likely to think of music programming,
talk shows, news, and sports. Why, then, is it useful to discuss it in a film textbook? Unlike television, which includes both visual imagery and sound and
which contains a great deal of narrative programming, radio has no visual
element and little narrative programming.

This, however, was not always the case. For decades before the advent of
television, radio was heavily programmed with narratives. Indeed, many radio
programs, such as *The Lone Ranger*, *Richard Diamond, Private Detective*,
The Green Hornet, and *As the World Turns*, eventually switched over to
television. Several careers are intimately linked with both radio and film. The
most famous is that of Orson Welles (see chapter 15), who was the voice of
the title character in *The Shadow* and whose radio version of *War of the Worlds*
(1938) is infamous for causing widespread panic when listeners mistook it for
an actual Martian invasion. Only three years later he directed and acted in
Citizen Kane, perhaps the most highly acclaimed American film of all time.
The Ozzie and Harriet Nelson family, including sons David and Ricky,
appeared on radio, television, and film. Groucho Marx of the Marx Brothers
comedy film team hosted *You Bet your Life*, a witty quiz show, on radio and
later on television.

Studying radio in relation to television and film sheds light not only on
important differences between these media but also on the issues of authorship and creativity discussed in chapter 9. Narrative radio programs typically
ran for half an hour, including commercial breaks and station identifications.
The strict time constraints obviously bear a relation to television, where programs must also fit into a predetermined time slot, whether half an hour, an
hour, or even two hours. Although most movies during any time period
typically adhere to approximately the same time frame (for example,
ninety minutes during the classical Hollywood period), they all vary
and some, such as *Gone with the Wind* (1939, figure 10.5), are over
three hours long.

It is instructive to continue along the lines adopted in chapter 9
and compare radio to film and theater. In theater, we discovered,
the creation of the artistic text belongs to the writer. William Shakespeare's words create the fictional world in *Hamlet*, including all
the characters, their dilemmas and fates, and the play's themes
about the nature of life and the world. In film, on the other hand,
we saw that the fictional world, the characters and themes, are

Fig. 10.5

created in a complex visual text of which the words spoken by the characters comprise only a part, and sometimes a very small part. Language in film does not create the **diegetic** world; it is part of it. For that reason, film directors may be much more important than screenwriters in creating an artistically complex fictional world. There is some truth to the old saying, "Theater is a writer's medium and cinema a director's medium." Where does radio fit into all this?

Of all the arts (theater) and media (television and film) that contain a performance element, radio is the ultimate writer's medium. As in the theater, the words the characters speak create the diegesis and tell us everything we know about the characters themselves, their dilemmas, and the nature of their world. The story, the plot, the themes – everything is directly attributable to the writer. In the theater, we at least see the actors performing, but on radio we only hear them. Indeed, the role of the radio director is limited to directing the actors' vocal interpretations of their parts and the added sound effects. If a character angrily leaves a room, for example, we might hear footsteps followed by a slamming door. While such performances were demanding on live radio, the important point here is that the role of the director was minimal in terms of creatively shaping the fictional world. Indeed, in comparison to theater, radio directors had little room to "interpret" the writer's script. Listeners did not see the sets or actors, they had to imagine much about the appearance of these crucial things, much like readers do when they read a novel.

Radio's total reliance upon the world of sound points to an area of potential creativity within the form. Movies, by comparison, frequently have memorable scenes that occur in visually dazzling and unusual locations. *North by Northwest* (1959), for example, climaxes with a shoot-out between a federal agent and the villains on Mount Rushmore (figure 10.6). Seeing the figures pursuing each other over the familiar facial features of past presidents of the United States is an arresting sight. Alfred Hitchcock knew this and reportedly wanted to place his characters there before he had any story justification to do so. He also realized the humor in the situation and at one point considered calling the film *The Man in Lincoln's Nose*. As if the danger of the situation were not enough, the film's heroine falls over the edge of the mountain and, in a tensely drawn-out scene, is rescued by the agent, who slowly pulls her to safety. If this scene had taken place on any precipice other than Mount Rushmore, it would have had an entirely different effect.

Visually dramatic settings such as Mount Rushmore in *North by Northwest* obviously have little impact on radio, but the medium does have the opportunity to use dramatic sound locations – places where sounds are exaggerated or omnipresent, or where unusual sounds are foregrounded. Thus, while a widescreen Western like *Man of the West* (1958) climaxes with a shoot-out staged on rugged, wide-open terrain that visually overwhelms the combatants, a shoot-out on a radio Western might be better staged in a

Fig. 10.6

canyon where we hear the echoes of gunshots and the sounds of bullets ricocheting off the hard rocks.

Shifting Roles of Writers, Producers, and Directors in Different Media

The differences between radio, television, and film outlined above account for the different places occupied by creative personnel within the industrial structure of these three media. In film, the greatest creative control lies with the **director**. Such control, which has varied historically, is certainly not total: directors frequently fight with writers and producers to get their way and they sometimes lose. Nevertheless, directing is the seat of power in filmmaking and, as a rule, directors have more creative control over film productions than anyone else. This extends beyond the actual shooting of the film and currently includes working with writers and set designers in pre-production and overseeing editing in post-production. Many directors even have approval over the final cut of a film, meaning that the studio cannot change it without the director's consent. Executive producers in film invest money in the productions, and producers oversee the logistics of film production, ranging from location shooting to having the extras ready as needed. Typically, however, it is the director who "calls the shots."

In radio and television, **producers** and/or **executive producers** have the greatest creative control. While the terms "producer" and "executive producer" have varied historically, we are using them to refer to the person or persons who create and determine the tone (and on television, the look) of the series. This means that they write at least the first episode, which introduces the premise, creates and introduces the central characters and their relationships, and establishes the style of the series. Many executive producers of television series also direct the pilot and, currently, television episodes end with the executive producer's name over the final image. These creators/producers hire and oversee the writers and directors on the series. Although some creators/executive producers return to the series from time to time as writers and/or directors, they expect the writers and directors they employ to maintain the originating premise, characters, and style of the series. Within this industrial structure, the creator/executive producer maintains script approval and the equivalent of "final cut." Other employees assemble the scenes that television directors shoot and, if the executive producer doesn't like the scripts or the direction, he or she can hire new writers and directors.

It is not surprising, therefore, that if we look at the careers of strong film directors who have also worked in radio and/or television, they typically fulfill different functions in these media. Michael Mann, the executive producer of the successful series *Miami Vice*

Fig. 10.7

(figure 10.7), became not a producer but a director when he moved into films (for example, *Last of the Mohicans*, 1992, *Heat*, 1995, and *The Insider*, 2000). Similarly, Glenn Gordon Caron was one of the most successful television creators and executive producers during the 1970s and 1980s: his *Remington Steele* was so popular that it positioned its star, Pierce Brosnan, later to portray James Bond in the popular film series, and *Moonlighting* was so popular that it positioned Bruce Willis to play the central character in the popular *Die Hard* series. Yet, when Caron moved into

Fig. 10.8

films, it was also as a director (for example, *Clean and Sober*, 1988, *Love Affair*, 1994, and *Picture Perfect*, 1997).

Likewise, when established film directors move into television, they do so primarily as creators and executive producers but not directors. David Lynch, the acclaimed director of such films as *Eraserhead* (1978), *The Elephant Man* (1980), *Blue Velvet* (1986, figure 10.8), *Lost Highway* (1996), and *Mulholland Drive* (2001), was, along with Mark Frost, the creator and executive producer of the cult television show *Twin Peaks* (figure 10.9). As is common in such situations, Lynch directed the pilot and a few further episodes but left most of the directing and writing to other people. The most recent well-known figure to follow this pattern is James Cameron.

Fig. 10.9

After directing *Titanic* (1997), the biggest grossing film of all time, he became the co-creator and executive producer of the television show *Dark Angel*, though to date he has not directed any episodes.

Blake Edwards, to whom we turn below, was the creator of and frequent writer for the *Richard Diamond, Private Detective* radio show, the creator and producer of the *Peter Gunn* television show, and the director of more than fifty feature films, including the highly successful Pink Panther series. Edwards's career is particularly illustrative of the issues with which this chapter deals, since creative control is essential to his image of himself as an artist. Although he frequently fulfills multiple functions as a writer, producer, and director, he positioned himself primarily as a creator and writer in radio, as a creator and producer in television, and foremost as a director in film. A look at one instance of his work in each – an episode of *Richard Diamond, Private Detective* for radio, one of *Peter Gunn* for television, and the 1982 movie *Victor/Victoria* – reveals a good deal about how these media work, differ, and interrelate.

Richard Diamond, Private Detective

Edwards created the popular radio series, *Richard Diamond, Private Detective*, which ran from 1949 to 1952, as a vehicle for its star, Dick Powell. In the 1930s, Powell had been a popular singing star in movie musicals such as

Fig. 10.10

Footlight Parade (1933) and *Flirtation Walk* (1934), but in the mid-1940s he changed his image into that of a wisecracking tough guy in *films noirs* such as *Murder, My Sweet* (1944, figure 10.10, see chapter 5). *Richard Diamond, Private Detective* capitalizes upon both aspects of his star persona. Richard Diamond is a tough, wisecracking private detective who sings.

Richard Diamond, Private Detective typically begins with Diamond waiting for work. Someone then approaches him with a case. This frustrates his girlfriend, Helen Asher, who wants him to spend time with her. The case frequently involves murder, sometimes of his client, and Diamond often seeks the help of police Lieutenant Levinson and his oafish assistant, Sergeant Otis. When the case is solved, he usually winds up at Asher's apartment, where he romances her and sings her a popular song of the day. Not only is the basic situation similar from week to week but so are the character relations. Asher constantly pleads for more time with Diamond and he constantly resists; Diamond constantly trades wisecracks with Levinson and mocks Otis's stupidity.

"Satire on Radio Detectives"

We will examine the November 5, 1949 episode, "Satire on Radio Detectives" (sometimes called "Richard Diamond's Singing Voice"), which was written by Edwards and, uncharacteristically, directed by him. This episode is more satiric and tongue in cheek than most episodes, but it provides a good introduction to the series.

It opens, unusually, with Diamond coming to Asher's apartment. He is showing off fifty-three letters from her neighbors praising his singing. When he starts to sing, however, Mr Lumpkin, a neighbor in a nearby building, starts screaming about how much he hates Diamond's singing and, unknown to Lumpkin, Diamond discovers he is losing his voice. Lumpkin is so angry that he hires a private detective, Pat Kosak, to stop Diamond from singing. The two later trap Diamond in a freezer and then in a steam room in the hope of making him ill. The episode ends with Diamond back in Asher's apartment. Although the cold and heat exposure was intended to ruin his voice, it has instead cured his cold, and he sings more vigorously than ever. Hearing this, Lumpkin throws Kosak out and screams in frustration.

Storytelling with Sound

This storyline could as readily be used for a television episode or even a movie as for a radio show, but the techniques used in presenting it here bear little relation to those used in television or film. The entire episode is structured around clever uses of different kinds of sound that repeatedly establish what may be termed different sound environments. In fact, each episode is intro-duced with a brief, whistled melody, which provides a "tag" or sound identi-fication for the series.

The episode begins with dialogue between Diamond and Asher about the letters. It also includes background sounds that provide cues as to the physi-cal space, her apartment, in which the dialogue occurs, such as the doorbell, her door opening as he enters, her piano when he plays it. As she reads the letters, we hear him doing comical singing exercises. He then opens the window and, when he sings, we hear Lumpkin screaming in the distance. This situates Lumpkin's apartment as being nearby and, in doing so, introduces a new kind of sound space, which gives a different significance to Diamond's singing. He is no longer just serenading a sweetheart; it is now an act of provo-cation to the grouchy neighbor. Diamond and Asher use mock British accents and banter as he decides to sing even louder and further irritate Lumpkin, but soon he loses his voice.

We then hear brief orchestral music followed by Diamond's voice-over nar-ration telling us that, while Asher was giving him hot drinks to cure his cold, Lumpkin was plotting against him. The music separates the scene of Diamond and Asher from the introduction of his voice-over, which is followed by a new sound space, a monologue from within Lumpkin's apartment during which Lumpkin wonders how to stop Diamond's singing. He telephones Kosak and they plot against Diamond, now extending the space of Lumpkin's apartment to the electronic space of the phone.

Kosak has a dry, business-like voice very different from either that of the joking and singing Diamond or the hysterical Lumpkin. This series not only uses different kinds of music and background sounds but also often uses vocal stereotypes to establish character: sometimes foreign accents (such as Diamond and Asher's mock British "stiff-upper-lip" banter), sometimes speaking styles that connote class (a soft-spoken, literate upper-class accent as opposed to a loud, lower-class "Brooklyn" accent) or physical condition (intermittent breathing to connote serious injury, slurring to indicate drunkenness).

The show's sound environment changes frequently, seldom staying with one location very long but switching rapidly and efficiently from Diamond's office to Asher's apartment to the police station to any number of other settings. This extends beyond simple dialogue cues (such as Diamond's announcing that he is going to Levinson's office) and into various environmental sounds. When he and Otis are locked in the steam room, for example, we hear the background "hisssss" of the steam as well as Diamond's jokes about Otis's uniform shrinking from the steam. The type of sound forwarding the narra-tive frequently changes, constantly moving from voice-over narration to dia-logue scenes to musical interludes to phone conversations, sometimes in the same scene. When Diamond is trapped in the freezer, for example, he is responding to a call to meet a client in a deserted warehouse. We hear his voice-over describing the warehouse but we also hear the sounds of his taxicab stopping and then driving off, thus giving us both the abstract, narrational space of the voice-over and the dramatic space of the street outside of the warehouse. His voice-over describes the dark interior of the warehouse. Then, however, we hear unidentified scuffling sounds followed by the muffled sound of Diamond's voice yelling, "Hey, what's going on? Where am I?" and banging as his muffled voice says, "Hey, let me out of here!" We then hear the clear, foregrounded voices of Kosak and Lumpkin, who have just locked Diamond in the freezer. The scene, then, has shifted its sound point of view from that dominated by Diamond's voice-over narration to that of the scuffle in the warehouse, and then to the point of view of Kosak and Lumpkin, for which Diamond's voice is now only muffled background noise.

We have an even more sophisticated version of this in the final scene. It begins in Lumpkin's apartment as he gleefully anticipates Diamond's inability to sing in Asher's apartment. We then hear her laughing and, without any break, the sound point of view shifts into her apartment. When Diamond says he will try to sing, we hear a loud "Ha!" from Lumpkin's apartment, but heard from the point of view of Asher's apartment. When Diamond sings, we hear the distant, frustrated screams of Lumpkin. We then hear Lumpkin attacking Kosak with a chair, and Diamond and Asher's enjoyment of the spectacle. The scene has shifted sound perspective in mid-scene. It begins in Lumpkin's apartment, where the activity in Asher's apartment is background sound, and then makes Asher's apartment the dominant sound space and Lumpkin's the background space.

Style

The jaunty whistling that provides the introductory "tag" for the series is only one of the devices used to establish a distinctive style for this show, giving it a personality that differentiates it from other detective series. In some cases, plots for different detective shows such as *Sam Spade*; *Pat Novak, for Hire*; *The Adventures of Philip Marlowe*; and *Martin Kane, Private Eye*, were virtually interchangeable. The shows' styles differentiated them. Diamond is associated with a number of stylistic flourishes that recur episode after episode. He not only sings but also speaks in a distinctive way. At the beginning of most episodes, he answers his phone with an impromptu, wise-cracking poem about the Diamond Detective Agency. This episode works variations upon that. When Lumpkin searches the phone book for detectives, he resentfully reads out such a poem in Diamond's ad, "Whoever you are, / Whatever you do, / If you're too dead to walk, / We'll come to you." Later, when Asher calls Diamond in Levinson's office, Diamond answers "Fifth Precinct. / Remember our motto. / A corpse in the morgue / Is worth two in your basement."

The issue of style extends to narrative patterns and character interactions. Much of this episode works variations with the standard patterns of the show and presumes audience familiarity with them. Diamond himself, for example, usually recites the poem identifying his agency. Since Asher usually pleads with Diamond to come to her, it is unusual to have the episode begin with him coming to her apartment, and she comments upon it. Diamond generally goes to Levinson's office with a hidden agenda, either access to privileged police information or Levinson's help in getting him out of trouble, so when he arrives just to "chew the fat," Levinson does not trust him and suspiciously asks questions like "Where's the body?" Lumpkin is a recurring minor character who is generally used for little more than a brief comic moment as he screams objections to Diamond's inevitable singing, but here the entire episode is built around his hatred of Diamond's singing.

When this episode ends, everything is in place for the next one. Diamond is ready for a new case and to sing again; Lumpkin can bemoan Diamond's singing again; Asher, Levinson, and Otis are precisely where they were at the beginning.

Peter Gunn: "Skin Deep"

The television series *Peter Gunn* (1958–61), which Edwards created and produced, also conforms to the basic series pattern of ending with the key character relationships returned to where they were at the beginning. We will examine an episode, "Skin Deep," that Edwards neither wrote nor directed. It was directed by Boris Sagal, who worked frequently on the series, and was written by Tony and Steffi Barrett. As we indicated earlier, this does not necessarily indicate a lack of creative control. Edwards receives the credit "Created and Produced by" which, within the industry practices of television, indicates his responsibility for the stylistic pattern of the series. While he did direct and write some episodes, he oversaw the others, ensuring stylistic continuity. Writers and directors working on the show operated within the narrative and stylistic parameters that Edwards established.

Fig. 10.11

The episode begins with no introductory "tag" whatsoever. We see the outside of a mansion at night and then a room inside in which a woman reclines on a couch and happily talks to her lover on the telephone (figure 10.11). We also hear a slow, insistent jazz beat on the soundtrack that grows more intense as the sequence proceeds. We then see a shot from the point of view of someone entering the room and secretly observing the woman. The intruder picks up a fireplace poker, which the camera follows in ominous close-up as it approaches the woman (figure 10.12). The music increases in volume and intensity as the poker is raised and she turns and sees it. As she is murdered, the camera, still holding the point of view of her killer, moves down her arm to show her hand drop the phone. Abruptly, the introductory credits appear, with Henry Mancini's blaring

Fig. 10.12

Fig. 10.13

"Theme from Peter Gunn" on the soundtrack. This is followed by a commercial break.

This sequence works differently from the introduction to *Richard Diamond, Private Detective*. It begins with a dramatic and unexplained incident in which Peter Gunn is not involved. The only thing contemporary viewers could use to link it with the series is Mancini's music, but this scene does not use the famous theme. Then the credit sequence aggressively announces the series with words, theme music, and distinctive abstract graphics, part of which appear and disappear with the pulsations of the music. The audience has, in effect, been thrown into a narrative without identification and then told it is watching *Peter Gunn*. Repeat viewers, however, would recognize this pattern as part of the style of the series.

Both *Peter Gunn* and *Richard Diamond, Private Detective* were half-hour, broadcast network shows, the standard for their genre and era, and had to tell their entire story in that brief time, made even shorter by commercial and station breaks. The shows were not only expected to engage their audiences immediately but also to hold their attention during the breaks. The *Peter Gunn* introduction demonstrates one strategy for doing this. It abruptly presents a dramatically photographed and unexplained murder – we know nothing about the killer or the victim, and the growing intensity of the music underscores the potency of the event.

This structure – the story event, the camerawork, the music – cues the viewer to stay for more, to learn what is unexplained, and to share in the implied dramatic intensity to come after the first commercial break. Another break is preceded by a similar mini-climax. Approximately midway through the program, Gunn is beaten up in a dark alley by hoods who warn him to stay off the case. As he lies in the alley (figure 10.13), the camera moves in on his face and the screen fades to black as the music increases in volume and dramatic intensity and is completed precisely at the moment the screen is black. Everything – the image and the soundtrack – stops. This mini-climax occurs as Gunn, the hero, is at his most vulnerable. As is typical of a television series, Gunn's fate is never really in doubt. We expect that he will stay on the case and even solve it, but we want to learn how he will reverse his fortunes and accomplish his goal.

Visual Style

The *Peter Gunn* introduction also differs from *Richard Diamond, Private Detective* in that sound is only part of its repertoire. While the Mancini music, the dialogue, the atmospheric sounds are all significant, they work with a dramatic and atmospheric image track. Techniques like the point of view shot of the murder are unavailable to radio and much of the style of *Peter Gunn* is highly visual. A look at the following scene illustrates this.

Fig. 10.14

Fig. 10.15

We see a high-angle night shot of a neon sign, "Mother's," and the dark and empty street below (figure 10.14). Inside Mother's, a jazz club, we see Edie, Peter Gunn's girlfriend, playing cards alone (figure 10.15). The club is obviously closed; a man is sweeping up and chairs are stacked on the tables. The door opens and Peter Gunn enters (figure 10.16). He nods at the owner, Mother, who nods back, and he walks up behind Edie. They exchange dialogue revealing that she is lonely waiting for him and it is obvious that this is a frequent event in their relationship. She then points out a hitherto unseen woman sitting at a back table waiting for Gunn. Gunn goes over to the woman, the attractive, wealthy Helena Mears, who tells him that her sister, Katie, has disappeared. He agrees to look into the matter for her and

Fig. 10.16

she leaves. Edie then laments that her deck of cards will be her date for the night and they kiss. He leaves and, exasperated, she flips the deck into the air.

The sequence is visually structured around the interrelation of Gunn, Edie, and Helena. At first, we see Gunn and Edie in close shot, then she points to the hitherto unseen Helena. We then see a shot with Helena in the foreground and Edie in the background (figure 10.17), and Gunn walks from Edie's into Helena's space. When Gunn and Helena talk in close-up, some shots show Edie in the rear of the shot (figure 10.18). And then, when Helena leaves, Edie walks into the foreground and we see Gunn and Edie together in close shot. Although the women exchange no dialogue, they are visually interrelated by the carefully orchestrated use of the background and the foreground

Fig. 10.17

Fig. 10.18

of the frame. They signify different aspects of Gunn, his private and professional life; the fact that Helena is blonde and attractive, like Edie, underscores temptations of his professional life as well as Edie's jealousy.

Interestingly, Edie is entirely irrelevant to the episode's narrative. She never appears again and has no role in the solving of the case. She is, however, a basic component of the series, like Mother and her club. Unlike movies, television and radio series episodes often include characters and locations irrelevant to the individual episode; their presence reaffirms the basic situation of the series. The characters and locations, even when not central to the plot, acquire a comfortable familiarity for the audience. Characters like Mother and Edie almost become old friends for the audience as well as for Gunn.

Other things such as the dark look are important to the visual style of the scene. The opening, exterior shot establishes the fact that it is night, and it is late, since the club is closed. The emptiness of the club and the dark shadows produced by the upturned chairs create an aura of darkness and atmospheric mystery reminiscent of *film noir*. This is characteristic of the series, many episodes of which occur at night and in dark, mysterious places. Exterior shots generally show dark, deserted streets with ominous shadows. Later, in fact, two thugs emerge from those shadows, drag Gunn into an alley, and beat him. The scene ends with a dark, ugly close shot of him unconscious on the pavement.

Gunn himself establishes a strong visual presence. He is nattily dressed in suit and tie, with jacket neatly buttoned. His close-cropped stylish hair, lean, athletic figure, and quietly elegant demeanor make him a maturely "cool" figure of the late 1950s. Unlike Dick Powell in *Richard Diamond, Private Detective*, Craig Stevens, the actor who plays Gunn, did not have a widely known persona prior to this role, and Edwards styled both his outer appearance and persona to recall that of Cary Grant. Gunn provides a quietly dignified presence and looks particularly aristocratic and upscale at Mother's and among the colorful underworld types with whom he associates.

The opening scene introduced material new to the series, and this scene re-establishes the familiar (Gunn, Edie, and Mother). The remainder of the show complicates and resolves the narrative. Gunn follows Katie's trail to her job, her boyfriend, a lonely hearts club where she met him, and Miguel's nightclub, and eventually he discovers that Helena killed her sister out of jealousy. Gunn tricks Helena into revealing the location of Katie's body.

Character Development and Television Style

The episode contains a good deal of narrative information that is developed efficiently in its short time format. This is made possible by aspects of television industrial practice. Television shows are shot much more quickly and cheaply than movies. They include longer takes, more close-ups and fewer long shots than films, techniques that save time and money while ensuring narrative clarity and visual impact on the small screen. Such shows also use a kind of narrative and characterological shorthand, often quickly establishing a distinctive new character with a few brief strokes during a scene whose main purpose is to advance the narrative.

"Skin Deep" has a number of scenes introducing such characters in a similar way; they open with a close shot of some object that characterizes the character, then the camera pulls back to show the character doing something revealing of his or her personality. At the same time, narrative information is given. In one instance, Gunn goes to the flower shop where Katie worked. The entire scene is shot in a single take. It opens on a shot of a bouquet of flowers and we hear the fussy voice of the shop-owner complaining about the arrangement. The camera pulls back and we see a large man holding the flowers and the smaller, exasperated, chubby shop-owner berating him for his lack of taste. Gunn enters from the rear of the frame, walks to the foreground, and solicits information, the main narrative purpose of the scene (figures 10.19 and 10.20). He leaves in the reverse way. The short scene has conveyed the necessary narrative information (the shop is doing poorly without Katie; Gunn learns the address of her boyfriend), and it has also quickly established a distinctive character.

Fig. 10.19

Fig. 10.20

This is followed by another scene done in a similar way, but with more cuts. It begins with a shot of a dresser top covered by framed photographs of women. Gunn looks at one and the camera pulls back, showing Katie's sweaty boyfriend exercising with weight pulleys in the rear of the frame. The photos, his concern with his body, his pencil mustache and thick, greasy hair establish him as a vain seducer, and also categorize him as sleazy when compared with the dignified and contemptuous Gunn (figure 10.21).

The *Peter Gunn* series was famous for its style, for the "cool" character of Gunn, for its dark look and mood, for Mancini's popular jazz score, and for its idiosyncratic minor characters. Although Blake Edwards later made *Gunn* (1967), a theatrical movie based upon the series, television and films remain very different enterprises. To further illustrate this, we now turn to his film *Victor/Victoria*.

Fig. 10.21

Victor/Victoria (1982)

Narrative Structure and Character Relationships

Unlike the "Satire on Radio Detectives" and "Skin Deep" episodes, *Victor/Victoria* (1982) neither presents us with familiar characters nor returns them at the end of the film to where they were at the beginning; to the contrary, they are changed forever. *Victor/Victoria* tells the story of Victoria Grant, a performer in Paris in the early 1930s. She befriends Toddy (plate 54), a gay man, who guides her into a successful career as a female impersonator; in other words, she becomes a woman pretending to be a man pretending to be a woman. King Marchand (plate 55), a Chicago gangster, sees her show and, before learning that she is supposedly a female impersonator, falls in love with "her." Disturbed by the homosexual implications of his "mistake," he determines to learn whether Victor is a man or a woman. He learns the truth but they remain a couple even as she continues the masquerade. When the police threaten to reveal the hoax, she is forced to relinquish her role to Toddy, who, at the end of the film, performs on stage in her place.

As is typical of film narrative form, all of the central character relationships are changed by the film's conclusion. At the beginning of the film, Victoria and Toddy don't even know each other, then they become friends, and then business partners. Likewise, King begins the film as a tough, heterosexual gangster traveling with Norma, an attractive blonde companion, and Squash, a bodyguard (plate 56). After he meets Victoria, he has a crisis about his masculine identity, which he resolves. By the end of the film they are united as a couple with the implication that they will soon marry. Victoria's career as a female impersonator is over now that her secret has been discovered. Even a minor character like Squash changes drastically when, much to King's surprise, he reveals himself as gay.

These characters and their relationships differ substantially from what they were at the beginning of the film. Victoria can neither continue her act nor remain business partners with Toddy; King can never return to his moment of doubt about Victoria's "true" sex after seeing her naked; Squash is "out of the closet"; and so on. The equilibrium with which the film ends is entirely different from the equilibrium with which "Satire on Radio Detectives" or "Skin Deep" ends. In the former, Diamond still has the same relationship with Helen Asher that he had at the beginning; and, in the latter, Gunn maintains the same relationship he had with Mother, Edie, and the police department.

It is unimaginable, for example, in the radio series that Lieutenant Levinson would announce that he was gay and form a relationship with Sergeant Otis or, in the television series, that Edie would announce that she was a lesbian and form a relationship with Mother, but that is precisely the kind of character development that occurs in *Victor/Victoria*. If *Victor/Victoria* were a television series, it would have to keep King in suspense week after week about Victor's true identity, Squash would remain in the closet, Victoria would have a continuing crisis about her attraction to King, Toddy and Victoria would continue to live their lives as a masquerade, and so on. In short, the original premise would be re-established at the end of each episode and the main narrative question – will King Marchand discover the truth and what will happen when he does – would be forestalled. In the movie, however, after delays and complications, the question is answered and the film ends. To return to those characters in a sequel would be to return to changed characters.

Visual Style

Much as the *Richard Diamond, Private Detective* and *Peter Gunn* series have distinctive styles, Blake Edwards's films also have one, but whereas the styles of his radio and television work derive primarily from his roles as creator, writer, and producer, the style of his film work derives primarily from his role as a director. The facts that Edwards uncharacteristically directed the *Richard Diamond, Private Detective* episode or characteristically did not direct the *Peter Gunn* episode are of little relevance to our analysis of them; any of the usual series directors would have produced essentially the same episodes. Edwards's direction of *Victor/Victoria*, however, is crucial to its style and highly reminiscent of the visual style of his other films. To illustrate this, we will look at the film's use of sight gags and screen space, one of Edwards's stylistic signatures.

Edwards is most famous for the successful Pink Panther films starring Peter Sellers as the inimitable Inspector Clouseau, and those films are most associated with physical, slapstick comedy. But it is slapstick of a certain style that is structured around sight gags. What is the difference? Slapstick simply refers to a vaudeville tradition of performers taking pratfalls and engaging in knockabout physical comedy. This tradition had its golden age in film in the silent era with comedians like Charlie Chaplin and Buster Keaton, who, as Edwards would later, encased their physical shenanigans within a complex visual style. The Three Stooges films, on the other hand, are examples of a crude slapstick style that lacks sophisticated sight gags. Their antics revolve around the manner in which they physically assault one another and incompetently perform their tasks.

Although Clouseau is also incompetent and sometimes physically assaults associates such as his domestic servant Cato (plate 57), there is a major difference: most of the comedy is contingent on careful orchestration of film space, camera movements, and cutting patterns. These filmic devices stage the gags within a complex visual environment where the physical comedy becomes part of elaborate spatial and temporal patterns that have nothing to do with actors and of which the characters themselves might even be oblivious. This is a far cry from Moe poking Curly's eyes, banging his fist on his head, and pulling his tongue. Our point is not to belittle the comic style of the Three Stooges but to indicate that, although they and Clouseau might both be termed slapstick, Edwards's style is quite different.

A simple example illustrates this important point. At the beginning of *The Pink Panther* (1964), Clouseau spins a large globe and then absent-mindedly leans on it and goes crashing to the floor – pure and simple slapstick. Edwards, however, frames the action in such a way that Clouseau falls out of the **frame** while the camera remains stationary. Moments later, Clouseau ludicrously rebounds up into the frame and proceeds as if nothing has happened (plates 58 and 59). The use of offscreen space to structure the simple gag gives it entirely new dimensions. This visual sophistication characterizes Edwards's style.

Although Sellers's Clouseau is commonly thought of as "inimitable," Edwards in fact imitates him quite successfully in *Victor/Victoria* in the role of a private detective hired to discover Victor's true identity. Dressed in a trench coat and hat reminiscent of Clouseau's, the detective bumbles his way through a series of misadventures equally reminiscent of Clouseau: he gets his finger squashed in a closet door, gets hit by lightning, and falls from a broken bar stool (plate 60). The manner in which Edwards shoots and edits all these scenes is visually complex, as in the Pink Panther films. We will now focus on a sequence without that detective and without any slapstick to illustrate a central aspect of the film's visual style.

Toddy and Victoria stay in the same hotel as King and Squash. Driven to know whether Victor is a man or a woman, King devises a plan to hide in Victoria's apartment: he pretends to be Toddy calling for extra towels and, when the maid brings them, he sneaks in behind her. Although the entire sequence is structured around sophisticated timing and use of **offscreen space**, we will concentrate on the hallway scene.

A stationary camera in the middle of the hallway shows an elevator at the end and doorways at the extreme right and left, the one on the right opens into Toddy and Victoria's room and the one on the left into another guest room (plate 61). This single hallway shot with a stationary camera will be used several times and will use five areas of offscreen space: that behind the elevator door which, when it opens and closes, suddenly reveals the new space of the elevator car and its passengers; an entrance from an offscreen hallway at the left, adjacent to the elevator; the space behind the camera from which the maid will enter; and the spaces behind the doors at the left and right of the frame into and from which various characters will come and go.

In one shot, we see King enter from the offscreen hallway at the left rear of the frame, directly by the elevator, and approach Toddy and Victoria's doorway. When the door at the left opens, he quickly leans against the left side of the hallway, trying to appear nonchalant. A guest in a bathrobe appears with a pair of shoes that he is about to leave outside his door for shining when he spots King and warily withdraws into his room (plate 62). As King detects the maid approaching, he rushes to the elevator and pushes the button. The maid enters from the offscreen space behind the camera and approaches the door at the right of the hallway. As she prepares to enter Toddy and Victoria's room, King once again tries to act nonchalant, this time pretending to be awaiting the elevator. As the maid enters the room, King rushes to the door in time to catch it before closing and, as he enters the room, the elevator arrives and the door opens. Just as King disappears offscreen right (plate 63), the operator emerges from the elevator and, bewildered, looks around for whoever called for it.

This single shot introduces all five areas of offscreen space: behind the camera, behind the elevator door, the hallway in the left rear, and the two rooms at the right and left of the hallway. It also includes elaborate timing involving the comings and goings as well as the actions, reactions, and glances of King, the maid, the guest, and the elevator operator. But, as is typical of Edwards's style of building sight gags, this is just the beginning.

Later he returns to the exact same camera set-up as Squash enters from the hallway at the left rear. He approaches the door to Toddy and Victoria's apartment and rings the doorbell. We see King inside the apartment responding with alarm and then cut back to the hallway, where Squash kneels and begins to pick the lock (plate 64). The door at the left opens and the man with the shoes once again appears but, once again spotting suspicious proceedings, quickly retreats. Just as Squash opens the door and enters into offscreen space at the right, the elevator door opens again and Toddy and Victoria emerge. As Toddy prepares to unlock the door, Victoria playfully raises the tails of his long overcoat and crawls under it. The door at the left again opens and the guest reappears with shoes in hand (plate 65). He exchanges looks with Toddy and, as Toddy and Victoria rush into their room, we see an increasingly bewildered expression on the guest's face. Edwards then cuts to a shot inside the room.

This part of the sequence has built on elements already introduced. Squash enters from offscreen in the same place from which King entered; the guest across the hall reappears twice in a continuing effort to leave his shoes; and the elevator operator arrives just in time to again miss someone surreptitiously entering Toddy and Victoria's room. As before, all of this occurs from the perspective of a perfectly stationary camera and with precision timing among the actors.

Edwards is still not done with this set-up. He returns to it once more, this time as Squash is leaving after an elaborate farce sequence involving both him and King hiding in the apartment. Squash has inadvertently been locked out on a snowy balcony. Edwards cuts to the exact same camera set-up as the previous times but this time the hallway is empty. The door opens at the left and the persistent guest, shoes in hand, once again reappears. Just as he is about to place his shoes on the floor, the door across the hall opens and Squash, covered with snow, appears (plate 66). He and the incredulous guest lock glances. "Do you have heat in your room?" Squash asks. "Yeah," the man replies. "Boy, you're lucky," Squash retorts and then dashes offscreen, leaving the man, shoes still in hand, staring after him in disbelief.

This last part of the gag is revealing in two ways: it demonstrates how Edwards structures these sight gags and it contains the only important dialogue throughout the running gag. Each time we see the man with his shoes, we think we have seen the joke. We do not expect to see him again; in fact, he is a nameless character who has not appeared previously in the film and will not appear again. The manner in which Edwards keeps returning to him conforms to Edwards's style of "topping the topper." In this style of visual comedy, just when you think you have seen the gag completed, it is "topped" and then topped again. Notice also that most of this running gag involves no dialogue; we only hear Henry Mancini's music.

Everything about this style of comedy is suited to cinema and would be difficult or nearly impossible on a television series. First, the entire style is based upon the assumption of an audience carefully watching every moment, not distractedly looking away and merely listening to some parts. The careful manner in which the gag is built takes long periods of time, all of which have to be observed by the spectator to gain the full effect. The careful use of offscreen space and split-second timing also depend for their success on a spectator who scrutinizes the image rather than one who casually glances at it.

In the "Skin Deep" episode of *Peter Gunn*, we noted how camera style functioned in several scenes such as the first scene in Mother's and the first scene in the flower shop. While Peter Gunn is interviewing his client at Mother's, we noted how in some shots Edie appears in the rear of the frame. While that is a nice touch, someone could follow the scene perfectly well by merely listening to the exchange between Gunn and the client. When one next glanced at the screen, there would be no confusion or sense of anything having been lost. Similarly, the scene in the flower shop is one long take, but it is not elaborate in the sustained manner of the shots described from *Victor/Victoria* and, again, one could follow all the significant developments by merely listening to the conversation Gunn has with the florist. As we noted, the *Peter Gunn* series does have a distinctive "look" to it, but involves different stylistic elements. By glancing at the sets, and at aspects of Gunn's appearance, such as grooming and dressing style, we can quickly take in this visual style; our appreciation of it is not contingent upon the sustained attention required of the visual style in *Victor/Victoria*.

Radio, television, and film are three distinct yet interrelated media. The *Richard Diamond, Private Detective* radio series, the *Peter Gunn* television series and the film *Victor/Victoria* were all successful with their respective audiences. While all three relate to Edwards's *oeuvre* in their reliance upon detective figures, for example, or their use of witty repartee, what most emerges from a careful study of them is how Edwards functions differently in all three of these media and how his success is contingent upon understanding how elements these media hold in common function differently in each one. Dialogue is not just dialogue, visual style is not just visual style, aural style is not just aural style, and a good narrative structure is not just a good narrative structure; the dialogue, visual style, and narrative demands of a television series, for example, are quite different from those of a feature film. If Edwards were to make a television series out of *Victor/Victoria*, it would need a different narrative structure, a different look, and different sound.

SELECTED READINGS

John Ellis discusses the differences between film and television, including narrative form, technology, and viewing context, in *Visible Fictions: Cinema: Television: Video* (Boston: Routledge and Kegan Paul, 1982). William Luhr and Peter Lehman analyze *Victor/Victoria* in relation to Edwards's career in *Returning to the Scene: Blake Edwards*, Vol. 2 (Athens: Ohio University Press, 1989).

11

REALISM AND THEORIES OF FILM

The Battleship Potemkin and *Umberto D*

Aesthetic Judgments

We have all had the experience of leaving a theater with a friend and arguing about whether the movie we had just seen was good or bad. During such arguments we are likely to say things like "It wasn't realistic" or "I didn't like the ending." Although we don't think of ourselves as theorists when we make such statements, we are on their turf. Aesthetic judgments about whether works of art are good or bad are part of theories about art. The crucial word here is "part," since theories are much more than simple judgments of taste. In fact, there is nothing simple about such judgments.

Fig. 11.1

Some people did not like the ending of *Basic Instinct* (1992) because it was ambiguous as to whether or not the central female character was the ice-pick murderer so crucial to the film's plot (figure 11.1). Some simply wanted a definitive answer, while others were cynical about the obvious set-up for a sequel. In both cases, those viewers considered complete narrative closure an important criteria for judging a movie, meaning that, by the end, we should know the answers to important questions that the film has raised. Similarly, some viewers objected to *The Birds* (1963) because the film, which is premised on brutal attacks by birds upon humans, never explains why the birds are attacking (figure 11.2) or whether or not the attacks will be brought under control. At the end of *Wolf* (1994), the central male character is transformed into a wolf and the female character, who forms a romantic couple with him, is also transformed into a

Fig. 11.2

werewolf who follows him into the wilderness (figure 11.3). Some critics objected to this far-fetched ending, which avoided resolving the central interpersonal relationships with which the film deals. For those critics, the ending of a film should grow out of the body of the film and satisfactorily resolve its main conflicts. If an ending seems tagged on or opens up new, unresolved issues, they consider it silly or weak.

Fig. 11.3

In order to explore such judgments, film theorists must consider many issues. Aesthetic judgments are linked to theoretical assumptions about such things as realism, originality, and stylistic unity. Why are there such a bewildering variety of styles? Why is it that, when we see some films operating upon different premises than those with which we are familiar, we find them boring or even incomprehensible and wonder why anyone would want to make such movies? In order to answer such questions, film theorists have to ask fundamental questions that may strike some of us as obvious. What is a movie? What is a camera? How do spectators watch movies? How are they affected by the movies they watch?

What is Film Theory?

Nearly everyone who watches movies makes aesthetic judgments, yet most viewers are not film theorists. What accounts for the difference? Theorists base their aesthetic judgments upon logical connections between what they think a movie is, how spectators watch movies and are affected by them, and what kinds of movies are good and what kinds are bad. A complete theory, in other words, involves much more than a judgment about whether a movie is good or bad; it involves an examination of assumptions and criteria underlying such judgments. If all filmmakers thought that movies were the same thing, they would all make similar movies. Obviously they do not. As a result, we are faced with a bewildering variety of movies either implicitly or explicitly based upon an equally bewildering variety of theories about film.

Since popular notions of realism are so pervasive in our culture and so profoundly affect our responses to movies, this chapter will explore those notions in relation to film theory. The following three chapters deal with gender, race, and class; it is essential that we understand the limitations and errors of popular notions of realism before exploring those other areas, since many people invoke popular realism in responding to them. It is also important that we understand the difference between popular, largely unexamined notions of realism and sophisticated, theoretical concepts of realism as well as how both relate to formalist film theories. The second half of this chapter will analyze Sergei Eisenstein's *The Battleship Potemkin*, a major formalist film, and *Umberto D* (1952), a major realist film directed by Vittorio de Sica. Realism and formalism are very different approaches to film; examining these films together

underlines some of the differences and reveals how important it is to appreciate the theoretical assumptions upon which films are made.

Questioning Theoretical Assumptions

Varying responses toward something as apparently simple as the ending of a
film shows how complex these issues are. They also reveal that many film
spectators make aesthetic judgments without questioning the theoretical
assumptions underlying those judgments. We all know whether or not we
think the ending of a film should explain everything, but few of us would have
a good answer to the simple question, "Why?" We might respond that we are
just used to watching movies like that and think that is the way they are supposed to be. Film theorists attempt to answer such questions, sometimes
making implicit, unexamined assumptions explicit.

Let's return to our other example of saying "It's not realistic." Instead of
objecting to the unanswered narrative questions at the end of *Basic Instinct*
or *The Birds*, some might reject those endings as unrealistic. The central male
character in *Basic Instinct* is a smart, experienced homicide detective. In the
course of the film, he witnesses a great deal of disturbing behavior on the part
of the central female character to whom he is sexually attracted even though
she is a murder suspect. Yet, at the end of the film, they are making love. The
spectator, but not the main character, sees an ice pick under the bed. Some
might think to themselves, "No detective would be so stupid as to put himself
in such danger again!"

As we have seen in previous chapters, our expectations about what is realistic changes with different genres (see chapter 5). Even though the parameters of what is considered realistic vary widely from genre to genre, notions
of realism are remarkably tenacious and operative in nearly all films. Even
though *The Birds* is a horror film, some think it ludicrous that the world would
be unexplainably threatened by animals that we live with everyday, which do
not ordinarily attack people, and are not even thought of as enemies of
humans. If we ask such people why they think everything they see in a movie
should be realistic, most would be at a loss to say anything other than, "That's
the way movies are supposed to be." If we ask them what they mean by
"realistic," we will get many different answers. It is easy to say a movie is
bad because it is unrealistic but difficult to say why it should be realistic or
even what it means to be realistic.

Style

Let's take an example from style rather than narrative. Many critics criticize
Brian De Palma's style as being derivative, obtrusive, and full of technical
razzle-dazzle. In *Obsession* (1976) he uses long, 360-degree pan shots where

Fig. 11.4

Fig. 11.5

the camera circles around characters in a manner that brings attention to the camera's movement. At the beginning of *Bonfire of the Vanities* (1990), the camera starts inside a car and, in one long take with moving camera, follows a character into a building, up an elevator, and through crowded rooms (figure 11.4). The sheer virtuosity of choreographing such a complex shot is likely to attract the viewer's attention. Or, at the other extreme, De Palma uses extensive editing during a shoot-out scene in *The Untouchables* (1987) that takes place on a staircase at a train station (figure 11.5). The editing style and even some of the images, such as a woman with a baby carriage (figure 11.6), refer to the famous Odessa Steps sequence (figure 11.7) from Eisenstein's *Potemkin*, which we will analyze later in this chapter. And no one can miss De Palma's trademark stylistic signature of literally splitting the screen as in *Sisters* (1973) and *Carrie* (1976, figure 11.8), where, side by side, we see two images filmed with different cameras.

Fig. 11.6

Fig. 11.7

Fig. 11.8

The objections to these stylistic flourishes take many forms, but they are all based upon a common assumption about the Hollywood **invisible style** of filmmaking. To object that a style is obtrusive or highly noticeable makes sense only with reference to a norm wherein style is usually not noticed. If a camera circles characters in a dizzying manner, or the screen suddenly splits into two images, or a shot seems to go on forever, or, at the opposite pole, suddenly there is an outburst of many shots held for only a brief time, we are likely to notice these things. Many critics have a related complaint with De Palma's baroque style: they argue that it is totally superficial, frequently borrowed from other directors such as Alfred Hitchcock, and unintegrated into the plot – in short, a form of cinematic pyrotechnics, all flash and no substance.

Even if this is an accurate description of De Palma's style, it does not necessarily justify a negative value judgment. If De Palma is interested, for example, in how the same scene may look from two perspectives simultaneously or from the perspective of circular motion in a manner that has nothing to do thematically with what is happening in the scenes, that is "bad" only if one assumes that narrative is always more important than style and should dominate it. Comparably, if De Palma's fascination with using circular camera movements can be traced to an exaggerated development of such moments in Hitchcock's films, such a link is "bad" only if one assumes that originality is always better than being derivative. While classical Hollywood films concern events and characters in what appear to be either real or totally imaginary worlds, De Palma's films, like the works of many modernist artists, are partially about other films. Should this render them invalid? Film theory has historically grappled with these and similar problems.

History of Film Theory

From cinema's origins in the late nineteenth and early twentieth centuries through the 1960s, theories about cinema tended to divide into the opposing camps of **formalism** and **realism**. Major formalist theorists include Sergei Eisenstein and Rudolf Arnheim; major realist theorists include André Bazin and Siegfried Kracauer.

Formalists emphasized the formal properties of cinema that shaped the way movies were made as well as our responses to them. They might observe, for example, that what we see in a movie is delineated by the four sides of the film **frame**, whereas what we see in real life tapers off into peripheral vision. This would support the conclusion that organizing screen space and offscreen space is an artistic activity that differs from our daily perception of space; a formalist approach emphasizes this difference. There is, for example, no such thing as an offscreen sound in real life. If we stand in a room and hear a strange sound, from elsewhere, we immediately turn our heads in that direction and may even investigate it. We would not do this in a movie theater. If sound emanates from an offscreen space to the right of where we are sitting, we do not turn sharply to search for its source. We understand the difference between film form and real life.

Realists, in opposition, stressed the mechanical, recording nature of cinema as well as the connection between the camera and the world in front of it. They might point out that, if Sarah Bernhardt performs in front of a camera, the camera will capture that performance on film. Although we may not have been present at the performance, a record of it remains.

Some have seen the difference between realists and formalists as analogous to the distinction between the film screen as resembling either a canvas or a window. Formalist filmmakers, who see the screen as a canvas, create a world within its frame using their own compositional rules and laws much as painters do; nothing significant exists beyond that frame. Realist filmmakers, however, work as if they look out of a window that frames a small part of a larger world lying outside our view.

Different styles were developed within both camps. Formalist theories of film developed first. Since film was a new art form, one way to gain respectability for it was to emphasize its relationship to established art forms. If films simply showed the world as it really was, then they were little more than recordings that required no special artistic skill and allowed no room for creativity. After film became a respected form, however, realist theories switched the emphasis to the recording aspect of the medium.

Realist and formalist theories of film were highly polarized, essentialist, and prescriptive. Theorists saw the essence of cinema as being either realistic or formalistic and championed styles of filmmaking that would support one or the other. By the late 1960s, this opposition broke down for a number of reasons. Theorists such as Peter Wollen and Noël Burch approached film by abandoning the old formalist/realist opposition and tried to create an inventory of, and understand, the full range of cinematic possibilities, citing diverse works by Sergei Eisenstein, Jean Renoir, and John Ford.

At the same time, a new generation of filmmakers made movies that did not conform to either paradigm. French director Jean-Luc Godard (*La Chinoise*, 1967, and *Weekend*, 1967) went so far as to turn one aspect of that paradigm on its head when he remarked that we should reverse the manner in which we regard two of the most important figures in the history of film, Georges Méliès (*Trip to the Moon*, 1902) and the Lumière Brothers (*Train Arriving at the Station*, 1895). Méliès traditionally is seen as pioneering fiction filmmaking, and the Lumières are seen as pioneering documentary filmmaking. Godard, however, suggested that the obvious contrivance of a film like *Trip to the Moon*, which, long before space travel was a reality, showed men travel to the moon and explore it, was really truthful in that it fooled no spectator into believing it was real, while a documentary like *Train Arriving at the Station*, which simply showed a real train arriving at a real station, made people believe that what they were seeing was just like what they would really see if they were there, which is a fiction, since the filmmakers decided where to place the camera, how to light the scene, what kind of film stock to use, and so on. In other words, all films have a style, and styles are properties of works of art, not the real world. We must understand how all styles shape our view of the world they represent.

Since the late 1960s, film theorists have discredited notions of realism that argue that any style is "like" the real world. They have come to see realist styles as just another form that favors certain techniques over others.

Popular Realism

Notions of realism govern the popular reception of film by both critics and the public. While there probably always will be a great deal of debate among film theorists about the nature of cinema, the term "realistic" as it is applied to movies in everyday usage has been thoroughly discredited, and it is important to understand why. When discussing theories of authorship in chapter 4, we pointed out that it is no longer tenable to view directors as geniuses who possess great insight into universal truths; rather, they are part of an historically specific cultural context of which they, like all mortals, do not have full understanding. Viewing the director as an ahistorical genius shuts off exploration of important aspects of films, which perpetuates dominant cultural notions about life and art.

A similar problem occurs with realism. When we argue that something is realistic, we mean that it is like "real" life. This is tantamount to saying that something is the way it is in a film because that's the way it really is in life. We do not have to question further. But who is to say definitively what "real" life" is? Different people have different perspectives. If a science-fiction film introduces a monster whose very sight makes a woman scream until the man she is with slaps her, many viewers accept this response as "realistic" by thinking that women actually get hysterical in dangerous situations while men stay calm and rational. Such a notion of women, however, has nothing to do with some essential characteristic of women but rather with a historically specific idea that some people hold about women. The distinction is crucial, since the former implies an unchanging truth about women and the latter implies an historically constructed and changeable concept.

If something is understood as being constructed within a specific historical and cultural context, we can ask questions that lead to a fuller understanding of both the art object and the time and culture in which it was made. We can then posit significant alternatives, both culturally and in representation, as part of a process of change. We can say that the notion of women as helpless hysterics is simply a sexist concept rather than an essential truth; furthermore, we can construct meaningful alternatives such as the heroines in *Alien* (1979) and *Terminator 2* (1991) who remain in control in the most terrifying of situations and do everything that a male hero traditionally does. We can also redefine the role of real women in the military; it is no accident that such a social change has in fact coincided in the United States with new representations of women in action films and such military films as *GI Jane* (1997).

Three of our examples have come from science fiction, a genre by definition not reflective of "real" life. Doesn't this exempt them from realistic criteria? Not at all. We have already discussed how such criteria differ in different genres but, at the same time, genres conform to many popular notions of realism. *King Kong* (1933), for example, posits the existence of a giant ape and then has it rampage through Manhattan. However, given this fantastic premise, the leading men in the film are dynamic and the main female character is entirely passive and desperately needs to be rescued by a strong man, who becomes her romantic partner. Furthermore, the film characterizes whites as civilized and urbane but blacks as jungle savages easily cowed by terrors the whites overcome. These gender and racial characterizations conformed with popular notions about reality at the time. If, however, *King Kong* had kidnapped a passive white man who was then rescued by an aggressive white woman working together with an intelligent, urbane black man who becomes her romantic partner, contemporary audiences might have been outraged.

They had no trouble dealing with a giant ape on 34th Street; other things might have struck them as more difficult and "unrealistic."

The next three chapters analyze the representation of gender, race, and class in films. It is important that we discard essentialist notions of realism that lead us to simply think such things as "That's the way blacks (or women or the rich) really are." Such a naïve position blocks exploration of the most urgent social and cultural issues in movies, and current film theory is dedicated to the full exploration of the medium.

Content and Realism

Common notions of realism frequently involve naïve notions of the relationship between content changes in films and increased realism. The history of censorship makes this clear. When censorship codes began to change in the late 1960s and allowed more nudity, profanity, sexuality, and graphic violence, filmmakers, critics, and the public alike frequently responded by hailing the new R- and X-rated films as being more realistic. *Midnight Cowboy* (1968), an X-rated movie dealing in gritty detail with the lives of marginalized, down-and-out characters, even won an Academy Award for Best Movie of the Year. From this perspective, profanity, sex, and nudity are all part of life and, adding appropriate amounts of them to movies makes them more realistic.

Such a crude content notion of realism conceives of films as containers into which we can shovel differing amounts of realism. Up to a limit, the more sex and profanity we throw in, the more realistic the movie becomes. Content notions of realism are dangerous because they block crucial questions about the representation of these new, supposedly "realistic" subjects. Since the ratings code changed in 1968, there has been a great deal of nudity in films, but that nudity is not equally distributed between male and female characters nor are nude men and women treated equally. Full frontal male nudity, for example, is much rarer than full frontal female nudity. Even with such "adult" films as *Last Tango in Paris* (1972, figure 11.9), critics and public alike accept this difference with regard to how Marlon Brando and Maria Schneider, the film's stars, are shown. But such a distinction has nothing to do with the "reality" of sex and nudity; it results entirely from social, historical, and institutional (the ratings board) constraints that must be questioned and understood. To simply accept the representation of sex in *Last Tango in Paris* as "realistic" is to stop the questioning process before it starts.

The same is true of race. The relaxation of censorship codes has led to a proliferation of urban blacks represented as foul-mouthed pimps, drug dealers, dope addicts, and criminals. Yet, as we showed in discussing Spike Lee in chapter 4, a film such as *Jungle Fever* (1991) challenges such a notion by showing a black professional family living in Harlem, reading *The New York Times* and generally

Fig. 11.9

interacting with one another in a manner that fits none of the above-listed "realistic" character traits of screen blacks. No matter how explicit the sex, violence, language, or anything else is in a film, we cannot simply accept it as realistic. We must examine how it is represented and the assumptions underlying those representations.

Realism and Progress

A final assumption underlying the concept of popular realism involves a belief that the contemporary moment marks an advance over earlier historical periods. This aspect of realism can refer to style, technology, and subject matter. We have all had the experience of watching an old Hollywood movie and thinking that it looks phony and that its content is simple and naïve. When we watch old horror films with monsters such as *Frankenstein* (1931), we may be more bemused than frightened by the monster, who pales in comparison with the high-tech, special-effects monsters of the 1990s. Such judgments are built on the implicit assumptions that things now look real rather than fake and that we treat subjects as they really are.

From this perspective, the contemporary moment always looks sophisticated and realistic and the past looks naïve and unrealistic. But the reason for this has nothing to do with representations becoming more realistic but, rather, with us accepting as realistic what we are used to watching. If we walk into an electronics store and see many televisions on at the same time and tuned to the same station, they all look different in terms of brightness and color. Which one is the most realistic? If we believe that one is more realistic than another it is because it approximates to the look of the television that we are used to watching at home or one that we think is the most technologically advanced. Someone else might say it is too bright because he or she is used to a different intensity on his or her set. If such is the case with the same technological form showing the same program, think of what happens when we consider different movies shot over widely varying time periods.

If we look at color films made in the Technicolor process during the 1940s and 1950s, reds and greens are saturated and strongly demarcated from other colors. Current color processes use more gradations of color, and those colors stand out less. The color in *Gone with the Wind* (1939), for example, now strikes us as looking more like Hollywood than like the real world. But the exact same thing is true for the color scheme we use now; thirty years from now it will strike viewers as looking like the first decade of the twenty-first century rather than looking like the real world. Norms that we are used to become invisible to us; it is only when a change takes place that we see them for what they are.

Documentaries are particularly revealing in this regard, since many people consider the entire genre realistic. During the 1930s and 1940s, however, such films as *The River* (1937) and *The Plow that Broke the Plains* (1936) were made with well-lit, carefully composed shots with a fine grain texture that resembled those used in Hollywood. Indeed, a socially serious film of the period, like *The Grapes of Wrath* (1940), which dealt with Depression victims, used similar compositions. In the 1960s, a new style of documentary filmmaking called *cinéma vérité* emerged. It favored hand-held cameras, which produced jerky and quickly changing compositions that were not lit in the classical style and often appeared grainy as a result. Within a few years this look seemed so realistic that the earlier documentaries looked fake and staged. Suddenly, "real" came to mean spontaneous and impromptu rather than carefully planned and composed. Now, *vérité* style in turn has come to look like a 1960s' notion of reality that is just as dated as the 1940s' style.

Special effects may make this particularly clear, since they probably change more quickly and dramatically than any other aspect of film style (see chapter 16). The *Star Wars* trilogy set the standard for special effects during the 1970s, but producer George Lucas released a new version with updated, computerized special effects in 1997. And after *Jurassic Park*, any films belonging to the same or related genres that do not use computer graphics are going to seem as unrealistic as painted backdrops from Hollywood movies of the 1940s and 1950s now seem!

The same is true with subject matter. Perhaps this is nowhere more clearly evident than with television situation comedies. When we watch episodes of *Father Knows Best*, *Leave it to Beaver*, or *The Ozzie and Harriet Show* we are likely to feel smugly superior to a simpler time when Americans believed in the ideal of the happy nuclear family with a working father, a housewife mother, a few kids, and no problem so serious that it threatened domestic bliss for long. Current sitcoms deal with teen sex, drugs, and single-parent homes in a manner that we are likely to consider a realistic portrayal that acknowledges the real problems of family life. Decades from now, however, that notion of the family will seem just as dated and unrealistic as 1950s' television families do to us now.

If we accept the current style or content as simply realistic, we will miss asking the most important critical questions about it. No aspect of film form, style, or content lies outside the analytical questions posed by film theorists. In the remainder of this chapter, we will discuss two films, *The Battleship Potemkin* and *Umberto D*, by exploring the ways in which Sergei Eisenstein analyzed the former and André Bazin the latter. The work of both theorists stands in opposition to classical Hollywood and makes us question rather than simply accept that style as a realistic norm. Eisenstein was a Russian who became a major filmmaker and theorist following the Russian Revolution of 1917. Bazin was French and came to prominence following World War II. Unlike Eisenstein, he did not make films but analyzed and theorized about those made by others. Eisenstein's formalism stands in strong contrast to the Hollywood classical style. Bazin's notions of realism and the films he championed contrast as much with typical Hollywood notions of realism as with Eisenstein's formalism.

The Battleship Potemkin (1925) and Eisenstein's Formalist Theory

Sergei Eisenstein's films, including *Strike* (1925), *The Battleship Potemkin* (1925), and *Ivan the Terrible, Parts 1 and 2* (1944 and 1946), were made in accordance with his theory that films need not follow the spatial and temporal laws of the real world. Through careful composition and cutting, they could create their own world. In *Ivan the Terrible*, for example, we see Ivan and his troops prepare for battle. The scene includes a visual motif of sunlike rays emanating from a central point. In a series of shots that are only moments apart in narrative time, Eisenstein shoots Ivan watching the proceedings with the sky visible behind him. Between two such shots, the pattern of clouds in the sky has changed in such a manner that now the clouds appear as rays emanating from Ivan's head. Realistically, no such change in the cloud pattern could occur in the time between the two shots but, for Eisenstein, the formal motif has prominence over any concern with the laws of the real world. Within the space and time of the film world, he makes them occur.

Eisenstein saw film as a construct that could be shaped by filmmakers in accordance with laws of artistic film form, not the real world. In Hollywood, such a noticeable and quick change in the clouds between the two shots would be considered a continuity error, but Eisenstein had different priorities. Although much of *Potemkin* is shot in continuity, glaring exceptions are not errors since Eisenstein did not consider film style subordinate to the spatial and temporal laws of the real world.

Eisenstein felt that filmmakers who carefully manipulated film form could produce desired effects in the film's audiences. He considered style not simple window dressing but fundamental to the shaping of viewer response to a film. For Eisenstein, **montage** (or editing, as it is commonly called now) was the fundamental tool of the filmmaker. By the standards of classical Hollywood filmmaking, his films have many shots cut together quite quickly and in a noticeable fashion. *Potemkin*, which uses these techniques, is one of the most respected films ever made.

Narrative and Character

Although *Potemkin* tells a story, it does so in a manner quite different from stories told in realist traditions. The film is divided into five parts with titles:

1 Men and Maggots
2 Drama on the Quarter-Deck
3 The Dead Man Cries for Vengeance
4 The Odessa Steps
5 Meeting the Squadron

Rather than presenting the film as a seamless whole, Eisenstein divides it into sections that emphasize that it is constructed out of parts. When watching a classical Hollywood film, we can forget that it was made because the invisible style is intended to make us feel as if we are looking at a world that unfolds magically and continuously before our eyes.

Fig. 11.10

Eisenstein creates complex formal relationships within and between the five parts. The entire narrative is structured around oppositions. Each of the five parts is itself divided into opposing parts. In "Men and Maggots," we see the men resting in their hammocks (figure 11.10). This restful mood gives way to one of unrest after they are awakened and face the oppressive conditions on the battleship. In "Drama on the Quarter-Deck," submissiveness turns to mutiny when the petty officers who are ordered to fire on the sailors refuse to carry out their orders. In "The Dead Man Cries for Vengeance," mourning turns to political protest; in "The Odessa Steps," fraternizing turns to slaughter; and in "Meeting the Squadron," tense waiting turns to unity and brotherhood. Just as each of the five parts is divided into opposing parts, the entire narrative of the film is similarly divided. The first two parts are separated from the last two by the comparatively brief section dealing with the dead sailor.

Like all narratives, *Potemkin* has characters, but they bear little resemblance to the types of characters we are used to in realist traditions. Most obviously, there is no central character. Furthermore, most of the characters are never even named. Not only do we not learn their names but we also learn nothing about them as individuals. This is even true of Vakulinchuk, one of the few sailors who is named and the one who falls onto a hook and dangles over the water when he dies (figure 11.11). Aside from his name, we learn nothing about his background, his personality, or his personal life, such as whether or not he has a girlfriend or wife. Most styles of realist filmmaking tell us such things as who characters are and what their backgrounds and motivations are. To varying degrees, we feel that we understand them psychologically and this allows us to identify with them.

Eisenstein wanted to block this type of realist character development because he felt it led to a near total emphasis on caring about individuals rather than large social and political issues. This film is about class and oppression. Just as the officers oppress and even attempt to kill some of the sailors, the government oppresses and even kills some of its people. Eisenstein tries to make us think about these issues rather than concern ourselves emotionally with what, for example, motivates an officer to perform a particularly oppressive act.

Psychologically developed characters are replaced in this film with highly generalized and recognizable types: for example, the tyrannical officer, the cowardly priest, and the courageous sailor. This shift from psychological character development to generalized types involves a corresponding shift in acting style. Eisenstein used the

Fig. 11.11

Fig. 11.12

Fig. 11.13

Fig. 11.14

movements and actions of the characters as compositional elements and visual motifs. Vakulinchuk, for example, falls to his death onto a hanging hook in a manner that recalls the rotten meat on a hook (figure 11.12) in an earlier scene showing the inhumane conditions aboard ship. The visual parallels imply that the oppressive officers treat the sailors like meat.

During such scenes as the mutiny on the ship and the massacre on shore at the nearby Odessa Steps, ways in which the actors move count for everything and conventional acting counts for nothing. In fact, many of the actors in *Potemkin* were not professionals and were chosen for their parts because of their appearance. Unlike actors in realist traditions, it is not their job to make us understand, believe anything about, or identify with their characters. Indeed, at times athletic and acrobatic skills are much more central than acting skills, as when Vakulinchuk is thrown overboard and when a man with no legs uses his arms to propel his flight from the Cossacks on the Odessa Steps (figure 11.13).

Space and Time

Space in *Potemkin* is frequently ambiguous and confusing. Near the beginning of the film, we see a brief shot of the entire battleship (figure 11.14) but neither that view nor the few others of it serve as an **establishing shot**. The first shot of the battleship looks like an establishing shot because it shows the whole ship, but it does not help us locate the space we see next. We never really get such a feel for the layout of the ship that we know where the captain's quarters are in relation to the sailors' sleeping quarters or the galley. We simply see these spaces abruptly introduced. The purpose of the **long shot** is to establish a formal relationship between the whole ship and its parts that functions thematically throughout the film. The film develops the theme of the growing revolution by first locating it in part of the ship, then having it spread to the whole ship and finally move from one ship to the other. The two ships joined in brotherhood at the end of the film stand for the revolution spreading throughout Russia.

Even when action is confined to one part of the ship, as happens when the petty officers are ordered to fire upon the rebellious sailors on the quarterdeck, we have little sense of who is where. After the captain orders those dissatisfied with the soup to be hanged from the yardarm, we see a series of shots of the sailors and petty officers turning and looking but the shots are so tight and follow in such rapid succession that we do not know who stands where in relation to whom or even precisely where they stand in relation to the yardarm. The act of turning and looking, in other words, is defined within the confines of the film frame rather than with spatial reference to the real

Fig. 11.15

Fig. 11.16

world. Exactly where they are in relation to one another does not matter any more than exactly who they are as individuals. The formal motif of looking does, however, recur throughout the film, as when the doctor inspects the rotten meat (figure 11.15), the mourners look at Vakulinchuk's body, and horrified onlookers watch the massacre on the Odessa Steps (figure 11.16).

Although the Odessa Steps are the space on which one of the film's most famous dramatic actions takes place, the space remains quite ambiguous as we watch the frenzied movement of civilians fleeing the machinelike column of Cossacks. Although we know the Cossacks start at the top of the stairs and march downward, and that the civilians are fleeing downward to escape the inexorable advance of the soldiers, we never know precisely where any of the specific episodes of horror or confrontation are located or even from where the observers watch. We see images of people running, falling, and looking, but exactly where they are is frequently impossible to determine and irrelevant.

Fig. 11.17

Furthermore, we see several of the spaces repeatedly traversed, and that makes it even more confusing. If there is one general and downward movement, how can we be back up where we had already been earlier? Wouldn't the people and the Cossacks be farther down by now? This spatial confusion points to a similar temporal confusion: stated simply, the action is drawn out in a manner that violates all realist expectations of how long it would take. The running and the marching seem never to stop or, to put it another way, no one seems to ever get anywhere. This is a clear example of how Eisenstein did not believe that cinema should be subordinate to the laws of the real world but should create its own. He creates dramatic conflict in part by extending the time and repeatedly showing characters traversing the same ambiguous spaces.

Another simple example occurs in the section "Men and Maggots" when we see shots of tables suspended on ropes swinging back and forth (figure 11.17) and, moments later, a shot of one of the tables perfectly still (figure 11.18). In Hollywood this would be considered a continuity error since the laws of nature are such

Fig. 11.18

Fig. 11.19

Fig. 11.20

that such extreme swinging could not stop in an instant. Yet for Eisenstein this is no error, since movement and stillness are properties of film with which he can do what he wants. If he wants to emphasize movement in one shot and stillness in the next, he can logically do so since he follows compositional laws, not the natural laws of the real world.

Composition

All aspects of **composition**, including shape, line, and direction of movement, were used by Eisenstein to construct the film in accordance with the governing concept of opposition and conflict. These principles can be seen in the Odessa Steps massacre. The people gathered on the steps are associated with round shapes such as hats, umbrellas, carriage wheels, and eyeglasses, and the Cossacks with the sharp, pointed shapes of their rifles with fixed bayonets. Even the tactility and materials of the shapes are involved. The tautness of the vulnerable umbrella, an image of which fills the frame at one point (figure 11.19), stands in opposition to the piercing sharpness of the bayonet blades (figure 11.20), and the fragile glass of eyeglasses is shattered in several images (figure 11.21). The parallel, horizontal lines of the steps conflict with the diagonal lines of the rifles thrust out in front of the soldiers.

Although the massacre appears to move in one downward direction, Eisenstein even creates conflict here by having a mother cradling her dead son move up the steps toward the advancing soldiers (figure 11.22). The upward movement of the vulnerable mother and the relentless downward movement of the Cossacks creates extreme tension. Everything – civilians and Cossacks, circles and pointed shapes, fragile materials such as cloth and glass in contrast to sharp and hard rifles and blades, parallel and diagonal lines, and upward and downward movements – is in opposition throughout the section.

Eisenstein the formalist uses every aspect of film form from narrative structure to composition to shape the conflict between the oppressed classes and their oppressors that lies at the center of the film.

Fig. 11.21

Fig. 11.22

Umberto D (1952) and Bazin's Neorealism

Narrative and Character

The story of *Umberto D* (1952, Vittorio de Sica), which deals with an elderly man facing eviction from his apartment, seems suitable for, and perhaps even typical of, a Hollywood film of social seriousness. This movie, however, strikes most American viewers as unusual and, for the film theorist André Bazin, the reason for this is crucial to understanding the film's realism. Although we consider Hollywood films highly realistic, Bazin objected to them on both narrative and stylistic grounds. Whereas Hollywood narratives build from one dramatic event to another until they achieve a climax, the plot of *Umberto D* levels rather than builds its dramatic action. This happens in two ways.

The dramatic events of the story are not causally integrated. When Umberto develops heart trouble and has to go to hospital, it is unrelated to his eviction. In *Written on the Wind* (1956), a typical Hollywood dramatic scene occurs when an elderly man suffers a heart attack because of his rebellious daughter's behavior. The attack occurs as he mounts a staircase to confront his daughter. The heart attack is not only dramatically staged on a staircase, which heightens the danger and spectacle of the collapsing man, but it is also the direct result of the daughter's disturbing behavior, which we have just witnessed; the one dramatic event causes the other.

Since Hollywood drama builds from one major event to another, it elides or leaves out anything insignificant to its narrative pattern. *Umberto D*, however, does the opposite. The character of the maid supplies an excellent example, and one scene was of particular importance to Bazin. In Hollywood films, maids and servants stay in the background unless they are integrated into a subplot. In *The Man who Shot Liberty Valance* (1962), for example, Tom Doniphon's servant Pompey comes to the fore only in so far as he relates to Doniphon either by helping him kill Liberty Valance or by remembering Doniphon after his death. It is virtually inconceivable that we would suddenly be presented with scenes dealing with Pompey's love for a sick mother, for example, unless that relationship directly affected the main characters. In *Umberto D*, however, something akin to that happens when the film deals with a maid's relationship with a soldier (whom we never see) and her resultant pregnancy (about which we learn nothing). The maid does not, for example, have an affair with Umberto or murder the landlady. The scenes dealing with her life are thus not dramatically integrated with the rest of the film.

Such lack of dramatic integration even occurs with extremely minor characters in the film. As Umberto lies sick in his bed at night, a guest attending a party given by the landlady accidentally walks into his room, discovers his mistake, and excuses himself. The action is very brief and leads to nothing significant. Umberto does not, for example, become friends with the man. Why even include it in the film? Within de Sica's aesthetic, which was part of a larger

Fig. 11.23

Fig. 11.24

movement called neorealism, such attention to seemingly insignificant characters and non-dramatic events contributed to the film's realism. We observe a wealth of detail that traditional dramatic writers and directors would eliminate.

A scene devoted exclusively to Maria, the maid, shows her awakening (figure 11.23) and going through the routines of getting out of bed, going into the kitchen, and making the morning coffee. Nothing is left out of the scene; no action or detail is considered too minor or insignificant to show. She stretches, she looks at the cats, she drowns ants, lights the stove, looks out the window, feels her pregnant belly, grinds the coffee (figure 11.24), kicks the kitchen door closed and so on. In contrast to Hollywood films, which go from major event to major event, de Sica breaks down this one event into much smaller components. And, remember, the scene is dealing with a minor character!

In Hollywood, if someone is going to make coffee, we generally see the beginning of the action and then cut to a later time when major characters are drinking the coffee and talking about something significant. Here it is reversed. We see a minor character go through all the details of making coffee and we do not even see her or anyone else drinking it. Absolutely nothing dramatic comes of it. Hollywood conceives of events on a large scale and, even when they involve a major character, something like awakening is expressed in a couple of brief shots and we see the characters immediately involved in significant actions that are fully integrated into the narrative and move it forward.

Space and Time

The style of *Umberto D* differs from that of both Hollywood and Eisenstein as much as its narrative structure and character conception do, and the scene of the maid Maria awakening and making coffee gives a key as to why and how. The decision to show everything that occurs involves style as well as narrative, since it means that no space or time will be elided. De Sica seeks to give a wholeness to the reality he represents. He does not break it down into parts, decide what is important and what is unimportant and then only show us the important part. He shows us everything in the belief that we can decide what is important. Thus, space and time must be whole, and certain aspects of film style contribute to that wholeness.

The classical style, which we discussed in chapter 3, uses a continuity system based on eliding unimportant parts of an action. If a character gets up and walks out of a room, for example, we may see her rise and walk toward the door and then cut to a shot of her emerging into the hallway. Although such a cut implies continuity of action, we do not see everything. The filmmaker has decided that watching the character walk across the room is boring and insignificant and that we can get on with the important action by showing what happens next. De Sica, on the contrary, believes we must watch every second of time and see every bit of space as Maria gets up and makes the coffee. Sometimes the camera follows her movements and at other times there is a cut, but the cut merely repositions the camera so that we may continue to observe everything. Both the space and time of the cut are continuous with what we have just seen.

In addition to cuts that do not elide any time or space, de Sica's style at times employs deep focus and long takes with a moving camera for similar effect. **Long takes**, meaning that a shot lasts for a long period rather than a few seconds, mean fewer cuts. During any given long take both space and time are whole and continuous. **Deep focus** refers to keeping the focus and clarity of the image far into the rear of the frame. The classical Hollywood style usually keeps a shallow focus, which directs viewer attention to the important foregrounded action; sometimes the focus shifts during a shot to redirect attention. But, as with cutting, such use of focus implies that some things are more important than others. Deep focus, then, shows more space within the shot, including background details and actions.

After Umberto returns home from selling his books, a scene occurs that concisely illustrates many of the film's neorealist stylistic tendencies. The camera is in the front hallway as Umberto enters. We hear music coming from the distance at the end of the hall and then the noise of a train accompanied by the flickering lights and shadows it casts (figure 11.25). Umberto approaches the camera and, when he is almost up to it, de Sica cuts to a shot from an angle 180 degrees opposite from the previous one. We now see down the long hallway with the closed doors to the landlady's room at the end (figure 11.26).

Umberto knocks on a door at the right of the frame, and Maria comes out. They stand talking (figure 11.27), he gives her the money for the landlady, and asks her to get the thermometer because he feels ill. She walks offscreen right into the kitchen, but the camera remains absolutely stationary. Umberto continues to talk to her, and she returns with the thermometer. Umberto now leaves at the left to go into his room, but again the camera does not move. Maria then walks down the hallway, which is fully in focus, and opens the door to the landlady's room (figure 11.28). De Sica cuts to a shot from inside the room as we see Maria opening the door and entering (figure 11.29). The cut is continuous, and no space or time has been elided.

Fig. 11.25

Fig. 11.26

Fig. 11.27

Fig. 11.28

Fig. 11.29

Fig. 11.30

The camera now follows Maria as she moves through an empty outer room, and then we see the guests and landlady sitting in the rear of the adjoining room. Maria moves from the left side of the frame toward the center and then continues to walk toward the landlady (figure 11.30). The camera follows her as she approaches the landlady, who sees her, gets up, and directs her to a side of the room. The camera again follows as the two stand in front of a window talking. We see the darkness suddenly lit up by the bright lights of a train entering the station. Maria explains that Umberto has part of the rent money now and will pay the rest later, but the landlady rejects the offer and we cut to a shot of Umberto in his bedroom.

The entire part of the scene in the landlady's room is shot in one long take with a moving camera. When the two talk, we see them both at the same time without the use of any **shot/reverse-shot editing**. The same is true during the earlier conversation between Umberto and Maria. Bazin admired these kinds of compositions because they presented the dialogue and characters within a continuous space and time and also because he felt the spectator was free to choose exactly where to focus within the scene, in contrast to both the Hollywood invisible style of shot/reverse-shot editing and Eisensteinian montage, which directed the viewer at precisely what they were supposed to see.

Unlike Eisenstein's use of space, de Sica always lets the viewer know where the characters are. There are several deep-focus shots in the film of the apartment hallway. We know from those shots precisely where Umberto's room is in relation to the kitchen across the hall and the landlady's room at the end of the hall. Sound as well as visuals contribute to this realist sense of space. We hear sounds layered in relation to where they are coming from. The singing down the hall, for example, sounds distant because of where it is coming from and because the door is closed. When Maria enters and approaches the source of the music, it gets louder. Similarly, the sound of the train heard in the hallway indicates the proximity of the station to the house. The film employs realist sound perspectives that let us hear exactly where things are coming from in a manner that compliments the visual strategy of letting us see where things are.

Just as offscreen sound contributes to the feeling that a "real" world exists beyond what we see in the frame, the offscreen light from the train that casts the flickering pattern in the hallway and then lights up the darkness we see through the window situates the station in relation to the house and gives us the feeling that real life is going on beyond our view. Although no action takes place at that station, due to the light patterns, sounds, and partial glimpses of the station roof through windows we know where it is spatially situated in relation to the house. It constantly reminds us of a larger world extending beyond the "window" through which we are looking.

The Hollywood invisible style counts on us not noticing or paying attention to the fact that we are watching many shots. When a dialogue scene uses shot/reverse-shot editing, for example, many spectators don't have the slightest idea how many cuts are taking place or even that they are taking place. Most of us accept this as realistic much as we accept dramatically integrated narrative structures as realistic. Bazin's concept of realism, however, is a perceptual one. The spectator should be aware of cuts, camera positions, and movements, and so on. Since for Bazin the camera records aspects of real time and space, filmmakers should use those techniques that maximize that spatial and temporal wholeness. This is true no matter what the subject matter of the film is. Bazin greatly admired *Citizen Kane* (1941, see chapter 15) because, even though it was a Hollywood film, it abandoned the usual invisible editing style and employed long takes with deep focus and moving camera.

Part of the magic of cinema for Bazin lay in movies that let spectators watch the events in all their spatial and temporal integrity; for Eisenstein, part of the magic lay in the manner in which movies could form their own spatial and temporal universe; for most Hollywood filmmakers part of the magic lies in making their style invisible so that spectators will lose themselves in the fictional world of the film. Different styles are based upon different assumptions, whether or not the filmmakers or audiences are aware of them. We cannot simply accept Hollywood movies as realistic. Both Eisenstein and Bazin and movies such as *Potemkin* and *Umberto D* can help us see the Hollywood style for what it is: not "reality," but a narrative and visual style like all others.

SELECTED READINGS

Eisenstein's major writings are collected in *Film Form* (New York: Harcourt, Brace, and World, 1949) and *Film Sense* (New York: Harcourt, Brace, and World, 1942). His analysis of the narrative structure and visual style of *Potemkin*, upon which we have drawn heavily, appears in *Potemkin: Classic Film Scripts* (New York: Simon and Schuster, 1968). André Bazin's major writings are collected in *What is Cinema?* (Berkeley, CA: University of California, 1967) and *What is Cinema?*, Vol. II (Berkeley, CA: University of California Press, 1971). In "*Umberto D*: A Great Work," which is published in volume II and upon which we have drawn heavily, Bazin analyzes that film's narrative structure and visual style. Peter Wollen theorizes about stylistically diverse films, ranging from classical Hollywood to Sergei Eisenstein and Jean Luc-Godard without pitting one against the other, in *Signs and Meaning in the Cinema* (Bloomington, IN: Indiana University Press, [1969] 1972). In *Theory of Film Practice* (Princeton, NJ: Princeton University Press, [1969] 1981), Noël Burch gives an inventory of all of cinema's stylistic possibilities and, rather than advocating one style over another, praises formal inventiveness wherever he finds it. In *Philosophical Problems of Film Theory* (Princeton, NJ: Princeton University Press, 1988), Noël Carroll observes that formalist theories were developed before realist theories because of the historical need to legitimize cinema as an art form.

12

GENDER AND SEXUALITY

The Silence of the Lambs and *American Gigolo*

We have different expectations about the roles of men and women when we see different kinds of movies. Action films, for example, have traditionally meant male action. Walter Hill, a director of male action films (*48Hours*, 1982, and *Red Heat*, 1988) has made several films in which women are virtually absent. Aside from a waitress in the opening scene, there is not even a minor female character in *Trespass* (1992), which is devoted to male action in an abandoned, inner-city building. In *Geronimo: An American Legend* (1993), we glimpse Native American women only in the background of a few shots.

Fig. 12.1

"Geronimo is here" is the only line spoken by a woman, and she remains unidentified as she introduces the legendary chief to another warrior (figure 12.1).

Most male action films give women minor roles in romantic subplots. Kevin Costner's *Dances with Wolves* (1990), for example, has its central male character fall in love with a Native American woman. But Hill's rigorous exclusion of women from even these marginal roles makes clear just how male-centered these films are. Precisely because of this marginality, James Cameron's efforts in *Aliens* (1986, figure 12.2) and *Terminator 2* (1991, figure 12.3), and Renny Harlin's in *Cutthroat Island* (1995) and *The Long Kiss Goodnight* (1996) to place women at the center of the genre are highly noticeable; we are not used to women wielding swords or high-powered automatic weapons and vanquishing the enemy in action films. Films like *Lara Croft: Tomb Raider* (2001) continue this current trend.

Fig. 12.2

These few examples raise many of the gender topics which we will explore in this chapter. Most simply, they show that men and women are not represented equally in films and that these representations, like all representations, are open to change. We cannot justify the depictions of these characters with reference to realism and real life. As we have shown throughout this book, everything represented in a film must be understood as shaped and formed by film rather than real life. We cannot

Fig. 12.3

dismiss the absence of women in *Geronimo* by simply saying that it is based on actual events and historical figures. Women lived 24 hours a day in the American West of the late nineteenth century just as men did. Their virtual absence as significant presences in Westerns is a narrative decision typical of the genre, which has traditionally chosen to tell stories in which women are largely absent or placed in the background and marginalized. In real life, women are not simply part of plots or subplots nor in the foreground or background. In movies, however, they, as all characters, are always represented in terms of such cinematic properties.

Action films also demonstrate that presence and absence is not the only significant aspect of gender representation. Another aspect involves the active/passive split. Many movies have active male characters who make the important decisions and perform the decisive actions. In *The Man who Shot Liberty Valance* (1962), for example (see chapter 4), Tom Doniphon, Ransom Stoddard, and Liberty Valance are active characters who set goals for themselves and fight for those goals. Hallie, on the other hand, is totally passive (figure 12.4). Tom calls her "my girl" at the beginning of the film, and it is he who decides to leave her with Ransom near the film's end. She

Fig. 12.4

is virtually passed from one powerful man to another; her function in the film is little more than an indication of the shifting power relations between these men. Similarly, the beautiful woman played by Michelle Pfeiffer in *Scarface* (1983, see chapter 1) is transferred from a powerful gangster leader to the gangster who deposes him (figure 12.5). What becomes most notable about the central female characters in *Aliens*, *Terminator 2*, and *Lara Croft: Tomb Raider* is not their presence but, rather, the active roles they play.

Fig. 12.5

These action films point to a dimension beyond even active and passive presence, that of the actual physical representation of men and women. During the 1980s such popular stars as Arnold Schwarzenegger (figure 12.6) and Sylvester Stallone set a new standard for male action heroes that emphasized a body-builder's physique. Earlier male action heroes such as John Wayne and Clint Eastwood (figure 12.7) did not look as if they spent their days

Fig. 12.6

Fig. 12.7

Fig. 12.8

working out in a gym and seldom even displayed their torsos in their films; later action stars such as Bruce Willis (the *Die Hard* series, 1988, 1990, and 1995) and Keanu Reeves (*Speed*, 1994), however, noticeably developed such physiques when they moved into action roles. By the 1980s an emerging notion of masculinity set off action heroes from mere mortals in a manner much more anatomically exaggerated than that during the 1950s or 1960s.

Similarly, Linda Hamilton, the central female character in *Terminator 2*, reveals rippling muscles. Yet, in *Point of No Return* (1993, figure 12.8), Bridget Fonda plays an assassin who looks like a conventionally beautiful and "feminine" woman rather than a highly muscled, masculinized one. Whereas the assumption in *Terminator 2* is that a strong woman should look like her male counterparts, the assumption in *Point of No Return* is that she can be just as strong without in any way physically resembling them.

In the first part of this chapter we discuss some of the common ways in which male and female characters are represented in movies, pointing to the cultural assumptions about femininity and masculinity underlying those representations. In the second part we analyze *The Silence of the Lambs* (1990) and *American Gigolo* (1980), two movies that depart significantly from many of the conventions and illustrate the point that gender representations are historically specific and subject to change.

The Mother/Whore Dichotomy

Women are frequently represented in movies as being either good, dutiful mothers and wives or independent and sexual beings. This polarization of women is often referred to as the mother/whore dichotomy, which implies that if women are not traditional mother figures, safely under the protection of a man, they are whores in spirit, if not profession. The sexual woman is usually represented as dangerous to herself and/or men. Let us examine five major examples from different periods in Hollywood.

Fig. 12.9

In *Way Down East* (1920), after a virtuous woman's father dies, a wealthy playboy pretends to marry her in a false ceremony, but abandons her when she becomes pregnant. Although entirely innocent, she is brutally cast out of her society as a fallen woman (figure 12.9). Without a male protector, she is driven to despair and nearly commits suicide, but an enlightened young man willing to marry her saves her. Throughout the film, she remains passively subject to the whims or good graces of active men.

Stagecoach (1939) supplies an illuminating variation on the classic split. Dallas, a prostitute, is evicted from the community. Ringo does not know her profession. During the stagecoach journey, another passenger gives birth to a baby and, when Ringo sees Dallas holding the baby (figure 12.10), he suddenly envisions her as the mother of his child. Immediately following the scene, he proposes marriage. Dallas is transformed from one pole to the other and ends the film safely under Ringo's protection.

Fig. 12.10

The Big Heat (1953) includes not only a highly sexual woman who is the mistress of a gangster but also a woman who is the wife of a federal agent who stays home, cooks, and takes care of the children. The only time that we see the agent's wife outside the home is when she prepares to pick up a baby-sitter. However, the moment she turns the ignition key in the car, she is killed in a car-bomb explosion. The other woman is first brutally scarred when a gangster throws hot coffee in her face and later killed in a shooting. Implicitly, the film categorizes the kitchen and the nursery as the safest place for a woman; a woman who leaves them courts disaster.

Fig. 12.11

In *Fatal Attraction* (1987, see chapter 1), a similar polarity exists between the central male character's dutiful wife, who stays home with the couple's child, and the aggressive career woman, who initiates an affair with the husband. In this film, the independent, sexual woman is mentally unstable and dangerous. She poses a danger to herself, to the man with whom she has an affair, and to his family. In the end, she is killed. *Single White Female* (1992) offers an interesting contemporary variation on this polarity. A young woman breaks up with her live-in boyfriend and, instead of getting involved with another man, advertises for a female room-mate (figure 12.11). Her room-mate turns out to be mentally unstable and dangerous (she even kills a pet dog much like the woman in *Fatal Attraction* kills a pet rabbit). In the end, just as the wife in *Fatal Attraction* kills the other woman, the woman kills the room-mate.

All of these films contain implicit messages strongly tied to these polarized images of women. They warn both men and women of the dangers of independent, sexual women and either place such women under the safe control of a powerful man or punish them with death. *Single White Female* proves the dictum "the more things change, the more they stay the same." Although the film may seem modern in its depiction of non-marital sex, it implies that the woman's decision that she does not need a man in her life and her replacement of him by close bonding with another woman is dangerous. Here the mother/whore dichotomy is replaced by a new dichotomy: good girl (heterosexual female in a monogamous relationship)/bad girl (mentally unstable, implicitly lesbian). The message stays very much the same: women who live outside the confines of a socially acceptable, safe relationship with a man are evil and dangerous; even "good" women who venture outside these confines place themselves in danger.

Recognizing such polarities also reveals how restrictive common representations of women are. The problem does not just lie within these stereotypes but in the manner in which they inhibit a much larger range of representations. Women need not be represented in this either/or fashion. Aggressive career women who initiate sexual relationships can also be represented as attractive and compelling characters.

The Active/Passive Split

Traditionally, men have been considered more active in our culture than women, so it is not surprising that this deep cultural division of active male and passive female has affected narrative structure. *Gone with the Wind* (1939) supplies an interesting example. In the second part of the film, Scarlett O'Hara, the central female character, assumes many conventionally masculine roles because of her father's incapacity and her husband's unmanliness. Despite warnings, she defiantly rides alone in a carriage and, on one such occasion, is attacked by destitute blacks. While the Southern white men actively seek revenge for the attack, the women at home passively read (see figures 9.3 and 9.4), even commenting that, if Scarlett had not transgressed, none of this would have happened.

Frequently, women's activity is restricted to the spheres of romance and/or the family. In *The Searchers* (1956, see chapter 4), the main female character has a minor role and waits at home while the men, including the man she loves, search for the kidnapped girl. In desperation, she chooses to marry another man but is stopped when her beloved returns from the search. Similarly, in *She Wore a Yellow Ribbon* (1949, figure 12.12), the only active choice the central female character has is between which of two young lieutenants she will marry, and this is largely determined by which one receives the approval of a father figure. Both of these female characters have little agency beyond the apparent choice between two men, and even this choice is severely limited by the fact that in both cases, one of the men is more conventionally masculine, and thus more attractive, than the other and he wins her affections.

These patterns are not exclusive to Hollywood cinema. We have seen, for example, in *Nosferatu* (1922, see chapter 9) from the German silent cinema that, even though the woman is the only one able to defeat the vampire, she

does so by being totally passive, even to the point of submitting to her own death. The men make virtually all of the major decisions in the film; her only plot-determining decision is to choose to submit to the vampire and die. In *Temptress Moon* (1997) from the contemporary Chinese cinema, the central female character, played by Gong Li, develops a reputation as an independent woman. The elder of her family repeatedly says that a "real man" is needed to control her. That "real man" does come along and she falls desperately in love with him. When she later tries to reject him, he poisons her. The last image we see of her is of her totally paralyzed; the family elders appear much more comfortable with her in this state.

Fig. 12.12

Of course, there are exceptions. Lee Tamahori's widely praised *Once Were Warriors* (1994) about urban Maori tribespeople in contemporary New Zealand, centers on a woman who finally has the courage to leave her brutally oppressive husband. This film praises a strong and active woman and critiques a widespread social presumption among the Maoris of male domination. Another New Zealand filmmaker, Jane Campion, has made a number of films that deal complexly with strong women as central characters, such as *Sweetie* (1989), *The Piano* (1993), and *Portrait of a Lady* (1996). While these characters may be oppressed by a male-dominated culture, they do not exist in the background of the films but rather occupy their center. There is also a tradition in Hollywood of films such as *Julia* (1977) about strong active women. Particularly since the 1960s, there has been a growing number of women holding important behind-the-camera positions, which might promise fundamental changes in representational patterns. But let us return for a moment to other dominant patterns of mainstream cinema.

Saving and Punishing Women

Closely related to the mother/whore dichotomy and the active/passive split is the fate that awaits women who, at the beginning of the film, lie outside the control of men. Normally we think of saving someone or punishing someone as being nearly opposite activities; the former is kind and humane and the latter is negative and cruel. Yet, for independent women in mainstream movies, these two common fates are similar since both lead to eliminating their independent status. In Alfred Hitchcock's *Marnie* (1964), the central male character is a powerful businessman who falls in love with Marnie, an employee who assumes false identities and robs her employers (figure 12.13). Knowing about her past, he catches her in the act and forces her to marry him, in effect saving her from prison. When she attempts suicide, he saves her from death. At the end of the film, he forces her mother into revealing the repressed childhood trauma that is responsible for Marnie's criminal behavior, thus saving her from repeating her criminal acts. Each time he saves her, he places her more firmly within his control. Indeed, by the end of the film, she literally owes her identity to him because she now has full memory of her past. Because of him, she knows who she is.

Death is a frequent form of punishment for highly sexual women. In *The Big Heat*, disfiguring the woman's face with scalding coffee is the first form of punishment, since the film stresses how the scars have ruined her beauty, which is the source of her power. But even this is not enough and she is later killed. In *Fatal Attraction*, a similar fate awaits the sexually aggressive, independent career woman, who is first apparently drowned and then shot.

The much-discussed ending of *Rio Bravo* (1958) makes unusually clear the nature of the narrative need to contain sexually inde-

Fig. 12.13

Fig. 12.14

pendent women. Sheriff John T. Chance spends much of the film trying to run Feathers out of town because she is a provocative woman associated with illegal gambling (figure 12.14). Her sexuality and independence threaten him. At the end of the film, he confronts her in her dressing room as she prepares to perform in a saloon wearing a tight, revealing costume. He says that if she leaves the room dressed that way, he'll arrest her. She replies emotionally that she thought he'd never say it and he asks, "Say what?" "That you love me," she replies. "I said I'd arrest you," he responds, to which she retorts, "It means the same thing." She happily succumbs to his wishes and they embrace. The way in which the film explicitly links romance to the power of the law makes unusually clear that love functions in many films as a form of power, authoritatively and frequently literally in the name of the law, bringing women under control.

Beauty and the Fragmentation of the Body

Issues of body representation go beyond body type and require careful analysis of cinematic form, including camera placement, cutting patterns, and lighting. Most movies do not represent men and women in the same manner. Conventionally, women's bodies have been displayed erotically more frequently and in different ways from men's bodies. Fashion styles, lighting, and close-ups can all be used to fragment a woman's body and place a particular emphasis on one part of it. Indeed, this tendency can be so strong that some actresses become identified with a part or parts of their body: Betty Grable was known for her legs, Jane Russell for her breasts, Marilyn Monroe for her curvaceous figure and blonde hair, and Veronica Lake for her long, wavy blonde hair, which fell over one side of her face. This overvaluation of a part or parts of a woman's body is called fetishism, a term borrowed from psychoanalysis. In general use, fetishism refers to using part of the body or clothing for visual erotic pleasure and usually implies a particularly male way of looking at women's bodies.

Sometimes, movies incorporate the erotic display of the female body into their stories by setting scenes in bars and clubs. In *Carlito's Way* (1994), one such scene occurs in a topless bar. The female character who dances in the bar is not a dancer in the novel upon which the film is based. Making her a dancer in the movie justifies the introduction of this erotic display of her nude body. Indeed, nude scenes make the patterns of erotic display of the female body particularly clear, since they usually occur more often than male nude scenes and, when they involve both men and women, they usually show more of the female body and show it longer.

Frequently, love-making scenes and their aftermath as well as such related scenes as showers become narrative pretexts for dwelling on the female body. *Single White Female* contains examples of both. Near the beginning of the film, the phone rings while the Bridget Fonda character is in bed with her boyfriend. She gets out of bed and walks to the phone while the camera lingers on her nude body. Later, she enters the bathroom while her room-mate, Jennifer Jason Leigh, is taking a shower and we see Leigh's nude body (figure 12.15). *Romeo is Bleeding* (1994) contains common variations. The central male character is a police officer who uses binoculars to watch people making love. Shots of him looking are followed by point-of-view shots of the nude lovers. He also has an affair with a young woman who, in a

Fig. 12.15

long scene, dances erotically in a négligé to arouse him. Again, point-of-view shots let the audience as well as the character watch her. In another sex scene, we see a woman dressed in black leather with her breasts exposed and, in a later scene, we see her from behind as she disrobes. A major plot-motivating device in *Titanic* (1997) is a nude drawing of Kate Winslet's character. When the drawing is made, we see Winslet erotically disrobe and pose for the artist who soon becomes her lover.

Such patterns of fetishizing women's bodies are not always so overtly sexual, but they function to similarly objectify their bodies for male visual pleasure. *An Unmarried Woman* (1978) supplies an important example because it was hailed upon its release for its progressive representation of the title character. Ironically, the film was advertised with an image of its star, Jill Clayburgh, wearing a revealing halter top and tight panties; the image comes from a central scene in the film. Alone in her apartment, she dances to express her inner feelings, yet the way she is dressed turns her dance into an erotic spectacle much like those in *Titanic, Romeo is Bleeding*, and *Carlito's Way*. The way in which the body is represented caters to male desire and fantasy and thereby contradicts the ostensible tone of the film, which is to celebrate this woman's independence from male domination. The visual style subverts the potential threat to male domination posed by the character in the narrative and makes her safe for, indeed desirable to, men.

Flashdance (1983) functions in the same way. Once again, the central female character is an independent, strong-willed woman. When she works out in her apartment she is dressed in a fashionably chic, highly erotic manner, and the character's private activity becomes a pretext to create a conventional spectacle out of her body. Rather than looking like she's doing grungy, hard work to achieve her personal goals, she looks like a sexual fantasy.

A final example comes from *Alien* (1979) and returns us to action cinema. Until the final scene, Sigourney Weaver plays an active, intelligent character who is treated similarly to the men; she even dresses like them. At the end of the film, however, when she prepares to enter deep sleep for the trip back to Earth, we see her dressed erotically in a small, tight halter top with a revealing pair of bikini underpants (figure 12.16). Although we see most of her body, the camera is very close to her and,

Fig. 12.16

in several shots, she looks much like a Playboy centerfold. The close camera position combined with the lighting and clothes draw attention to her breasts and groin and make an erotic display out of her body.

At the beginning of the film, we had seen shots of male crew members awakening from their deep sleep, but that scene has an unerotic, clinically distanced tone, entirely different from the shot of Ripley near the film's end. Furthermore, immediately after her body is displayed erotically, Ripley is terrorized by the alien creature. Although she ultimately succeeds in ridding her craft of the alien, the display of her body and the terrorization of her character are conventional ways of erotically representing and punishing women. Some scenes in a film, then, may contradict much of the rest of the film and it is important that we pay careful attention to the entire movie.

The Masculine Spectacle and its Collapse

Just as the mother/whore dichotomy structures many representations of women, male characters in movies are frequently polarized as being powerful spectacles of masculinity or the pathetic and sometimes comic image of its ruin. In *True Lies* (1994), Arnold Schwarzenegger plays a character who embodies an awesome masculinity. In a subplot of the film, however, his wife nearly has an affair with a used-car salesman who pretends to be a powerful government agent. When he is caught and threatened for his deceit, he pathetically blurts out that he has to act that way since he has a small penis; then he urinates in his pants (figure 12.17). At the end of the film, he reappears only to once again panic and urinate in his pants. Our cultural concept of masculinity is highly quantitative; how "much of a man" someone is frequently comes down to size, as illustrated by Schwarzenegger's bulging muscles or the used-car salesman's small penis. The former is supposed to impress us, and the latter becomes the butt of humor for not living up to the masculine ideal.

Stars of classic male action genres such as the Western (John Wayne, Gary Cooper, and Clint Eastwood) or the contemporary action film (Schwarzenegger, Stallone, and Steven Seagal) are, within the standards of their time, typically large, strong-looking men. A comic tradition exists, on the other hand, with small actors like Charlie Chaplin, Woody Allen, Dudley Moore, and Peter Sellers playing men who fail to live up to such cultural standards of masculinity. Just as the action hero's excess of masculinity is figured in his powerful body, the comic hero's lack of masculine power is figured in his slight body. An Arnold Schwarzenegger character in an action film cannot credibly joke in such a way that we believe that he is the only man he knows who suffers from penis envy, but Woody Allen's character says precisely that in *Annie Hall* (1977). We accept this in a comedy where

Fig. 12.17

masculinity is under siege, but in a Western or action film where it is to be taken seriously, we expect powerful men to look strong and imposing. As we mentioned in chapter 6, when Sean Connery as James Bond in *Goldfinger* jokes that he carries a gun because "I have a slight inferiority complex," the audience readily accepts it as a joke because of Connery's powerful presence. Were Woody Allen to say the same line, however, the effect on the audience would likely be very different.

Fig. 12.18

Wounding and Scarring the Male Body

Since muscles, agility, and speed are attributes that characterize male power, loss of power is figured on the male body differently than it is on the female body. Whereas a woman's loss of power is frequently represented via a scar that mars her beauty, such as that of the woman in *The Big Heat* who has hot coffee thrown in her face, male scars usually function to empower by implying that the man has been tested and is tougher for it. Once again, a variation on this occurs in *True Lies* when a powerful government agent played by Charlton Heston wears an eye patch. Although loss of vision is normally a sign of weakness in men, here it hints at some combat experience.

Scars do not typically function to weaken men because they are merely passive attributes of appearance. Since masculinity is defined in active terms, wounds to the legs that limit mobility and symbolically imply a loss of sexual power are a common sign of weakness. The powerful lawyer Bannister in *The Lady from Shanghai* (1947) walks with crutches. His disability signifies a lack of sexual potency, since his beautiful wife plots against and eventually kills him. In *Rio Bravo*, an old man is named Stumpy in reference to his wooden leg and noticeable limp (figure 12.18). This sign of his loss of masculine power is related to a larger pattern that links him to stereotypical female characteristics and positions; he is always chattering and making small talk in comparison to the verbal reserve of the other men; he also cleans and cooks. At the end of *Rio Lobo* (1970, the last in the trilogy of films of which *Rio Bravo* was the first), the villain is first wounded in the leg and then blinded; moments later he is killed by a woman whose motivation is revealing. Earlier in the film, the villain has sadistically scarred her face with his knife: after killing him, she reveals how the large scar has marred her beauty for life. Were she, for example, to have her mobility impaired, it would not matter so much since her worth, unlike a man's, is not measured in that way. Losing her beauty is the ultimate price she can pay.

The Display of the Male Body

Men's bodies are displayed in films for different purposes and in different ways from women's bodies. Certain male action genres such as gladiator films, war

Fig. 12.19

films, Westerns, and the contemporary male action film frequently create opportunities for showing nearly naked men engaged in combat and, often, that display is accompanied with or followed by severe punishment of the male body. In *Rambo: First Blood Part 2* (1985), for example, the Sylvester Stallone character is sadistically tortured. The scene graphically dwells on his muscular and nearly naked body, which is visible throughout the torture. In *The Good, the Bad, and the Ugly* (1966), the Clint Eastwood character is tortured by the villain who makes him walk in the hot desert with no shade or water until he collapses, his face horribly blistered and bleeding (figure 12.19). Whereas erotically displaying women's bodies assuages male fears by making the woman desirable and less threatening, displaying the male body upsets the active/passive division. At times, this serves the plot function of justifying extreme retaliatory violence on the part of the brutalized hero. It may also arouse anxiety in men who homophobically fear the implications of the pleasure they derive in looking at the bodies of other men and who then take pleasure in seeing those bodies punished. Finally, it may have a masochistic appeal to the male spectator who enjoys the spectacle of powerful men being punished and stripped of their power.

Although there has been an increasingly overt display of the partially nude male body in movies since the early 1970s, such scenes usually function quite differently from the erotic display of the female body and can be understood in relation to the larger historical and cultural context that includes *Playgirl* and male stripping. In all cases, the male body is usually represented as much more powerful and active than its female counterpart. Not surprisingly, Arnold Schwarzenegger appears nude near the beginning of *Terminator* (1984) and *Terminator 2* (1991), and Sylvester Stallone also appears nude near the beginning of *Demolition Man* (1993). In all three cases, however, camera position, lighting, and body placement conspicuously conceal the genitals while emphasizing the muscled torso. This pattern supplies a key to understanding much about the display of the male body, which attempts to impress us with the symbolic display of power rather than the literal display of sexuality.

An entire tradition of "beauty and the beast" films exists wherein a deformed or ugly man falls in love with a beautiful woman. In the course of the film, she learns that to see with her heart is more important than with her eyes. *Cyrano de Bergerac* (1950) and the recent French remake (1990) as well as *Roxanne* (1987), a modern retelling of the Cyrano story, all fall into this tradition, as does the Disney animated feature *Beauty and the Beast* (1991) and the *Beauty and the Beast* television series. In all of these examples, the deformed man possesses some extraordinary physical and/or mental powers that compensate for his physical appearance. If he lacks beauty, he has an excess of conventional masculine power. In *Cyrano de Bergerac* (1950), the title character, whose face is deformed with a large nose (itself a symbolic sign of an excess of virility) is both an outstanding poet and swordsman. Language and fighting are the twin domains of traditional male power, and he excels in both realms. In this film, a young woman loves a handsome soldier, but he is tongue-tied and cannot woo her. Cyrano devises a ploy whereby he can supply the lover the words that will win her heart and, in a scene where she says that because of the darkness, she cannot see, she falls under the power of Cyrano's words (figure 12.20). Like all "beauty-and-the-beast" narratives, this film teaches a woman that what she sees does not matter.

Fig. 12.20

All popular "beauty-and-the-beast" films involve a deformed man and a beautiful woman. Although they seem to offer the touching humanistic message that looks are not as important as the inner person, they are in fact gender-specific movies. They tell us that how a man looks is not important to a woman; his possession of male power is what matters. As if this were not bad enough, such films simultaneously imply that beauty counts for everything with women. This deformed or ugly man never falls in love with an ordinary-looking woman; it is always a beautiful woman. Although she has to learn to love him for his power, he loves her for her appearance. These films illustrate that physical appearance functions differently for men and women. The handsome soldier in *Cyrano de Bergerac* provides an ideal example. He is characterized as vacuous and superficial because all he has to distinguish himself is his appearance. For women in such films, however, that is all they need.

We turn now from defining a few of the central characteristics governing the conventional representation of males and females in movies to examining two movies that show that all such tendencies involve significant exceptions and historical change. The first, *The Silence of the Lambs* (1991), contains a significant deviation from traditional patterns of representing women, and the second, *American Gigolo* (1980), from patterns of representing men.

The Silence of the Lambs (1990)

Breaking Stereotypes

The Silence of the Lambs tells the story of Clarice Starling (plate 67), a young woman training to become an FBI agent who gets assigned to a case involving "Buffalo Bill," a serial killer. On many levels, the film is noticeable for the manner in which Starling is represented; she is intelligent, independent, career-oriented, and has an engaging personality. Furthermore, the film lacks a conventional romantic subplot even though it establishes the expectation of one when Starling is assigned to work with an older male agent. Many films, such as *In the Line of Fire* (1994), where the Clint Eastwood character is an older Secret Service agent assigned to work with an attractive, younger female agent, develop those working relationships into the film's love interest. At the end of *In the Line of Fire*, the two form a romantic couple.

Nothing of the sort happens in *The Silence of the Lambs*. In fact, the older agent never even attempts to initiate a relationship with Starling. As if to further highlight the elimination of romance and love-making scenes from the film, two other characters make advances on Starling, only to be firmly rejected. When she first visits the notorious criminal, Hannibal Lecter, in his cell in a high-security ward for extremely dangerous and mentally ill criminals, the director of the institution makes advances and, similarly, when she visits a museum to gather information for her case, a young expert who helps her does the same. Remarkably, her outright rejection of these men does not mark her as having something wrong with her nor does it make her character un-attractive to the audience. On the contrary, this film makes the powerful men who presume it is their right to treat an attractive woman in such a manner seem offensive and even sleazy. Starling's relationship with Lecter, however, takes on an intensity that suggests that it is a replacement for the lack of a more conventional romantic subplot. In a sense, Starling falls under Lecter's charismatic power.

The visual style of the film also avoids common ways of eroticizing and fetishizing women's bodies. Starling is never once shown wearing a revealing outfit nor is there any gratuitous nudity. Once again, a scene raises traditional expectations. Starling is interrupted with business after taking a shower. Yet, when we see her, she is wearing a plain bathrobe that fully covers her body; there are no shots of her showering or leaving the shower, and the bathrobe is neither revealing nor stylish (plate 68). This strategy contrasts strongly, for example, with the shots of Bridget Fonda walking nude to the phone or Jennifer Jason Leigh showering and exiting the shower in *Single White Female*.

Throughout the film, then, Starling is a sympathetic, active woman who remains independent and uninvolved with men (aside from the bizarre rela-tionship she develops with Lecter) and whose body is not subjected to fetishis-tic, erotic, conventional representation. At least until the end.

Reinforcing Stereotypes

Although *The Silence of the Lambs* intelligently avoids many of the commonly limiting ways of developing its central female character and of representing her body, it does contain several disturbing elements. Near the end of the film, the male FBI agents have been misled to close in on what they believe to be the location of the serial killer. As they discover their mistake, agent Starling, in a different location, enters his house without any awareness of who he is or the dangers awaiting her. When she realizes the situation, she draws her gun on the killer but he mysteriously vanishes. She follows him down to the basement, where he turns out all the lights, leaving her terrorized in pitch darkness. He then puts on a pair of night-vision goggles, and we see his point-of-view shots of Starling as he approaches to kill her (plate 69). At the last moment she hears something, turns, and shoots him.

Starling's literally blind terror becomes a spectacle for the audience by means of the killer's point-of-view shots and bears comparison with the manner in which Ripley is terrorized by the alien at the end of *Alien*. In both cases, the scenes coming at the end of the films graphically prolong the heroine's terror ordeal; aside from providing conventional audience suspense, they serve as a punishment for the extremely independent behavior the women have shown throughout the film, behavior that accounts for the predicament in which they find themselves. Indeed, before the climax in *The Silence of the Lambs*, we see Starling following leads and investigating the case by herself. She is alone when she discovers the clues that lead her to the killer's house.

The blindness that Starling endures in the basement is not her only failure of vision in the scene. The manner in which the killer eludes her upstairs is virtually inexplicable; one moment she covers him with her gun drawn (plate 70), and we see him standing in front of her (plate 71), the next he lurches behind a doorway to her left, disappearing in front of her eyes. Her vision cannot hold him upstairs, and then it fails her totally downstairs. This failure of vision relates to the manner in which women are enculturated to be the object of vision rather than the subject of strong, controlling gazes. Indeed, Starling's terror, rather than fetishized beauty, becomes the object of both the killer's vision and the audience's. At this moment, blinded and specularized, she is represented in a totally conventional manner.

The end of the film furthers this punishment. We see her graduating and receiving her status as a regular agent. During the reception following the ceremony, however, she receives a phone call. Much to her and our surprise, it is from Hannibal Lecter, the monstrous killer who escaped during the course of the film. Her relationship with Lecter stems from the fact that she has consulted him on the "Buffalo Bill" case because he has been convicted of similar crimes. Now he is on the loose and about to strike another victim. To no avail, she begs him not to hang up, and the final shots of the film show her powerlessly holding the receiver (plate 72) and then Lecter walking off in pursuit of his victim (plate 73). Although this is much milder since she is not in immediate danger, once again Starling is powerless. In fact, the images of victimization in both scenes derive from the contemporary horror film. In such films as *Halloween* (1978) and *Friday the 13th* (1980), victims are frequently sighted through the moving point-of-view shots of their approaching killers. Images of women being terrorized on the telephone and helplessly pleading into the receiver are commonplace in films and central in horror films; there is also a tradition of films about terrorized blind women including *Blink* (1994) and *Wait until Dark* (1967).

But Starling is not the only character in the film whose representation includes disturbing gender and sexual elements: the perverse killer Jamie Gumm, nicknamed "Buffalo Bill" for the manner in which he skins his female victims, is a sexually confused transvestite. In one scene, we see him put on make-up and parade around with his penis tucked between his thighs, giving the appearance of a woman (plate 74). Once again, there is a cinematic tradition of equating homosexuality, lesbianism, and transvestism with criminal behavior. This includes a homosexual in *The Naked Kiss* (1964), so titled after what the film calls the kiss of the pervert; a killer who turns out to be both a homosexual and a transvestite in *Gunn* (1967); and a lesbian who is ambiguously implicated with murder and dangerous lifestyles in *Basic Instinct* (1992).

Careful consideration of these images points to some of the complexities of gender studies. On the one hand, the existence of this tradition is disturbing because it repeatedly implies that what our dominant culture considers abnormal sexuality is dangerous and criminal. On the other hand, some of these films implicitly grant that some forms of sexuality are truly different from dominant heterosexual monogamy and that that difference is frightening and threatening to the norm.

From this perspective, films like *Gunn* and *Basic Instinct*, in which middle-aged, white heterosexual detectives are troubled by the world they encounter, cannot simply be dismissed as negative for their portrayal of homosexual and transvestite lifestyles. They may, in fact, be more complex, honest, and useful in acknowledging difference and the fear it arouses than seemingly "positive" images that are based upon the assumption that all of us, regardless of sexual orientation, are alike. It is easy, in other words, to accept "others" if we believe they are "just like us." But some forms of sexuality do involve major departures from the norm of heterosexual monogamy, and many in our culture find it hard to acknowledge that difference without condemning it. The point is not that all gays and lesbians lead what to many appear to be "exotic" lifestyles different from their own, but that those who do are not perversely ill and dangerous.

Part of the problem with the representation of Jamie Gumm in *The Silence of the Lambs*, then, cannot fully be grasped by just considering the film itself. If this were an isolated instance of a person of confused gender and sexual orientation being a dangerous criminal, the implications would be different. Since this is a common way of representing such a person and since significant alternatives are virtually non-existent, we tend to fix a connection between certain kinds of people and danger. A good part of the problem is that we need a much wider range of representations than we currently have. Jonathan Demme, the director of *The Silence of the Lambs*, seems to have implicitly recognized this when, a few years later, he made *Philadelphia* (1993), a film that attempts to represent gays in a positive manner.

However, *Philadelphia* also drew some severe criticism for its representation of homosexuality. Two common complaints were that it propagated stereotypes by representing gay men as overly sensitive to the emotional aspects of opera and that it did not represent romantic or sexual physical contact between gay lovers as Hollywood films typically do with heterosexuals. By implication, showing such physical affection between men would be disgusting. Understanding the responses to *The Silence of the Lambs* and *Philadelphia* helps us understand an important lesson in gender studies. The issues are much more complex than so-called positive or negative images. As we will see in chapter 13 on race, much of what we commonly accept as positive should be questioned, criticized, and rejected, and sometimes what we consider as negative should not simply be condemned but rather understood within a complex context. Ultimately, the notion of positive and negative images is too simplistic to help us understand the complex constructions that films are and the complex relationship they have to society. They neither simply reflect society nor cause events, but, if we take the time to analyze them, they can help us understand complex social issues such as how heterosexual women or gays and lesbians are represented.

American Gigolo (1980)

The Display of the Male Body and the Active/Passive Split

A moment perhaps without precedent in the American cinema at that time occurs in *American Gigolo* (1980). After a love-making scene, Julian (Richard Gere) gets out of bed, walks over to the window and, as he stands talking to Michelle, the woman with whom he has just made love, we see a frontal nude shot of him as she looks at him. This seems to be a reversal of the usual pattern of women being photographed in such a manner. But is it? And if it is, what are the implications of such a reversal? Does it correct the male/female power imbalance and treat both equally?

The scene in question is preceded by a highly stylized love-making scene with Julian and Michelle. In nearly all the shots, he is moving over her body, kissing and stroking it (plate 75). The actress playing Michelle, Lauren Hutton, a beautiful and famous fashion model, remains highly passive and fetishized. Within this context, the later moment of passive display of Julian's nude body is atypical. Furthermore, at precisely the moment that Julian's body is most fully on display, there is a cut to an extreme long shot that obscures our view of him (plate 76). This cutting pattern also strongly separates our view of Julian's body from Michelle's. In fact, the camera has been placed so far back that her body is visible near the middle of the frame. The somewhat jolting cut back denies Michelle's point of view, once again minimizing the importance and power of female vision and simultaneously de-emphasizing Julian's exposed body.

What Julian says is also of importance. He tells of the extraordinary long time he devoted to sexually satisfying an older woman whose husband had long ignored her needs and of his sincere concern with her pleasure. Although he doesn't speak in a bragging tone, his speech can also be read as an affirmation of his masculine prowess. The speech, combined with the cutting pattern in the scene, deny the objectification of his body by the look of the woman who is paradoxically entranced by the seriousness of his concern for women's pleasure. Julian's speech makes us care about him as a person rather than as an erotic object. The way he looks out of the window before talking makes him appear thoughtfully preoccupied, and the speech virtually ennobles him. This is a far cry from the manner in which women's bodies are typically eroticized and objectified.

If we compare the nude scene with an earlier scene that displays Julian's body, the situation becomes even more complicated. We see Julian dressed in shorts with no shirt exercising in his apartment, with fragmented shots of his body as he adjusts his ankle grips (plate 77) and grabs the exercise bar, swings himself up and locks his ankles into place. As he exercises while hanging upside down, we see several views of his body with muscles straining. While he works out, he listens to a foreign-language tape and repeats phrases. We hear his heavy breathing as well the repeated Swedish phrases. The phone rings and he drops to the floor, answers it, and continues exercising and moving about. As he looks at himself in a mirror, he flexes his upper torso and neck and, when he resumes moving, does two strong leg kicks (plate 78).

All the fragmented body shots emphasize the hard, masculine exercise equipment and the muscles either poised for action or in action. Even when he is talking on the phone, he is in constant action. His heavy breathing stresses his exertion, and the foreign-language lesson shows that he is exerting his mind as well as his body. In this scene Julian is represented in totally conventional masculine ways that seem to overcompensate for the static display of his body in the later love-making scene. This kind of tension and contradiction surrounding Julian is not confined to these two scenes but affects the entire film.

Julian Associated with Femininity

Throughout the film, Julian is associated with femininity: his nickname is "Julie"; he is a prostitute, a profession normally identified with women; he places an extraordinary emphasis on fashion and has a closet full of beautiful clothes; and, perhaps most significantly, he is a victim who at the end of the film is saved by a woman. A weak character for much of the film, he constantly seeks help from women. He pleads for an alibi with the older woman he was with at the time of a murder for which he is a suspect and he asks help of the woman who runs the prostitution service for which he works.

He finally begs a powerful black man who heads another prostitution service to help him, but the man refuses. In desperation, he rushes the man from behind and pushes him over a balcony, catching him by the legs as he is about to fall. Although he wants to scare the other man into agreeing to his demands, Julian panics and loses control of the situation. Ironically, he ends up begging the man not to fall since he needs his help. Gradually he loses his grasp and impotently clutches the empty boots as the man falls to his death (plate 79).

Julian's failure at this moment of typical masculine endeavor is almost unimaginable in a comparable moment in a John Wayne, Clint Eastwood, Arnold Schwarzenegger, or Sylvester Stallone movie. Indeed, a scene of this type occurs in *True Lies* when Schwarzenegger and his partner hold a man on the edge of a precipice above a river to get him to talk. He does and they pull him to safety. In *LA Confidential* (1997, see chapter 13), Russell Crowe holds a terrified district attorney out of window by his legs to get him to reveal information and, when he does, Crowe brings him back in. In *North by Northwest* (1959), Cary Grant pulls a woman to safety from atop Mount Rushmore.

The only other scene in *American Gigolo* in which Julian attempts typical masculine behavior is equally revealing. He catches a spy who has been trailing him and scares and humiliates the young man by aggressively writing a message on his forehead (plate 80). The spy, however, is a comically inept kid who works for a senator and seems qualified to be a page but not a spy. Julian's victory is no victory at all.

Instabilities of Representations of the Male Body

The passive display of the nude male body in *American Gigolo* is symptomatic of the profound instabilities that erupt in our culture when the male body is erotically objectified. Such objectification is conventionally reserved for the female body, and perhaps this film can place the actor, Richard Gere, in that position since his character is placed in feminine positions throughout the film. The prostitute Julie, who is finally saved by a woman, is a character in a narrative trajectory far removed from that of the Schwarzenegger character in *True Lies*, who boldly frees himself from a small army of captors and rescues his wife and daughter.

The representation of masculinity and the male body in *American Gigolo*, then, is complex and contradictory. On the one hand, it dares to display the nude male outside the usual forms of glimpsing it while engaged in stereotypical male activity such as in *The Deer Hunter* (1978) when Robert De Niro runs naked down the street or *Women in Love* (1969) when Alan Bates and Oliver Reed wrestle. Furthermore, *American Gigolo* conceives of the male body as a source of pleasure and satisfaction for women. However, it is troubled and contradictory in how it actually represents that body and a woman's look at it; it virtually denies the woman's vision and the audience's look at the body and in a schizophrenic manner hysterically over-masculinizes and at other times feminizes the male character.

Just as *The Silence of the Lambs* has to be contextualized within the early 1990s' efforts to create new action heroines in the American cinema, *American Gigolo* has to be placed within the late 1970s cultural context of eroticizing men's bodies for women's pleasure. *Playgirl* magazine and the newly emergent popularity of male stripping were all part of a "turnabout is fair play" mentality. While such a mentality may give pleasure to some women for getting back at men who have been looking at *Playboy* for years and going to strip shows, it points to a complex truth about the male/female power imbalance in our culture: where there is a true power imbalance, a simple reversal will not correct it.

Playgirl celebrates the same male power that oppresses women in their real lives, and male stripping similarly presents highly active, muscled dancers who attempt to impress their audience in a manner far removed from the erotic display of female strippers. The extent to which *American Gigolo* shares some of this context can be seen in the exercising and love-making scenes. Many of the shots in the former, including the emphasis on athletic equipment, strained muscles, and muscles poised for action, and in the latter of a man preoccupied with lofty thoughts, had direct parallels in *Playgirl*. All of these images attempt to make men appear physically and mentally active rather than acknowledge them as passive objects of erotic display.

American Gigolo and *The Silence of the Lambs* in this regard have some common characteristics that should caution us as to how we respond to issues of gender in movies. No matter how challenging they are, movies seldom offer representations of men or women that we should hail as simply progressive. However well intentioned or challenging to stereotypes they may be, they are likely to have their own limitations and even contradictions.

SELECTED READINGS

In her ground-breaking article "Visual Pleasure in the Narrative Cinema," *Screen* 16, no. 3 (Autumn, 1975), pp. 6–18, Laura Mulvey first brought attention to the manner in which women's bodies are fetishized in cinema, the active/passive split in narrative construction, and the manner in which female characters are contained through being punished or saved. Richard Dyer discusses the instabilities surrounding the erotic display of the male body in "Don't Look Now: The Male Pin-up," *Screen* 23, nos 3–4 (September/October, 1982), pp. 61–73. A collection of essays analyzing gender issues in *American Gigolo* appears in *Gender: Literary and Cinematic Representation*, ed. Jeanne Ruppert (Gainesville: University Presses of Florida, 1994).

13

RACE

Out of the Past, LA Confidential, and Boyz N the Hood

If we bring up the topic of race in film, many people will make three assumptions. First, they will presume that the issue concerns the representation of people of color such as African Americans, Asians, Hispanics, or Native Americans in such films as *Lethal Weapon* (1987), *Do the Right Thing* (1989, figure 13.1), *Black Rain* (1989), *The Joy Luck Club* (1994), *Dances with Wolves* (1990, figure 13.2), and *Powwow Highway* (1989). Second, they will think about how such representations hurt or help members of those races. This points to a related assumption: that there is a clear-cut and important distinction between positive and negative images in films and that the former are desirable for the good effects they have upon society and the latter deplorable for the bad effects. Third, most people will assume a significant distinction in how race is represented between films directed by a white, such as *Lethal Weapon* (Richard Donner) and by an African American, such as *Do the Right Thing* (Spike Lee).

Fig. 13.1

People of Color and Whites

These three assumptions may seem obvious and beyond question. In this chapter, however, we will question and, in various ways, qualify them. Let us start with the assumption that, when we talk about race, we talk about people of color. The very popular *Lethal Weapon* series might strike us as a good example because it features Danny Glover, an African American actor, in a prominent role. *Victor/Victoria* (1982), however, is unlikely to come to mind since

Fig. 13.2

it features no prominent parts for people of color. Indeed, most viewers would be hard pressed to remember if people of color appear in the film at all. The assumption is clear: white is not a color! As such it becomes an **invisible norm** against which other people are defined as colored.

Our point is not that it is a mistake to analyze the representation of people of color but that it is a mistake to exclude whites from such analysis. The *Lethal Weapon* films are particularly interesting within this context. They are part of a long-standing American popular culture tradition that bonds a white male with a male of another race. The nineteenth-century American novel was full of interracial male bonding between such characters as Huck Finn and Jim in *The Adventures of Huckleberry Finn*, Ishmael and Quequeg in *Moby Dick*, and Pathfinder and Chinachgook in *The Last of the Mohicans* and other *Leather-stocking Tales*. In the twentieth century such bondings have appeared widely in radio, television, and film.

A popular radio, television, and film series, *The Lone Ranger*, united the white hero of the title with Tonto, his faithful Native American sidekick. Notice the significance of the last term. Tonto is almost always referred to as a sidekick, a term indicating his placement within the narratives. The Lone Ranger is the central character, and the Native American is the minor character who supports him. The series never questioned this relationship or the benevolent manner in which the Lone Ranger treated Tonto. Far from seeming a racist, he appeared to be a kindly companion.

Two changes are immediately apparent with the *Lethal Weapon* films. The African American character is not a sidekick; he is of equal importance with the white character played by Mel Gibson. Of even more significance is the change in the usual stereotypical representation of whites and African Americans in Hollywood films. Glover plays a solidly middle-class family man (figure 13.3) and Gibson plays an unstable, single man whose mental health is precarious; he seems likely to explode into violent behavior at any moment (figure 13.4). In short, we don't learn something just about the representation of African American men in this film; we also learn about the representation of white men.

Fig. 13.3

Even this situation may not be quite as simple as it seems at first. Although Glover's character may seem a refreshing departure from common negative stereotypes about black men, the films in the series cast his comfortable, middle-class lifestyle as one in which he has lost his vitality. Much is made about his aging and this, combined with the excessive domesticity, gives negative connotations to what in other circumstances would be positive. One implication is that Glover's character has to escape his stable, "good citizen" domesticity in order to revitalize himself. Since our culture values potency in men, Glover's seemingly "positive" image is in many ways sad. Paradoxically, he needs to be saved from the very things that mark him positively.

Fig. 13.4

The **star system** also plays a role here, since Mel Gibson enjoys a "heart-throb" reputation that Danny Glover does not have. Furthermore, Gibson gets the first screen credit and is better known to the public as a superstar commanding huge salaries for his roles. Clearly, the Gibson and Glover characters are not in all ways equal in the *Lethal Weapon* series. Nevertheless, Glover's character shares an equal position with Gibson's within the films' narrative structures; it is in this that their relationship differs markedly from that of the Lone Ranger and Tonto.

Fig. 13.5

All too often, recent American films represent black men as threatening figures (violent gang members, drug addicts, pimps) and white men as the unquestioned norm against which the blacks appear unstable and undesirable. In *Bonfire of the Vanities* (1990), for example, a character makes a wrong turn and accidentally drives into a New York inner-city neighborhood. The experience becomes a nightmare that is immediately characterized by the appearance of threatening African Americans (figure 13.5). They materialize in this urban desolation like vultures waiting for innocent victims, and that is all we see of their neighborhood or their lifestyle.

Another way of stating this issue is that blacks are frequently seen as different from whites, and the difference is exotic and undesirable. In other words, they are the strange characters and the whites the normal ones. But black characters could just as easily be presented as the norm against which whites appear exotic, or the white norm could be represented in such manner as to make it undesirable or frightening. A variation on this occurs in *White Man's Burden* (1995), in which blacks are represented as the dominant social class and whites as the oppressed underclass. The racist industrialist, played by the black actor Harry Belafonte, has a white factory worker, played by John Travolta, unjustly fired. The desperate Travolta character then kidnaps the Belafonte character to show him how the other half lives. Clearly, this movie differs from our other examples, since its premise is one the audience will immediately recognize as "unrealistic" as opposed to that of, say, *Boyz N the Hood* (1991), but they share the strategy of reordering traditional representational priorities and questioning stereotypes. Much of the effect of *White Man's Burden* comes from seeing actors behave in ways that deviate severely from stereotypes of their race; its value may be in provoking its audience to question racial stereotypes. But while the film's intentions are praiseworthy, its simple role-reversal strategy is based upon the premise that, under the skin, we are all alike; this ignores the individuality of both groups. The blacks dress and behave like stereotypically bigoted upper-middle-class whites, and the whites behave like ennobled working-class blacks. Furthermore, the use of an actor of Travolta's star power in the sympathetic starring role, while intended to evoke sympathy for a black underclass, may in fact build sympathy for the whiteness of the actor, and the casting of Belafonte in a villainous role may associate the actor's race with villainy.

Stereotypes

As with *White Man's Burden*, discussion of race invariably turns to **stereotypes** and evaluations of characters as negative or positive. What are stereotypes and why are they important to understand? Stereotypes characterize a group of people in a highly repetitive fashion with the same few characteristics. The groups can be defined by age, class, race, ethnicity, gender, sexual orientation, profession, hair color – virtually anything. Common examples of the above, respectively, are elderly people as senile, extremely wealthy people as unhappy, blacks as oversexed, Jews as stingy, women as hysterical, gay men as effete, professors as forgetful, and blonde women as stupid.

These stereotypes are not consistently present in the history of American cinema, and at times there is a significant difference between stereotypes that circulate in the culture at large and those that appear in films. Although some films of the silent era, such as *The Birth of a Nation* (1915), represented blacks as sexual threats who were also given to violent behavior, films of the sound era until the late 1960s seldom represented them in this manner and instead portrayed them as harmless, marginalized characters generally seen in menial positions. And how many stingy Jews come to mind during the classical era? Yet those stereotypes were active in the culture at large during those years. Clearly, films mediate cultural racial stereotypes in complex ways. The effectiveness, for example, of such organizations as the National Association for the Advancement of Colored People and the Anti-Defamation League to protest demeaning stereotypes clearly affects cinematic practices.

The absence in films of certain widespread stereotypes does not mean that those stereotypes are not operative in other ways. *The Searchers* (1956, see chapter 4), for example, deals with fear of miscegenation between white women and Indian men and can be seen as an indirect engagement of black–white racial tensions. American Indians were a marginal and largely invisible group to white Americans in the mid-1950s. Fear of the sexual potency of black men and strong racist reactions against interracial coupling of black men and white women, however, were strong at that time. Thus, the film engages extremely touchy racial fears of the time by displacing them from blacks to Indians and from the present to the nineteenth century.

Some degree of stereotyping is inevitable, so why is it of such importance? What's the difference, for example, between a stereotype of a black man and one of a white man? Or of one between a blonde woman and a black woman or a professor and a pimp? Whites are frequently cast as either villains or heroes, so what's the big deal? There are at least two major differences between stereotyping whites and people of color; one deals with films and the other with society. First, whites are represented in a full range of roles and characterizations in Hollywood films. At times they certainly are represented as one-dimensional villains (Luke Plummer at the right in *Stagecoach*, 1939, figure 13.6), but they are just as likely to be represented as the one-dimensional hero

Fig. 13.6

Fig. 13.7

or "good guy" in the same film (The Ringo Kid played by John Wayne, figure 13.7). The same is true in *Dirty Harry* (1971, see chapter 7) where a white psychotic killer (figure 13.8) is counterpointed by Clint Eastwood playing the detective of the title (figure 13.9). Some white men might be ridiculed for sexual incompetence as is the pathetic used-car salesman (itself a stereotype of a profession) in *True Lies* (1994), but, as in *Stagecoach* and *Dirty Harry*, that figure is offset by the hero, played by Arnold Schwarzenegger.

Fig. 13.8

With such a wide variety of white characters, the entire race is not characterized by any one of them. No one watches *True Lies*, for example, and concludes that all white men are pathetic lovers, just as no one watches *Stagecoach* and concludes that all white men in the old West were villains in black hats or watches *Dirty Harry* and concludes that all contemporary, young white men are psychotic killers. Other images in those very films prevent such generalizations. Yet, if in film after film,

Fig. 13.9

people of color are represented as marginal characters and as servants or as dangerous and undesirable, people may conclude that they characterize their race. If one sees enough films with Native Americans as nothing other than screaming savages or Asian Americans as nothing other than houseboys and launderers or African Americans as nothing other than poorly educated, one might begin to think of those races in such a manner.

In *Higher Learning* (1994), the African American filmmaker John Singleton casts Laurence Fishburne as a black college professor of the highest intellectual and moral character. This reverses the stereotype of black men as uneducated. At the same time, however, it perpetuates one of the most familiar stereotypes of professors: the character constantly smokes his pipe (figure 13.10). Similarly, a gang of white male neo-Nazi "skinheads" are the troublemakers, not the black gang members who simply protect themselves from abuses

Fig. 13.10

they suffer at the hands of whites, including a stereotypically racist police officer. The film also perpetuates stereotypes of lesbians, including the idea that lesbianism is caused by being raped. Thus, this film paradoxically challenges some stereotypes while reinforcing others. Yet, as this brief list indicates, all are not equally serious issues. Most people would quite rightly be more concerned with the social implications that white police officers are racist or that lesbianism is caused by rape than by the association of college professors with pipe smoking.

Even if *Higher Learning* fails to avoid stereotyping, it points to the need to expand the range of representations of African Americans in films. It also points to the need for us never to uncritically accept images. However well-intentioned Singleton is, he perpetuates many stereotypes of varying degrees of importance that resemble the ones the dominant cinema perpetuates about African Americans. Victims of stereotyping are not necessarily free from employing similar stereotypes themselves. Many critics felt that Spike Lee perpetuated anti-semitic stereotypes in his depiction of money-grubbing Jews in the jazz world in *Mo' Better Blues* (1990).

Social and Cultural Power

The above-described range of images is purely a question of cinematic representation. Are races and groups of people characterized by a limited or by a wide variety of characteristics? We cannot adequately answer this question by simply discussing movies. Let us assume for the moment that excessively wealthy white businessmen and beautiful blonde women are stereotyped as completely and as negatively as black male drug dealers and black prostitutes. Shouldn't we be as upset by the way in which the whites are stereotyped as by the way in which the blacks are? The answer to this question might very well be no – and not because we are insensitive to the plight of white businessmen or blonde women.

Both white groups possess real power within their society and culture. Far from being marginalized, white businessmen enjoy a great deal of cultural privilege, authority, and wealth. How they are represented in movies is unlikely to harm them significantly, and many people may even have a great deal of trouble feeling any sympathy for them. Similarly, blonde women are commonly fetishized as the ideal of American beauty. Like white businessmen, they are in this regard culturally well positioned.

The situation is different with racial minorities. Because of long-standing histories of economic and social discrimination, many racial minorities have been oppressed and marginalized within our society. They have not had equal access to education and the professions and in many ways lack the cultural power that white businessmen enjoy. Anything that contributes to demeaning their image may help perpetuate the unjust social circumstances in which they find themselves. If many believe that all African Americans are either drug addicts and criminals or suitable only for menial jobs, and that is all they see in movies, they might very well consider the movies to be evidence for the validity of their beliefs. If, however, they see black doctors, lawyers, and professors, such beliefs are challenged.

Positive and Negative Images

Opposing doctors, lawyers, and professors to servants, drug addicts, and gang members raises the crucial issue of positive versus negative images. Are not some images simply positive and others simply negative? Wouldn't we be better off if we simply characterized racial minorities in positive ways? As appealing as it might be to answer the second question with a simple yes, the situation is once again more complicated.

In the 1980s, a cynic quipped that there were more black women judges on television than there were in real life. Clearly, one could herald black women judges on television as superb role models for black girls. It might inspire some to set similar career goals. But there are problems with this simplistic approach. If in fact we live in a society that makes it difficult and unlikely for black girls to grow up to become judges, the disparity between the reality and the television representation may actually mask ugly social prejudices and problems. An overly "positive" view of the world may candy-coat disturbing issues and may in fact make it more difficult for some people to achieve their goals if those goals are unrealistic and lead to increased frustration.

Role Models

A role model is someone whom we think young people should admire and model their lives upon. Once again this may seem like such an admirable concept that there is no need to question it, but nothing could be further from the truth precisely because of the difference between a real-life role model and one from movies or television. In effect, people who argue for the value of positive role models in films are urging young people to uncritically accept the image of a fictional character (for example, the professor in *Higher Learning*) or the equally fabricated public image of the actor (for example, Laurence Fishburne playing the professor).

Throughout this textbook, however, we have argued for the value of a highly critical, analytical response to every aspect of movies. We emphasize the word "every" since, however well intentioned the motive, we cannot exempt any element from scrutiny. The concept of role modeling is indeed wonderful if young people model themselves on teachers, doctors, or lawyers whom they know. It is an altogether different and precarious activity when they model themselves upon media heroes.

Many members of the African American community have long been disturbed by the fact that nearly all the media role models available to black male children today are athletes and rock singers. It is for this reason that, when a variety of allegations or revelations about ethical and criminal misconduct are leveled at such figures, there is such shock. Such moments reveal that we know little about these celebrities and that we have simply been accepting constructed media images as truths. The solution to this problem is not to find the right celebrities to emulate but to recognize that all media figures are similarly constructed and that we should understand such constructions rather than simply accept and emulate any of them.

The same situation holds for characters in films. As we have stressed, it is important that a wide variety of characters of any race or minority group be represented regularly in films, including both good and bad characters and, perhaps more importantly, complex characters who resist such easy classifications. It would be a mistake to simply identify positive characters and praise the films in which they appear. Furthermore, we should always question what at any point in time our society considers positive. How many such "positive" images in the past have included people of color or gays and lesbians? Many of the white heterosexuals in positions of power in our society have simply assumed heterosexuality to be a positive, desirable trait.

In chapter 7, we saw how playing positive characters was actually a limiting experience for an African American actor like Sidney Poitier in the 1950s and 1960s when he carried the burden of demonstrating black nobility. From this perspective, Wesley Snipes's opportunity to play a one-dimensional villain opposite Sylvester Stallone's hero in *Demolition Man* (1993) indicates an increased range of opportunity for an African American actor in the 1990s. Snipes does not feel he has to carry the burden of representing all blacks with every role he takes. He has remarked in interviews how much he enjoyed playing such an evil character, something that would have been almost unimaginable for Sidney Poitier around the time of such films as *Lilies of the Field* (1963) and *Guess Who's Coming to Dinner* (1967).

Historical Change and Representations of Race

Fig. 13.11

As the above example of the difference in the roles available to Poitier and Snipes indicates, it is important to analyze race in historical terms. In the 1930s and 1940s, for example, no black stars in Hollywood were featured in leading roles such as Poitier had in the 1960s. Successful African American actors like Stepin Fetchit and Hattie McDaniel were relegated to comparatively minor parts such as Fetchit's shuffling "darkie" in *Steamboat 'Round the Bend* (1935) and McDaniel's robust "Mammy" in *Gone with the Wind* (1939, figure 13.11). This does not mean that we should ignore the accomplishments of these actors any more than we should overlook Poitier's accomplishments. It means rather that we have to situate the roles in relation to the options available when the films were made. Although they were all talented actors, Poitier had opportunities that Fetchit didn't have and, today, Snipes has opportunities that neither of them had.

Historical shifts can also be seen in **genres**. During the 1970s and 1980s, for example, the horror film was largely preoccupied with issues of teen sexuality and family life. Race was not usually a central issue, although there are important exceptions such as *Night of the Living Dead* (1968) and *Dawn of the Dead* (1978) in which African Americans had starring roles. The seemingly endless series of *Halloween* and *Friday the 13th* films, along with such classics as *The Texas Chainsaw Massacre* (1974), however, were much more typical of the genre. Horror and (mostly white) teen sexuality went hand in hand.

Beginning with *The People Under the Stairs* (1991, see chapter 14) and continuing with *Candyman* (1992), *Candyman 2: Farewell to the Flesh* (1995) and *Demon Knight: Tales from the Crypt* (1995), a number of important recent horror films have shifted their focus from teen sexuality to race issues. Indeed, teen sexuality is absent from these films. In *The People Under the Stairs*, a pre-teen, African American boy is the hero (figure 13.12); in the *Candyman* films, the title character is the monster, though, in a complex shift, he is an African American who had been the victim of horrible racism that he has returned from the dead to avenge; and in *Demon Knight* both a major and a secondary part are filled by African American women, one of whom becomes the hope for the future of the human race.

Related developments appear in other genres such as the Western. *Posse* (1993) is centered on an heroic group of African Americans in the West who must deal with racist whites. *Dances with Wolves* (1990) is a revisionist Western concerning the mistreatment of American Indians during the settling of the West. It portrays them as the "good guys" and the whites as the "bad guys." *Dances with Wolves*, directed by Kevin Costner, has major problems in its depiction of race, however. The central character is a white man played by Costner, then an extremely popular star (figure 13.13). Thus, while the film seeks sympathy for the Indians, it does so without ever questioning white centrality and dominance; it is still "about" the white man and his experiences. The film also helps raise an important question: what are the differences between films made by whites and those made by members of racial minorities? Of the recent horror films dealing with race mentioned above, only Ernest Dickerson's *Demon Knight* was directed by a filmmaker of color.

Fig. 13.12

Dickerson had been Spike Lee's cinematographer and directed *Juice* (1992), a serious social drama about inner-city youth. After that, however, he switched to more established genre filmmaking. *Surviving the Game* (1994) is a male action

Fig. 13.13

film and *Demon Knight* a horror film. Dickerson's career development shows that, much as African American actors are now pursuing a wide variety of roles, filmmakers of color need not confine themselves to socially serious films; they can now make genre entertainments and, as Dickerson has shown in both films, feature black characters and themes. It is hard to imagine Lee a decade earlier making an action film for his second film and a horror film for his third. In that short time, Lee helped create a new social context with more options, and in 1995 he produced *Tales from the Hood*, which combines the horror genre with socially serious drama. More recently, Keenan Ivory Wayans has had great popular success with his parodies of horror films, *Scary Movie* (2000) and *Scary Movie 2* (2001). And the acclaimed African American directors, the Hughes Brothers, have made *From Hell* (2001), a film about Jack the Ripper set in Victorian England and starring Johnny Depp. It was, upon its release, treated by most critics as simply another mainstream Jack the Ripper film. Although it does not have a single black character in it, the film provides a trenchant critique of the self-destructive and self-consuming nature of British white power at its peak in the late Victorian age.

Minority Filmmakers and Minority Aesthetics

Many people intuitively think that it is important for women, gays, and racial minorities to make movies as well as to be represented in them. And for good reason. Members of a group have a wealth of experience that outsiders do not

Fig. 13.14

Fig. 13.15

and they may bring a different perspective to bear. It is equally important to emphasize, however, that the simple fact that one belongs to an oppressed minority does not necessarily give one insight into that or other forms of oppression. Indeed, members of minorities may perpetuate stereotypical beliefs within their culture. Spike Lee's films, for example, have been criticized as misogynistic by fellow African Americans, and Lina Wertmuller has been criticized as sexist by feminists for films such as *Swept Away . . .* (1975).

Nevertheless, a glance at the films of such African American filmmakers as Spike Lee and John Singleton confirms that they bring different experiences and perspectives to them from those available to white filmmakers. Scenes of urban, domestic life in the African American community such as those in *Jungle Fever* (1991, see chapter 4, figure 13.14) and *Boyz N the Hood* (figure 13.15) have a richness and detail lacking in mainstream Hollywood depictions. Both films present African American neighborhoods as places where loving families with strong moral values live, not just violent streets with drugs and crime. They do not deny the existence of drugs and crime, but neither do they reduce the neighborhoods to exotic settings or backdrops as they are in so many Hollywood films.

The films of Lee and Singleton, among others, challenge and provide alternatives to dominant racial stereotypes. Lee's work in particular confronts the issue of stereotypes and racial representation in diverse ways. He has made fictional films, such as *Do the Right Thing* (1989) and *Jungle Fever*, films based on historical figures, *Malcolm X* (1992), as well as fictional films set during historically significant times, *Get on the Bus* (1996). He has also made documentaries, such as *4 Little Girls* (1997) and *The Original Kings of Comedy* (2000). His *Bamboozled* (2000) confronts the history of American racist representations, as well as changing responses to those representations within the African American community. Are the films by artists such as Lee and Singleton, however, simply different from those produced by the white mainstream? Once again, the answer to this question is more complex and involves aesthetics as well as social issues. A film's relationship to the mainstream is in part determined not just by who makes it but also by whom it is made for, who finances it, who distributes it, and who exhibits it.

If the person who directs a film belongs to a racial minority but most of the other components are part of the dominant production, distribution, and exhibition systems, then the filmmaker is confined by certain parameters and expectations. While such films might aesthetically look somewhat different and might have somewhat different characters and themes, they in many ways participate in the dominant style. The characters are not so different, for example, that we do not recognize them as resembling characters in films made by whites. Similarly, the plots resemble the plots of most Hollywood films. *Sister Act 2: Back in the Habit* (1993), a comedy directed by Bill Duke and starring Whoopi Goldberg, both African Americans, provides an example of such a mainstream film. However, even the films of Lee and Singleton, which are much more socially "serious" and explicit about the racial issues they engage and are at times stylistically experimental, also conform to many features of the mainstream. To look for extreme differences, however, we must go outside mainstream production and turn to independent, experimental films like *Tongues Untied* (1989) by Marlon Riggs, an African American filmmaker. This film about male homosexuality in the African American community has no traditional plot or characters.

From this perspective, such Oscar Micheaux films as *Ten Minutes to Live* (1932) are revealing. Micheaux, an African American, originally made low-budget films targeted at a black audience. These films were made within a highly segregated social and economic context. They were only shown in black neighborhoods and were produced, distributed, and exhibited outside the dominant system. After Micheaux's production company went bankrupt in 1928, it was reorganized to include white Harlem theater owners. Although no longer fully independent, Micheaux nevertheless made films distinctively different from those of the white mainstream. For these reasons, Micheaux's films were overlooked by dominant film histories; even most academics had never seen or even known about them. Only within recent years have these films been screened and written about within the dominant culture. What strikes one today is how creatively different from the mainstream they are.

Dominant Culture

We began this chapter by noting how the color white is commonly an invisible norm against which other people of color are measured. Similarly, it is common to think that the sole purpose of analyzing the representation of race in films is to better understand how people of color have been represented or, perhaps more accurately, misrepresented, and to attempt to improve such representations. But there is an entire dimension missing from this formulation: the dominant white culture. Instead of just studying what we can learn about African Americans in films, we should also study what we can learn about the white culture to which these disturbing representations have been so central. The history of much American culture, including cinema, nineteenth-century literature, popular fiction, radio, and television, is preoccupied with racial others, particularly African Americans. This is not just a problem for people of color, but also one for the whites who create, dwell on, and need these images. These images can tell us much about them.

With this in mind, we now turn to two films within the Hollywood tradition known as *film noir*, *Out of the Past* (1947) and *LA Confidential* (1997), and *Boyz N the Hood*, one of the important recent films by African American filmmaker John Singleton. Whereas the pairing of the first two films shows changes in racial representation within a single genre, *Boyz N the Hood* offers many new, challenging perspectives.

We have chosen the two *films noirs*, made fifty years apart, to show that racial representation is neither a simple thing nor historically fixed. Both are Hollywood films made from the perspective of the dominant culture. *Out of the Past* has neither a moment of racial conflict nor any explicit thematic engagement with racism. However, and reflective of its era, it reveals troubling presumptions about race and exoticism. *LA Confidential*, which is set in the same time and place but made fifty years later, uses white racism as a central theme, and contains scenes of racial conflict.

We have chosen *Boyz N the Hood* because, aside from Spike Lee's groundbreaking films discussed in chapter 4, it received the most attention and praise of recent African American films at the time of its release. The fact that it was Singleton's first film made it even more remarkable. Made by a young director who had just graduated from film school, *Boyz N the Hood* is an excellent example of the serious examination of social issues that characterizes much of the work of current African American filmmakers. If the two *films noirs* show the need to understand and be aware of the assumptions about people of color in dominant filmmaking, *Boyz N the Hood* demonstrates the importance of films made by members of racial minorities that challenge many spectators' expectations.

Out of the Past (1947) and *LA Confidential* (1997)

Film noir, possibly the most original and enduring American film style, first appeared in the early 1940s, has undergone many changes, and remains a strong presence in today's movies (see chapter 5 on genre). Two films from that tradition, *Out of the Past* (1947) and *LA Confidential* (1997), although set in the same place and era (the post-World War II US), were made fifty years apart. This difference makes them illustrative of shifts during the inter-vening half-century in US perceptions of the relationship of Anglo culture with the cultures of various peoples of color, both within and beyond US borders.

"*Noir*," meaning black, refers both to the dark look and the grim themes of the films; racial issues often figured in both that look and those themes. Both films discussed here are presented from the points of view of white males in the US; both show those males undergoing erosions of their presumed cul-tural privilege. Differences in the ways in which the films present the "other" peoples and "other" ways of life that the central characters encounter reveal a great deal about changes in American film and culture between the 1940s and the 1990s.

The two films present their "others" in radically different ways. *Out of the Past* reveals a conservative stance that laments the loss of white male power, a loss it associates with a powerful woman (a sexual other) as well as with people of color and with Mexico. *LA Confidential*, to the contrary, might be described as liberal. Unlike *Out of the Past*, it explicitly condemns white racism and asso-ciates evil not with peoples of color but with the white power structure.

In *Out of the Past* a white male crosses the border from the US into Mexico, a movement that symbolically triggers other crossovers, involving gender, race, and class. The film presents those crossovers in terms of loss, as transgressive and emasculating deviations from a white, male, rural, middle-class ideal. It presents the decline of its central male character in terms of pain that comes from the degree to which he embraces the exotic.

Jeff Bailey (Robert Mitchum) is hired to track down Kathie Moffat (Jane Greer), who wounded and robbed her New York mobster boyfriend, Wit (Kirk Douglas). Bailey pursues her to Mexico where he falls in love with her, uncharacteristically betraying his boss as well as his partner. Why did this happen? Bailey had a reputation for integrity and intelligence, which was why Wit hired him. His motivation for throwing it all away is never explained beyond his telling us on the soundtrack that he suddenly fell in love. The film, however, indicates in its symbolic use of exoticism that much more is involved.

The film's use of the exotic is evident in its selection of Mexico as a setting. On a story level, there is really no need for the film to include Mexico at all; its entire justification is that it is simply a place outside of New York to which Kathie flees. The film uses locales all over the US – New York, San Francisco, Lake Tahoe, and so on, so why cross the border into Mexico? The answer exists on the symbolic level, where the film has every reason to go "south of the border" since it presents Mexico as a profoundly exotic place, more so than anything the US offers. Furthermore, it becomes the symbolic locus for other exotic associations. Bailey pursues one kind of exotic, a seductive and murderous woman above his class, into an exotic place, Mexico, and influenced by both, he crosses other borders. As a result, he loses his masculinity. At the end he is literally and mortally shot in the groin. His integrity, his career, his very identity (he changes his name and occupation), as well as his American dream, shown as a working-class life running a gas station in rural Bridgeport, California with a clean-cut blonde girlfriend, are all lost.

The film presents Mexico as an exotic place marked by racial, linguistic, and cultural difference. When Bailey crosses into it, he enters a place of temptation, feminization, indolence, and sensual overload, a place where "such things happen." And when they do, Bailey is doomed, although the film implies that, in a less exotic environment, Bailey might not have so readily lost control over his life. In fact, at a crucial moment, Jeff is unable to telegraph his boss that he has finally tracked Kathie down because the telegraph office is closed for siesta. Businesses in New York or Bridgeport, California do not close for siesta. Had Bailey been in either of those places, he would have sent the wire, thereby completing his assignment; he could then have returned to his old life. But he is in Mexico, and the siesta gives him time to reconsider; it is one more thing that distances him from his duty. He never sends the wire, but flees with Kathie instead, thereby sealing his doom.

In another instance of the film's selection of a setting with little narrative but great symbolic justification, Bailey begins his search for Kathie by briefly questioning her maid in a black jazz nightclub. Neither the maid nor a black cultural environment reappear in the film and the information Bailey elicits is minimal, so why the locale? Its exotic associations with people of color and with jazz in 1947 make it an appropriate place for Bailey to begin his journey away from the securities of his culture. That journey leads him to Mexico (shown in the very next shot), which becomes his "heart of darkness" and changes him forever.

Later he seeks a way back. He changes his name and starts over in rural Bridgeport, California. But his past catches up with him, and he returns to Kathie. He is not alone; the gangster she shot and robbed also returns to her. She will eventually kill both men. The film not only depicts a woman who becomes more powerful than its men but it also shows the men returning repeatedly to the woman who betrayed them, fully aware that she is likely to continue doing so.

Although Bailey tries to reclaim his life, the film indicates that, once you have crossed the border, there is no going back. The exotic appeal of what lies across the border masks its ability to corrupt; its very pleasures erode Bailey's ability to reintegrate himself into the US. When he finds out how far he has fallen, it is too late. This sentiment reflects US xenophobia of the 1940s and also appears in the popular World War I era song opposing plain and simple American life with the exotic European experiences of returning

American soldiers, asking how are you going to keep them down on the farm once they have seen Paris. The implication is that, once innocent Americans taste corrupting foreign pleasures, they will never again be satisfied with "home sweet home." Much of *film noir* exhibits such xenophobia. *The Maltese Falcon* (1941), for example, presents all of its villains as either foreign in origin or as having traveled to exotic places, and implies that their evil and their foreign associations are linked. In *Out of the Past*, Bailey's new life is ruined as the consequences of his Mexican trip emerge "out of the past" into his present.

As is common with many forms of prejudice, racism in the film is covert, never overt. Neither people of color nor Mexico are ever characterized as actively evil in *Out of the Past*; rather, they are associated with evil exclusively on a subtextual level. The blacks in the jazz nightclub have no overt connection whatsoever with the Latinos in Mexico. Their only relationship is symbolic; they are people of color; they are not white males. Furthermore, no black or Hispanic does anything evil or even menacing; they are benign. This does not, however, give them equal status with the white characters. The film associates its people of color with Kathie, who betrays and kills white men. Kathie employed the black maid, Kathie chooses to travel among Hispanics in Mexico, and those people of color and foreign places become symbolically, although never causally, associated with her evil.

From a racist and sexist perspective, danger is easy to spot in *Out of the Past* because it is visible – it comes from across the border, from another race, another country, another gender. But what if it is not so easy to spot, what if it lies *within* the border, as is the case in *LA Confidential?* One reason it is not so easy to spot is that the meaning of the exotic has changed in the fifty years between the two films. It is obvious by now that issues such as the meaning of the exotic and race in film cannot be studied in isolation because they are intertwined with other important issues, such as class (see chapter 14), representation, and history. The social meaning of race changes over time, partially because things intertwined with it change.

Such a change is evident in the two films discussed here. Both are Hollywood films that center on white males, but the relationships of those males with people of color, primarily blacks and Hispanics, function in opposed ways. *Out of the Past* weaves people of color into a racist subtext of exoticism that corrupts white males; in *LA Confidential*, however, precisely the opposite happens. People of color do not work as a subtext but figure overtly in the film's themes, which explicitly condemn white racism. The film presents white males who reject racism as good; those who do not as corrupt. Furthermore, corruption comes not from the exotic place across the border but from within white male power, and one of its ugliest manifestations is white racism. Reasons for this shift in racial signification, from the 1940s to the 1990s, involve historical and genre change.

Examined together, the two movies point to a shift within Hollywood from associating people of color with evil to identifying with them. Our understanding of this shift can be aided by social history. The history of US political demonology, or the tendency to characterize certain types of people as "devils" and thereby blame all that goes wrong in society on them, has been categorized as having gone through three stages. The earliest stage began in colonial America and was overtly racial. It pitted whites against people of color and its targets were the red and black peoples of frontier America. Such demonization was used as a rationale to enslave blacks and conquer Native Americans. The second stage of demonization, a reaction to the waves of immigration, particularly from eastern Europe, in the late nineteenth century, was class and nation based. In this stage, the demons might have been white, but "they" were readily identified by physical and linguistic markers. In the post-World War I "red scare" round-up and deportation of subversives by Attorney General A. Mitchell Palmer (and his subordinate J. Edgar Hoover), Palmer described his targets as "alien filth," with "sly and crafty eyes . . . lopsided faces, sloping brows, and misshapen features." He considered them the working-class "savages" of newly urbanized America. The third stage of demonization shifted the danger from the visible body to the mind. During the Cold War, communists looked no different from white, US males. A popular television series of the period was *I Led Three Lives* (1953–6) in which the central character, a white male, appeared as a "normal" US citizen, an FBI agent, and a communist spy (really an FBI double agent). However, whether he was appearing as a "normal" Boston advertising executive, an agent of justice, or an agent of foreign evil, he looked exactly the same. The message was clear: demons were no longer easy to spot because they looked like "us."

In *LA Confidential* the enemy does, indeed, look like "us." The film concerns a massacre in a diner for which three African American youths are arrested; the real culprits, however, are members of the Los Angeles Police Department. Furthermore, the department has a secret component that brutally intimidates and ejects dangerous outsiders, such as gangsters and drug dealers, ostensibly to keep LA pure, especially from drugs. It turns out, however, that the police themselves are engaged in the drug trade, and eject or kill outsiders not for the public good but to consolidate their own hold on corruption. The police captain, Dudley Smith (James Cromwell, figure 13.16), appears to represent the best traditions of his department, but in fact stands at the center of the corruption. He even murders members of his own department.

His LAPD is composed entirely of white males and the film shows incidents of ugly white racism. In one, a mob of drunken officers, acting on an unsubstantiated rumor, stampedes into the station's jail to savagely beat a group of jailed Chicanos. In another, police frame three African American youths for murders performed by police officers. Unlike *Out of the Past*, this film deals explicitly with racism and condemns it. The officers who resist it are its heroes.

Fig. 13.16

In *LA Confidential*, the danger comes not from outside the white power structure but from within it. The dangers associated with exotic people and places that seduced and destroyed the central characters in the 1947 movie are, here, no dangers at all but a smokescreen for white male corruption. The system has turned in on itself. The enemy is now "us."

Why the change? Part of the reason can be explained in relation to the above-described pattern whereby the notion that the body, "theirs" or "ours," no longer provides reliable proof of demonism. Another is the sea change in US culture that took place in the 1960s and 1970s resulting from Watergate, the Vietnam War, the empowerment movements for women, various racial and ethnic groups, and gays and lesbians. It is no longer so easy to blame others for problems in the country, and the integrity of the power structure is no longer inviolable.

Film noir has changed also. The initial movement died in the mid-1950s but it has provided a resonant touchstone for American culture and has, from the late 1960s on, been revived in a number of ways. The post-1960s' films tend to be shot in color instead of black and white; they also deal explicitly with aspects of sexuality and race that censorship codes forced the earlier films to make implicit. But, more importantly, the new films are often "period" films, about our past, where the earlier ones were about the "today" of their era. In ways the earlier films never did, the new ones combine nostalgia for that era with a cynical exploration of our national and cinematic past. In them, the nature of the exotic has changed in fundamental ways. The earlier films commonly presented the exotic as powerful women, other races, other nations, and political beliefs. This was not confined to *films noirs*. In horror films of the 1930s (*Dracula*, 1931, *Frankenstein*, 1931, *The Werewolf of London*, 1935, for example), evil came from "somewhere else," foreign places. Films made after the mid-1960s, such as *LA Confidential*, *Chinatown* (1974), and *Mulholland Falls* (1996) work differently. Their exotic is the world of the earlier films – the clothing styles, the music, the cars, the colors, even the white males in fedoras. These movies tend to present race in a post-1960s' "liberal" manner and characterize foreign nationals and people of color as victimized by white racism rather than as symbolic of exotic, sinister dangers. Evil in these films lies not on the fringes but at the center of the power structure; evil comes, as in many horror films after the mid-1950s (*Invasion of the Body Snatchers*, 1956, *Psycho*, 1960, and *The Texas Chainsaw Massacre*, 1974, among others), not from "somewhere else," but from "here"– the mainstream US. It would be difficult to find a recent Hollywood film that uses white association with people of color or foreigners to imply white villainy or degradation. It would be comparably difficult to find a recent film that uses belief in communism to do the same thing. The message of many of these recent films is that white society is often corrupted by its very power and needs careful examination. Times have changed.

As the third stage of demonology characterizes evil as looking just like "us," *LA Confidential* has a central concern with deceptive appearances. Things are not as they appear; benevolent cultural traditions, such as the LAPD, are not as righteous as they present themselves. The three central and ultimately heroic detectives demonstrate this. Each finds something horribly wrong in the traditions he was raised to revere. Ed Exley (Guy Pearce), the proud son of an honored LAPD officer, wants to follow in his father's tradition, now embodied in Captain Smith. Exley is horrified to learn of Smith's corruption and ultimately kills him. Bud White (Russell Crowe) was abused and abandoned by his father, who also murdered his mother. He repeatedly goes out of his way to brutally punish abusers of women. Jack Vincennes (Kevin Spacey), while himself corrupt, is the advisor for *Badge of Honor*, a popular television show glorifying the LAPD, modeled on *Dragnet* (1952–9, 1967–70). But while he presents himself to the public as the "real life" model for the noble and righteous detectives on *Badge of Honor*, he also covertly accepts bribes from *Hush Hush* magazine for his participation in high-profile and possibly fraudulent celebrity arrests. When he attempts to reform and prevent the framing of a gay man, however, Smith murders him.

Not only are the righteous images of public institutions and social traditions deceptive, but so also are the physical appearances of characters. Kim Basinger plays a prostitute made up to look like a 1940s' movie star, Veronica Lake (figure 13.17). She turns out to be a "down-home" Texas woman. In one scene, Exley accuses a woman who looks like Lana Turner of being a prostitute associating with a gangster, only to learn it is the *real* Lana Turner, who is, nevertheless, dating a gangster. The very title of the film refers to a sleazy tabloid whose mission is to expose the underbelly of Hollywood glamor, to gleefully show that all is not as it appears on the surface. Over and over, the message is reinforced – appearances are unreliable. Danger cannot be presumed to come from without; it is neither visible nor exotic.

LA Confidential opens with nostalgic film footage, Johnny Mercer's rendition of "Ac-cent-tchu-ate the Positive," and narration by a gossip columnist (Danny DeVito) for *Hush Hush* magazine describing post-war Los Angeles as a "paradise on earth" holding unlimited promise. He says that this image is created by the media – radio, television, film – but that the mainstream media does not show "trouble in paradise;" that is the job of *Hush Hush*. He describes the underbelly of Los Angeles as the criminal empire ruled by Mickey Cohen and says that, now that Cohen has been sent to prison, a power vacuum has opened up. We later learn that that vacuum will be filled by the police.

Fig. 13.17

Fig. 13.18

The opening footage establishes the movie as being "about" the American past. The movie closes with a black-and-white image of a stereotypical 1950s' white, suburban nuclear family watching *Badge of Honor* (figures 13.18 and 13.19) on television. The shots are strongly ironic because the entire film preceding them has shown that the image of the LAPD in *Badge of Honor*, as well as the image of un-troubled 1950s' suburban family life, is a hypocritical and carefully manufactured lie. A significant point of commonal-ity between both of them, and one that the movie criticizes, is glorified whiteness – the police in *Badge of Honor* are white, the idealized family is white. The movie makes it clear that the post-war US was very different from the idealized images it presented of itself, whether in the nostalgic footage opening *LA Confidential*, or in the idealized families and police in television shows of the era.

Fig. 13.19

Throughout this book, we stress the importance of looking critically at all movies. Even though *LA Confidential* critiques white racism, we should realize that its perspective is also white. Every important character in the film, good or evil, is white; they, and never people of color, are the film's norma-tive figures of identification. Although the three central detec-tives are presented as ultimately heroic, all commit serious crimes against people of color or women. The movie presents these crimes, but then implicitly glosses over their importance by the end. While Bud White defends abused women, he also murders a black rape suspect in cold blood. Furthermore, we see him savagely brutalize a black youth during an interro-gation. White forces him into a terrifying variation of Russian Roulette by shoving a pistol into his mouth and pulling the trigger repeatedly (figure 13.20). While Jack Vincennes tries to prevent the framing of a gay white male, he has a long history of corrupt activity. He also participates in the beating of Chicano men during a drunken riot at the police station (figure 13.21). Although Ed Exley defies Smith, he also uses his methods when he shoots Smith in the back. Fur-thermore, he rapes a woman. But regardless of these crimes, the film invites us to sympathize with all of these characters by its end.

Fig. 13.20

Fig. 13.21

From this perspective, the manner in which the film centers whiteness makes it more similar to than different from *Out of the Past*. We now turn to *Boyz N the Hood*, a film that does not have an invisible norm of whiteness and develops a radically different perspective.

Boyz N the Hood (1991)

Writer/director John Singleton's first film, *Boyz N the Hood* (1991), represents a major trend in African American filmmaking. Released by Columbia Pictures into a mainstream market, it resembles the work of Spike Lee (see chapter 4) in being a film dealing with African American life, made with African American filmmakers in dominant creative roles, and yet part of mainstream production and distribution. This is a far cry from black involvement in films during the classical era, when blacks worked primarily as performers in marginal and generally servile roles. Singleton's film differs also from the 1970s' "blaxploitation" films, which were also directed by blacks, starred black actors, and were set in black environments. "Blaxploitation" films, such as *Shaft* (1971), *Superfly* (1972), and *Cleopatra Jones* (1973), often dealt with black life under white oppression but did so in a highly formulaic, generic manner, often reinforcing stereotypes of blacks as hyperviolent or hypersexual. Interestingly, Singleton revisited that genre in his remake of *Shaft* (2000). Finally, *Boyz N the Hood* differs from black-controlled films produced and distributed entirely outside dominant production and distribution venues such as the recent experimental films of Marlon Riggs or the early films of Oscar Micheaux. Artists like Singleton, Lee, and Allen and Albert Hughes (*Menace II Society*, 1993) signal a new wave for black filmmaking and representation.

One of the major issues posed by this chapter is the significance of having people of color behind the camera. As we have pointed out, it varies with the filmmaker as well as the production and distribution circumstances, but *Boyz N the Hood* provides one instance of a profoundly important way of representing people of color in mainstream film. One of the most evident things about the film is that, in it, black is not an exotic color as it is in most classical films. The movie deals almost exclusively with black people in a predominantly black environment. There is no invisible norm of whiteness, since whites are hardly represented and those who appear are in marginal roles. The word "nigger" is used a great deal, but always by blacks, so its significance is intra-racial instead of interracial. The movie presents no significant white characters as norms of identification, positive or negative, for the mainstream audience.

This also affects the film's use of stereotypes. Since it occurs within a black community, its stereotypes are those reinforced by that community, not those imposed from without. Furthermore, no one character or group of characters bears the weight of representing all African Americans; all are seen as involved in a complex layering of social roles and forces. Many recognizable stereotypes appear but are presented within a context different from that of mainstream cinema.

The film in no way ignores or sugarcoats problems within the black community or offers a simplistic and triumphant optimism about its future; rather, it presents a strong critique of problems of African American life mediated by a profound sense of value and struggle within the black community. In this it resembles Singleton's 2001 companion-piece to the film, *Baby Boy*, which is set in the same neighborhood. The approach of *Boyz N the Hood* is perhaps most evident in a title that introduces the film by telling us that one in twenty-one black American males will be murdered and that most will die at the hands of another black male. We hear the horrifying sounds of a drive-by shooting on the soundtrack before we see an image, and the first image we see is a stop sign. The movie focuses on the waste of black male youths and pleads for a stop to it.

Plate 65

Plate 66

Plate 67

Plate 68

Plate 69

Plate 70

Plate 71

Plate 72

Plate 73

Plate 74

Plate 75

Plate 76

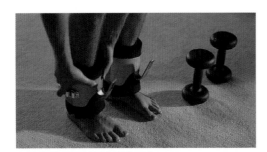

Plate 77

Plate 78

Plate 79

Plate 80

Plate 81

Plate 82

Plate 83

Plate 84

Plate 85

Plate 86

Plate 87

Plate 88

Plate 89

Plate 90

Plate 91

Plate 92

Plate 93

Plate 94

Plate 95

Plate 96

Plate 97

Plate 98

Plate 99

Plate 100

Plate 101

Plate 102

Plate 103

Plate 104

Plate 105

Plate 106

Plate 107

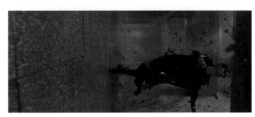

Plate 108

Plate 109

Plate 110

Plate 111

Plate 112

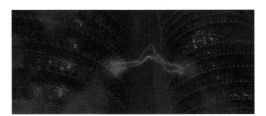

Plate 113

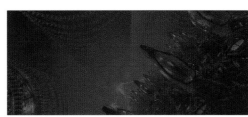

Plate 114

Plate 115

Plate 116

Plate 117

Plate 118

Plate 119

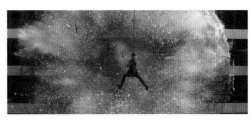

Plate 120

Plate 121

Plate 122

Plate 123

Plate 124

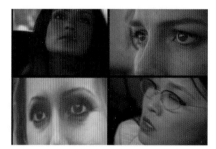

Plate 125

Plate 126

Plate 127

Its plot concerns the coming of age of Tre Styles (Cuba Gooding, Jr plays Tre as an adult; Desi Arnez Hines II plays him as a 10-year-old) in the black community of South Central Los Angeles. It begins in 1984 when Tre is around 10 and ends seven years later when he is about to go to college. In the first part, he has difficulties in school and his mother (Angela Bassett) takes him to live with his father (Laurence Fishburne); in the second part, seven years later, he falls in love, sees a close friend murdered, and avoids the social dangers that destroy many of his peers. His peers consider him a success story, and the film associates that success with the influence of his parents. Although divorced, they both care deeply for him, provide responsible role models, and instill in him a profound moral code. This is most evident when, after seeing his friend Ricky (Morris Chestnut) murdered, he flees his father and girlfriend and goes seeking revenge with Doughboy (Ice Cube), Ricky's brother. Doughboy and two other friends are heavily armed and drive around town hunting Ricky's killers. After hours of searching, however, the troubled Tre asks Doughboy to pull over and he leaves the car. No one objects. Doughboy and the others soon murder Ricky's killers, but the next day Doughboy tells Tre he does not hold it against him that he left the car, that he understands and respects Tre's moral code. A title at the end of the film says that Doughboy himself was murdered two weeks later. Tre, then, by being able to remove himself from the pattern of violence and retribution at a moment of intense temptation not to do so, avoids Doughboy's fate. A closing title tells us that he went on to college.

Interestingly, the film's climax avoids narrative temptations common to classical and "blaxploitation" films. A more traditional narrative strategy would be to allow Tre to engage in retributive violence, especially since he saw his friend murdered in cold blood, and then declare that part of his life over and go on to college. In other words, having it both ways – giving the audience the spectacle of triumphal violence and still allowing it to feel good about the now-matured, gentle hero. But Singleton removes Tre from the retribution scene and then further complicates expectations. Tre returns home to his anxious father, but neither says a word. After looking at each other, they go to separate rooms, giving the audience no alternative scene of triumph through cheerful paternal approval; in fact, we never see the father again. Furthermore, the retribution scene is not triumphal but sad and ugly. Doughboy and his friends mow down the three fleeing and defenseless killers with an automatic weapon, and then Doughboy walks up to two who are still crawling and shoots them in cold blood. And we learn he is murdered soon after. The violence is sad and cyclical: they killed Ricky, Doughboy killed them, somebody kills Doughboy, and on it goes. Only Tre escapes by leaving the cycle and not, as is more traditional, by triumphing within it. We never see him fight, or even fight back. The film systematically avoids the traditional temptations of using heroic violence to signify success.

A scene at the beginning gives a good sense of the movie's layering of social pressures upon Tre; it is also the only scene in which black/white social tension appears. We see 10-year-old Tre walking home from school toward the camera on a suburban street (plate 81). On the soundtrack, we hear a tense telephone conversation between his mother and his white teacher. Between Tre and the camera, a group of rowdy older boys gambles and blocks the sidewalk. As Tre walks around them (plate 82), violence breaks out and three of them beat the other two (plate 83). Tre continues to walk home and never mentions the incident. Clearly, explosive violence is part of his daily experience.

Singleton intercuts shots of Tre's mother on the telephone (plate 84). The teacher tells her that Tre is intelligent but has a bad temper and that she recommends therapy. The mother declines, and the teacher tentatively asks if there is a problem in the home, if she is employed. The mother's anger builds; she tells the teacher it is none of her business but then retorts that she is employed and is also working for her master's degree. The teacher's voice indicates surprise that the mother is educated. We soon see Tre enter the home and in the frame for the first time with his mother (plate 85), who tells the teacher that Tre will not be returning to school but will be going to live with his father. To the teacher's surprised "Father?" the mother responds "Yes, father, or did you think we made babies by ourselves?" and hangs up. When Tre asks her if she told the teacher to jump in the lake, the mother angrily points to a written contract she and Tre had made about not getting into fights, and says that, since he broke it, he will be going to live with his father.

The layering is complex. We have seen that Tre's teacher is well meaning but ineffectual and barely comprehends his world. Tre also has trouble with some of his peers and, coming home from school, he avoids dangers from older boys. His mother recoils at the teacher's racist assumptions that black families are incomplete because the father has abandoned the family or that single black mothers are unemployed, uneducated, and so sexually promiscuous that they either do not know or have no ongoing relationship with their children's father. And, yet, she does not allow Tre to take pleasure in denouncing the teacher; rather, she chastises him and decides it is time to let him live with his father, who will teach him to become a man. Her decision is reinforced in a ride through a run-down part of Los Angeles where she says that she loves Tre and doesn't want to see him dead, in jail, or drunk, fates that she sadly anticipates for many of his peers. Tre's maturation, then, involves personal and social pressures from a number of directions (teachers, peers, parents, and social dangers), and his mother herself also negotiates a complex network of tensions, some of which involve race. The film's characters deal with many of the problems of a social minority, but they are defined by many things besides their race.

When Tre and his mother park in front of his father's house, we see an image unusual for films about black youth at the time – the father is raking the lawn (plate 86). On a number of levels, this film challenges stereotyped images about black youth dominant in the 1970s and 1980s. The movie is set on streets with single-family homes and lawns, not the usual inner-city tenements.

We see few flashy cars, and Tre's father has a Volkswagen bug convertible, the same type that Tre himself later drives. Drugs and prostitution are present but not a dominant issue. Tre does not conform to the stereotype of hypersexual black youth; an attractive, popular high-school senior, he admits to a friend that he is a virgin. His girlfriend, Brandi (Nia Long), values her Catholicism and intends to save her virginity until marriage. When Tre's parents discuss his future, they meet at a stylish restaurant (plate 87), where she orders espresso and he *café au lait*. They are neither *nouveaux riches* drug dealers throwing money around nor poorly educated people touring out of their class, but cultivated people entirely comfortable and relatively inconspicuous in the upper-class restaurant. The film has no pimps, no drug dealers in flashy cars, no overdoses, no racist white police.

In fact, the only confrontationally racist scenes involve a black police officer. After Tre's father shoots at a burglar, an arrogant black officer (plate 88) tells him that it is a pity he didn't hit the burglar since there would then be "one less nigger around here." The officer's embarrassed white partner stands nervously by. Seven years later, the same black officer stops Tre's car, sadistically holds a gun to his throat (plate 89), and taunts him, saying he enjoys Tre's terror, that he became a police officer because he hates "niggers" like him. The image of a black who hates his own race is politically charged; seldom found in mainstream film, it is more often found in works produced from within the minority group and engaging problems not always accessible to outsiders.

This film, then, avoids many stereotypes of African American life, gives new perspectives on others, and introduces images largely new to mainstream film. Related to this, one of its central concerns is the establishment of role models. Tre is considered a role model for his peers. The film's second part opens at a party celebrating Doughboy's release from prison. As Tre enters, Doughboy's mother (Tyra Ferrell) asks Tre to talk with her son, indicating that she considers him a positive influence. And Tre's role model is his father, Furious Styles. His father is firm, politically aware, and caring. He repeatedly instills into Tre the importance of responsibility, especially for children in an environment where absentee fatherhood is a common occurrence. Seven years before, in a talk with his 10-year-old son about sex, he stresses this, saying that any man can sire a child but only a "real man" can stay around to raise his children. He stresses his awareness of himself as a role model, saying that he wanted to be someone Tre could look up to, and that desire influenced life-altering decisions such as joining the army.

While the film does not represent overt black–white racial conflict, it does not ignore the issue, and it is most vocalized in Tre's father's declarations on issues such as the effects of gentrification on the African American community, drugs and guns in South Central Los Angeles as opposed to Beverly Hills, and racism in the army. He is respected in his community, by Tre's friends, and even by his ex-wife. He does not seem to be a happy man but one with a strong awareness of racial oppression and of the need to contain his anger and frustration. His first name is "Furious," and we repeatedly see him rolling two stainless steel balls in his hand, presumably his way of displacing tension. When his ex-wife asks how he is, he says, "I'm living. That's enough for me" as if he fully realizes that a happy life under his circumstances of constant struggle is not likely, but that sheer survival is a value.

Boyz N the Hood, as a mainstream film about and by people of color, would not have been possible fifteen years earlier, yet now is part of a significant trend. It signals a new phase in the representation of race in American film. Unlike *Out of the Past*, *LA Confidential*, or for that matter, most of Hollywood cinema, it does not present its people of color from the point of view of whites or represent whites as normative figures of identification – it lets its characters stand on their own.

SELECTED READINGS

Richard Dyer discusses the importance of understanding the invisible white norm in "White," *Screen*, 29 (4) (Autumn 1988), pp. 44–64. Toni Morrison stresses the importance of turning the dominant representation of African Americans back upon the white culture that produced them in *Playing in the Dark: Whiteness and the Literary Imagination* (New York: Vintage Books, 1992). Leslie Fiedler has analyzed the tradition of interracial, homoerotic male bonding in American culture in *Love and Death in the American Novel*, rev. edn (New York: Stein and Day, 1966). In *Redefining Black Film*, Mark A. Reid discusses the history of Oscar Micheaux's productions and criticizes what he considers the deplorable ideology of Spike Lee's films, including their misogyny. Reid also delineates the economics of white-controlled production and distribution of films made by blacks. Michael Rogin develops the different stages in the history of US political demonology in *Ronald Reagan: The Movie and Other Episodes in Political Demonology* (Berkeley, CA: University of California Press, 1987).

14
CLASS

Pretty Woman and *The People Under the Stairs*

Why can't Bruce Willis's character, after saving thousands of lives in three *Die Hard* movies, get a better job, haircut, and clothes? Why does Sylvester Stallone's Rocky, after five films in which he makes millions of dollars in the boxing ring, wind up in *Rocky V* (1990) with little money, wearing his same ratty, beaten-up hat in the working-class Philadelphia neighborhood from which he began, and yet feeling triumphant? These two actors are among the highest paid in the world, making $20 million or more for some of their movies, and their lives are chronicled in obsessive detail by the media. Why do they grunge themselves up for movies over which they have considerable control? Why not make movies in which their characters, like themselves, enjoy a life of spectacular luxury? Wouldn't the public have the same interest in seeing in movies what they follow obsessively in the media? The answers to these questions have a great deal to do with issues of class.

We all have used the terms high class and low class. High class conveys the meaning of good or stylish, and low class means bad or without style or morals. If we refer to someone as having "class" or as a "class act," we mean that we admire them and feel that we can depend upon them; a low-class person is someone we would do better to avoid. But these vague terms rest upon cultural assumptions that often seem contradictory. A look at the way in which class is represented in film will help us understand some of those assumptions and also show us how issues of class are linked to those of race and gender.

What is Class?

One precise meaning of class involves **economic status**. The upper class is generally considered to be a small percentage of people with the greatest wealth.

Many picture them as having the biggest houses, the fanciest cars, servants, expensive consumer goods, and unlimited access to travel and exclusive places such as country clubs. Many picture the lower class as also a small minority, but one that lives in crowded ghettos in squalor. They either struggle to survive or are wholly irresponsible and perhaps even drug addicts or criminals. Most film viewers, regardless of their actual economic status, tend to identify with the middle class, which ranges from the lower middle class (which has minimal comfort) to the upper middle class (which has a good deal). Middle-class people are not excessively rich – they have to work, but they do not have to worry about basic sustenance.

This seems pretty simple. A basic corollary of this would seem to be that lower-class people in movies are successful if they rise into the middle class and middle-class people if they rise into the upper class. But it is not that simple. In *Wall Street* (1987), Charlie Sheen plays a young man taken under the wing of a financier played by Michael Douglas, who offers him the promise of a fabulously wealthy life and entry into the upper class. In contrast to this lifestyle, that of the Charlie Sheen character's father, played by Martin Sheen, looks shabby. His father belongs to the working class. He dresses in off-the-rack workman's clothes instead of the custom-made suits the Douglas character wears, is active in his labor union, and hangs out at the local tavern. Charlie Sheen's character gradually learns that the Douglas character is corrupt and he becomes disgusted by him; he also comes to respect his father's integrity.

Fig. 14.1

Fig. 14.2

He helps to get the Douglas character indicted, and his father stands solidly by him in his difficulties.

The film is centered on a character who aspires to the upper class but ultimately rejects it. It does not turn out to be what he dreamed it to be. Part of his upward path involved a deal that would have devastated his father's labor union, a group of working people. The son learns that the wealth of the few is often based upon immoral greed and the destruction of many decent, hard-working people. He comes to value not the class to which he aspired but the one from which he tried to escape.

Let us compare this with *The Wizard of Oz* (1939), a beloved movie that at first seems to have nothing in common with *Wall Street*. Little Dorothy is transported to the wonderful land of Oz, which holds all sorts of fantastical creatures and sights. Where her home life in Kansas is photographed in black and white with its connotations of realism at the time (figure 14.1), Oz is in glorious Technicolor with connotations of fantasy (figure 14.2). She and the friends she picks up along the way take the yellow brick road in the hope of meeting the fabled Wizard, who will make their dreams come true. The Wizard, like the Douglas character in *Wall Street*, turns out to be a sham. The end of the film finds Dorothy back on her poor farm in Kansas with her plain and simple friends and family; like the beginning, it is photographed not in Technicolor but in black and white. And yet, a jubilant Dorothy exclaims, "There's no place like home!"

While *Wall Street* deals explicitly with class contrasts and issues, *The Wizard of Oz* does not. Both films, however, contain the implicit message that it is dangerous to aspire above one's station in life. In Hollywood films, rising above one's class is often ruinous, whereas adapting to the lower class of one's "roots" is often revitalizing. Why?

The Invisible Class Norm

The reasons are complex. We approach them in this chapter by showing how mainstream movies tend to presume an **invisible norm** of middle-class life and values; they also present contemporary class structures as justifiably fixed and use class prejudice and stereotypes (which are related to racial and gender stereotypes) to reinforce these beliefs. They displace notions of justifiable class warfare or change on to foreign countries or into the past and, in doing so, present such class warfare or change as valuable only in so far as it paves the historical or cultural path to the contemporary American middle class. Class issues are central to many genres, and notions of what makes up the middle class have changed over time.

The notion of an invisible class norm is comparable to the norms we discussed with race, in which whiteness is the invisible norm against which other races are categorized; with sexuality, in which heterosexuality is the norm from which homosexuality is seen to deviate; and with gender, in which masculinity is the norm against which women are frequently categorized as being mysterious or troublesome. In Hollywood films, the presumed class norm is the middle class. Other classes are measured against it and generally found to be lacking. Upper-class people are often portrayed as exotic, crazy, corrupt, immoral, selfish, and unhappy; lower-class people as desperate, dangerous, and also immoral. Whether they depict the ghettos of Harlem or South Central Los Angeles, or the mansions of Nob Hill or Park Avenue, films frequently represent non-middle-class locales as being as exotic as the Taj Mahal.

These locales differ in fundamental ways from those frequented by the middle class. But how? As we saw with *Wall Street*, class is not simply a matter of money; it is associated with other things. Perhaps the most obvious of these is that middle-class life is often linked with moral strength, while either excessive or insufficient wealth is often portrayed as morally erosive. The dream of bountiful wealth and privilege in *Wall Street* becomes a nightmare because it is linked with limitless greed and moral corruption. Similarly, in *Chinatown* (1974), the wealthy patriarch played by John Huston turns out to be not only a murderous villain but also the rapist of his own daughter. The central character in *Titanic* (1997) is disgusted at the emptiness and vanity of her upper-class peers, and finds happiness and love only with a penniless young man from steerage. Even when a wealthy character is charming and benign, as the title character in *Arthur* (1981), he is so out of touch with the realities of life that he is incapable of supporting himself. Arthur is an irresponsible and childish alcoholic, but the film makes him appealing because he has the sense to fall in love with a working-class woman instead of the arrogant debutante to whom he is engaged.

The message of an entire subgenre of films dealing with the extremely wealthy, such as *You Can't Take it with You* (1938) and *It Could Happen to You* (1994), is not only that money can't buy happiness but that one is better off without the inevitable misery that accompanies wealth. If the title of *You Can't Take it with You* implies the limitations of wealth, *It Could Happen to You* uniquely dramatizes this concept as its main characters go instantly from the working class to the upper class when they win a shared lottery ticket. A police officer who doesn't have money for a tip tells a waitress that, if he wins the lottery, he will share the prize with her. He does win the lottery and, true to his decent, working-class ethic, he returns to the restaurant and shares his winnings. By the time the film is over they fall in love and learn that all the money in the world can't bring them happiness: all they need is each other.

Upper-class life is often linked not only with wealth but also with familial estrangement and sexual deviation – people with "too much time on their hands" – whereas middle-class life is associated with nuclear family cohesion and the ennobling effects of hard work. Lower-class life, as in *The Grapes of Wrath* (1940) or *Midnight Cowboy* (1968), is associated with deprivation, despair, vulnerability to exploitation, and often intolerable stresses upon the nuclear family.

Class is also associated with race. Images of the "filthy" rich seldom include people of color, while images of the lower class often focus upon black ghettos and Latino *barrios* as places of economic deprivation, substance abuse, and violent crime. The shock implied in the title of *Guess Who's Coming to Dinner* (1967) is that a black man is coming to dinner not as a waiter but as a guest in a white, upper-class home and, even worse, he intends to marry the upper-class daughter. The fact that this man, played by Sidney Poitier, holds great social prestige is largely irrelevant to the cultural assumption of the time that African Americans "belong" in the lower classes and have no place in white, upper-class homes unless they are servants. He is perceived as a danger because class is associated with more than simple economics; it is presumed in some ways to be fixed and therefore associated with "knowing your place," and place includes racial status.

An interesting variation upon this occurs in *Ransom* (1996), which deals with the kidnapping of the son of an extremely wealthy white man. The FBI agent assigned to the case is black and, in a revealing moment, he confides to his wife on the telephone that he is glad they are not rich. The implication is clear: even though his culture positions him by means of race and class "below" the rich white man, he prefers his middle-class status to the dangers he associates with upper-class life.

When Hollywood films depict other countries and cultures, those lands appear exotic not only in terms of geography, language, and culture, but also class. Such films depict either the exotic environs of the wealthy, as in *To Catch a Thief* (1955), *The Pink Panther* (1964, figure 14.3), or *The Comfort of Strangers* (1991), or the equally exotic but often primitive environs of the pathetic or angry poor, as in African safari films like *Mogambo* (1953) or political films like *Salvador* (1986). Some depict both

Fig. 14.3

upper and lower classes, as *The Year of Living Dangerously* (1983). Most of these films show foreign lands as having no significant middle class. An implicit message in them is that foreign lands, like the upper and lower classes, might be interesting to visit and dream about but, as Dorothy says in *The Wizard of Oz*, "There's no place like home."

This also works in reverse. Many American films portray people in foreign lands as desperate to partake of American life. One example is the sad old Polish woman in *Torn Curtain* (1966) who offers to help the main characters escape the Iron Curtain police if only they will sponsor her immigration to the United States. The desirability of American life is often presented as not only freedom from police states but also access to consumer goods. In *Moscow on the Hudson* (1984), the Robin Williams character lives in squalor in Moscow but, on a trip to New York, defects in Bloomingdale's department store. In one scene, he is dazzled by the wealth of consumer goods in an American supermarket, a shocking contrast with their virtual absence in Moscow. *Jet Pilot* (1957) concerns the defection of an ace Russian pilot to the United States; it sums up the attraction of American life to her at the end with a shot of a sizzling steak.

Fixed Class Structure

By and large, Hollywood films present the contemporary class structure as justifiably fixed. As opposed to many other national cinemas (such as that in Russia in the 1920s or many recent Latin American cinema movements), Hollywood film has little interest in depicting or espousing class warfare or class change in positive ways. When this does occur, it is almost always in films set in the past and often involves notions of progress from imperfect class structures toward the idealized system of the present. In other words, class change is good if it paves the way for the system that we have now, in which class change is not desirable. *Gone with the Wind* (1939) is set in the Civil War era and depicts a genuine change in the class structure of its society through violence. Scarlett O'Hara, its central character, shifts her loyalties from the feudal, pre-war South represented by Ashley Wilkes (figure 14.4) to the capitalistic, post-war South represented by Rhett Butler (figure

Fig. 14.4

Fig. 14.5

Fig. 14.6

Fig. 14.7

14.5). Where Wilkes was a cultured aristocrat, Butler is a rugged, self-made man much more attuned to the coming twentieth-century middle class than the dreamy Wilkes could ever be.

This works in the opposite way in the major Civil War epic of the silent era, *The Birth of a Nation* (1915, figure 14.6), which depicted the class changes brought about by the war in a negative light and presented the founding of the Ku Klux Klan as a way of restoring the feudal values of the pre-war South. It is significant that both films are set in the historical past. Films set in the present usually presume that virtually all challenges to the existing class structure are undesirable and that people are better off by learning to adjust to their own class and station in life.

Few films are more explicit about this than the perennial Christmas favorite, *It's a Wonderful Life* (1946), in which the central character, played by James Stewart (figure 14.7), is so unhappy with his life that he intends to commit suicide. His misery comes not from frustrated class aspirations but rather from a feeling that his lifelong sacrifices in service of his strong middle-class sense of community responsibility have come to naught. An angel shows him how miserable his community would have been had he not lived and convinces him that his life is in fact wonderful. At the end his situation is largely unchanged but he is a very happy man. Over and over, the message is to value what you have and where you came from.

Class Origins

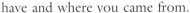

The notion of "where you came from" works differently in different cultures. Characters like Tarzan and Robin Hood (figure 14.8) take root only in lands with a hereditary monarchy like England. Much of the logic underlying most Tarzan stories and films, for example, is that Tarzan is the superior creature that he is because he has aristocratic British blood. According to such logic, he

Fig. 14.8

survives in Africa not because of what he does but because of what he is – a blue-blooded Englishman and consequently superior to other peoples. His class is his birthright, and his superiority emerges even though he was stranded in Africa before he learned of his birthright. Comparably, Robin Hood is a successful bandit leader because he also comes from the aristocratic class. At the end of many of the films, after risking all to defeat the villain Prince John, he readily gives over the kingdom to King Richard. This may at first seem odd, since Richard has put the country in the bad state it is in by ignoring his duties as king and irresponsibly going off on Crusade. Robin feels that Richard deserves to be re-enfranchised, however, simply because he has royal blood.

Fig. 14.9

Few American myths function in this way. Heroes of the land or heroes who engage in class warfare, like those in *Shane* (1953), *Young Mr Lincoln* (1939, figure 14.9) or *The Alamo* (1960), are heroes from the past who paved the way for today's middle-class values. Their pedigree is unknown or irrelevant; their merit comes not from royal blood but from skill, hard work, vision, and class solidarity. Americans do not see their roots in an aristocratic past, as the British do, but in an almost *sui generis* rising from the earth. They do not trace their mythical lineage to the revolutionary period in the eighteenth century in which the traditional heroes like Washington, Jefferson, and Franklin were financially well off, dressed like

Fig. 14.10

aristocrats, and had strong links to Europe; rather, Americans trace their lineage, their "roots," to the cowboys and the mountain men of the nineteenth century who often dressed in animal skins and lived off the land. There has never been a feature film about George Washington, but there have been many about Davy Crockett, Daniel Boone, Jesse James, and Wyatt Earp. Relatively few films deal with the revolutionary period, in which the basic law of the country was established; those that do appear, like *Jefferson in Paris* (1995) tend to garner little popular interest. The Western, however, has been a major genre since the beginning of films. American culture has little sympathy for the aristocratic culture that many founding fathers represented but much for the self-made culture of Western lore. The middle class in films sees its roots in a working and often immigrant class.

Films like *The Godfather, Part II* (1974) reinforce such a notion. It presents the powerful criminal Don Vito Corleone as ennobled because he stayed close to his roots in Sicilian peasant culture (figure 14.10) and to his family. His son Michael, however, betrays his roots in his rise in class and becomes corrupt; he divorces his wife, murders his brother, and becomes the antithesis of his father. A film like *The Firm* (1993) casts doubt upon the central Tom Cruise character because, in his eagerness to join a prestigious law firm, he denies his roots by concealing the fact that he has a brother in prison. His redemption is partially signaled by his acknowledgment of that brother.

Class Stereotypes

While class issues are implicit in all movies, many films engage them by explicitly contrasting life in different classes. D. W. Griffith's *A Corner in Wheat* (1909), for example, indicates the destructive effects of the excesses of the wealthy upon the lives of the poor by showing the opulent dinner party of the "Wheat King" in contrast with shots of the starving poor waiting on line for bread, the price of which keeps rising. The Wheat King is ultimately smothered to death under his own wheat. Such films, while appealing for sympathy for the lower and downtrodden classes and condemning the excesses of the wealthy, often reinforce class **stereotypes**. In this, more recent films like *Losing Isaiah* (1995) are little different from very old ones like *The Kleptomaniac* (1905). *Losing Isaiah* begins with a black, single mother who lives in squalor, has no supportive nuclear family, is drug-addicted, and prostitutes herself for money. She leaves her baby in a garbage receptical while hunting for money. Garbage collectors take the infant to a hospital where a white, middle-class woman adopts it. When the black woman later discovers that her child is alive, she initiates a custody battle and tries to "better" herself by adopting a lower-middle-class lifestyle. The film contrasts her dark, unstable, and crime-infested ghetto environment with the well-lit, stable, fashionable, nuclear family environment of the white woman and characterizes the two environments as essentially unchangeable worlds. Similarly, *The Kleptomaniac* shows women of different classes caught shoplifting. The wealthy one steals from a department store; the poor one impulsively steals a loaf of bread. The wealthy woman escapes the consequences of her crimes while the poor one is sentenced to jail, indicating that the legal system is class biased, but, again, each conforms to the stereotypes of her class.

Instead of simply seeking to evoke sympathy for members of a fixed and stereotyped lower class, some filmmakers consistently confront class stereotypes. Spike Lee, for example, has made a number of films that avoid ghetto stereotypes and are set in the African American middle class. *School Daze* (1988), for example, contradicts the image of African Americans as poorly educated and homogeneous as a group by showing internal divisions within an all-black college. *Jungle Fever* (1991, see chapter 4) has as its central character an upper-middle-class black architect who reads *The New York Times* and encounters both class and racial difficulties in his relationship with a lower-middle-class Italian woman. Furthermore, the film sees little value for either character in returning to his or her roots, which are deeply troubled and at times destructive.

Class and Genre

Class is a significant factor in understanding many **genres**. *The People Under the Stairs* (1991), which we will examine in detail later in this chapter, evokes much of its horrific atmosphere from the fact that it is set in a place without a middle class. Implicitly, "we" are threatened or irrelevant, and the world has become a chaotic and confrontational mix of upper and lower classes. A threatened or absent middle class has, by and large, always been a component of horror films. A distinguishing aspect of the flowering of American horror films in the 1930s was the fact that, in them, horrific events usually take place "someplace else," generally in foreign lands and among the upper classes. *Dracula* (1931) occurs in Transylvania and England; *Frankenstein* (1931) in Germany; *Dr Jekyll and Mr Hyde* (1932), *The Invisible Man* (1933), and *The Werewolf of London* (1935) in England. Dracula is an aristocrat and the British people with whom he interacts are well to do; Dr Frankenstein's father is a baron and he is a doctor; Jekyll is also a doctor and seeks to marry into an upper-class family; the title character in *The Invisible Man* is a well-to-do British physician; and the title character in *The Werewolf of London* is so well off that he travels to exotic locations.

Fig. 14.11

After World War II, things changed and many American horror films involved domestic threats. *The Invasion of the Body Snatchers* (1956, figure 14.11) is exclusively a film of the middle class, but the middle class is being taken over by aliens. In the 1970s and 1980s, many films like *The Texas Chainsaw Massacre* (1974, figure 14.12) and *The Hills Have Eyes* (1977) took as their premise the ill-advised intrusion of middle-class people into lower-class, "white-trash" environments. The people there are presented as primitive and savage, virtually uncivilized. In this the films resemble dramas like *Deliverance* (1972), in which a group of men from the city vacationing in the wilderness encounter a hellish nightmare with "hillbillies." Many later horror films set in middle-class environments, like the *Nightmare on Elm Street*, *Halloween*, and *Friday the 13th* series, have those environments threatened by monsters who either come from or resemble the lower classes. Thus, whether the horror movie is set in a foreign land or in the very backyards of the American middle class, an implicit and disquieting element of them is either the absence or endangerment of that class. Monsters often have strong "other" class associations. Dracula is an aristocrat; Frankenstein's monster resembles a peasant but is created by an aristocrat; the murderous families in *The Texas Chainsaw Massacre* and *The Hills Have Eyes* are "white trash."

Fig. 14.12

Film noir may be seen in linked class and gender terms. Many of its films, like *Double Indemnity* (1944, figure 14.13), *Murder, My Sweet* (1944), and *The Maltese Falcon* (1941), involve women who aspire above their "place" in both gender and class. Neither submissive nor maternal, they exploit their sexuality to manipulate and often destroy men in their ruthless attempts to rise in class. *Film noir* was strongly influenced by and at times indistinguishable from

Fig. 14.13

Fig. 14.14

Fig. 14.15

the gangster film, which has as a standard pattern the precipitous rise in class of a violent and generally doomed criminal. Such films as *Little Caesar* (1930, figure 14.14) and *Scarface* (1932, see chapter 1, and 1983) often derive humor from the gangster's low-class notion of high-class life, his *nouveau riche* behavior and vulgar sense of style. His doom explicitly comes from his criminal activities, but implicitly from his refusal to "know his place."

Another popular genre, the Western, has also traditionally dealt with class change. It repeatedly re-enacts its basic scenario of the taming of a savage nineteenth-century country for the coming twentieth-century middle class. The appeal of the form lies mainly in its violence, but the form justifies that violence as necessary to pave the way for the twentieth century. This is often explicitly stated, whether in the shift of power between the rugged gunfighter to the literate senator in *The Man who Shot Liberty Valance* (1962, figure 14.15), the gunfighter Shane fighting the local warlord to make way for the peaceful farmers in *Shane* (1953), or the world of the strong man giving way to that of the strong woman in *Cimarron* (1931). In this, gender is important. Women are characterized as agents of the middle-class world to come – disapproving of the man's temptation to violence and, in many cases such as *The Virginian* (1929), *High Noon* (1952), and *The Searchers* (1956), explicitly trying to stop it. They represent the more feminized middle class of the next century.

Economic Class and Social Class

Class is signified in a variety of ways and class cues are complex. Why is Burt Reynolds's southern, working-class, "good ol' boy" character in *Smokey and the Bandit* (1977) and other films presented in a positive light but the "good ol' boys" in *Mississippi Burning* (1988) are presented as evil? Why is Edward G. Robinson's lower-class Italian gangster in *Little Caesar* (1930) presented as hysterical and demented, but Robert De Niro's immigrant-class Italian gangster in *The Godfather, Part II* as noble? All of the characters are of the same class, but they are not all presented in the same way.

During the 1994 Winter Olympics a great deal of media coverage was devoted to the potentially disabling attack upon the ice-skater Nancy Kerrigan. One of her competitors, Tonya Harding, was implicated in the attack. While both Kerrigan and Harding come from working-class backgrounds, the media represented them as coming from different classes. Kerrigan's tasteful, polite behavior made her seem to embody respectable middle-class values, and some commentators characterized Harding's tawdry, often crude image, heavier figure, and revealing clothing as low class. Kerrigan's image of tasteful beauty was widely glorified, while Harding's lifestyle became the subject of countless tabloid exposés. Thus, class is often represented as less of an economic issue as one of social issues such as taste and morality. The implication frequently is that, whatever one's financial status, one can choose the **social class** one wants by an act of will; the further implication is that the preferred values to embody are those of the middle class. One of the many reasons why the De Niro gangster is presented in a positive manner is his commitment to wife and family; the Robinson gangster has no such commitment.

The Reynolds "good ol' boy" is somewhat different. He is part of a long tradition in American film and literature of valorizing the male adolescent impulse, seen in the middle-class ethos as the period before "settling down." Whether cowboy or racecar driver, his rootless, traveling life has often been valorized, but it is significant that this lifestyle is totally inaccessible to women. Apart from highly publicized exceptions like *Thelma and Louise* (1991), there is virtually no place in American film for the valorizing of women in such a lifestyle. Their "place" is to embody the domestic values of the middle class.

Somewhat comparable with the ways in which Tonya Harding and Nancy Kerrigan have been represented, the differences between Dr Jekyll and Mr Hyde have generally been mapped out along class lines even though they are the same person. In *Dr Jekyll and Mr Hyde* (1932), the Hyde character wears the clothes of the upper-class Jekyll (figure 14.16), but through make-up looks physically deformed and monstrous, traits often associated with lower-class physiognomy. Furthermore, the first place he goes to after having transformed from Jekyll to Hyde is a lower-class music hall, where he starts a relationship with a woman who performs in it. Unlike Dr Jekyll, who attends upper-class dinners, Mr Hyde acts in a manner associated with degrading stereotypes of the lower class.

These mixed signals go a long way in answering the questions posed in the first paragraph about the characters that actors like Bruce Willis and Sylvester Stallone choose to play in their films. Both actors lead lives of extreme wealth and privilege and yet, generally, play characters of the lower middle class with resolute middle-class values, the presumed values of their audience. Their films often emphasize this by giving villains in the *Die Hard* movies or *Rambo: First Blood, Part II* (1985) or *Cliffhanger* (1993) upper-class characteristics and having them sneer at the middle-class heroes. Comparably, the Planet Hollywood restaurant chain that they and Arnold Schwarzenegger invest in and visibly support is not an upper-class environment with sophisticated French cuisine but a burger and beer place with movie memorabilia. All of these actors realize the importance of appealing to middle-class values, of telegraphing the message that they have not lost their middle-class roots and are still one of the guys, regardless of their actual financial status. They want to show that their heart lies with the right class.

In the following section of the chapter, we analyze the representation of class in *Pretty Woman* (1990) and *The People Under the*

Fig. 14.16

Stairs (1991). *Pretty Woman*, a huge box-office success, both perpetuates class stereotypes and candy coats serious class issues such as the likelihood of making the transition from being a prostitute to being the fiancée of a successful businessman. Although *The People Under the Stairs* belongs to the horror film genre which is not rated highly by critics, it analyzes and critiques such class issues as the unjust distribution of wealth between landlords and ghetto dwellers. The two films supply a valuable contrast in the ways in which Hollywood films can both perpetuate class stereotypes and challenge them. Both films also show how race, class, and gender issues are frequently intertwined in films. Finally, neither film represents the middle-class invisible norm. Even when the middle class is absent, however, its values dominate mainstream cinema. These two films depict a strong contrast between upper- and lower-class life and, even though no middle class is represented, its values are implied as preferable to those of the other classes.

Fig. 14.17

Pretty Woman (1990)

Class Stereotypes

Pretty Woman (1990), an enormous box-office success, is a fairy tale in which Edward Lewis, a fabulously wealthy financier (Richard Gere), pays Vivian Ward (Julia Roberts), a desperately poor prostitute, to spend a week with him. They fall in love and, at the end, plan to live happily ever after. Both characters conform to many class stereotypes. He is well dressed (figure 14.17), cultured, supremely confident, and used to the finest locales and entertainments, but so distanced from "normal" life that he hardly knows how to drive a car. She is loud, vulgarly dressed (figure 14.18), poorly educated, desperate for money, confused, and has low self-esteem, but knows more about cars than he does. He stays in the penthouse of an exclusive Beverly Hills hotel (figure 14.19); she shares a cramped apartment (figure 14.20) with a room-mate, and must sneak down the

Fig. 14.18

Fig. 14.19

Fig. 14.20

fire escape to avoid paying the rent she does not have. What they have in common is that they feel unfulfilled in their personal lives. Edward's class privilege does not help him here and, in fact, a common stereotype of the rich is that their wealth does not bring them happiness. Like Vivian, he comes from a dysfunctional family and is not part of a couple.

When she first walks through the lobby of his hotel (figure 14.21), everyone notices her. Her cheap, revealing clothes with thigh-high vinyl boots, her make-up and wig, and her comportment all instantly identify her as not belonging there. Conversely, his car (not even his but his lawyer's, which he can't drive well) makes him stand out in her domain on Hollywood Boulevard. Neither belongs in the other's world.

Fig. 14.21

Class Privilege

The movie's title song, Roy Orbison's "Oh, Pretty Woman," plays on the sound-track at two moments of particular celebration of class privilege. We first hear it over shots of Vivian joyously shopping at an expensive boutique (figure 14.22). She is learning to look and act like an upper-class "pretty woman." We hear it again when her "dream" comes true. At the end of her week with Edward, she refuses his offer to set her up as his mistress in an expensive condo, telling him she wants "the fairy tale," implicitly marriage. They seem to have separated forever when he pulls up to her apartment building in his limousine and they embrace (figure 14.23).

She feels triumphant in both scenes. In the first, she is not only exulting in a stereotypical female activity – shopping for expensive clothes – but the activity also compensates for a degrading humili-ation. A day earlier, Edward had given her cash to buy an appro-priate dress for dinner with him. Still dressed in her street clothes, she entered a fashionable boutique. The shopwomen sneered at her and refused to serve her. One told her that she was obviously in the wrong place and asked her to leave.

Fig. 14.22

When Edward learns about this, he takes her to a comparable shop, tells the manager that he intends to spend an obscene amount of money on her, and demands some major "sucking up" on the part of the entire staff. They grovel with abandon, even to the extent that, when she says she wants the tie a salesman is wearing because it would be perfect for Edward, the manager immediately makes the salesman give it to her. After this, she stops in the store that snubbed her, identifies herself, and lets the saleswoman know that she made a "big mistake." The song, then, is associated with her rise into the pleasures of privilege.

When it plays for a second time, she rises from a comparable low. Before he pulls up, she feels she has lost Edward. She had told him

Fig. 14.23

Fig. 14.24

Fig. 14.25

that her fantasy was to be locked in a tower and to have a noble knight on a big horse come to rescue her. Although Edward is afraid of heights, he climbs her fire escape. He asks, "So what happened after he climbed up the tower and rescued her?" She replies, "She rescues him right back."

We see his chauffeur watching and beaming with joy (figure 14.24). He clearly likes them; he feels they belong together, that they both have "class." The film also has many shots of hotel employees looking at Edward and Vivian with pride (figure 14.25) – they all know class when they see it. The entire hotel staff, particularly the manager, functions as a kind of servant class; their lives revolve around catering to the wealthy, and the film develops no sense of class conflict or resentment. These people seem contented in their "place" and take pleasure in watching the upper class enjoying themselves in ways inaccessible to them.

But, to return to the final scene, how can Vivian "rescue" Edward? This goes to the heart of the film's notion of class. Edward clearly returns to her because he feels that she has something to offer that women of his own class do not. But what?

The "Need" for Middle-class Values

After Edward meets Mr Morse, an elderly shipbuilder who resists Edward's brutal corporate takeover, Vivian tells him she thinks he liked Morse. Edward replies that he never lets emotion interfere with business. She agrees, saying that she never gets involved when she turns tricks, that it makes sense to be like Edward, to stay numb and not get involved. He replies that they are similar, that they both "screw people for money." His phrasing suggests a growing unease with his life.

But things are changing. Later, after a fight, she leaves without taking the agreed-upon money he has placed on the bed. This moves him to ask her to return. Soon after this, Edward decides not to destroy Morse's company but to help him fulfill his dream of maintaining his company intact. He tells Morse, "I find myself in unfamiliar territory. I want to help you." He then goes to walk barefoot in the grass in a public park and, after that, he goes for Vivian.

What she has to offer Edward is commitment to the middle-class dream – the "best things" in life, which are of course depicted as beyond the power of money or class. By opening himself up to these things, Edward gets what he doesn't have, a loving mate (her) and a father figure (Morse). Edward's life had great wealth and power but was stereotypically empty. His father had recently died, but Edward had not seen him in fourteen and a half years and was not at the deathbed. In effect, he never had a loving father. But now, after

Edward refuses to destroy Morse's dream due to Vivian's influence, Morse places his hand on Edward's shoulder in a fatherly gesture and tells him that he is proud of him. Furthermore, Edward has an ex-wife, and his workaholic ways have estranged him from girlfriends, who complain that they spend more time talking with his secretary than with him. And, anyway, the women of his class are generally shown as catty and vicious. Now, however, Vivian offers love and family values, and she can even tie his tie because she used to do it for her grandfather. She has proved her commitment by being willing to give up a life of wealth when not offered in traditional terms of respectable marriage. Clearly, wealth is not enough, and money cannot buy happiness.

The film begins with a dark screen and we hear a voice say, "I don't care what they say, it's all about money." The first image we see is of hands and gold coins. The movie goes on, however, to indicate that "it" is not all about money. In fact, the movie implies that only by renouncing money will its characters find happiness. Edward stands to lose money by helping Mr Morse, but he will gain what the film asserts money cannot buy. But the film has it both ways. It exults in the privilege and excesses of wealth and, at the same time, indicates that the very wealth that provides that privilege threatens happiness. Similarly, the characters have it both ways. Both Edward and Vivian make gestures of sacrificing money for love and family, but they still wind up fabulously wealthy, and with a limo waiting.

The film presents both his and her life as equally exotic and distanced from "normal" life. He is able to spend astounding amounts of money on a single date with her – buying her expensive dresses, taking her to the airport in a limousine and then by private plane to San Francisco for an opera opening. She prostitutes herself, lives in desperate poverty, and learns that a fellow prostitute has been murdered and dumped in a garbage bin. Her room-mate steals the rent money to buy drugs and is so broke that she eats drink garnishes (such as orange slices and cherries) in a bar for nourishment. Yet Vivian and Edward take great pleasure from things as simple as a walk in the park. Thus, it is important that, later, when Edward makes the deal bonding him with Morse (and infuriating his greedy lawyer), he returns to the park, rolls his trousers up, and walks in the grass with bare feet. Implicitly, Edward does not lift Vivian up into the upper class but, rather, they meet in the middle, the only class able to sustain meaningful human contact.

"Fairy Tales" and Class

Is there anything wrong with this? It is not "real," but the film does not claim to be "real." In fact, it doubly announces itself as a dream: first, when Vivian sets the terms for their relationship as those of a fairy tale, and, secondly, by a street person who, early on and at the end of the film, walks around proclaiming that this is Hollywood, the place where everyone with dreams comes.

Although the movie declares itself a fairy tale, that does not mean it cannot reveal a great deal. Fairy tales have heroes and villains, gender roles, and social priorities just like "realistic" stories. The story of Snow White works out well for Snow White, but not for the queen, and the story of Little Red Riding Hood does not work out well for the wolf. For those characters, the stories hardly take on the fairy-tale connotations of dreams come true. The question to ask with *Pretty Woman* is whose dreams come true, why, and at whose expense?

Let's return to the two scenes over which the title song plays. Both appear to show Vivian triumphing across class barriers. Where class prejudice caused her to be denied the pleasures of extravagant shopping, she returned to indulge in it fully. Where she rejected a compromised life of wealth for her dream of "the fairy tale," she ultimately gets the fairy tale. Is she not, then, the "pretty woman," proving all class barriers irrelevant? Not really. While these scenes at first appear to erase class barriers, they really reinforce them, and with a vengeance.

After Vivian is rejected by the first boutique, she returns to her hotel and things get worse. The manager, recognizing her as a prostitute, tells her that she is inappropriate for the hotel, that she is there only by the grace of Edward's prestige, and that after Edward leaves, he does not want to see her there again. Beginning to cry, she shows him the money Edward gave her and describes her lack of success in getting a dress. He picks up the phone. She presumes he is calling the police but instead he is calling another boutique and arranging for her to be treated royally. She feels better, but her treatment has nothing to do with her. Rather, the manager wants Edward to be happy when he returns. At that moment, Vivian literally does not know whether she will be arrested or sent to Rodeo Drive. Her "triumph" has little to do with her except inasmuch as she is a pawn of those with class privilege.

When Edward takes her on the shopping spree the next day, all in the shop grovel to her in deference to him. At one point he even tells the manager not to direct his groveling toward him but toward her, and the manager instantly complies. At the end, the "rescue" is entirely in his hands. She has no alternatives and does not wait a second before rushing to him. And yet she says she will rescue him.

The film presents the things that count as being beyond class, as being inaccessible to those without the vision and courage to choose them. Vivian's room-mate, Kit, says that even when Vivian was on the street she did not really fit in. Kit is coarser and more aggressive and incapable of holding out for, or even understanding, her "dream." She has "no class." Stuckey, Edward's sleazy but wealthy lawyer, wants to ruthlessly destroy Morse's dream and even beats and tries to rape Vivian. He, like Kit, has "no class." Vivian and Edward, on the other hand, come to recognize what is important and are willing to sacrifice for it. They choose their class, and the employees at the hotel adoringly recognize it.

Class and Race

The employees, the servant class, appear happy with the way things are, and the film's representation of the way things are, as we have pointed out in previous chapters, involves not only class but other issues such as those of race and gender. Everyone who counts in this movie – Edward, Vivian, Kit, Stuckey, Mr Morse – is white. People of color only appear as contented members of the servant class or as street people. The manager is played by an Hispanic actor, the chauffeur by a black one, a carhop by an Asian one. The film reinforces traditional stereotypes of the upper classes as being exclusively white and the servant classes as being people of color. At one point, Edward is on the phone talking to his lawyer and Vivian is in the bathtub, singing along with a Prince song and mimicking an ethnic accent. The lawyer asks who is singing and Edward answers, "Housekeeping is singing," indicating that only someone of color and of the servant class would be interested in a rock song by a black artist. Edward, by comparison, plays classical music on the piano and takes Vivian to the opera. This film places its people of color very much in their "place," and that place is happy servitude. Furthermore, the races do not mix.

Class and Gender

The film is not only reactionary in its presentation of class and race but also in its construction of gender. To return finally to the Orbison song, if one listens to it in a distracted fashion on the soundtrack, it simply seems to reinforce the notion of Vivian's beauty and happiness. But the song actually conveys a male point of view, a male who is lonely and desperate for the attentions of the pretty woman who holds power over him, whom he pathetically hopes is "lonely just like me." When she turns her attentions to him, he is ecstatic. Nothing could be farther from Vivian's situation in this film where women are secretaries, servants, or prostitutes – all positions of power are exclusively male. Even Vivian's fairy-tale dream places her in a totally powerless situation awaiting rescue by a strong man. Edward is happy to find a father figure, but no mention is made of a mother figure. Furthermore, Mr Morse is trying to groom his grandson for his business. No mention is made of his wife, daughter, or granddaughter.

In the shopping scene over which the Orbison song runs, Vivian's pleasure exists because Edward wills it; at the end, it is his decision to return. Her very value comes from his approval, and we see this depicted in a single shot. When they go to the opera, it is her first. He tells her that a person's response to her first opera reveals whether she has it in her blood. We see her watching and enjoying it, but the real focus of the scene is him, sitting next to her and silently watching her in an approving way (figure 14.26). This

Fig. 14.26

Fig. 14.27

validates her taste, her value. He has set up the terms for approval and then he gives his approval. She has nothing to say about it, and the film indicates that that is the way things should be. In an earlier scene, while he is taking her shopping, she says she is nervous because she fears everyone is watching her. He smugly tells her not to be concerned, because they are all watching him. Within the power structure of the film, he is right.

After the success of *Pretty Woman*, Julia Roberts became one of Hollywood's most popular female stars, a fact that gave her considerable control over her career. In 1999 she appeared in *Notting Hill*, which in many ways uses the same formula and class presumptions as *Pretty Woman*, but with the genders reversed. In *Notting Hill* Roberts plays the most popular movie actress in the world; Hugh Grant plays a simple bookstore owner. They meet when she wanders into his shop to purchase a book. She has a boyfriend, played by Alec Baldwin, also a successful film star, but corrupted by success and power. Arguments are constantly made in the film that Roberts and Grant can never be together because of the gap in class between them, but the film contrives to show that they have found "true love," and they end up together. Furthermore, the "fairy-tale ending" happens when she literally picks him out of a crowd, when he thought he had lost all hope. It is a gesture that appears to erase class barriers in favor of love, but, as in *Pretty Woman*, it is the person with the power who does it, thus reinforcing those barriers.

Pretty Woman contrasts upper- and lower-class lives and implies that they really have little to do with one another, that true happiness comes outside of class. Only with Mr Morse's statement that he wants his company kept intact because he cares about the lives of those who work for him is there any indication that there might be any relationship at all between the power of the upper class and the deprivation of the lower one. Aside from that, the relationship is more like the one implied during a polo game. After the game, we see the wealthy spectators go onto the field in their expensive clothes and high heels in a traditional and playful gesture of "stomping the divots," or restoring the clumps of earth the horses have overturned (figure 14.27). One member of the polo club even takes Vivian's shoe to polish it, citing this also as a tradition. This is work as a game and seems the closest any of these people can come to real labor. The upper class seems to have no relation to the working class. Nothing could be further from the case with *The People Under the Stairs*.

The People Under the Stairs (1991)

Although fans of horror films attend them to be scared and entertained, the movies also often engage important social and cultural issues. Put simply, things that scare us tell us much about ourselves and our society. In *The People Under the Stairs* (1991), class issues lie at the center of what is horrific. Unlike *Pretty Woman*, which disturbingly reaffirms many traditional notions about class, *The People Under the Stairs* critiques such notions and offers strong social criticism. The film tells the story of an inner-city family that is evicted from its apartment after being three days late with the rent. The landlord wants to clear the building so he can raze it and replace it with more lucrative condominiums. Poindexter, a boy about 12 years old, is talked into robbing the landlord's house in order to get money.

The Ghetto

The beginning of the film stresses the economic definition of class, carefully delineating the upper-middle-class owners from the poor people living in what the film repeatedly calls the ghetto. At the beginning of the film, Leroy, a man who apparently is a family friend, characterizes the landlord as an evil man who, despite his knowledge that Poindexter's mother is critically ill, coldly evicts the family: "He knows; he don't care." Even the mother's illness is directly related to money concerns. Leroy tells Poindexter, "You know your mama got a cancer in her she can't afford to have taken out . . . thing any doctor could take out just like that, but you ain't got no money." When Leroy describes his burglary plans to Poindexter, he does so without naming the target of the plan. He simply describes the victim as someone who "deserves to be robbed . . . someone who don't care nothing about families or about the neighborhood. He just wants to bring the wrecking ball in so he can line his pockets." "Who you talking about?" the boy asks. "The landlord, that's who," comes the reply. Leroy adds that the landlord owns "one-half the buildings in the ghetto."

The entire plot of this film, then, is set in motion by class issues. The first characters we see are the "have-nots" who live amid such poverty that they cannot afford the medical treatment they need to save their lives. Even before we see them, the "haves" are described as coldly calculating business people who lack human decency and who own a disproportionate part of society's wealth.

Fig. 14.28

The Middle Class

Nearly the entire film takes place in two settings: the ghetto apartment (figure 14.28) and the landlord's home (figure 14.29). The contrast turns more on the "families" that live within those homes than on the startling difference between the impoverished apartment and the spacious two-story house. The occupants of neither, it turns out, are a traditional family. The ghetto apartment appears

Fig. 14.29

Fig. 14.30

to be shared by Poindexter and his mother, both of whom are African Americans, and Ruby, who has children. Although Ruby could be Poindexter's sister, this is never made clear, and she looks Hispanic rather than African American. No husbands or fathers are present or even referred to, although Leroy's place in the group is not clear. What is clear are the strong bonds of familial love between the ghetto family members, especially Poindexter and his sick mother. The boy will do anything for his mother, and the scenes between the two as she lies on her deathbed are genuinely affecting (figure 14.30). By contrast, the landlord lives with what initially appears to be his wife and daughter, Alice. In place of any affection for either of her parents, Alice reveals only terrified obedience. Indeed, her relationship to her "mother" is nearly the reverse of Poindexter's relationship with his mother: Poindexter saves his mother's life while Alice helps kill hers. But we learn near the end of the film that the upper-middle-class family is far from what it seems to be. The man and woman, who have no names and who simply call each other Daddy and Momma, are really brother and sister; Alice, whom they kidnapped, is not their daughter.

Incest and the Middle Class

Fig. 14.31

The white middle-class family is characterized by an obsessive turning inward, the logical result of which is incest. The film represents the suburban family as a twisted parody of its traditionally affluent normality. The house, a former funeral home with connotations of death, is constructed not only to keep outsiders out but also to prevent those inside from escaping. It is both a fortress and a prison and, as such, symbolizes the bizarre extremes to which the upper-middle class has gone to protect itself from the lower-class elements. All the wires on the windows and the electronic locks on the doors recall the manner in which many American homes have for decades tried to keep burglars and criminals out. Far from being a bizarre aberration, the unnamed upper-middle-class "family" in this film is a logical extension of widely held middle-class values and beliefs.

The manner in which the house and its occupants parody the norm becomes crystal clear in the scene in which the police come to investigate reports of child abuse. Daddy dresses in a sweater and sports cap and smokes a pipe (figure 14.31) while Momma serves coffee and cookies to the police officers (figure 14.32). The iconography of the scene recalls that of the cheerful, supportive, suburban families of such 1950s' and 1960s' sitcoms as *Leave it to Beaver*, *Father Knows Best*, and *The Ozzie and Harriet Show*.

The idea that the middle classes have turned inward in a bizarre effort to save themselves achieves literal expression in the many

Fig. 14.32

images of Daddy running around his house shooting his shotgun at the inner walls! The people referred to in the film's title are "children" who have disappointed Momma and Daddy and have had their tongues cut off and been imprisoned in the basement. One of them, Roach, has escaped and lives in the spaces between the walls. Daddy hunts him through his own house (figure 14.33), blowing gaping holes in the walls where he thinks he has heard Roach. In a parodic version of the manner in which many Americans have bought guns to protect themselves from intruders, Daddy has turned the gun inward, hunting someone who haunts his house. Such a context of sealing the family off from the outside world in an effort to preserve it has an ideal symbolic parallel in incest. Incest, of course, is a sexual turning in to replace society's mandate that sexual relations take place with those outside the family. The incest taboo, which forms the cornerstone of society, ensures a healthy, socially interactive culture. It is the ultimate paradox that in this film, the upper-middle-class family, while trying to protect itself from the lower classes, has destroyed the very thing it seeks to protect. The "normal" family and the house in which it lives has become a demented group of prisoners within their own fortress.

Fig. 14.33

Fig. 14.34

At the beginning of the film we see Daddy sitting in front of the fireplace eating a huge rack of ribs (figure 14.34), which, by the film's conclusion, we can only conclude are human ribs. Near the end of the film, we see his mouth red with blood as Leroy, an intruder who has become a victim, hangs on a hook like a slab of meat. Cannibalism is the perfect symbol of eating, which correlates with the incestuous family that shoots up the interior of its own home. Everything has turned in on itself.

Race and Class

Thus far, we have described the main conflict in the film as one of economic and social class; the upper-middle-class family exploits the poor people and erects a barricade between them. One class belongs in the inner city and the other in the suburbs, with the fortified home serving as a barricade to keep out the ghetto-dwellers, who try to break in. While this class issue is the film's main premise, it is of necessity linked to issues of race, since people of color have long been the occupants of America's inner cities and whites the occupants of the suburbs. *The People Under the Stairs* is an excellent film to demonstrate how important issues of race and class are inextricably linked together.

Near the beginning of the film, when Daddy receives news of what has happened to his liquor store, he remarks, "Some niggers robbed the store." Although that is the only time in the film that we hear the racial epithet, it foregrounds the connection between race and class: the lower classes are not just poorer, they are composed of racial minorities. This theme reappears when the police investigate the mysterious van parked at Daddy and Momma's home. Momma tells the officers, "It's just there's been an awful lot of robberies lately. The neighborhood's changing. Has us all a bit on edge." The phrase "the neighborhood's changing" has more meaning than just economic; it's a phrase white Americans have used for decades to complain of ethnic and racial minorities moving into their neighborhoods.

The upper-middle class in *The People Under the Stairs* is synonymous with the white upper-middle class. The film equates preserving the ideal of the middle-class family with preserving whiteness. All others must be kept out of the neighborhood. This notion of the middle class is inherently racist. Once again, this is taken to such extremes that, when Poindexter first meets Alice, he realizes that she has never seen a black person before. When he refers to himself as a "brother," she mistakenly thinks he is talking about himself as her sibling. Indeed, Alice has no notion of any neighborhood, since her entire life has been directed inward. Taken to its logical extreme, the white middle-class desire to keep "others" out would mean a world where they could raise their children without any awareness of people of color.

Indeed, the people of the title, confined to the cellar, are exaggeratedly white and pale. They serve as a reminder of the connection between racial whiteness and the perverse goings on within the home: this is a particularly white form of class madness. Not surprisingly, Momma and Daddy have a particular fear of the developing relationship between Alice and Poindexter, two children on the verge of puberty. When they realize that Poindexter is in the house, Momma says, "He's in there right now with our little Angel." Later, making her fear of miscegenation even more explicit, she cries out, "She did it with him, I know."

Fig. 14.35

The end of the film celebrates the collapse of both an economic notion of class and a racial notion of class. Poindexter discovers a vault in the basement with piles of paper money and gold coins (figure 14.35). "No wonder there's no money in the ghetto," Poindexter exclaims in a line that summarizes the film's critique of a grossly unjust economic system. All that money in the basement of a white upper-middle-class home is one of the true horrors of this horror film. But the film further indicts this economic system. Daddy sadistically tells Poindexter about the pleasure he has had thousands of times counting the money and rolling it through his fingers. This money, exploited from the people of color in the ghetto who need it, is simply hoarded for the perverse pleasures of its owner: it serves no social function and leads to no social good.

The final images of the film bring all these themes together. Poindexter blows up Daddy in the vault, in the process blowing the money sky high so that it rains down on the people from the ghetto who have come demanding justice (figure 14.36). Furthermore, the excessively white people from under the stairs run outside and

Fig. 14.36

mingle with the people of color. All of the barriers have been broken down in this utopian vision of the collapse of class difference: the people from the ghetto have broken out of their neighborhood and the people under the stairs have broken out of their imprisonment within their house, while the money that has been so unjustly gained and perversely hoarded falls on those who need and deserve it.

Gender and Class

The end of the *The People Under the Stairs* also celebrates something else – the formation of a couple in the figures of Alice and Poindexter, and this points to how gender issues as well as race issues are linked to class. The film is in some ways as much a parable about gender as it is about class and race. At the beginning of the film, Poindexter's mother, referring to her illness, tells him, "You're the man of the house now." Poindexter's decision to join Leroy in the robbery plan is itself a form of assuming masculine responsibility for bringing money home. When Leroy, Poindexter, and Spenser, the third accomplice, case the house for the break-in, Poindexter fails in his mission to get inside the house. Spenser responds, "Send a boy to do a man's job, that's all you got." Later, when Leroy breaks open the door to the house, he refers to it in sexual slang, and when Leroy and Poindexter get inside the house, Leroy tells Poindexter about the awkward age he is at in terms of having sexual relations.

Fig. 14.37

As in many Hollywood films, a heterosexual couple is formed at the film's conclusion. Poindexter's relationship with Alice actually begins before he enters the house when he catches a glimpse of her watching him from a second-story window. The two are quickly paired and, after Poindexter escapes from Daddy, he returns to rescue Alice. When he succeeds in getting the money for the surgery that will save his mother's life, he also rescues Alice from her nightmare life, in the process outsmarting and killing Daddy. Consequently, Poindexter proves his masculinity to both his mother and Alice; the final scene of Poindexter in the film shows him united with Alice in a manner that suggests they are now a couple (figure 14.37). This coupling also relates to the film's racial themes. Earlier, we see Poindexter and Alice embracing (figure 14.38). The prospect of couples like Poindexter and Alice having children destroys the incestuousness of the white middle class and suggests a union of the ghetto with suburbia and white with black.

Although in the last three chapters we separated gender, race, and class issues for pedagogical purposes, all three must be studied together. As *The People Under the Stairs* so well illustrates, we risk simplifying films if we separate these issues. In this case, a film that offers an intelligent critique of race and class issues also reinforces conventional gender structures; an active boy proves his manhood

Fig. 14.38

by rescuing a passive victim who becomes his girlfriend. Many films are complexly contradictory, containing both progressive and conventional or even reactionary elements.

As we have stressed throughout this book, we can never stop thinking critically about movies if we want to maximize what we can learn from them. In the next chapter, we summarize the many critical methods and skills that we have learned by applying them to *Citizen Kane* (1941), the film most often canonized as the greatest of American movies. We will then conclude with a chapter on the ways in which new technologies are fundamentally changing the world of film as we know it.

SELECTED READINGS

Since film studies does not have a body of literature on class comparable to that on gender and race, we have relied upon our own ideas and analyses in this chapter. Those interested in further reading should refer to Linda Dittmar's "All that Hollywood Allows: Film and the Working Class," *Radical Teacher*, 46 (Spring 1995). Dittmar notes the scarcity of materials on class issues in film studies and outlines a course unit on the representation of the working class in film. The Tonya Harding and Nancy Kerrigan affair is analyzed from a variety of critical perspectives, including that of economic and social class, in *Women on Ice: Feminist Responses to the Tonya Harding/Nancy Kerrigan Spectacle*, ed. Cynthia Baughman (New York: Routledge, 1995).

15

Citizen Kane: AN ANALYSIS

Citizen Kane

From the moment of its appearance in 1941, Orson Welles's *Citizen Kane* has been **canonized** in American cinema. This means that, just as no one can study nineteenth-century American literature without reading Herman Melville's *Moby Dick* or study nineteenth-century classical music without listening to Beethoven's Ninth Symphony, no one can study American cinema without seeing *Citizen Kane*. Such canonization, while perhaps inevitable, is both good and bad. On the positive side, it brings attention to major works and artists and ensures that they will be of lasting importance within their culture. On the negative side, such canons are just as noteworthy for who and what is excluded as they are for who or what is included. Women, minorities, and despised genres, for example, are likely to be excluded, while the works of white male artists working in recognized "high" art genres are likely to be included. Beethoven, Melville, and Welles are all clear examples of the latter.

In this book, we have included a number of canonized films, such as *Rashomon, Rules of the Game, Nosferatu, The Searchers, Psycho*, and *Umberto D*, as well as a number of virtually overlooked films, such as *The People Under the Stairs*. We have also included recently canonized films, such as *Jungle Fever* and *Boyz N the Hood*, that reveal a current critical context in which the predominantly white male canons of the past are being challenged and augmented by adding people of color, women, and gays and lesbians to the list. We have also included a number of fairly recent box-office hits like *Jurassic Park, The Sixth Sense, Fatal Attraction*, and *Pretty Woman*. We have chosen this wide variety of movies for two reasons. First, an introduction to film should include many kinds of films. Second, by including many recent and commercially successful films, we hope to engage the interests of readers by referring to films that many will have seen and loved while, at the same time, expanding their repertoire with older, more obscure titles. In the end, the individual films are less important than the critical methods used to analyze them, since all of us can use those skills to think about any movies.

Canonization risks another danger. Once something is canonized, we are likely to place it on a pedestal and simply revere it. The main thread that has run through this book, however, has been the need to think critically about all movies, and that includes the canonized ones. Which brings us to *Citizen Kane*. The purpose of this chapter is to summarize the critical issues and methods of the previous chapters by analyzing one film. Obviously, we could use any film. By choosing *Citizen Kane*, we hope to show how an understanding of this most canonized of American movies not only justifies some of the high critical praise it has received but also requires a keen awareness of its limitations. The circumstances surrounding the making and reception of this film also make it uniquely suited to our purposes of touching on nearly all of the many issues we have raised.

In the first part of the chapter, we situate the film in relation to its makers, audiences, reception contexts, and other arts and media; in the second part, we supply a detailed textual analysis of the film, pointing to both its formal achievements and its ideological limitations. Since a detailed analysis concludes this chapter, early references to the film's plot and characters are brief and assume some familiarity with the film. Those who have not seen the film might want to read ahead to the "Narrative Structure" section to familiarize themselves with major plot patterns.

Authorship

Forty years after *Citizen Kane* appeared, critic Pauline Kael ignited an **authorship** controversy over it in a *New Yorker* article by claiming that Herman J. Mankiewicz, co-screenwriter with Welles, was responsible for much more of the screenplay than had hitherto been acknowledged. She also raised the issue of claims for Mankiewicz as author of the film itself.

We have discussed the complexity of film authorship, as well as the inadequacy of the notion of simply attributing it to screenwriters, in chapters 4 and 9. Kael was correct in claiming that Mankiewicz's contributions to the script had historically been slighted but, given the nature of film authorship, even if Mankiewicz had written the entire script, Welles's claim to authorship of the film would remain intact.

Welles has become a model for authorship studies, and one could hardly find a better instance to support such an approach than *Citizen Kane*, in which he receives formal **credit** as director, star, co-writer, and producer (figure 15.1). His work on the film (he was twenty-five when it was released) reinforced his "boy wonder" reputation as an innovative creator and performer in both theater

Fig. 15.1

and radio. Although a first-time director, he came to the film with a contract giving him almost unprecedented creative control (including final cut). The film was, and is, widely perceived as a distinctive achievement reflective of his unique artistic vision.

Before further outlining reasons for Welles's pre-eminence in authorship studies, it is useful to point to qualifications for such claims. Commentators have often discussed his authorship more in terms appropriate to a poet or novelist – totally creating the work – than in terms suited to a dominant participant in a collaborative process. Welles did a great deal on the film but he also wanted to be seen as having done virtually everything and that is not the case. Historical evidence indicates that, both at the time of the film's production and after Kael's article appeared, he tried to diminish Mankiewicz's role in the screenplay and reinforce the image of himself as near-total creator.

Fig. 15.2

But he did not make the film alone. He worked with top Hollywood talent, such as cinematographer Gregg Toland, and some of the innovative deep-focus photography for which *Citizen Kane* is often cited can be seen in earlier Toland films with which Welles had nothing to do, such as John Ford's *The Long Voyage Home* (1940). Furthermore, the music, art direction, special effects, and editing were done by accomplished industry professionals.

Aside from the fundamentally collaborative nature of commercial filmmaking and the historical contributions of personnel involved, the film's very construction and look, so often cited as daring and innovative, draws from pre-existent traditions. The faux newsreel chronicling Kane's life that appears near the beginning of the film imitates recognizable newsreel practices of the time (figure 15.2); the expressionistic look of the opening Xanadu sequence (figure 15.3) uses German expressionistic practices of the 1920s; and so on. The very collage-like structure of the narrative was both new for its time and evocative of pre-existent styles. Although Welles certainly used many of these things in innovative ways, he did not create them. In fact, he acknowledged his debt to past work when he said he learned how to make the movie by repeatedly watching John Ford's *Stagecoach* (1939, figure 15.4).

Fig. 15.3

Citizen Kane is often cited as the one film project in which Welles's authorial genius was in full bloom. The remainder of his career was plagued with troubled, unfinished projects. His authorial image shifted from that of a boy wonder to that of a tragic, wasted genius. Many theories have attempted to explain his decline but, whether he was a visionary too innovative for a constrictive studio system that cast him aside or the victim of his own excesses and ego, most of the theories fit the pattern of the troubled "great man," the Romantic genius brought down by a world unfit for him or by his own human limitations.

Fig. 15.4

Fig. 15.5

When the *auteur* theory became prominent in the 1950s, Welles was commonly cited as a pre-eminent example. He was categorized as an innovative artist whose work in an admittedly collaborative system distinguished itself by numerous stylistic and thematic continuities. *Citizen Kane* provided an ideal illustration. While made within the **studio system**, it used a number of non-traditional formal strategies in its sound, lighting, camerawork, and cutting. It also used a cast largely new to Hollywood but drawn from theater and radio. Such deviations from standard filmmaking style and practice were cited as evidence of Welles's individual authorship.

Furthermore, the film reveals thematic concerns that pervade Welles's career. Charles Foster Kane is a tormented and doomed figure of excessive male power played by Welles. Such figures recur again and again in films written and directed by Welles; examples include Franz Kindler in *The Stranger* (1946), Macbeth in *Macbeth* (1948), Mr Arkadin in *Mr Arkadin* (1955), and Hank Quinlan in *Touch of Evil* (1958, figure 15.5).

A flamboyant and diversely creative figure in the Romantic mode, Welles cultivated the biographical image of himself as the brilliant author of his works. We must resist such a notion of the author, however, if we are to gain critical insight. Attributing authorship of the film to Welles is not equivalent to hailing him as a genius who had universal insight into the human condition. Far from it. It is simply to acknowledge his unifying creative presence in the making of the film, which, like all others, was caught within many of the assumptions of the times in which it was made.

Genre

Citizen Kane does everything it can to avoid the demeaning connotations of the term "genre entertainment." In chapter 5 we discussed genre's use of **convention** and **invention** and *Citizen Kane* systematically tries to avoid the conventions of its time and foreground its inventiveness, its uniqueness. It presents itself as a serious, artistically constructed, fictional biography with great contemporary relevance. Just as it deviates from traditional formal practice, it also deviates from traditional genre practice.

Fig. 15.6

The opening illustrates this. At first, it looks and sounds like a horror movie. We see expressionistic shots of the exterior of Xanadu with a number of exotic-looking or jungle-like or mysterious environments, underscored by Bernard Hermann's dirge-like music. We then see the dark, gothic interiors of Xanadu and Kane's death (figure 15.6), although we have no idea of who he is or what his dying word "Rosebud" means. It is all somber, mysterious, and ominous. But then the film abruptly switches into a different genre entirely, the blaring sound and rapid-fire narration of a newsreel, incorporating different kinds of faux documentary footage of Kane's life from what appear to be professional silent and sound newsreels

Fig. 15.7

Fig. 15.8

Fig. 15.9

to "hidden camera" shots of the elderly Kane (figures 15.7 and 15.8). The newsreel is accompanied by blaring, military music. Now, nothing is mysterious, everything is clearly presented and redundantly interpreted for us by the newsreel's narrator. The expressionistic conventions of the horror genre have given way to those of the newsreel.

Then the newsreel stops and we see its makers unsatisfied with it (figure 15.9); they feel it needs a new "angle" to make it engaging to its audiences. They decide to search for what Kane meant by "Rosebud," and the film then switches into a kind of detective story with the reporter, Mr Thompson, pursuing clue after fruitless clue. We have, then, the styles of three different and largely incompatible genres evoked early in *Citizen Kane*, but this collage, by evoking many genres, allies itself with none.

Citizen Kane does resemble some widely known **genres** of the time, perhaps the most obvious being the historical biography. Such films tended to show a past or contemporary figure involved in some "great" and heroic enterprise against a background of historical change. They also showcased *tour-de-force* performances by prominent actors, often using a great deal of make-up: for example, Paul Muni in *The Story of Louis Pasteur* (1936), *The Life of Emile Zola* (1937), and *Juarez* (1939); Edward G. Robinson in *Dr Ehrlich's Magic Bullet* (1940); Raymond Massey in *Abe Lincoln in Illinois* (1940); Alexander Knox in *Wilson* (1944); and Spencer Tracy in *Edison, the Man* (1940).

Citizen Kane was widely considered to be a thinly veiled biography of the still-living newspaper magnate William Randolph Hearst, but it deviates from the biographical genre in being more of an exposé than an inspirational biography. Furthermore, it does not give a single, defining meaning to Kane's life but rather provides barely resolved diversity. However, like the inspirational films, it is also rooted in a masterful acting performance with a great deal of make-up against a changing historical background.

The movie also bears comparison with the newspaper film, like *The Front Page* (1931), *It Happened One Night* (1934), *Meet John Doe* (1941), *Nothing Sacred* (1937), and *His Girl Friday* (1939, figure 15.10), but newspaper films

Fig. 15.10

Fig. 15.11

Fig. 15.12

Fig. 15.13

usually focus on investigative reporters and on getting the "scoop," and this does neither. It deals little with traditional reporting and is rather a tale of media power and, ironically, the media's inability to explain someone's life to us. After reading a newspaper article about the life of a famous person or seeing a newsreel of that life, we might think we know who they are but, according to this film, that is a simplistic delusion.

Finally, *Citizen Kane* has often been compared with *The Power and the Glory* (1933), a dark study of a callous tycoon's rise to power that uses a flashback structure. Not really part of a widely recognized genre, this film, written by a writer–director like Welles, Preston Sturges, does bear a number of significant resemblances to *Citizen Kane*.

Citizen Kane, perhaps because of its deviation from mainstream practice, has remained aloof from much genre criticism; it does not easily fit any genre. Unlike a film such as *Stagecoach* (1939), which developed a reputation as a classic Western, *Citizen Kane* has developed the reputation of a "great film," but not a "great fictional biography" or a "great newspaper film," and it has not produced a recognizable tradition of similar films. It is significant that, when Ted Turner, then the owner of the TNT television network, received notoriety for colorizing the films in his library for broadcast, the one film he said he would not colorize was *Citizen Kane*, implicitly classifying it in the popular mind as unique. Critics generally respond to genre entertainment as being different from and, at least implicitly, inferior to serious art. From this perspective, the manner in which *Citizen Kane* does not fully conform to any highly popular genres probably relates to the serious reputation it has as being a one-of-a-kind artistic accomplishment.

Audiences and Reception

In *Citizen Kane*, the title character is characterized as both a hero and a villain, as both a fascist and a communist, among other contradictory classifications. The differences in the descriptions of Kane reveal as much about those describing him – from Mr Thatcher to Mr Bernstein to Susan Alexander to Jed Leland (figures 15.11– 15.14) – as they do about Kane. They evoke different Kanes, and the film lets us know enough about the describers to show why they do so. The film's treatment of Kane is thus analogous to the manner in which different audiences see different things in the same film.

The **reception context** for this movie was complex and dramatic. Part of it was shaped before the film's release by Welles's reputation as a boy wonder and a ground-breaking genius in theater and radio, not only someone with prestigious artistic credentials but also with enough of a hold on the popular audience to have created a highly publicized panic with his *A War of the Worlds* radio broadcast less than three years earlier. Film was another new form for him to conquer, and *Citizen Kane* would be that film. At the same time there was substantial resentment against Welles within the Hollywood community for the virtually unprecedented power that his RKO studio contract gave him and the fact that much of the performance talent he brought in for the film consisted of Hollywood newcomers. Some considered Welles a brash interloper from New York who deserved to be cut down to size. Consequently, there was a pre-release climate hoping for the film to be either a major success or a resounding failure.

Fig. 15.14

Two responses dominated the movie's release. One was the widespread critical praise given to it as bold and artistically significant; the other was its reputation as a veiled attack on the newspaper magnate William Randolph Hearst. The powerful Hearst syndicate refused to advertise the film (and, for a short time, all RKO films) in its newspapers and even tried to have all prints destroyed before release. Louella Parsons, one of Hollywood's most powerful gossip columnists and a Hearst employee, stormed out of a private screening while the film was still running. Hearst purportedly attempted, in a number of ways, to tarnish Welles and his film.

A third aspect of the film's reception involved the industry and had nothing to do with either the critical response or with Hearst. Hollywood set designers canonized it throughout the 1940s as a model of how to give a film an expensive "look" on a limited budget (figure 15.15).

The Hearst opposition and the critical acclaim generated considerable publicity for the film in major cities but, fairly soon after its release, another aspect of its reception became all too evident – outside the big cities, people were not attending the film. The reasons are complex. Some distributors purportedly refused to book it in their theaters out of fear of Hearst. Some people purportedly felt that it simply was not a film for mainstream audiences; its non-linear, quasi-resolved and downbeat narrative, its experimental techniques, its largely unsympathetic main character, and lack of a romantic subplot probably alienated popular audiences. Furthermore, although it was nominated for nine Academy Awards, it only received one (best original screenplay). The poor Academy Award showing may have reflected industry antagonism to Welles and denied the film the box-office boost that Academy Award recognition can sometimes give a film.

RKO declared a $150,000 loss on the film in 1942. Not only was the movie played very little in the United States between 1942 and 1956 but its critical reputation also diminished. However, when released in France in 1946, it was a critical success and, shortly thereafter, André Bazin and the *Cahiers du Cinéma* critics made it and Welles a cornerstone of the *auteur* theory. After 1960, *Citizen Kane*

Fig. 15.15

began to develop a reputation as one of the greatest films of all time, perhaps *the* greatest film of all time, in a number of international polls. It has since been canonized in academic circles as a prestigious film and is almost universally taught in film courses and written about in academic texts, like this one.

Film Theory

One of the above-mentioned reception contexts of *Citizen Kane* was its 1946 première in Paris where a young critic named André Bazin saw it. A few years later, Bazin published his first book on Welles, the first monograph ever devoted to the films of a single director. It is not in this *auteurist* context that Bazin's response to the film had its biggest impact but, rather, in his later highly influential essays on the nature of cinema in which *Citizen Kane* figured prominently. Bazin, as discussed in chapter 11, became the proponent of what he termed "neorealism" and of a style of filmmaking associated with long takes with moving camera and **deep focus cinematography**. Bazin championed the films of Vittorio de Sica in Italy, Jean Renoir in France, and Orson Welles in the United States.

Citizen Kane held a particularly important place for Bazin for a variety of reasons. As a Hollywood film, it abandoned the usual invisible style of editing in favor of what at times was an elaborate reliance on extremely long held shots with, as we shall see below, entire scenes constructed out of a few such shots. This style was of theoretical importance to Bazin because it preserved spatial and temporal continuity, meaning that all the space and time within a scene are presented. Nothing is cut out because it is boring and unimportant. Bazin argued that this kind of filmmaking gave spectators the opportunity to perceive the fictional world of the film in its wholeness and decide for themselves what was important. The dominant style of filmmaking determines what is important ahead of time, elides the insignificant, and then cuts up the rest in a manner that tells the spectator what is the important action, reaction, or dialogue at that particular moment.

Bazin became internationally renowned as a film theorist, and the manner in which he hailed *Citizen Kane* as forming part of a significant trend in post-World War II cinema became a dominant context in which the film was viewed. Along with such films as Eisenstein's *Potemkin*, *Citizen Kane* is one of the key films invoked and referred to in film theory debates about such crucial issues as realism in the cinema. It is also rewarding when examined with reference to a number of other issues discussed in this book, such as that of film acting.

Actors and Stars

Citizen Kane provides good examples of differences between actors and stars. Welles is a model of an actor in the stage tradition. He never established a solid persona in films but rather, like Laurence Olivier or Dustin Hoffman, appeared in a multitude of diverse roles. And, like Olivier, he never became a star who could draw large audiences. By contrast, the movie contains a film star, but in a very minor, uncredited role. Alan Ladd, who appears briefly as a reporter at the end of the film (figure 15.16), went on to become one of Hollywood's top stars of the 1940s and 1950s, mainly in urban tough-guy films and, after *Shane* (1953), Westerns. While he had a limited acting range, he later developed a highly marketable star persona, more so than anyone else in *Citizen Kane*.

Fig. 15.16

Although *Citizen Kane* was made at the height of the studio **star system**, it featured no stars. In fact, it was the first film for many of the actors, including Welles, who came mainly from radio and theater. Furthermore, aside from Welles, no actor featured in the film would achieve film stardom, although many (like Joseph Cotton, Agnes Moorehead, Everett Sloane, and Ruth Warrick) would have substantial careers in film and television.

Welles's performance in the film is a pyrotechnical one. He is on screen for most of the film and ages about half a century, from a young man to a very old one. He constantly and convincingly changes his appearance, through make-up, body shape and posture, and voice (figures 15.17 and 15.18), and such an ability has often been cited as one mark of a certain kind of "great" actor. Nothing could be further from a film star with a consistent persona such as Alan Ladd, who looked and spoke very much the same not only within any given film but from film to film. Ladd thus appeared to be playing the same character or "himself" over and over.

Fig. 15.17

But, unlike Ladd, Welles also directed himself. Many actors have long relationships with directors, and a few, like Charles Chaplin, Laurence Olivier, and Clint Eastwood, have even directed themselves. Welles's multiple roles of director, writer, producer, and actor, here and in other films, combined with his history of comparable involvement and success in radio and theater as well as his powerful visual and aural dramatic presence, bring to his acting a larger-than-life creative presence.

Fig. 15.18

Citizen Kane, released in 1941, was the high point of Welles's acting career. By the late 1940s he had more or less left Hollywood and spent much of his time in Europe, acting in American and European films as well as on stage and in television. Some of his roles, such as Harry Lime in *The Third Man* (1949, figure 15.19), garnered him critical accolades, but he also developed the reputation of a wasted genius and appeared primarily in supporting roles. He became obese in the 1950s, which added to his "larger than life" image, but also to his dissipated one. One critic cruelly commented of his presence in *Falstaff* (1966) that he may have been the first actor in history too fat to play Falstaff. Yet his image, in

Fig. 15.19

which *Citizen Kane* played a legendary role, continued to command a great deal of prestige, and his roles included famous men of history (*A Man for All Seasons*, 1966) or villains (*Casino Royale*, 1966). Having attained the status of a cultural icon, he also appeared frequently on television talk shows and even wine commercials as himself.

Film and the Other Arts

The opening sequences of *Citizen Kane* with its expressionistic shots of Xanadu, followed by the newsreel, clearly establish this as a film using the formal properties unique to the form. To an extent, the film can be seen as Welles's way of announcing to his audience that, even though he came from the theater and radio, he was not going to approach this film as either an illustrated radio drama or a filmed play; he was going to produce a uniquely cinematic work.

Language of any kind has little to do with the first sequence, aside from the "No Trespassing" sign outside Xanadu and the spoken word "Rosebud." The effect is visual and aural. The centrality that language holds in fiction, radio, and theater has little relevance here. The newsreel sequence has, to the contrary, too much language, language that is soon declared by characters within the film to be inadequate. The final revelation, that "Rosebud" is Kane's childhood sled now being burned, is told visually, the only language being the word on the sleigh itself (figure 15.20).

The complex visual and sound texturing of this film extensively uses formal properties that differentiate it from the other arts. Although Welles was at the time a renowned stage actor and director, no one could mistake *Citizen Kane* for a recording of a stage performance. Its patterns of montage and camera movements, for example, create a unique cinematic space far removed from stage space and one in which acting functions rather differently from in the theater.

Welles was also known as an innovator in radio, itself a new form when he entered it, and in theater. He had staged the widely discussed black *Macbeth*, set in Haiti, for the Negro Theatre in Harlem in 1936 as well as the modern-dress, anti-fascist *Julius Caesar* in 1937. As he did in films, he sought creative control and commonly served multiple functions in both radio and theater, often including acting, writing, and directing.

Its uniqueness as a film notwithstanding, *Citizen Kane* bears relation to a number of other forms. One example is in its non-linear and overlapping narrative structure, which emphasizes different subjective points of view. While this was unusual for mainstream film, it has many analogues in fiction, certainly from the mid-nineteenth century with popular novels such as Wilkie Collins's *The Woman in White* and, later in the century (as discussed in chapter 9), with *The Strange Case of Dr Jekyll and Mr Hyde* and *Dracula*.

Fig. 15.20

Such narrative techniques became central to the twentieth-century modernist tradition in novels like James Joyce's *Ulysses* and *The Sound and the Fury* by William Faulkner. Furthermore, the movie illustrates how cinema can incorporate other art forms and deals explicitly with the process and apparatus of artistic production in its use of opera. Kane tries to make his second wife, Susan Alexander, into an opera star and involves himself in virtually all stages of the process of operatic production (figure 15.21). He oversees her vocal training, builds a major opera house, and finances a production featuring her. During a performance we see backstage, stage, and audience perspectives of it. In addition, Kane attempts to use his newspapers and critics to generate a positive reception climate for her performance. He is also presented as a compulsive collector of art objects.

Fig. 15.21

Citizen Kane, then, not only reveals careful attention to the properties of its form, but it also has significant relationships with other art forms, and it takes as one of its themes the process of artistic production and the relationship of art and power.

Film and Radio

Orson Welles was able to make *Citizen Kane* primarily on the strength of his success in radio. Many of the people he brought with him, from production personnel like John Houseman to much of the cast, had also worked with him in radio. He also remained involved with radio for more than a decade after this film. This extensive involvement provides a number of contexts for discussing the film.

The first involves creative control. Welles was not only a popular radio actor but also served on many of his projects as adaptor, director, narrator, and actor (examples are *First Person Singular* for CBS in 1938, *The Mercury Theater on the Air* for CBS in 1938, and *The Campbell Playhouse* for CBS in 1938–40). This is paralleled by his work on the stage, and his multiple functions in *Citizen Kane* are part of an authorial pattern.

The trailer for the movie shows all of the cast except for Welles; he is represented solely by a microphone on a boom and by his dominating narrating voice, which recalls his radio career and underlines the influence of radio in the film. While the sound era in films was in full bloom by the 1930s, the 1940s have been seen as the time in which the soundtrack became sophisticated. One example would be Welles's use in this film of flashbacks with multiple and complex point-of-view narration, which while innovative for the time, later became common practice, especially in some genres like *film noir*. It is likely that his extensive experience in radio influenced this.

Broadcast radio began in the 1920s and became enormously popular in the 1930s and 1940s, decades often referred to as the "golden age" of radio. It produced not only a new generation of artists, like Welles, and technicians,

Fig. 15.22

Fig. 15.23

but also an audience attuned to the sophisticated use of sound for storytelling. By 1941, radio's influence was beginning to show itself in film, and *Citizen Kane* is a good example in narrative technique, performers, and the sophistication of the soundtrack. In the party scene for the *Inquirer*'s staff, for example, the set was constructed with muslin ceilings so as to enable live sound recording (figure 15.22). A number of scenes include complex use of sound such as that of Kane's wedding announcement, which employs overlapping dialogue, and others use ambient effects, such as the hollow, echoing sounds of Kane and Susan talking inside Xanadu. She appears lost in a gloomy, cavernous space as she sits doing a puzzle, and the hollow sounds supply a perfect aural corollary to this visual image (figure 15.23).

Finally, the film thematically deals with the power of the mass media. Welles had created a panic in his 1938 *War of the Worlds* broadcast, and *Citizen Kane* claims that Kane created the Spanish-American War through the power of his newspapers. Like his recasting of H. G. Wells's nineteenth-century novel, *The War of the Worlds*, into a series of contemporary news broadcasts, Welles's use of newsreels at the beginning of *Citizen Kane* gives contemporary media relevance to the material.

Narrative Structure

Citizen Kane has what, in 1941, was an unusual narrative structure: the story is told largely through a series of **flashbacks**. An occasional flashback was, in itself, not unusual in classical Hollywood cinema, but *Citizen Kane*'s narrative is structured around them. In fact, everything we learn about the title character we learn after his death; very little of the film is set in the present. The opening scene shows Kane's death, but then the film cuts directly to a newsreel account of the famous man's life. The next scene takes place in the screening room where the newsreel makers discuss the film we have just seen. The boss decides that they need to know more about the life of the man and lands on the idea that they should find out the meaning of Kane's last word, "Rosebud." He assigns Mr Thompson to interview people who knew Kane and Thompson's assignment supplies the narrative structure for the rest of the film.

Thompson goes to the El Rancho nightclub to interview Susan Alexander Kane and then to the Thatcher Library, where he reads a manuscript about Kane, then to Bernstein, Leland, back to Susan, and finally to Xanadu itself, where he interviews Raymond, Kane's servant. With the exception of the first visit to Susan, during each following interview and during the reading of the manuscript in the library, we see flashbacks about key episodes in Kane's life. This flashback structure is further complicated by the fact that the episodes are not in chronological order. When Thompson interviews Leland at a hospital, the old man recounts, among other things, the première of Susan's opera career. We see and hear preparations for the opening night, the curtain rising, Susan singing, stagehands indicating their disapproval, and Leland, attending as music critic, bored by the performance. We then see a scene where Leland falls asleep at the typewriter, unable to finish typing the negative review he wants to give to this performance. Kane himself finishes the review as he thinks Leland would have and then fires his longtime friend.

After interviewing Leland, Thompson returns to Susan and the film jumps back in time to scenes of her getting her voice lessons preparatory to her career as an opera singer, the disastrous consequences of which we have just seen. Thus, *Citizen Kane* departs from the usual linearity of the classical Hollywood cinema in two significant ways: instead of beginning in the present and having one event lead logically to the next, it begins in the present and then hops back and forth, leading to a further disruption of linear time when even the past events are presented out of chronological order. A more linear narrative would have shown Susan first training to become an opera singer and then failing in her debut.

Citizen Kane does, however, use a device common to **classical Hollywood narration** discussed in chapter 2: the film poses a central question (What does "Rosebud" mean?) and, when that question is answered, the film is over. In this regard, *Citizen Kane* resembles a detective film where Kane's death scene poses a mystery that must be solved. We see the dying man drop a glass ball containing a snow scene (figure 15.24) and we hear him utter "Rosebud." What is Rosebud and what connection exists between the dying word and the dropped ball? Thompson is analogous to a detective assigned to the case and, true to the classical style of narration, the central questions are answered in the film's final scene, but with significant variations.

Thompson offers Raymond a thousand dollars for information about Kane but is dissatisfied with what he hears. The interview takes place as the contents of Kane's estate are being boxed and prepared for removal. Disappointed that he has not learned what he came for, Thompson leaves with several other reporters as we see workmen throw worthless items into a roaring fire. A workman picks up a sled and Raymond orders, "Throw that junk in." As the man complies with the order, the camera moves in on the sled sur-

Fig. 15.24

Fig. 15.25

rounded by flames and we see the word "Rosebud" written on it. The film ends with exterior views of the mansion with black smoke pouring out of the chimney.

Although Thompson, Raymond, and the other characters in the film never learn what Rosebud is, we do. Earlier in the film, we see Kane as a little boy playing in the snow outside his parents' boarding house. When the little boy learns that Thatcher has come to take him away from his home, he uses his sled to push the strange man away (figure 15.25). The memory of happily playing with his sled has been cherished by the adult Kane throughout his life, and the memory explains both the glass ball with snow and the word "Rosebud:" Kane dies holding a visual remembrance of his lost childhood as he utters the word he associates with those happy days. Within the classical Hollywood narrative style the main characters usually accomplish their goals and learn the answers to questions posed to them. Although *Citizen Kane* is a variation on this, it still fulfills the main requirement of Hollywood narratives that the audience leaves knowing the answer to the main question posed at the beginning. At the simplest level, Kane's dropping the glass ball and uttering the dying word "Rosebud" are explained in the last scene.

The last scene also points to another feature of classical narration: it rhymes with the first scene. The film opens with exterior images of Xanadu and the camera gradually moves through a series of **dissolves** closer to the mansion until we are inside, where we see Kane die. The film ends by going from inside to outside with a series of dissolves recalling those at the beginning as the camera gradually moves farther away until it is outside the fence with a "No Trespassing" sign visible. In a sense, the whole film has been an effort to trespass on Kane's privacy. This image, combined with the book-end rhyme with the film's opening scene, gives the film a strong, classical sense of dramatic, formal, and thematic closure.

Formal Analysis

Formally, *Citizen Kane* departs significantly from the classical Hollywood style. As we noted in chapter 3, the Hollywood "invisible" style of **editing** relies heavily on a system of shot/reverse-shot editing based upon action, reaction, and dialogue. When characters say or do important things, we cut to shots of them, and when others react, we cut to shots of their reactions. Typically, this style of editing also elides small bits of time and space deemed unimportant. If a character leaves the room, for example, we may see him or her get up and start to walk toward the door and then cut to a shot of him or her in the outer hallway; we do not see him or her walk across every inch of the room, open the door, and walk through it.

Key scenes in *Citizen Kane*, however, reject this editing model in favor of employing **long takes** with moving camera and deep focus, somewhat like those discussed in *Rules of the Game* (1939) in chapter 3. In all or most of these scenes, every inch of space and every second of time is represented in its entirety. Two such scenes are the childhood boarding house scene and the first interview scene between Thompson and Susan.

The boarding house scene

The boarding house scene begins with Kane playing in the snow. He throws a snowball, and there is a cut to it hitting the boarding house sign and then another cut back to the boy. From this point, the remaining portion of the scene until the last shot employs two long takes. As we see the boy in long shot playing, the camera pulls back through an open window where we see Mr and Mrs Kane and Mr Thatcher. Mrs Kane stands looking out of the window, then turns and leads the way to a table farther back in the room. Mrs Kane and Mr Thatcher sit at the table and Mr Kane remains standing in the mid-ground at the left side of the frame. The window is open in the rear of the frame and through it we see and hear the boy playing. The adults discuss the boy's fate, and Mr Kane emotionally opposes Mrs Kane's plans to give custody of their son to Thatcher (figures 15.26 and 15.27).

Fig. 15.26

Fig. 15.27

In a conventional cutting pattern of the time, when Mr Kane makes an emotional plea to keep his son we would see his face and then, when Mrs Kane responds, we would cut to a shot of her face. Similarly, when Thatcher reads important parts of the legal document or answers an important question, such as the one Mr Kane poses to him as to why Mrs Kane has the full decision-making power about the boy's future, we would cut to a shot of him.

Welles, however, shoots the scene in such a manner that all the adults are clearly framed and in focus throughout the conversation, enabling the spectator to look around the frame at the participants. Furthermore, the deep focus even extends into the far rear of the frame where, through the window, we see the boy playing. He comes and goes, disappearing then reappearing. This activity, combined with the intermittent sounds, also draws the spectator's attention to that portion of the frame.

Remarkably, the shot continues when Mr Kane walks to the window and closes it, shutting out the sounds of the boy playing. Mrs Kane gets up and, followed by Thatcher, walks to the window and opens it. As she does so we immediately hear the boy again and, just as she finishes raising the window, the film cuts to a view from the other side of it. Now we see Mrs Kane standing in the right foreground facing the camera with Thatcher in the left rear and Mr Kane in the right rear (figures 15.28 and 15.29). Their conversation continues.

Fig. 15.28

Fig. 15.29

The nature of this cut is revealing. Welles cuts because it is a technical necessity to set up a **tracking shot** from inside to outside the house. He does not cut in order to emphasize a line of dialogue, an action, or a reaction. In fact, the cut repositions all three characters in such a manner that we can once again see all of their faces. The cut is also a match on the action of Mrs Kane raising the window so that not a moment is left out. As the adults prepare to go outside, the camera tracks back and, in one motion, goes from inside the house to the yard outside. We see the adults emerge through the front door and approach Charles.

This second long take continues as Charles learns about his fate. Initially, we see Thatcher and Mrs Kane in the left foreground with Charles at the right and Mr Kane in the rear center of the frame. The boy starts back toward his father but is recalled. When he returns, Thatcher stands at the left, Charles in the center, and his mother now at the right. His father remains in the rear. Charles reacts emotionally to the news that he is going away with Thatcher, pushes him over with the sled, and tries to run away. As the family and Mr Thatcher regroup, the last cut in the scene takes place: we see a close-up of Mrs Kane with her arm around her son, and the camera moves down to a close-up of his face. The shot then dissolves to one of the sled, lying covered with falling snow (figures 15.30–15.32).

Nearly all of this complicated scene is done in two shots. The second, like the first, frames an elaborate interchange among all of the characters as they try to explain things to the boy. Again, in a typical Hollywood film, we would

Fig. 15.30

have seen a close-up of the father's face when he tells the boy how exciting the trip will be or of Thatcher's face when he first explains the trip to Charles or of Charles's face when he figures out what is going on. But until the last shot of the scene, Welles resists this. Only at the end of the scene do we get a close-up of Mrs Kane's face, with the camera moving to then frame Charles's face in close-up. In contrast to the previous two shots, at these moments the spectator's undivided attention is directed at the mother's face and then at the son's.

Welles's style requires elaborate timing between the actors and the cinematographer. In the conventional cutting style, an actor is on

Fig. 15.31

Fig. 15.32

screen for a brief time and then a new shot is set up; here, however, the actors are all on screen throughout the long take. This style is also challenging to spectators since they have so much to look at and listen to. Rather than one person dominating a composition, many people and their interactions vie for the spectator's attention.

Thompson interviews Susan Alexander

This scene begins with a shot of a billboard of Susan from which the camera cranes upward and moves toward a rooftop sign for the El Rancho nightclub. The camera moves through the sign and then cranes down toward a skylight through which we can see Susan sitting alone at a table. The camera passes through the glass just as a lightning flash obscures things momentarily. Now inside the club, the camera continues to descend toward Susan's table. She sits at the left and Thompson enters; after a moment, he sits down with his back to the camera. The shot continues as the two talk and, when Susan becomes irate and yells at Thompson, he rises to leave and the camera follows his actions. The *maître d'* enters and nods for Thompson to follow him to the right rear. Once again, the camera follows. A waiter enters the frame and the *maître d'* explains Susan's condition to Thompson, who leaves to telephone his boss. He walks offscreen right, where we hear the sound of a coin dropping into a pay phone followed by the sound of dialing. The *maître d'* talks to the waiter.

At this point the only cut occurs in the scene. In the new composition, we see Thompson in the phone booth in the lower right foreground of the frame, the *maître d'* and the waiter behind him, and Susan at the table in the left rear. The *maître d'* approaches Thompson, who alternates between speaking into the phone and speaking to the *maître d'*. In the rear, we see the waiter serving Susan a drink. When Thompson is connected with his boss, he closes the booth's glass door. The *maître d'* continues to wait in the middle area of the frame and Susan continues to sit in the left rear. In fact, a diagonal line could be drawn through the frame, extending from Thompson in the right foreground through the *maître d'* to Susan. When Thompson finishes his conversation, he opens the booth door and continues to talk with the *maître d'*, asking whether he knows anything about Kane's dying words. The *maître d'* replies in the negative, and the scene ends as the shot fades to black (figures 15.33–15.36).

This entire scene is shot in two long takes. The first one moves from exterior to interior and then remains stationary throughout the conversation between Thompson and Susan before moving again to follow Thompson. The logic of the cut once again dictates

Fig. 15.33

Fig. 15.34

Fig. 15.35

Fig. 15.36

absolute spatial and temporal continuity. The camera is repositioned in such a manner that no space is omitted. We still see Susan sitting at the table where Thompson entered the scene and we simultaneously see the space with the *maître d'* from which Thompson has just exited. As in the boarding house sequence, the long take with deep focus enables the spectator to shift attention between Thompson, the *maître d'*, and Susan.

This scene, like the boarding house scene, relies heavily on dialogue. The Hollywood shot/reverse-shot editing style is perfectly suited to such scenes. The normal cutting pattern of the time would show a shot of Thompson as he asks a question and then a shot of Susan as she responds. A similar pattern would emerge in the exchange between the *maître d'* and Thompson; when Thompson is in the phone booth we would most likely see a shot of him talking into the phone and then a cut to a shot of the waiter serving a drink to Susan. Welles has resisted this ingrained formal style of the classical cinema, replacing it with a complex visual style that includes elaborate camera movements and deep-focus compositions with multiple planes.

Gender, Class, and Race

In both its narrative structure and its formal style, *Citizen Kane* broke new ground in the American cinema. Its status as a classic is undeniable, but this should not prevent us from thinking critically about its representation of women, people of color, and class. We conclude our analysis by raising some issues about the film's ideology. Our point is not that *Citizen Kane* has been overrated (although that is also a possibility) but that, like all films, it should be comprehensively critiqued and not merely placed on a pedestal.

Gender

Citizen Kane is a film first and foremost about the man of the title; everyone else is secondary. One of the many genres in which *Citizen Kane* could be placed is the "great man" genre. Such films are centered on the actions of important men and implicitly relegate women to a secondary status. *Citizen Kane* is no exception. The film's only interest in women is in so far as they relate to the life of the protagonist. Indeed, the film does not even concern itself with the women in the lives of Kane's associates Bernstein, Leland, and Thatcher. The fact that only Kane counts emerges strongly in the scene where Thompson interviews Bernstein in his office. The old man starts out by relating an incident that occurred years earlier when, as a young man, he caught a fleeting sight of a beautiful woman he has never been able to forget. He never met her, never learned her name, and the film never again refers to her. Furthermore, when Bernstein talks about his own life, the film gives us no flashback; the flashbacks begin only when he talks about Kane.

Who, then, are the women in Kane's life? There are primarily three: his mother and his two wives. His mother is seen briefly in the boarding house scene, where she is represented as a dominating woman overly protective of her son and coldly dismissive of her husband. Kane's first wife also has a minor role and is most memorably present in the famous breakfast **montage** sequence showing the decline of the marriage (figure 15.37), which sets up Kane's introduction to Susan Alexander. Although Susan is featured more prominently than the other two women, her character is developed only in so far as their relationship sheds light on him.

Fig. 15.37

Susan's voice lies at the center of their relationship. Language and voice have received much attention in feminist film theory. In a male-dominated society, women can be alienated from language and their opportunity to voice themselves can be severely restricted. To command language and have a voice are real power issues. When women are silenced, their power is curtailed. *Citizen Kane* supplies an interesting variation on silencing women's voices in Susan Alexander: her voice is not so much silenced (in fact, it is amplified) as it is taken away from her and torturously reshaped. Kane forces her into the mold of an opera singer and, when it becomes clear that she does not have the talent for it, he persists in his demands that she succeed. This leads to the sad spectacle of her male singing teacher forcing sounds from her at the command of her powerful husband. In one scene, we see Kane demand the teacher continue with the lessons that even the teacher wants to abandon.

After taking her voice away from her and reshaping it to suit his vision of her, Kane humiliates Susan in public by insisting that she debut in opera even though it is clear to everyone that she is not prepared to do so. This combination of having her voice removed from her control and being publicly humiliated makes her suicidal.

Class

The relationship between Kane and Susan points to the role of **economic** and **social class** in the film. Indeed, the film's representation of class, like its representation of gender, is remarkably conventional. *Citizen Kane* is another film in which the middle class is not represented but in which the values of that class still dominate. When Kane first meets Susan, he is one of the world's most powerful men and she is a working woman living in a modest rooming house. Indeed, part of Kane's attraction to her is the fact that she does not even know who he is. Of all the scenes of him as an adult in the film, Kane is the happiest the night he and Susan meet; they console each other as he makes her laugh by creating shadow figures on the wall.

Citizen Kane belongs with those films that represent the lives of the rich as sad and empty; this is evident in Kane's relationship with Susan. Both of them are almost childishly happy while entertaining themselves for free in a

Fig. 15.38

boarding house room. This contrasts sharply with the later scene in Xanadu where Susan sits by the fireplace of the living room playing with a puzzle, virtually lost in the monstrously dark space of the mansion. She whines about the fun normal people are having out on the town while she is trapped in this grotesque mansion. The image of people going to theaters and restaurants is precisely that image of middle-class happiness that we never see in the film but that stands in bold contrast to Susan's nightmare of wealth.

Kane responds to Susan's complaint by saying that they will go on a picnic, and we then see his idea of what a "picnic" is: a huge caravan with large tents, servants, roast pigs, and a jazz band (figure 15.38)! If ever a word had middle-class connotations, it is "picnic." For most, a picnic is an unpretentious cold meal in a basket shared with loved ones on a blanket on the ground. The "picnic" we see in *Citizen Kane* is meant to appall us precisely in so far as it departs from this norm. Its decadent excess is just another sign of how the rich cannot have fun, not even on something as simple as a picnic.

Susan goes from being a happy, unpretentious, working-class woman to being the miserably unhappy wife of one of the world's richest men. And the trajectory of Kane's life is similar. There are two boarding houses in the film: the one Susan lives in and the one Kane lives in as a boy. Part of the film's nostalgia for Kane's boyhood life is class based. Much as Susan would have been happier had she stayed where she was and not met Kane, Kane would have been happier had he stayed in Colorado with his parents. The innocence of his childhood is also the innocence of a working-class environment. When Thatcher virtually buys Kane from his parents by giving them a monthly income for the rest of their lives, everything changes instantly. It is no exaggeration to say that "Rosebud" is, among other things, a class term.

Race and ethnicity

Citizen Kane places not just any man at the center of its narrative, but a white man. Like most Hollywood films of the time, *Citizen Kane* presumes that all significant things in its world happen to white people. People of color are virtually absent from the film and a glaring exception proves the rule. Kane's idea of a picnic includes a jazz band, and the main images of blacks in the film are the black musicians in that band, not one of whom speaks a word (figure 15.39). The film propagates the stereotype of linking blacks with jazz and marginalizes them to such an extent that their sole function is to perform for the pleasure of rich white people. These musicians are, in a sense, servants for Kane and his rich white guests.

The African Americans in *Citizen Kane* are marginalized even more than the women. They are not given a trace of a life of their own, have no language, and are so peripheral as to occupy only a

Fig. 15.39

few fleeting moments of screen time. *Citizen Kane* is a film made by whites for whites and one that, like most Hollywood films of its time, assumes that only white characters are of interest.

This relates to the presumption of white as the invisible color in racial issues, the unquestioned norm against which all other colors are measured. And a certain kind of white – white, Anglo-Saxon Protestant. Interestingly, the film contains a scene critical of racial prejudice. During the famous breakfast scene depicting the decline of Kane's first marriage, Mrs Kane refers with contempt to a toy that Mr Bernstein bought their son and indicates that she does not want it in the nursery. Kane replies that Bernstein is likely to visit the nursery now and then and, therefore, the toy must be displayed. His wife asks if it is necessary that Bernstein visit and Kane sternly indicates yes.

Bernstein has long been a name associated with Jews, and though Mrs Kane never explicitly mentions Bernstein's Jewishness, her facial and bodily expressions along with the tone of her voice indicate a disdainful anti-semitism, one that Kane understands and severely refuses to countenance. We have, then, with this film a critique of ethnic prejudice and at the same time a wholesale acceptance of a privileged white norm. This seeming contradiction in such a renowned classic is an indication of the need to maintain a critical perspective on all films, a goal underlying this book's approach to film.

Conclusion

Citizen Kane is a particularly good film with which to encapsulate the approaches developed thus far in this book. It relates to every aspect of film studies that we have covered, with the sole exception of chapter 6, "Series, Sequels, and Remakes." Boldly innovative in its narrative and formal devices, it helped redefine several genres and catapulted Orson Welles into legendary fame as an *auteur*. With his background in theater and radio and his use of Mercury Theater actors, it also focuses attention on the relationship of film to both the other arts and the other media. The manner in which André Bazin championed the film made it central to the development of film theory. It has been hailed ever since its release and interpreted in many ways over the decades.

Yet, despite its astonishing level of achievement, the film's treatment of women, blacks, and the wealthy reminds us that no films lie outside the ideology of their time and culture. Thinking about movies means thinking about all aspects of all movies. Such a project of analytical and critical thought is by definition never completed. Who knows what important areas of *Citizen Kane* will be brought to light now that we have entered the twenty-first century? Race, class, and gender issues were, for example, not part of the film's original 1941 critical reception context nor of the 1950s' and 1960s' *auteurist* veneration of the film, but they should be part of any current consideration of the film.

The process of learning how to think about movies in many ways expands our enjoyment and appreciation of cinema. At the beginning of this book we cautioned that we should not assume that critical and analytical awareness of cinema kills the fun of going to movies. To the contrary, paying attention to formal and cultural matters makes us more discriminating, active viewers. It is fun to challenge movies and not just uncritically accept what the filmmakers and producers want us to. Thinking about movies means being an active, aware viewer, and that maximizes the enjoyment we can take from this unique art form.

In the next chapter we turn to a topic that would have been unimaginable at the time that *Citizen Kane* was made – the impact of computer, digital technology on film. Such technology has dramatically revolutionized the way in which films are made and the way they look from the time period in which *Citizen Kane* was filmed.

SELECTED READINGS

Robert L. Carringer's *The Making of Citizen Kane* (Berkeley, CA: University of California Press, 1985) has provided us with extensive information on the preparation, making, and reception of the film, on Welles's role in the scripting and producing of it, and on its image within the film industry. Carringer also has a visual essay on the film included in the Criterion Collection laser edition of *Citizen Kane*. Pauline Kael's "Raising Kane" (*The New Yorker*, February 20, 1971, pp. 43–89, and February 27, 1971, pp. 44–81) gives her perception of Herman J. Mankiewicz's role in the writing of the script for *Citizen Kane*. The Orson Welles special issue of *Persistence of Vision* (Number 7, 1989) gives extensive credits for Welles's stage and radio work.

16

DIGITAL TECHNOLOGY AND FILM

The Matrix and *Timecode*

When *Gladiator* (2000) opened, it was widely publicized in the media that the Roman coliseum where many of the film's central scenes take place was entirely constructed from digital images (plate 90). Although no full set of the coliseum was ever constructed, viewers of the hugely successful film saw many shots of the entire coliseum, often filled to the brim with cheering spectators watching the bloody spectacle taking place before them. Of course, the spectacle was not taking place "before them" because they were never there. It is only through digital technology that we see the fighting gladiators and the cheering crowds all in the gigantic coliseum at the same time. Hollywood does not try to hide the fact that, in some sense, the audience is being "cheated," but rather revels in advertising the miracles of digital technology. Furthermore, many DVDs have special features demonstrating how the digital images were created, showing the various stages of the construction of the final image. When *Forrest Gump* (1994) was initially released on video, an extra feature showed how a scene with Gary Sinese playing an amputee was shot. Rather than use conventional techniques of tying his legs back and hiding them from sight, the scene was shot showing both legs which were then digitally removed (plate 91).

The Cultural Impact of Digital Technology

Young people are so used to this form of "movie magic" and are so aware of when and how it is accomplished that to them it is no big deal. They may have trouble understanding why their parents think the "realistic" dinosaurs in *Jurassic Park* (plate 92) are so extraordinary since for them they appear quite ordinary. This points to a central paradox of this chapter: most of the students reading it have grown up during the era of digital and computer technology and know more about some aspects of its subject matter than their teachers. For many of their parents, however, the arrival of the era of home computers signaled a social and cultural revolution that drastically changed the world in which they live. As book authors, we remember the "old days" of handwriting a manuscript, taking it to a typist, hand correcting the typed manuscript and returning it to the typist. For a co-authored project such as this one, an added step involved xeroxing the manuscript at every stage and mailing it back and forth, along with lengthy, costly telephone conversations. With this book, of course, there is no typist and nothing was mailed between the co-authors; the word-processed files were constantly revised and instantly e-mailed as attached files. Most of the "talking" was done on e-mail rather than the telephone. Even the images from the films existed only as digital files throughout most of the process and were not printed on paper until the book was printed.

If the impact of digital technology on book publishing has been considerable, it has been equally if not more so on filmmaking and viewing. Every aspect of how films are made, viewed, and thought about has been affected by digital technology. This is just as true for home viewing of movies as for theatrical **exhibition**. In chapter 10, we discussed the differences between film and television. We saw that there are profound differences between watching a small, low-resolution image with poor sound fidelity in a distractive home environment and watching a high-resolution, large image in a darkened auditorium with high-quality, stereo-surround sound speakers. Those differences also help account for the different narrative strategies of film and television.

Home Theaters

While those differences between film and television still hold true, the emergence of the "home theater" is once again changing things. Growing numbers of people now watch movies at home on DVD (digital video disks) with higher resolution, larger TV screens and stereo sound. Some even have digital projectors that, as in a theater, project a large image on the wall in a darkened room. Increasingly, people are hooking their DVD players up to digital stereo **5.1 surround sound** equipment which copies the elaborate sound systems in movie theaters by supplying left, right, and center separation in the front speakers and left–right separation in the rear speakers. In addition to those five separate stereo sound sources, the sub-woofer (the "0.1" of digital stereo 5.1) amplifies certain frequencies, at times enabling the spectator to even feel sound vibrations while watching the movie.

However, even for people sitting at home and watching a higher-resolution, larger image with stereo-surround sound, there are still differences between home theaters and movie theaters. Most obviously, theaters usually project 35 mm film on a much larger screen with much better sound equipment. Furthermore, going to the movies still involves a social dimension that home theaters can never duplicate. Going out to the movies and sitting with a large audience of strangers is a different experience from staying home to watch a movie alone or with a small group of family or friends.

Home theaters are not likely to replace television as it is commonly understood. People will still watch television in highly distractive environments, even if their screens are larger and have better resolution and sound. Some will even continue to watch movies in a casual, home environment while talking to others, answering the phone, and doing chores. Yet the fact remains that, due to digital technology, it is now possible for people to approximate some aspects of the theatrical experience in their homes in a manner that simply was not possible twenty-five years ago. At the rate at which things are changing, it is likely that, much as many students now have never experienced using a typewriter to type on paper, or making carbon copies with carbon paper (historical artifacts), many students in the near future will never have placed a VHS video tape into a VCR. Before long, with the advent of high-definition TV (HDTV), many will never have seen small-screen, low-resolution televisions.

Digital Video and Independent Film Production

In the first part of this chapter, we will survey some of the impact that digital technology has had on film production, exhibition, and distribution; we will then look at the effect it has had on the manner in which we think, talk, and write about film and cinematography. Aside from its widely publicized use with visual effects, one of the most evident influences of digital technology on film-making is the manner in which it enables fast, comparatively low cost, feature film production. Shooting 35 mm film is expensive for many reasons, the film stock being only one of them. Expensive cameras and equipment have to be rented, film has to be exposed during all takes, a time delay is involved in developing the film so that "dailies" can be viewed, etc. The development of digital video cameras greatly reduces these costs, potentially placing the means of feature film production in the hands of those previously excluded from it. *The Anniversary Party* (2001) provides a good example. It was co-directed by Jennifer Jason Leigh and Alan Cumming. Leigh is mostly known as an actress in independent films and, although she appeared in such Hollywood productions as *Backdraft* (1991), is not a mainstream mega-star like Julia Roberts. As opposed to stars like Barbra Streisand and Jodie Foster, it is unlikely that, within the corporate Hollywood filmmaking climate, a star like Leigh would get the financial backing to direct a film. The same holds true for Cumming, and yet they were able to make *The Anniversary Party* on digital video. It is not a film with obvious special effects; in fact, nothing about it would strike the average spectator as in any way different from a film shot conventionally on 35 mm film. Indeed, had it not been advertised as being shot on video, few would have noticed anything and, with a higher budget, the same film could easily have been shot on 35 mm film. Within this context, one already existing influence of digital video is that now films like *The Anniversary Party* are being made by directors like Leigh and Cumming. Similarly, Ethan Hawke, another actor, directed *Chelsea Walls* (2001), another digital video production.

Digital technology also enables low-budget independent films that are boldly experimental and do not closely follow conventional narrative form or visual style. *Conceiving Ada* (1997) falls into this group. Written by Lynn Hershman Leeson and Ellen Jones and directed by Leeson, the film is a feminist account of the relationship of a contemporary woman with an historical figure, Lady Ada Lovelace. Ada, the daughter of the nineteenth-century Romantic poet, Lord Byron, was a mathematical genius who helped design the first computer. Leeson not only uses digital technology to make her film but also makes it part of the theme of her film. *Conceiving Ada* tells the story of a contemporary female computer scientist who, while working on her computer (plate 93), accidentally stumbles upon Ada's life in a previous century. Within this science fantasy film, the contemporary woman is not only able to see scenes from Ada's life but also to interact with Ada and intervene in her life.

Leeson did a great deal of historical research for the film, including taking photographs of houses that accurately reflect the nineteenth-century setting of many scenes. Then, somewhat like her heroine, she used digital technology to re-create the scenes with Ada. None of these scenes took place on actual sets; they were all digitally constructed, enabling the photographs to be placed in live video. The still photos were digitized and altered in various ways in Photoshop, a computer software program. Several computers were then used to add mattes and alter perspective and size. These were then placed on digital videotape while the actors were performing in a "virtual environment." The actors, while being photographed against a **blue screen**, could place themselves within that environment by looking at a computer monitor (plate 94).

Leeson's techniques were new to feature filmmaking and reveal important aspects of digital filmmaking. In the past, all these visual effects would have had to have been done in post-production, that part of the filmmaking process that takes place after the completion of principal photography. Leeson's method, however, enabled the actors to respond to both their real and virtual surroundings while the film was being shot.

Leeson's use of digital technology is particularly illustrative for us in relation to the gender issues we discussed in chapter 12. In that chapter, we noted that dominant patterns of representing men and women in films are strongly tied to cultural assumptions about gender, such as men being active and women passive. Another cultural assumption about gender involves technology, which is conventionally considered the domain of the masculine. Indeed, the common expression "boys with toys," referring to the manner in which many young men, including some film production students, love to immerse themselves within the world of equipment and technology, points to how our culture encourages boys rather than girls to pursue such activities. In *Conceiving Ada*, Leeson explores the feminist theme of recovering a "lost" historical figure and restoring her to prominence. Within the film this is accomplished by a female computer scientist who uses digital technology and, similarly, Leeson herself accomplishes this by using state of the art digital technology to make her film, thus challenging common assumptions that women are not adept with technology.

Established, independent-minded filmmakers are increasingly turning to digital video. Wayne Wang, the director of the highly praised film, *The Joy Luck Club* (1993), shot *The Center of the World* (2001) on digital video. The film has only three actors and focuses almost exclusively on two of them. Furthermore, it deals with disturbing sexual subject matter. Even an established director like Wang might have encountered difficulty making such a film on 35 mm film, especially since none of his actors is well known.

Digital Technology and Big-budget Hollywood Films

If digital technology has affected low-budget, independent filmmaking, it has also had a huge impact on mainstream Hollywood films. Indeed for many people, digital technology is synonymous with spectacular special effects. *Armageddon* (1999), a successful blockbuster, supplies an excellent example. The film tells the story of an asteroid on a crash course with earth. If it hits, the world will be destroyed. Manned shuttles are sent into space to blow up the asteroid before the doomsday scenario occurs. The film is filled with major sequences that are the result of complex digital effects, including all the shots of the shuttles and asteroid (plate 95), a sequence showing the destruction of Paris (plate 96), and the final explosion at the film's climax (plate 97). We will use as our primary example here the shuttle and asteroid shots.

Although the term **special effects** is commonly applied to a wide range of effects, the industry distinguishes between special effects and **visual effects**. Special effects are those that can be accomplished on the set and visual effects are those that cannot. Blowing up a car, for example, is a special effect because it often involves an actual car and a genuine explosion. Showing a shuttle land on an asteroid, however, is a visual effect because neither the shuttle nor the asteroid actually exist in the same space and time on the set. Realistic-looking images of them require models and computer graphics. It is the latter with which we are concerned here. The person in charge of these effects is credited in the film as the visual effects supervisor. A big-budget effects film like *Armageddon* may have several visual effects supervisors, each working on separate sequences. Richard Hoover was the visual effects supervisor for the shuttles and asteroid sequences in *Armageddon*.

The image of the asteroid in *Armageddon* originated as a sketch on a napkin. The image was then digitized and refined and colored in Photoshop. Then an actual foam model of the asteroid was constructed. Many shots were taken of the model which were then loaded back into a computer where other effects such as gasses, debris, and rocks were added. Then another, larger model was built. Through a complex technological process, it was possible to wire the model in such a manner that the computer would "know" every nook and cranny of the asteroid three-dimensionally.

The final images in the film are constructed of multiple layers of digital imagery. Many scenes have fifty to a hundred layers of film! *Armageddon* could have been made years ago using conventional, optical printing cinematography. In that method, however, black and green lines are often visible, for example, around a person standing in such a shot. The computer can eliminate such lines, making the composite process invisible to the spectator. Obviously, this affects the believability of the image for many spectators, especially since the Hollywood style generally conceals any signs of the filmmaking process (see chapter 3) in order to give the spectator the impression of watching a "real" and not a constructed event. Some have dubbed the classical Hollywood style of shooting and editing films "the invisible style." Digital effects make the process so much easier that it is more likely that films like *Armageddon* will get made. Whereas once a film like Cecil B. DeMille's *The Ten Commandments* (1956) was a rare occurrence in Hollywood because of the daunting, expensive nature of the effects, now such effects-laden productions flood screens yearly, and have come to constitute a major portion of the summer blockbusters. *Armageddon* was directed by Michael Bay who followed it up with *Pearl Harbor* (2001), another effects-laden summer film. It had the second biggest Memorial Day weekend in box-office history, second only to *Jurassic Park* – a film that, itself, helped set the standard for "realistic" visual effects.

The Changing Status of the Pro-filmic Event

As a movie like *Armageddon* makes clear, much of what we now see in Hollywood films never existed in front of the camera and this has had a profound effect upon how we think about movies. Traditionally, movies have been thought of as a filmic record of something that actually occurred in front of the camera. This **pro-filmic event**, as it is called, includes sets and actors. Spectators traditionally believed that those things were "really" there and that the film in some manner recorded their presence.

Special and visual effects have always been with us and spectators have known about them. One common effect is the use of a **painted backdrop** or a rear-projected photographic image to represent a location that is not "really" there. Actors on a **soundstage** in Hollywood might stand in front of the backdrop showing the Eiffel Tower, acting as if they were on location in Paris. At the end of *Marnie* (1964), for example, we see the main characters played by Sean Connery and Tippi Hedren emerge from an apartment into the street. In an extreme long shot, at the end of the street, we see a dock where a large ship is anchored. It is, however, obvious that the dock scene is a painted backdrop (plate 98).

Filmmakers use painted backdrops for various reasons, the most common being to save money. The cost of shooting an exterior location shot to which cast, crew, and production personnel have to travel and to which equipment has to be sent is immense and time consuming. It can be done more easily and cheaply in the studio with a backdrop. There are many technological variations of the backdrop, including having the actors stand before a **blue screen** upon which other images will later be placed. Although such techniques may appear more "realistic" to most spectators than a painted backdrop, they still are usually perceived as "fake" because of differences in contrast, depth, or the presence of lines around the composite figures.

We add a note of caution here with reference to our discussion of **reception contexts** in chapter 8. It is highly likely that some spectators of *Marnie* at the time of its release did not notice the painted backdrop for varying reasons, including absorption within the narrative. Nor are we suggesting that the visual effects in *Jurassic Park* will never date so that spectators will see them as crude and "fake." Indeed, the improvements in the dinosaurs in *Jurassic Park III* (2001) are part of the reception context for that film. We are, arguing, however, that one of the profound shifts that occurs with digital manipulation of images is that no one can see the manipulation, no matter how trained and sophisticated their eye.

This is perhaps best illustrated with reference to the legal system where the nature of photographic evidence is changing. By the late nineteenth century, photographs were commonly accepted as legal evidence in court, evidence that what the photograph showed had actually occurred. By the late twentieth century, however, their evidentiary value had declined. With some digital image processing techniques, even experts cannot tell whether or not the image has been manipulated. If people once, however naively, believed that photographs told the truth, we now live in a world where people believe there is little or no relation between a photographic image and the truth. A television commercial shows Martin Luther King delivering his famous "I have a dream" speech on the mall in Washington, DC. Although it appears that we are watching actual historical newsreel footage, the mall is empty at the beginning of the speech while, at the end, it is filled with a huge crowd. Our eyes have deceived us. It is not an "actual" historical image but a manipulated one. The point of the commercial is that no matter how good or important your message is, it is useless without a reliable way of reaching your audience. For our purposes, the manner in which the commercial flaunts its use of digital image manipulation is significant. It makes clear what it is now common knowledge: that it is easy to manipulate actual footage by, for example, removing people from an image who were present when the film was shot. In much the same way, films like Woody Allen's *Zelig* (1983) showed how a figure can easily be added to old newsreel footage. In *Zelig*, we see Woody Allen standing next to Adolf Hitler in newsreel footage of a Nazi rally. It is clear to the spectator that it is not an actor playing Hitler (as, for example, is the case with an actor playing President Dwight D. Eisenhower in the film *IQ*, 1994), but rather that it really is Hitler. And the spectator knows that the middle-aged Woody Allen could not have been present at one of Hitler's rallies, let alone standing next to him.

Digital Technology and Realism

Although digital technology is in some sense an extension of previous filmmaking techniques, it has also opened up entirely new approaches. Where in some cases, it simply embellishes the **pro-filmic event**, in other cases digital effects sometimes virtually replace the pro-filmic event by constituting much or even all of the setting. Perhaps Oliver Stone's *Natural Born Killers* (1994) was the first major Hollywood film to tell a story in such a manner as to make it clear to viewers that they were watching a complexly constructed, highly manipulated image much of the time rather than a simple recording of what allegedly happened in front of the camera (plate 99). *Natural Born Killers* is particularly interesting since the subject matter does not dictate the style, as is commonly the case, for example, in science-fiction films. Showing futuristic spacecraft zipping through space and engaging in fights with other ships requires some sort of visual effects since everyone knows that those things do not exist. But *Natural Born Killers* is the story of a young couple on a crime spree and it could easily have been shot in a conventional manner with most of what we see resulting from film footage of pro-filmically staged action. Many other crime films have been made in such a style.

Natural Born Killers points to another aspect of the digital revolution: most Hollywood films employing digital technology are made within a **realist** style. Realism is a problem that has haunted film theory and criticism for a long time (see chapter 11). Many critics use the term naïvely, as if any film could be "realistic" in the sense of being like real life. We all live twenty-four hours a day, for example, but movies don't show every minute in the life of any of their characters, let alone in the lives of all of their characters. Even if a camera photographed someone for twenty-four hours of a day, it would *represent*, not *be*, that person's "reality." It would give only one view of the person or that person's world at any single moment; other camera angles are possible.

Different genres establish different norms of reality. Traditional Westerns typically concentrated on their white male characters even though women's lives and the lives of Native Americans were just as "real" in the American West of the late nineteenth century as the lives of white males. When people traditionally watched a Western, they used the word "realistic" to judge whether or not the characters dressed in appropriate period costumes and engaged in activities, often violent, that, due to other films in the genre, they considered "realistic" for the era. Many were not bothered by the lack of attention to the concerns of women or of Native Americans because genre conventions had conditioned them to believe that such concerns were minor. Genre codes of realism also change over time and can incorporate things previously excluded from the genre, as we have seen in chapter 5 with films like *Dances with Wolves* (1990) and *Posse* (1993).

We also commonly use the word realistic to refer to how the world looks in a film with regard to **composition**, lighting, editing, and so on. Once again, there is no possibility of true "realism" since we don't see the world in long shots followed by close-ups. Nor do we see it in various degrees of graininess. Our world is not edited and does not involve quick jumps between angles of perception. Nevertheless, there are analogies between the classical style of filmmaking and how we see the world. Space and movement are represented coherently in a manner that recalls how we look at and move through space in our everyday lives. Films that maintain such a hold on vision, we call realistic. If the camera suddenly starts spinning so that everything gets blurry, it is because someone is dizzy from being drugged or hit on the head. In this sense, we can say the film looks realistic.

What we call realism is a style like any other style. If we look at realism as a style rather than as something that reproduces the world, we can understand how digital visual effects have affected this style of filmmaking. Most visual-effects movies employ the dominant narrative style whereby we can judge what the characters say and do by comparing them to our lived experience, no matter how unrealistic the circumstance. For example, at the end of *Armageddon*, the Bruce Willis character sacrifices his life to blow up the asteroid that threatens the earth. Judging the realism of such a sacrifice is no different in kind than judging a similar sacrifice in a World War II film, even though World War II really happened and no one has ever been sent to an asteroid, let alone blown one up with himself on it. Similarly, we can rely upon our sense of space and motion on this planet to judge whether the shuttles flying through the asteroid are realistic or not. In these regards, digital visual effects can and frequently are employed within the realist tradition of filmmaking. Paradoxically, the most common use of visual effects has been not to create challenges to the world we know but, rather, to make unknowable worlds (like the past in *Jurassic Park* or the future in *Armageddon*) more realistic and believable.

There is yet another notion of realism that is film-based. We have traditionally assumed that film is in some way real because of its nature as a photographic record; our own experience with amateur snapshots reinforces this belief. We know that light rays make an imprint on the film in the camera and presume that the film has captured something real which appeared in front of the camera. In this view, what the film records is somehow linked to the real world in front of the camera. Naïve versions of this form of realism have always underestimated how all photographic images are, in fact, constructed, and not simply recorded. Film doesn't just show us what is out there, but rather shows it to us in a certain way. Furthermore, it has always been possible to manipulate the image. From the early twentieth century onwards, popular carnival attractions have been wooden mock-ups that enable people to stick their heads through holes in the rear of full-scale paintings in order to be photographed. Those people appear in the finished photograph to be the figures in those paintings, from muscle men to bathing beauties. Viewers of such photographs have always realized that the image has been manipulated, as do viewers of current images of the starship *Enterprise* in space battles. In an era of digital visual effects, no one really believes that they are always seeing what's "out there." Increasingly, film audiences are aware of the fact that the films they watch are less and less a photographic record of a pro-filmic event and more and more a digital visual construction of something that exists nowhere except in a computer until it is printed onto film. But if those virtual worlds are represented using perceptual cues like those in our real world and if the characters behave in a manner consistent with our expectations based upon lived experience, we can find those worlds believable and realistic.

Digital Technology and Film Distribution and Exhibition

Shooting films on digital video and using digital visual effects are not the only manner in which digital technology affects cinema. Due to digital technology, alternative forms of distributing and exhibiting films are now possible. All of these things in turn are linked to a raging aesthetic debate about the merits of film versus digital video.

When we go to the movies, we nearly always watch a **35 mm** film being projected. Recently, however, there have been several highly publicized theatrical screenings of films using digital video projectors. One theater in Phoenix, Arizona, for example, premièred *Mission to Mars* (2000) on one of its screens using digital video. This requires a special projector since no film is used at any point in the distribution or projection process. The film is digitally encoded and can be sent to the theater in a number of ways, including via satellite signal. As with so many developments within the film industry, the move toward digital projection is economically driven. Making and shipping 35 mm prints around the country and the world is very costly. It is not uncommon for important films to open on over 3,000 screens in the US. Every one of those screens needs a separate print. Prints cost roughly $1,800 each and, after the first few months of distribution, most prints wind up as surplus. The major studios spend an almost unimaginable average of $800 million a year making prints! With digital projection this annual cost would virtually disappear, though, of course, there would be a start-up cost for theaters having to be equipped with new projectors.

These experiments have attracted a great deal of critical attention for a number of reasons. Ever since the advent of the digital era, many people have been predicting the end of film. Indeed, even referring to films shot and/or projected on digital video as "films" is a curious misnomer, like referring to CDs as record albums. As we have seen, there are strong economic imperatives to shoot, distribute, and project films on video. But there are other issues as well. A major one is that film and video look different and the gap is never likely to be closed. This has touched off a critical debate about whether video is as good as film. Like many such debates, it is often misdirected. The two are different and it is important to understand the differences. To argue which is better is like arguing whether silent film is better than sound, or color better than black and white. Given the history of a medium driven by complex economic and technological forces, aesthetics seldom becomes the basis for determining such industry issues. Rather, aesthetics develop in a complex interplay with technology and economics.

Some critics and industry professionals have argued that the dreamlike magic of 35 mm film is missing from digital video. If that is true only in an aesthetic sense, it is unlikely that the industry will find such an argument compelling. If, on the other hand, attendance drops because the magic of the dreamlike experience is central to motivating filmgoers to attend theatrical screenings, then the industry will respond. If and when video becomes the standard, aesthetic changes will take place in how films look. During a transitionary period, some filmmakers will resist the change and others will embrace it. George Lucas is currently the most visible filmmaker embracing digital video. He widely publicized his intent that *Star Wars: Episode II* (2002) be shot entirely without film. Steven Spielberg, on the other hand, has voiced his commitment to 35 mm film.

Even if shot on 35 mm and then projected digitally, a film like *Mission to Mars* looks noticeably different from how it does projected on 35 mm film. It has a very bright, clear, clean, crisp look about it. And it retains that look after repeated screenings since, unlike a 35 mm print, there are no scratches, dirt, splices, and so on, on the film as a result of projector wear and tear. Blake Edwards once remarked of *Victor/Victoria* (1982) that people who did not see it on its opening day, did not see the film he made. He was referring to nuances of print quality that would disappear with repeated screenings. An aesthetic plus of digital video is that no such print deterioration occurs.

As of now, very few people have had the chance to see an all-digital production projected digitally. But even if something is shot on video and projected on film or shot on film and projected on video, there is a perceivable difference, though many spectators may not be consciously aware of it. Film involves a random, shifting chemical process whereby silver halide crystals are embedded in the emulsion on the film's surface. Video, on the other hand, involves a chip and patterned pixels. The analogue chemical process of film enables a range of subtlety with regard to light, color, and sharpness that exceeds the capacity of patterned digital pixels. How important this difference will be in the future of shooting and projecting film remains to be seen.

We turn now to an examination of two films that illustrate quite different aspects of the digital revolution: *Timecode* (2000) was shot on digital video and uses digital technology in a highly experimental manner, while *The Matrix* (1999) was shot on 35 mm film and incorporates digital visual effects into a mainstream Hollywood narrative.

The Matrix (1999)

The Matrix is a futuristic film with a simple premise: the world that people think is real is actually a computer program. Such a premise would have been virtually inconceivable prior to the saturation of modern industrial societies by computers, especially personal home computers, in the 1980s. The recent pervasion of computer technology has changed virtually everything about our world, particularly the ways in which we communicate with each other. People born in the early twentieth century witnessed a massive revolution in transportation and communication. Automobiles, airplanes, space travel, movies, television all transformed their world in a short period of time. Some people literally lived from the "horse and buggy" era to that of space travel. Medicine made similar strides with new technologies for diagnosing and treating illnesses. It became a cliché that the dazzlingly fast manner in which scientific breakthroughs had transformed the world could never be repeated again. But the advent of fast, portable, and comparatively cheap computers changed that. Indeed, computers promised a social and cultural upheaval that would not only equal but also dwarf the changes of the twentieth century. It is only within this context that *The Matrix* can be understood. Its premise that computer reality has replaced the "real world" is itself a sign of the virtually limitless potential of the computer to change – or even replace – our world.

The Narrative

The Matrix has developed a cult following among young people who are poised to live in this new digital era, a prospect that is both exhilarating and terrifying. In the film, which is set in the twenty-first century, the world has been ravaged by war between humans and "AI" (artificial intelligence) machines. The planet is a wasteland. The machine life form has taken over the earth when it is discovered that humans are an excellent source of energy for the machines. Humans are raised as a crop and then harvested, their bodies turned into a liquid form of energy to be absorbed by the machines. To keep people docile, however, an elaborate computer program known as The Matrix is developed. It conceals reality from humans, who think they live in the civilized world of the late twentieth century where they work, play, and enjoy life as humans always have. But, of course, none of these things exists. The planet is a desert.

At the time of the creation of the computer program, a man is born inside The Matrix with the ability to change it in any way he wants. He freed a number of humans and taught them the truth before dying. An Oracle then prophesied that he would return, destroy The Matrix, and liberate the human race from computer tyranny. Morpheus (Laurence Fishburne) is one of those freed by the man born inside The Matrix. He leads a small band of renegades in a battle with The Matrix to find the chosen one. They feel that Neo (Keanu Reeves), himself a computer operator, might be that chosen one. They rescue him from The Matrix and bring him aboard their spacecraft.

Morpheus and his crew possess an amazing computer program of their own called "the construct." They can load anything they want into it, including training programs, weapons, and mental projections of a person's "digital self." Using this program, they teach Neo the skills he needs to re-enter The Matrix and defeat its manipulators. The Matrix, however, is patrolled by a special force of police agents led by Agent Smith (Hugo Weaving) who attempt to identify the chosen one and destroy him before Morpheus can successfully recruit him.

Even this brief summary indicates how much *The Matrix* is about digital **visual effects**. In some ways, the film can be summarized as a battle between two computer programs: The Matrix *v.* "the construct." Much of what we actually see in the film is comprised of elaborate effects that represent The Matrix, "the construct," or "the real world" – the name given the destroyed planet whereon the machines harvest their crop of human babies.

It is ironic that this film relies heavily upon digital visual effects to create this nightmare vision of a world that is, in fact, nothing but digital visual effects. The opening shot of the film shows enigmatic green characters on a computer screen (plate 100). We learn later that what we see on the screen is The Matrix program, an elaborate code wherein each mark or character represents some aspect of this phantasmic world. Someone who knows the code, for example, can recognize a woman in a red dress by simply looking at the screen.

The Fight Scenes

Although *The Matrix* employs many elaborate visual effects, perhaps the simplest of them supplies the film with some of its most memorable images – the ballet-like beauty of bodies soaring through the air in flight and in combat. The opening sequence of the film involves both kung-fu fighting and flight and pursuit. An extended kung-fu sequence occurs when Morpheus trains Neo within "the construct"; several later scenes involving kung fu occur when Neo and Trinity (Carrie-Anne Moss), one of Morpheus's crew members, enter The Matrix to free Morpheus, who has been taken captive.

Kung fu itself requires no special or visual effects: trained actors or stunt doubles can make the moves as part of a pro-filmic event recorded by the camera. In fact, some stars associated with various related forms of action cinema, such as Bruce Lee, Jackie Chan, Chuck Norris, and Steven Seagal, pride themselves on their martial arts skills. Their publicity gives the impression that they seldom use stunt doubles but perform most if not all of their stunts pro-filmically. Kung fu was used extensively in the Hong Kong action cinema that became very popular in the United States in the early 1990s. John Woo, one of the leading proponents of Hong Kong action cinema, even migrated to the US where he made such successful films as *Face/Off* (1997) and *Mission: Impossible 2* (2000). The Wachowski Brothers, who directed *The Matrix*, were strongly influenced by the Hong Kong action cinema and hired Yuen Woo-Ping, a leading Hong Kong kung-fu choreographer for the film.

For two reasons, however, the kung-fu style employed in the making of *The Matrix* does involve visual effects. First, some of the moves extend the capability of human beings with regard to how high and how long they soar through the air or are suspended in the air. Other moves that defy human capability involve jumping straight up to great heights or running on walls. Second, the Wachowski Brothers wanted to use the actors rather than stunt doubles as much as possible. This means that, in many of the film's most spectacular fight and flight sequences, we can see Laurence Fishburne, Keanu Reeves, and Carrie-Anne Moss performing their own stunts. How is this possible?

The basic technique that Yuen Woo-Ping employed involved wires and a body harness around the actors' bodies. Thus when the actors jumped or flipped, they were aided and guided by the wires, which pulled them up, held them up, or moved them across a space. Then, after the film was shot, the wires were digitally removed from the image. As discussed above, this digital process leaves no trace and it appears to the spectator that the actors are magically sailing through the air unaided. Even though digital visual effects were essential, the process was also physically demanding upon the actors. Yuen Woo-Ping trained the cast for months prior to the filming of *The Matrix*. The final scenes that we see in the film, then, are the result of pro-filmic actions in which the actors, not stunt doubles, performed superhuman feats aided by the wires that were then digitally removed from the image.

For four memorable examples let us briefly consider the opening sequence, the training scene, the lobby shoot-out sequence, and the final confrontation between Neo and Agent Smith in a subway station. In the opening sequence, Trinity is in The Matrix on a mission watching Neo. She is discovered and police attempt to arrest her. A fight breaks out, at the beginning of which we see her jump straight up in the air with her legs pulled up. The image freezes momentarily (plate 101) before she kicks the policeman. Moments later, she runs up and around the wall (plate 102) before killing another of the policemen. She escapes but is pursued by Agent Smith and other officers. As she flees, she jumps from one roof to another on the opposite side of the street. We see a high-angle shot of her as she jumps from the roof at the left and sails through the air to the roof on the right (plate 103). As she moves, it appears that she is running on air. Far below on the street, we see traffic.

One sequence of the film actually deals with learning kung-fu techniques. In order to teach Neo, Morpheus fights him inside a training program within "the construct." At one point, we see Morpheus high in the air, his legs pulled up as he sails across the room in slow motion. In the same shot, we see Neo lying on the floor in the lower left of the frame (plate 104). Later, Neo runs up a wall (plate 105) and, high in the air, leaps off. Facing the ceiling, his body sails parallel to the floor (plate 106) before he flips down to the ground. Morpheus then kicks him and he sails across the room (plate 107). For a brief moment, we see him in slow motion and then in regular speed as he crashes into the wall.

Near the climax of the film, Neo and Trinity enter The Matrix to save Morpheus. As they enter the building where he is held captive, they battle armed soldiers who guard the lobby. As the fighting breaks out, Trinity runs and jumps on a wall, her body parallel with the ground (plate 108). We then see her leap off the wall and do a flip; at one point, her head points straight down at the floor (plate 109). Within the same shot, she lands on her feet (plate 110).

A climactic fight between Neo and Agent Smith takes place in a subway station. The two men have fallen on to the tracks where they continue fighting as a train approaches. Suddenly, Neo breaks free and performs a back flip from the tracks to the platform (plate 111), landing on his feet (plate 112). A split second later, Agent Smith is hit by the train.

Visual Effects Scenes

Much of the aesthetic effect of these fight scenes comes from the ballet-like motions of the human body gracefully moving through space and time in physically impossible ways. Digital **visual effects** make these motions look "real" by erasing the signs of how these moves were staged and shot pro-filmically. But, of course, *The Matrix* includes more spectacular digital visual effects as well. For example, the first time Neo is in the "real world," a point-of-view shot shows two huge, tower-like buildings with currents of electricity jumping between them (plate 113). In the same shot, the camera tilts down to show the humanoids being harvested for energy (plate 114). The complexity of the elements within the shot – large-scale structures, electric currents, fields of humanoids, and dramatic shifts in camera perspective and movement from low angle to high angle – all require elaborate visual effects. Moments later, Neo is attacked by a creature-like machine that places its tentacles around his neck.

Another part of Neo's training requires entering the "jump" program within "the construct" to learn how to jump in a manner that defies gravity. First, a dramatic visual effect shows Neo and Morpheus landing on a tall rooftop.

Morpheus then leaps an impossible distance from one building to the next. We see him soaring through the air in a manner that recalls Trinity's escape in the opening scene as well as some of the fight choreography. Neo attempts the same jump and falls to the ground. In one shot, we see him jumping from the building and apparently running through the air (plate 115). In the next shot, he suddenly starts to fall directly toward the camera (plate 116). Then we see him hit the cement that miraculously turns into a soft, sponge-like material that cushions his fall (plate 117) and springs him back up into the air and out of the frame. Finally, we see him land again with a thud upon hard cement. Everything about the sequence, from the camera positions, to the bodily movements, to the street turning into a cushion, is dependent on digital visual effects.

Perhaps the most memorable visual effects sequence involves the battle on the rooftop when Neo and Trinity attempt to rescue Morpheus. Visual effect highlights include an image of sculptural beauty as Neo leans back to dodge bullets, his long coat-tails hanging to the ground. We see the path the bullets take as they move toward and past him in slow motion (plate 118). After Morpheus is rescued, we see Neo and Morpheus dangling from a helicopter as it flies through the urban landscape (plate 119). Later, one of the most spectacular digital visual effects shows the helicopter crashing into a glass high-rise building and exploding (plate 120).

Romance and Gender

In short, much of the action and the settings in *The Matrix* are the result of digital visual effects. In its subject matter, theme, and visual style, the film is fully a product of the digital era. Nevertheless, we want to conclude with a caution about simply succumbing to the cool, digital veneer of this movie that looks more like the future of Hollywood than its past. For all its cutting-edge digital style and subject matter, the film has much in common with conventional Hollywood filmmaking. As we discussed in chapter 2, Hollywood films frequently have a romantic subplot and this one is no different. During the course of the film, Trinity clearly falls in love with Neo and it is her love for him and the kiss she gives him that literally brings him back to life at the film's climax when it seems Agent Smith has killed Neo. The formation of a romantic, heterosexual couple at the end of a film is one of the oldest, most conservative narrative techniques in Hollywood.

In relation to the gender issues that we discuss in chapter 12, however, the film challenges other conventions. Most notably, Trinity is one of several current female action heroes who challenge traditional norms of female passivity (for example, *Lara Croft: Tomb Raider*, 2001). She is strong and fights in a manner equal to that of Neo. And it is she who saves him at the end. Nevertheless, she does not do so in the typically active male manner of rescuing him physically but rather by falling in love with him. Outward appearances notwithstanding, in many ways the powerful characters in the film are three men, Morpheus, the leader of the rebellion; Neo, the chosen one; and Agent Smith, the chief defender of The Matrix. Trinity might be capable but she becomes a supporting character who falls under the sway of powerful male characters. In one scene, we see her romantically looking on as Neo trains. Despite *The Matrix*'s new and futuristic look, then, it is important, as with all films, to think critically about it. While aspects of it are new and challenging, other aspects are solidly linked to the pre-digital Hollywood era. In some regards, Hollywood proves the old adage that the more things change, the more they stay the same. We turn next to *Timecode* (2000), an experimental film that offers a different notion of how digital technology can change both how films are made and how they look.

Timecode (2000)

In many ways *Timecode* (2000) is the opposite of *The Matrix*. Most centrally for our immediate purposes, it lacks any special effects. It is, however, as reliant upon digital technology, if not more so, than *The Matrix*. How can this be?

The Narrative

The story of *Timecode* seems ordinary enough. The main plot involves Alex (Stellan Skarsgård), a married film producer who is having an affair. His wife Emma (Saffron Burrows) is in analysis dealing with their marital difficulties. Rose (Salma Hayek), with whom Alex has his affair, is also simultaneously involved in a lesbian relationship with Lauren (Jeanne Tripplehorn), who suspects the affair. The entire story takes place within 90 minutes of one day during the production of one of Alex's films. Although there are many minor characters and plot threads, including an actress trying out for a part, an agent and his client who pitch a new film idea to the production company, a director of the current production, and a security guard, the main action is as follows.

Lauren accompanies Rose to the offices of Alex's production company. Along the way, she secretly places a small microphone in Rose's purse to monitor her activities. At the same time, Emma comes to the office to tell Alex she is leaving him. He has sex with Rose and Lauren hears it on her headphones. Determined to seek revenge, Lauren enters a production meeting and shoots Alex.

Summarized in this way, the story is quite traditional in its mixture of personal melodrama (multiple affairs, secret surveillance, personal confrontations, murder, and so on) and workplace melodrama (casting problems for the film, the director's history of drug abuse, Alex's difficulty in concentrating on his work due to personal problems, and so on) On top of all of this, a number of earthquakes momentarily disrupt the action. The personal and workplace problems plus the earthquake all add up to a fairly conventional theme: Hollywood is a crazy place to work, full of unstable people. The earthquakes, which the characters hardly notice, are themselves a sign of the chaos and insanity that characterize Hollywood. The film also develops the theme of digital technology invading and transforming the lives of the characters. Cell phones are used throughout, emphasizing how desperately these people are trying to communicate with one other. As Alex lays dying, his cell phone rings and he asks assistance in answering it from a woman who is shooting his death on digital video (plate 121)!

Visual Style

The story and themes of *Timecode* are, then, quite traditional; what distinguishes it is the manner in which the story is told and the themes are developed. In chapter 2, we made an important distinction between story and plot. The plot in *Timecode* is unique in the history of narrative cinema because, throughout its 90 minutes, it is presented from four simultaneous points of view. Traditional narrative and formal structure afford us one view of the action at a time. *Timecode*, however, divides the screen into equal quadrants, each of which shows us different perspectives on the overall action, each photographed by a different camera. Consequently, we are always looking at four images. The camera style of all four images is equally astonishing: from the beginning of the film to the end, each image is one **long take**. There are *no* cuts within the film. Any "editing" that occurs results from the viewer moving his or her eyes and attention between the quadrants. Consequently, two viewers watching the same film do not see the same film – their shifts in focus have made them see it differently. Furthermore, the same viewer seeing the film twice is likely to see it differently!

Director Mike Figgis's technique is not entirely without precedence. Andy Warhol's *Chelsea Girls* (1967) used dual projection throughout its approximate 3 hour running time. Shot in 16 mm, the film incorporates random perspectives into its design since, each time it is projected, the order of the reels may vary. The viewer is always watching two images projected side by side, but the relationship between them is not predetermined. Furthermore, the film lacks a conventional narrative since the reels are only loosely connected by the fact that the "characters" all share one thing in common – they occupy various rooms of the Cheslea Hotel in New York's Greenwich Village.

Shortly after Warhol's experiments, Brian De Palma incorporated the **split-screen** technique into such narrative films as the thrillers *Sisters* (1973) and *Carrie* (1976). Unlike Warhol, De Palma used the technique sparingly and integrated it into a conventional narrative structure, at key moments intensifying suspense or horror with the dual images. The technique was also used in documentaries of the era, such as Michael Wadleigh's *Woodstock* (1970), primarily to present multiple perspectives upon a live performance or the event itself.

Figgis's style differs markedly from those of both Warhol and De Palma. On the one hand, like Warhol, he structures the entire film around multiple projections (four instead of two) while, on the other hand, like De Palma, he fully integrates the technique into a conventional narrative. Like Warhol, he relies upon improvisations and long takes and, like De Palma, he relies upon moments of startling unity between what we see in the varying images. As is always the case in the history of any art form, nothing appears without antecedents and influences, and *Timecode* is no exception. It is both unique and part of film history. But what does any of this have to do with digital technology?

Production

Timecode was shot on digital video rather than 35 mm film and this enabled things impossible in film. First and foremost, each of the four camera perspectives runs for the full 90 minutes without a cut. This is literally impossible with 35 mm film where the longest take can only last about 10 minutes due to the physical length of the film reel. Alfred Hitchcock's *Rope* (1948) gained notoriety for appearing to be shot in a single long take although Hitchcock, in fact, "cheated" to accomplish this look. At the end of each 10-minute reel, the camera comes to rest on a close-up of something, such as the back of a character's sports jacket, that totally blocks the view of anything else. In production, the filmmakers then stopped, placed a fresh reel in the camera, and started the action again. When the camera moved away from the object that blocked its view, or that object moved, it appeared to the viewer as if no time had passed in a single shot. Photographed and edited in this manner, the completed film gives the illusion of one, uninterrupted shot. Digital video, however, enables the shooting of 90 minutes of film time in real time with no edits and no stopping and starting of the camera.

Digital video also enabled Figgis to make fifteen complete versions of *Timecode*! The cost of doing this in 35 mm would have been prohibitive and nothing like it has been done in the history of cinema. The low cost of shooting digital video also enabled Figgis to structure the production in a manner different from that of conventional 35 mm cinema. Any style of long-take cinematography affects the actors' relationship to the director and the camera. In a conventional shooting style, if the actor forgets lines or flubs in some manner, the consequences are slight. If such a mistake came near the end of shooting the complicated, 8-minute, long take that opens Robert Altman's *The Player* (1992), for example, the consequences would have been substantial. The entire take would have to have been reshot. Actors typically speak about the added pressure of working in such a style and some directors value long takes precisely because of the added pressure brought to bear on actors and the potential of such pressure to heighten their performance. The actors in *Timecode* had to stay in character and hit their marks for a full 90 minutes, somewhat like stage actors, or actors performing in live television.

Improvisation

Digital video also affected the acting style of the production by enabling extensive improvisation. Improvisation is not new to filmmaking but, due to cost and technical demands, it has been used sparingly throughout the sound era. Some unconventional directors, like Robert Altman and John Cassavetes, are known for using it a great deal in the preparation and even the shooting of their films. Others have at times used it in the conceptualization of films that are then shot in a conventional manner. Blake Edwards, for example, while making *The Party* (1968) with Peter Sellers, improvised a great deal while shooting with video. Then, after having come up with what he wanted, he rehearsed the scenes in a conventional manner and shot them on film. He extended this technique with *That's Life!* (1986), which in some respects originated in a manner similar to *Timecode*. Its fifteen-page script was only a barebones outline of the action. The actors improvised and then a traditional script was developed. By the time they shot on film, they had finished improvising. The improvisation in *Timecode*, however, was not confined to preliminary stages; the actors improvised for all fifteen versions of the film. None of them knew exactly what the others were going to do or say. This led to drastically different events in the various versions. In version 1, for example, Alex sits at a meeting in a somber, drugged state as he listens to someone pitch a film (plate 122). In version 15, however, he rudely interrupts the pitch with laughter, calling the project pretentious (plate 123). Such a change not only affects the action of the film but the other actors as well who had to adjust to this unexpected response. In this scene, the actor playing the filmmaker who makes the pitch has to decide how to take this rude interruption (plate 124).

The Script and the Finished Film

In order to make the film with 90 minute, uninterrupted, improvised digital video takes, Figgis developed a unique version of a shooting script. In conventional scripts, dialogue is normally written out and sometimes camera positions are indicated; at times, shots are even storyboarded (sketched). Figgis found this method inadequate for this production. Although he was able to summarize the overall direction of the story, his decision to use extensive improvisation meant that neither the dialogue nor the action could be written out with the kind of specificity important to preparing the practical aspects of production.

In chapter 9, we discussed film in relation to the other arts. We observed that, unlike music, filmmaking has no notational system. Figgis has, however, challenged even that with *Timecode*. Drawing upon his background as a musician, Figgis decided to use manuscript paper to create a kind of score for the film. All of the bars represented a fixed period of time and he used four different colored lines to represent the four cameras. He predetermined where each camera would be at key moments and the score indicated the patterns. This placed the actors in the position of improvising around a predetermined structure. They knew, for example, that they would have to exit a room within a certain number of minutes and the camera operator knew where the camera would be positioned at that moment. This method of scoring rather than writing a film enabled the development of formal patterns. For example, at one moment in version 15, a close-up of eyes fills each of the four quadrants (plate 125). This was indicated in the "score."

Similarly, this enabled complex movement patterns to be worked out in advance, showing actors simultaneously in two different quadrants and/or moving from one quadrant to another. Once again, the colored lines in the "score" indicated these complex moments. This happens, for example, with the massage therapist (Julian Sands) when he initially enters the building (plate 126), and when an agent (Kyle MacLachlan) initially approaches the building (plate 127).

The DVD and the Impact of Digital Technology on Home Viewing

Digital technology is already affecting more than the ways in which films are made; thanks to digital video discs, it is affecting the way we watch films. As is predictable with any new technology, the changes initially seem minor. Many DVDs include "extras" such as a featurette on the making of the film or on some aspect of the film such as special effects. They might offer the option of watching the film while listening to a commentary by people involved in its making as well as deleted scenes and theatrical trailers. Even these features have begun to affect how people watch films. If, for example, one listens to what the director had in mind when he or she made the film, that becomes part of the reception context of watching the film. In terms of our discussion of **reception** in chapter 8, listening to the filmmaker's commentary is likely to encourage the viewer toward a preferred reading. Learning how special effects are accomplished is likely to make viewers less naïve about the reality of the photographic image. Seeing deleted scenes gives viewers a glimpse of how, as we discussed in chapter 2, stories are shaped into plots. DVDs offer the viewer the opportunity to learn some things about movies that heretofore have been the privilege of industry insiders or of students taking college film courses. Some DVDs even include critical commentary that might encourage **negotiated** and **oppositional readings**, although the latter are few and far between and are normally restricted to old films where box office and video rentals will not be affected by such criticism.

Impressive as the above DVD features are, they still protect the integrity of the original theatrical film. The really radical potential for DVDs to change the manner in which we watch movies is only now beginning to appear. The television ad for the DVD of *Thirteen Days* (2000), for example, focuses more on the DVD and its interactive features than it does on the theatrical film, which was a box-office failure. The ad makes it sound as if it's more fun to play with the movie on DVD than to watch it in a theater.

Timecode affords an excellent example for understanding this aspect of the digital revolution. It contains the usual "extras," such as a video diary of director Mike Figgis talking about the making of the film. But it also contains a host of interactive options, some of which are as revolutionary as the film itself. The least innovative interactive option enables the viewer to watch the film and, when an icon appears on the screen, click to see a portion of the video diary before returning to the feature. A more innovative feature enables the viewer to choose which quadrant of the film to listen to at any given time. *Timecode* was shot with continuous sound on all four cameras and then a sound mix was made for the theatrical version. That mix fixes what we hear when we watch the film. The DVD interactive feature enables us to choose what we want to hear at any given moment while watching the film. We could watch the entire film, for example, only listening to the sound coming from the upper right quadrant. We can, in effect, watch a limitless number of versions of the film by changing our listening patterns. Indeed, it is highly improbable that, if we watch the film with the remote in our hands switching from quadrant to quadrant, we will ever watch the same film twice. The film offers countless versions.

But versions of what? Incredible as this question sounds, the DVD of *Timecode* has two complete versions of the film, version 1 and version 15. Viewers have the same limitless sound options on both versions. This creates yet another interactive option of sorts since watching them both changes the meaning of each. Knowing alternative versions of what characters say and do in version 1, for example, affects how we respond to the variation in version 15.

This raises yet another question about the impact of DVD on how we watch films: which version is the "true" one? Version 15 is the one that was released theatrically but does that necessarily privilege it on the video? Many DVDs offer "director's cuts" along with theatrical release versions or restored versions. Even the deleted scenes relate here since all of these options question the traditional notion of one true version of a film. Historically, the theatrical release version has been thought of as the privileged version, if for no other reason than that was the only version most people could ever see. DVD gives new meaning to the proverbial saying about things ending up on the cutting-room floor. In the past, most filmgoers never saw an example of what ended up on the cutting-room floor in their lives; now nearly all DVD viewers have.

This proliferation of versions of films and glimpses of deleted scenes, including alternative endings, has eroded the notion of *the* text. For many viewers, DVD has created a whole new awareness of what films are, how they are made and remade for distribution, and even how they can be further remade and manipulated by the viewer at home. In short, DVD affects how we watch, question, and enjoy movies at home in previously unimaginable ways.

SELECTED READINGS

Ty Burr discusses digital projection in "Reel Gone?," *Entertainment Weekly*, May 11 (2001), pp. 25–8. John Bailey, the cinematographer on *The Anniversary Party*, analyzes the differences between 35 mm and digital video in "Film or Digital? Don't Fight. Coexist," in *New York Times*, Sunday, February 18 (2001), pp. 9, 20. The visual effects supervisors of *Armageddon* demonstrate how the visual effects were accomplished on the "Disc 2: Supplement" DVD in the Criterion Collection DVD edition of *Armageddon* (1999). Stephen Prince analyzes the impact of digital technology on classical film theory in "True Lies: Perceptual Realism, Digital Images, and Film Theory," *Film Quarterly*, 49(3) (Spring 1996), pp. 27–77, and Kevin J. Corbett analyzes the impact of digital television on movie theaters in "The Big Picture: Theatrical Moviegoing, Digital Television, and Beyond the Substitution Effect," *Cinema Journal*, 40(2) (2001), pp. 35–56. Information on visual effects in the fight scenes in *The Matrix* can be found in the featurette on the making of the film on the Warner Home Video DVD release (1999). The DVD also contains material on visual effects. Mike Figgis talks about the production of *Timecode* in the "Video Diary" on the Columbia/Tri Star DVD release of the film (2000).

GLOSSARY

allusionism References in a film to other films, frequently those canonized by film critics and other scholars. *See* pp. 125–6.

art cinema European, Japanese, and other foreign or US independent films that differ in narrative, style, and theme from mainstream Hollywood cinema. In the art cinema, events and actions that are normally clear in Hollywood may, for example, be ambiguous, confusing, or even unknowable.

aspect ratio The ratio of the frame's width to its height. It can vary from the traditional Academy ratio of 1.33 : 1 to 1.85 : 1 to widescreen ratios of 2.5 : 1.

auteur (French for "author") In film theory, it commonly refers to the director as the author of, or the one most creatively responsible for, a film. To call a director an *auteur* is a sign of recognition that he/she makes film with personal vision and style.

author / authorship Although film is a collaborative art form, authorship is generally attributed to the director who is frequently the most powerful creative figure involved in the production. Placing a film within the perspective of its director's other work can provide valuable insights.

blue screen A translucent screen used in rear projection. Actors standing in front of such a screen can be made to appear to be standing in whatever background (Paris, a tornado, ancient Rome, Nairobi, urban traffic) is projected onto the screen from the rear.

bound motif *see* motif.

canonized films (canon) Films widely considered masterpieces. The **canon** is a body of films that those wishing to become knowledgeable in cinema should view.

cinematography Motion picture photography.

classical Hollywood narrative style In this style, established around 1915, a film's plot should have a clear forward direction and no irrelevant plot elements. A film need not have a happy ending, but it has a clear resolution of the main participants' goals.

close shot or close-up *see* shot.

composition The different elements that compose the film image, including camera placement and arrangement of the people and objects in the frame.

convention The expected and formulaic elements of different film genres. For instance, the conventions of urban action/adventure films include car chases and explosions; the conventions of Westerns include white civilization against Native Americans and the resolution of disputes by use of the six-gun. *See also* invention.

credits   The list of filmmakers and corporations involved with the film that appears at the beginning and/or end of the film.

cross-cut   *see* cut.

cut (intercut, cross-cut)   A cut marks the abrupt transition from the end of one shot to the beginning of the next one. A shot is said to be **intercut** into another when the film returns to the first shot, as when we see a close shot of a character's face, then a flashback memory that the character is having is intercut into the facial shot, and when the flashback is over, the film returns to the facial shot. **Cross-cutting** occurs when the film cuts back and forth between, or among, parallel actions, as in a chase scene.

cutting   *see* editing.

deep focus cinematography   Keeping the focus and clarity of the image constant from objects appearing close to the camera to those far into the rear of the frame, which enables the viewer to see more space within the shot, including background details and actions.

diegesis   The fictional, narrative world represented within a film (e.g., space, time, sound, characters). Music coming from a radio is diegetic; exciting sound-track music in a car chase scene can be non-diegetic.

digital technology   Recently developed, computer-based technology by means of which images and sounds are digitally encoded, as opposed to the more traditional analog photographic and magnetic sound technologies. Digital technology increases the ease with which the image may be manipulated in a hard-to-detect or undetectable manner.

director   The figure most responsible for determining and coordinating the various elements (camerawork, sound, acting, set design, and so on) that comprise the finished film. *See also* executive producer; producer.

dissolve (match dissolve)   A transition from one shot to the next in which the images overlap for a time, sometimes used to ease the visual abruptness of the transition (as from a darkly lit cave scene to a brightly lit snow scene) and at other times used to suggest an association between the two images (as from a letter addressed to a character to a shot of that character reading the letter). A **match dissolve** is one in which graphic elements of the two images match, as with the close shot in *Psycho* (see chapter 6) of a murdered woman's eye and a shot of a circular shower drain.

distribution (distributor)   The practice of placing the finished film into theaters for exhibition. The **distributor** is the person or company responsible for this.

dolly shot (tracking shot)   A shot taken from a camera mounted on a moving platform, or dolly. *See also* shot.

dominant meaning of a film   The meaning of a film that the filmmakers and publicists intend. Audiences are encouraged to respond to the film in the way projected by the filmmakers, distributors, and exhibitors. *See also* negotiated reading; oppositional reading; preferred reading.

economic class / status   How much wealth a person has determines his/her economic class. Economic class is usually categorized as upper-class, middle-class, and lower-class, sometimes called working-class.

editing (montage and cutting)   The ways in which separate pieces of film are joined together. **Montage** is the French term for editing, or cutting, but also carries connotations of the creation of meaning through editing patterns. Hollywood montage commonly refers to the rapid cutting together of multiple shots, often using many dissolves, to create the effect of the rapid chronicling of the passage of time, as from a character's youth to maturity.

establishing (or master) shot   An extreme long shot that shows (or establishes) the entire space in which the ensuing scene will take place. Many scenes begin with such shots to orient the viewer. Sometimes there are two establishing shots, one exterior and one interior.

executive producer   In film, executive producers invest money in the productions, while producers oversee the logistics of film production, ranging from location shooting to having the extras ready when needed. In radio and television, producers and/or executive producers have the greatest creative control. *See also* director; executive producer.

exhibition   The practice of showing the completed film to audiences.

eyeline match   The establishment, often through cutting, of the direction of a character's gaze. At times a shot will show a character looking, and a second shot will show what that character is looking at. At other times the term is used to refer to the directionality of characters' lines of vision within shots.

film noir   A French term meaning "black film," with "black" referring both to the look of the movies and to their mood (e.g., scenes of lurking danger at night on rainy streets). *Film noir* first appeared in America in the early 1940s and has been considered both a genre and a style.

5.1 surround sound   A sound system which supplies five separate stereo sound sources in addition to a sub-woofer which amplifies certain frequencies, enabling the spectator to feel sound vibrations while watching a movie.

flashback   A jump in narrative time from the present into the past. Rather than proceeding chronologically through the story, flashbacks allow filmmakers to jump back and forth between past and present events.

formal properties / structure   The elements of a film, such as screen space and offscreen space, sound, and editing, which shape and structure what we see and hear when we watch a film. The formal properties of films make them different from other art forms.

formalism   A film theory that emphasizes the formal properties of cinema that shape the way movies are made. Formalists recognize, for example, that organizing screen space is an artistic activity that differs from our daily perception of real life. Major formalist theorists include Sergei Eisenstein and Rudolf Arnheim. *See also* realism.

frame   The borders of the projected image.

free motif   *see* motif.

genre   A category of film: for example, Western, horror, musical, romantic comedy. Genre study relates films to other works of the same type.

high-contrast lighting   A form of lighting that creates a dramatic contrast between brights and darks.

high resolution   A clear, highly defined and detailed visual image.

intercut   *see* cut.

invention   The new, surprising, or unexpected elements of a genre movie, in contrast to the expected elements dictated by the conventions of the genre. *See also* convention.

invisible norm   Many US movies presume an invisible norm when representing race, class, and gender: masculinity is the gender norm, the middle-class is the economic norm, and white is the racial norm.

invisible style   A norm of filmmaking in which style is not usually noticed, based on the assumption that narrative is always more important than style and should dominate it. Such devices as not crossing the 180-degree line and cutting on action, reaction, and dialogue contribute to this invisible style.

long shot   *see* shot.

long take   A shot that lasts for a long period rather than a few seconds. During a long take both space and time are whole and continuous.

master shot   *see* establishing shot.

match dissolve   *see* dissolve.

melodrama   A genre traditionally devalued due to assumptions that it is based on emotion and aimed predominantly at women. In the 1940s and 1950s they were referred to derogatorily as "women's weepies."

montage   *see* editing.

motif   A recurring visual image or sound that forms a pattern. For the distinction between **free** and **bound** motifs see pp. 33–4.

narrative   The manner in which the story events of a movie are organized and structured; the way the story is told.

negotiated reading   A reading of a film that accepts most of the dominant meaning that the filmmakers and publicists want the audience to receive, but that inflects a film further with meanings of particular value for certain segments of the population, for example, men, women, homosexuals, or working-class people.

offscreen space   The six potential areas of space surrounding the image we see on the screen at any moment, i.e. the spaces at the left, right, top, and bottom of the image, as well as the space behind the camera and the space beyond the horizon.

180-degree line   An imaginary line drawn between the camera and the actors/action which the camera does not cross in order to prevent viewer disorientation and maintain the invisible style. *See also* invisible style.

oppositional reading   A reading of a film that opposes the preferred reading offered by filmmakers and producers. Critics and spectators who view films oppositionally do so with knowledge of what the filmmakers want them to accept but reject those readings and choose quite different ones. *See also* negotiated reading; preferred reading.

painted backdrop   A painted image of a background that actors stand in front of on a soundstage, thus making them appear to be on location.

plot / story   The term "story" refers to the events that must be narrated; the term "plot" refers to the arrangement of those events as they are told. Story events occur in chronological order; plot events occur in the order the filmmakers choose to present them.

preferred reading   Audience reception of a film that corresponds to that encouraged by the filmmakers, distributors, and exhibitors.

prequel   A film whose story takes place in a time prior to the story events in a previously made film. A character who is an adult in the first film might be a teenager in the prequel.

producer   The person responsible for coordinating all the various aspects of a film production, including extras, transportation, catering, costumes, location shooting, and so on. The producer is also responsible for overseeing the budget. Some producers put projects together by matching scripts with actors and directors; others work for a director. *See also* director; executive producer.

pro-filmic event   What is filmed in front of the camera, including sets and actors. Increasingly, what audiences now see in Hollywood films never existed in front of the camera, but consists of visual effects added with the aid of digital technology.

reaction shot   The cut to a listener or participant in the action to show their reaction to an event or dialogue. *See also* shot/reverse-shot editing.

realism   A film theory that emphasizes the recording nature of cinema, as well as the connection between the camera and what is in front of it in real life. Major realist theorists include André Bazin and Siegfried Kracauer.

reception context   The way in which a film is received by its audience. It can be shaped by pre-release publicity or by unexpected events and changes over time.

release print   The finished 35 mm version of a film that is sent or released to theaters for exhibition.

remake   A new version of an earlier film, often using similar characters and storylines.

scene   A scene is a narrative unit determined by unity of time and space. The events in a scene occur in one place at one time. A later scene, for example, may occur in the same place at a different time.

sequel   A film that starts where a previous film left off.

series   A number of movies that usually employ the same basic characters, situations, and style as the original movie. The James Bond series is a prime example.

set design   The style and appearance of a film's sets. Set design may, for example, include decisions on where to put doors and windows and what style and period of furniture will be in a room.

shot (close shot or close-up, medium, long, two-shot, tracking and dolly)   A shot is an image in the film uninterrupted by cuts or other transitional devices. The terms close shot (or close-up), medium shot, and long shot indicate the distance of the camera from the central object being photographed. With a person, a **close shot** generally shows the face and perhaps the shoulders; a **medium shot** will show the person from the waist up; and a **long shot** will show the person's full body. A **two-shot** is one that features two characters equally. **Tracking** or **dolly** (or dollie) shots are ones in which the camera moves. It was traditionally mounted on a moving platform, or dolly, and would follow or "track" a moving object, such as a walking character or a galloping horse. Tracking or dolly shots can also move through a set (like a haunted house) in which nothing is moving, giving a complex sense of depth to the shot.

shot/reverse-shot editing   A pattern of editing which shows, first, one character and then a cut to a reverse shot that allows us a nearly opposite view, typically another character who is talking or interacting with the first. Many scenes simply go back and forth between such shots until all the significant dialogue has been spoken and all the action has occurred.

social class   Unlike economic class, which is determined by the amount of money someone has, social class is determined by his/her style and values. A working-class person can have upper-middle-class values.

soundstage   A large, interior space where films are shot. Lights can be suspended from the ceiling and microphones can record sound while filming takes place.

special effects   Effects that can be accomplished on the set, such as blowing up a car, which involves an actual car and a genuine explosion. *See also* visual effects.

split screen A technique whereby two or more images are seen next to each other at the same time. A line may divide or split the screen into its various parts.

star image A set of characteristics that has great popular appeal and that make an actor a known and desired quantity. Some stars maintain a fixed image, while others are prized for the variety of roles they play.

star system A system of casting that privileges stars over ordinary actors. This includes the placing of stars under contract by the major studios in the period from the 1930s to the 1950s, and even the creation of stars by means of carefully assigned film roles and publicity campaigns.

stereotypes The characterization of groups of people, often defined in terms of age, class, race, ethnicity, and sexual orientation, in a highly repetitive way with the same few characteristics. Films can mediate cultural stereotypes in complex ways.

studio system During the 1930s to the 1950s Hollywood was predominantly organized around studios that had stars and directors, among other personnel, under contract. The studio system gave a certain amount of power to the business people who ran the studios and who could determine what films would be made, what roles contracted actors would play, who would direct, how long the film would be, what scenes would be cut, and so on.

stylistic norm The stylistic features of filmmaking at a particular time. Departures from the stylistic norm can be used to good effect by creative filmmakers because they come as a surprise.

subplot A subsidiary plot to the main plot, often involving a romantic or comic element.

subtext A theme or set of ideas that are not overtly and explicitly dealt with in the film but which, rather, emerge through the use of such devices as connotations, symbols, *double entendre*, and so on.

35 mm The most common theatrical film gauge is 35 mm, indicating that the width of the film strip measures 35 mm.

tracking shot *see* shot.

two-shot *see* shot.

visual effects Effects that cannot be accomplished on the set of a movie, but are added afterwards with the aid of models and computer technology.

visual motif A recurring visual image that forms a pattern, such as the doorway motif in some films directed by John Ford.

widescreen The most common aspect ratio in contemporary Hollywood. Widescreen films as measured by width and height are 1.66:1 or 1.85:1. *See also* aspect ratio.

INDEX

FILM STUDIES TITLES FROM BLACKWELL PUBLISHING